Quiet Water
New York:
Canoe and Kayak Guide

The Staff of AMC Books

Bryan Davidson, Production Manager   **Vanessa Torrado, Senior Editor**
Eric Hague, Editorial and Production Assistant

The AMC is a non-profit organization and sales of AMC books fund our mission of protecting the Northeast outdoors. If you appreciate our efforts and would like make a donation to the AMC, contact us at Appalachian Mountain Club, 5 Joy Street, Boston, MA 02108.

http://www.outdoors.org/publications/books/

Cartography by Vanessa Gray 2nd Edition; Ian Duncan 1st Edition.
Cover Design by Eric Edstam
Front-Cover Photograph: Paddler near Japanese Tea House, Osgood Pond © Nancie Battaglia.
Back-Cover Photographs: (left to right) © Nancie Battaglia, © Jerry and Marcy Monkman.
All interior images copyright of the authors unless otherwise noted.

Library of Congress Cataloging-in-Publication Data

Hayes, John.
   Quiet water New York : canoe & kayak guide / John Hayes and Alex Wilson. -- 2nd ed.
     p. cm.
   Includes bibliographical references and index.
   ISBN-13: 978-1-929173-73-0 (pbk. : alk. paper)
   ISBN-10: 1-929173-73-3 (pbk. : alk. paper)
   1. Canoes and canoeing--New York (State)--Guidebooks. 2. Lakes--New York (State)--Guidebooks. 3. Ponds--New York (State)--Guidebooks. 4. New York (State)--Guidebooks. I. Wilson, Alex, 1955– II. Title.

  GV776.N7H39 2007
  917.47--dc22

                                             2006103172

10 9 8 7 6 5 4 3 2 1

Quiet Water New York: Canoe and Kayak Guide

2nd Edition

John Hayes and Alex Wilson

Appalachian Mountain Club Books
Boston, Massachusetts

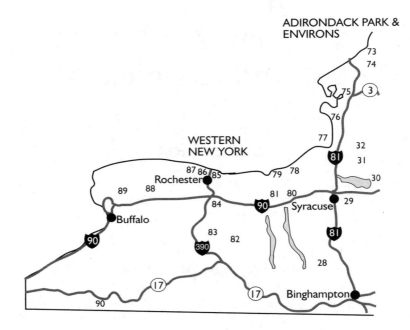

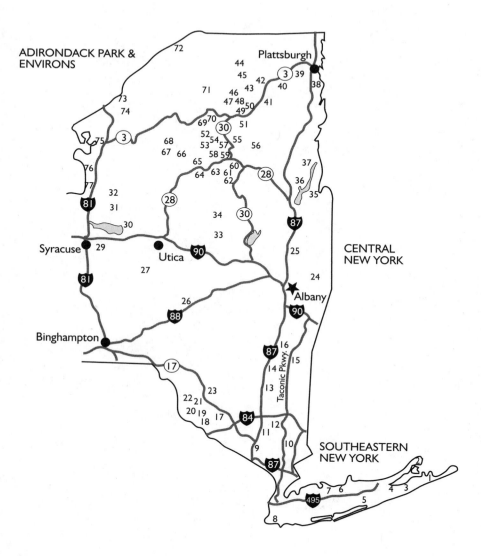

ADIRONDACK PARK &
ENVIRONS

72

Plattsburgh

44
45   42   3 39
71 46 43 40   38
47 48 50 41
49
69 70 51
30
52 54 55
68 53 57 56
67 66   58 59
65   60
64 63 61
62   28
37
36
35

32
81 28   30
31   34   30
30   87
Syracuse 29   33   CENTRAL
Utica 90   NEW YORK
27   25
24
81   90
Albany

26   88   87 16
Binghampton   15

17   13

23   Taconic Pkwy.
22 21   84   12
20 19   17   11
18   10
9   SOUTHEASTERN
87   NEW YORK
7 6
495   4 3 1
5
8

Contents

Central New York

Adirondack Park and Environs

Nature Essays

Key to Maps

⌒	Tent site
◀	Lean-to
⌐	Picnic area
Λ	State or federal campground
Δ	Private campground
⌣	Boat access
P	Parking area
⋰⋱	Marsh
☀	Peak
═══	Interstate highway
▬▬▬	State highway
▪-▪-▪	Paved road
═══	Less-traveled road
= = = =	Rough dirt road
....	Footpath
→ ═══	River
← ───	Stream

(Arrows indicate direction of flow)

Foreword

Let's get one thing straight. If as a paddler you have a yen for exploits on the Upper Hudson and the Colorado's Grand Canyon, if the more challenging the waters the more you are satisfied, if, in short, heroism is your aim, this book is not for you. It is a book not for heroes who seek to dominate the natural world but for pilgrims who seek it humbly for understanding and harmony.

Quiet Water: New York is a handbook for natural history as well as a practical guide to getting there. It will open your eyes to the richness of perception that awaits the casual paddler on New York State's lakes, ponds, and flatwater streams. The authors are competent guides. Alex Wilson is a naturalist and writer of three other quietwater guidebooks. John Hayes is a professor of biochemistry and environmental science and a leader of natural-history field trips. You may not have their luck of spotting four bald eagles at once, adults and fledglings, at a nest on Deer River Flow. But there is a good chance that they will draw your attention to cavorting river otters; to the spectacular flight of the peregrine falcon; to damselflies leaping off the landing pads of floating vegetation as your boat glides by; to the intricate mechanism by which carnivorous plants—sundew, pitcher, and bladderwort—feed on insects. And in the forever-wild forests of the Adirondacks and Catskills, Wilson and Hayes will assist in transporting you back to an early time on this continent.

—PAUL JAMIESON
Author of *Adirondack Canoe Waters: North Flow*

Preface to the
Second Edition

The first edition of *Quiet Water: New York*, published in 1996, was the fourth in a series that includes guides to New Hampshire and Vermont; Massachusetts, Connecticut, and Rhode Island; Maine; and New Jersey.

The first edition enjoyed great success, but lake and pond descriptions inevitably go out of date. We took this opportunity to add new material, including five new trips: Little Tupper Lake; West Branch Sacandaga River; Jamaica Bay; Tivoli Marsh; and Catskill Creek and Ramshorn Marsh. We also eliminated the section on Massawepie and Grass Creek because of difficult, seasonal access.

We rechecked the original bodies of water to ensure that new housing developments had not crowded the shores, and we revised directions to reflect new road names. When possible, we tried to avoid bodies of water with substantial development, but for the most part, we worried more about the effect of personal watercraft and high-speed boating on safety, the quietwater experience, and the environment.

Through publication of this expanded guide, we hope to draw attention to the need to preserve these wonderful places. All quietwater paddlers should work together at local and state levels to bring added protection to these precious resources.

Acknowledgments

For the second edition, we owe a debt of gratitude to Vanessa Gray, who drew the new maps and revised the existing maps. We also thank the staff of AMC Books for their contributions to improving the look and content of this edition. In particular, we thank Vanessa Torrado, senior editor; Bryan Davidson, production manager; and Eric Hague, editorial and production assistant.

Acknowledgments from the first edition: We are indebted to many individuals for helping to create this book. First and foremost, we thank our families, Jerelyn, Lillian, and Frances Wilson, and Joanne, Andrew, and Stefanie Hayes.

For providing us with suggestions of bodies of water to visit, we thank Mary Ellen Jones of the Nissequogue River Canoe Club, Bill Marosz of the Whalers of Suffolk County, Diana Dreeben of Peconic Paddler, Dave Cilley of the St. Regis Canoe Outfitters, Beth Tickner of Tickner's Adirondack Canoe Outfitters, Larry MacIntosh of Wildwater Outfitters, John Kowalski of the Canal View Café in Sylvan Beach, Jonathan and Nancy Fairbanks, Hudson Barton, Steve Bluestone, and Diane Arndt.

For putting up weary paddlers, we thank John and Phyllis Conley, Stanley and Irma Selengut, Sandra Pell and Sherman Taishoff, Ellin Randel, Jonathan Ortip, Kim and Dan Woodbury, and Lee Gratwick. For paddling companionship, we thank Sally Andrews, Ian Duncan, Philip Demay, Lee and Lucy Gratwick, and Jill Hulme. Also, a special thanks to Dick Forrestal for mechanical assistance with Alex's car during a visit to Long Island.

For information on wildlife, we thank biologists Pete Nye, Bob Miller, and Michael Mathews with the Bureau of Wildlife at the New York State Department of Environmental Conservation and Bob Engel of Marlboro College. Thank you to Ian Duncan for his fine cartographic work, to Marrin Robinson for the pen-and-ink wildlife illustrations, to Mark Lamoureux for photographic printing, to Nadav Malin for assistance with mapping, and to Gordon Hardy and his superb staff at the Appalachian Mountain Club.

Finally, on behalf of all paddlers who enjoy canoeing the Adirondack's wild rivers and lakes, we offer a heartfelt thanks to Paul Jamieson, coauthor of *Adirondack Canoe Waters: North Flow*, who reviewed and commented on portions of our manuscript. Over the past 50 years, Paul has undoubtedly done more than anyone else to promote paddling and to ensure public access in the Adirondacks.

Introduction to Quietwater Paddling

New York offers outstanding paddling opportunities. Indeed, many people think that the lakes, ponds, and rivers of New York's Adirondack Park offer the finest canoeing and kayaking in the Northeast. Although few places in the U.S. surpass the wildness of Adirondack lakes and meandering flows, New York offers many other outstanding paddling destinations. From the tidal estuaries of Long Island, to the historic Erie Canal in the central part of the state, to the wild and marshy inlet creeks of Lake Ontario, tremendous paddling exists near and far—places just right for a several-day expedition or for a half day of paddling near home.

The peaceful solitude of out-of-the-way lakes and ponds lures us to quietwater paddling. This guide will lead you to wood ducks swimming through early morning mists, to playful antics of river otter as you round a bend in a winding inlet channel, to the thrill of spotting moose—mouth full of pondweeds—as it repopulates the northern part of the state, to old-growth white pine towering above crystal-clear ponds that help us imagine what our forests looked like centuries ago, and to the loon's haunting wail wafting off the water as afternoon settles into dusk.

With quietwater paddling, you can focus on *being* there rather than on *getting* there. You do not need a lot of fancy high-tech gear—though a light canoe or kayak makes portaging over beaver dams a lot easier. Binoculars and field guides to fauna and flora make up our most important gear.

This guide will lead you to a body of water and describe why you might want to paddle it. Generally, we tried to include places that have abundant wildlife or extensive marshlands or beautiful scenery; most entries have all three. We hope that our research will allow you to spend your valuable time paddling, instead of driving around for hours trying to find elusive accesses. We designed the *AMC Quiet Water Guides* for paddlers of all experience levels, to help you better enjoy our wonderful water resources.

THE SELECTION PROCESS

This guide includes only a small percentage of New York's lakes, ponds, estuaries, and slow-flowing streams. In our selection process, we looked for great scenery; limited development; few motorboats; a varied shoreline with lots of coves and inlets; and interesting plants, animals, and geological formations.

We include a variety of water types: big lakes and rivers for longer excursions, and small, protected ponds and marshes for when you have limited time or when weather conditions preclude paddling larger bodies of water. To make the book as useful as possible, we paid particular attention to lakes and ponds in more populated regions, even though many more remote locations in northern New York better fit our ideal-paddling-spot standards.

We asked people about the best places to paddle, we consulted maps from DeLorme's *New York Atlas and Gazetteer*; we bought other books about paddling in New York, including the superb guides from the Adirondack Mountain Club (see Bibliography), and we systematically examined the 850-plus U.S. Geological Survey (USGS) 7.5-minute topographic maps of New York.

Though we tried to include the very best places to paddle, we doubtless have missed some really good locations. If you have suggestions of other lakes, ponds, and streams to include, please let us know (Alex Wilson or John Hayes, c/o AMC Books, 5 Joy Street, Boston, MA 02108).

SAFETY, EQUIPMENT, AND TECHNIQUE

We all long for the idyllic paddle on mist-filled, mirror-smooth surfaces of quiet ponds at daybreak. But if you spend any time paddling New York's lakes and tidal rivers, you will also encounter far less tranquil conditions. Estuaries can have swift tides that, coupled with wind, can be very dangerous. On larger bodies of water, strong winds can arise quickly, whipping up 2- to 4-foot waves in no time—waves big enough to swamp an open boat. If you capsize in cold water even a moderate distance from shore, hypothermia—a cooling of the body's core that can lead to mental and physical collapse—can set in quickly. If you have just driven a long way to reach a particular lake and find it dangerously windy, choose a more protected body of water, or go hiking instead.

SAFETY FIRST

All Northeast states require each boater to carry a U.S. Coast Guard-approved (Type I, II, or III) personal flotation device, or PFD. A good PFD keeps a person's face above water, even after losing consciousness. Children twelve and under must wear their PFDs, which must be the right size so that they will not slip off; adult PFDs are not acceptable for children. Although the law does not require adults to wear PFDs, we strongly recommend that you do so, especially when paddling with children. A foam- or kapok-filled PFD will also keep you warmer in cold water. If you do not normally paddle wearing a PFD, at least don it in windy conditions, when crossing large lakes, or when you may encounter substantial motorboat wakes. It could save your life.

You should also bring along a waterproof first-aid kit. The best kit is one that you assemble yourself; make sure that it has bandages or moleskin for blisters, an antihistamine for allergic reactions, sunscreen, an extra hat, a pain reliever, and any special medications that you might require.

As for clothing, plan for the unexpected. Even with a sunny-day forecast, a shower can appear by afternoon. On trips of more than a few hours, we bring along rain gear and dry clothes in a waterproof stuff sack as a matter of course. Along with rain coming up unexpectedly, temperatures can drop quickly, especially in the spring or fall, making conditions ripe for hypothermia. Lightweight nylon or polypropylene clothing dries more quickly than cotton, and wool slows heat loss even when wet. Remember that heads lose heat faster than torsos—bring a hat.

Avoid shallow, marshy waters during waterfowl-hunting season. For hunting-season dates, check the New York Department of Environmental Conservation Web site: www.dec.state.ny.us.

Other safety issues include the following:

- Getting off the water during lightning storms—lightning almost always strikes the highest object in the vicinity, which would be you in a boat out on a lake

- Knowing what to do and having experience doing it if you capsize

- Avoiding dehydration by drinking plenty of liquids

- Avoiding areas with a lot of high-speed boating

- Checking the weather forecast before going out

PADDLING WITH KIDS

When canoeing with kids, try to make it fun, and keep calm. Even though you may be plenty warm from paddling, children may get cold while sitting in the bottom of the boat. Remember that everyone should have PFDs on at all times, and PFDs will help keep children warm. They also need protection from sun and biting insects. Watch for signs of discomfort. Set up a cozy place where young children can sleep; after the initial excitement of paddling fades, a gently rolling canoe often puts children to sleep, especially near the end of a long day. Also, for those longer excursions, make sure to bring dry clothes for everyone in a waterproof sack.

EQUIPMENT

For quietwater paddling, avoid high-performance racing or tippy whitewater models. Borrow a boat before buying; selection will be easier with a little experience. Whether canoe or kayak, look for a model with good initial and secondary stability. A boat with good initial stability and poor secondary stability will tip slowly, but once it starts it may keep going.

Insist that children wear life vests (PFDs). We recommend that everyone wear a PFD when paddling.

The best canoes for lakes and ponds have a keel or shallow-V hull and fairly flat keel line to help track in a straight line, even in a breeze. Kayaks perform extremely well in rough water, particularly if equipped with a foot-operated rudder and a sprayskirt to keep from taking on water.

If you like out-of-the-way paddling requiring portages, get a Kevlar boat if you can afford it. Kevlar is a strong, lightweight carbon fiber. We paddle a rugged, high-capacity, 18-foot, 4-inch Mad River Lamoille canoe that weighs just 60 pounds, a 15-foot, 9-inch Mad River Independence solo canoe that weighs less than 40 pounds, a 14-foot Wenonah Wigeon kayak that weighs 38 pounds, and a 14-foot Wilderness Systems Chaika kayak that weighs 32 pounds. If you plan to go by yourself, consider a sea kayak or a solo canoe in which you sit (or kneel) close to the boat's center. You will find paddling a well-designed solo canoe far easier than a two-seater used solo. The touring or sea kayak—with its long, narrow design, low profile to the wind, and two-bladed paddling style—is faster and more efficient to paddle than canoes.

A padded portage yoke in place of the center thwart on a canoe is essential if you plan on much carrying. With unpadded yokes, wear a life vest with padded shoulders. Attach a rope—called a "painter"—to the bow so that you can secure the boat when you stop for lunch, line it up

Sally Andrews paddles a sea kayak as she explores a wooded shore.

or down a stream, and—if the need ever arises—grab onto it in an emergency. We both have embarrassing stories about not using a painter to secure the boat—wind can cause Kevlar boats to disappear very quickly!

Choose light and comfortable paddles. For canoeing, we use a relatively short (50-inch), bent-shaft paddle. Laminated from various woods, the paddle has a special synthetic tip to protect the blade. Bent-shaft paddles allow more efficient paddling, because the downward force converts more directly into forward thrust. However, straight-shaft paddles also work well. Always carry at least one spare paddle per group, particularly on longer trips, in case of breakage or a porcupine getting hold of one.

PADDLING TECHNIQUE

On a quiet pond, does it matter if you use the proper J-stroke, the sweep stroke, or the draw? No. Learning some of these strokes, however, can make paddling more relaxing and enjoyable. We watch lots of novices zigzagging along, frantically switching sides, shouting orders fore and aft. People have told us about marriage counseling sessions devoted to paddling technique.

If you are new to the sport and want to learn canoeing or kayaking techniques, buy a book or participate in a paddling workshop, such as those offered by the Appalachian Mountain Club, equipment retailers, and boat manufacturers. Books we recommend on canoeing are Jacobson, *Basic Essentials Canoeing*, 2nd ed. (Globe Pequot Press, 1999); and Roberts and Salins, *Basic Essentials Canoe Paddling*, 3rd ed. (Falcon, 2006). For kayaking, good books include Seidman, *The Essential Sea Kayaker*, 2nd ed. (Ragged Mountain Press, 2001); Hutchinson, *Basic Book of Sea Kayaking*, 2nd ed. (Falcon, 2007); and Hutchinson, *The Complete Book of Sea Kayaking*, 5th ed. (Falcon, 2004).

Start out on small ponds. Practice paddling into, with, and across the wind. On a warm day close to shore, with your PFD on and others to help you out of difficulties, practice capsizing. Intentionally tipping your boat will give you an idea of how easily it can tip over. Try to get back into the boat away from shore. Getting the water out of a kayak while treading water is impossible without a hand pump; you can mount one permanently on your boat or carry a portable one. You should be able to right a canoe with two people, getting most of the water out (keep a bailer *fastened* to a thwart). Getting back in is another story. Good luck!

How to Use This Book

For each body of water, we provide a short description, a map, some natural history, and other useful information.

Maps. We recommend that you use the DeLorme Mapping Company's *New York Atlas and Gazetteer*, www.delorme.com. We key each lake to the DeLorme atlas, which divides the state into 80, detailed 10- by 15-inch maps at 1:150,000-scale. The maps include most—but not all—access locations, campsites, road names, campgrounds, parks, and other pertinent information. For more detail and information on topography, marsh areas, and so on, refer to the 7.5-minute, 1:24,000-scale USGS topographic maps listed in each section.

Area and River Length. We include river lengths and areas of lakes and ponds. Choose larger bodies of water and longer rivers when you have more time and a good weather forecast. Under windy conditions, paddle smaller bodies of water or rivers.

Habitat Type. We describe the type of environment that you will encounter. Most entries include substantial shallow-water marshlands.

Fish. Where we could glean the fish species information from New York state publications or from local anglers, we include the prominent sport-fishing species.

Expect to See. Here we describe the predominant animals and the type of vegetation that you should see.

Camping. We include nearby public campground locations, keyed to the list in Appendix A of New York state parks and forest preserves. For information on private campgrounds, see the extensive list in the DeLorme atlas.

Take Note. This section describes any substantial development or hazards to avoid.

Getting There. We give directions from the nearest city or major highway to the access. We provide distances between points, with the cumulative distance given in parentheses. We assume that you will use a detailed highway map, such as DeLorme's *New York Atlas and Gazetteer*.

Happy paddling!

Stewardship and Conservation

Diverse wetlands—among the richest, readily accessible ecosystems—provide wonderful opportunities to learn about nature. You can visit salt-water tidal marshes; deep, crystal-clear mountain ponds; and unique bog habitats. You can observe hundreds of species of birds; dozens of mammal, insect, turtle, and snake species; and literally thousands of plants. Some quite rare species—such as a delicate bog orchid or a family of otters—provide a real treat when you observe them. But even ordinary plants and animals lead to exciting discoveries and can provide hours of enjoyable observation.

We have described a few interesting plants and animals that you might encounter. We interspersed these descriptions—and accompanying pen-and-ink illustrations by Marrin Robinson—throughout. By learning a little more about these species, we hope that you will find them more interesting to observe.

DO WE REALLY WANT TO TELL PEOPLE ABOUT THE BEST PLACES?

People have asked us how we could, in good conscience, tell others about the more remote, pristine, unspoiled places—after all, increased visitation would make these places less idyllic. We spent many an hour grappling with this difficult issue as we paddled along. We believe that by encouraging people to enjoy these places—people who value wild, remote areas—support will build for greater protection of these waters.

New York's diverse wetlands—lakes, ponds, rivers and streams, wooded swamps, bogs, fens, freshwater marshes, salt marshes, brackish marshes, and floodplains—cover 2.4 million acres or 7 percent of New York's surface area. In contrast, Maine, a state with only 57 percent of New York's area, has 5 million acres of wetlands (25 percent of its area). Although Maine has lost comparatively little of its wetlands, New York may have lost as much as 60 percent non-lake and river wetlands since 1780.

Extremely important ecosystems, wetlands recharge groundwater, help control floods, support fishing and waterfowl hunting, and provide habitat for many rare and endangered species, as well as for hundreds of other species. Even low-impact uses such as canoeing or kayaking can substantially affect fragile marsh habitat. Paddling can disturb nesting loons and eagles, rare turtles, and fragile bog orchids. And even a canoe or kayak can carry invasive weeds and zebra mussels from one body of water to another—use care to clean off your boat before you visit other water bodies.

You can go even further than the adage, "Take only photographs, leave only footprints." Carry along a trash bag and pick up the leavings of less thoughtful individuals. If each of us does the same, we will enjoy more attractive places to paddle. Motorboaters tend to have a bad reputation when it comes to leaving trash, but paddlers should have the opposite reputation—which could come in handy when seeking restrictions on high-impact resource use.

For information on low-impact camping and other uses of fragile habitats, see Hampton and Cole, *Soft Paths: How to Enjoy the Wilderness without Harming It*, 3rd ed. (Stackpole Books, 2003) or Lanza, *Ultimate Guide to Backcountry Travel* (AMC Books, 1999). Also, visit Leave No Trace—an organization dedicated to teaching us how to have minimal outdoors impact—www.lnt.org.

Besides reducing our impact on the environment, we can actively work to protect fragile bald eagle, osprey, otter, loon, and other wildlife populations. If we want to preserve these species and their habitats for future generations, we will demand that elected and appointed officials make wildlife preservation and ecosystem protection a higher priority. We can also join conservation organizations—such as AMC, Adirondack Mountain Club, Sierra Club, The Nature Conservancy, New York Audubon, and many others—so that when those organizations speak about preserving the environment, their voices carry the weight of tens of thousands of like-minded members.

PUBLIC ACCESS

Private land abuts many waterways, and to ensure continued access, we must respect private property. Never camp or picnic on private land without permission. In many places, adjacent landowners also own the riverbed or lakebed, which means that even if you may paddle there, you may not have the right to fish there.

New York's Department of Environmental Conservation has done a good job of providing public access to state waterways, either by establishing conservation easements or by outright land and water purchase. Two areas worthy of discussion: Adirondack Park and Long Island.

Adirondack Park. Private inholdings—much of it owned by paper companies—have kept some lakes and waterways off limits. Paul Jamieson, who wrote the forward to this book and who we mention frequently, for 60 years has been a strong advocate for increased access. Recently, the state has made great progress, procuring access to an outstanding resource in Little Tupper Lake, part of Whitney Park. With the purchase in 1999 of 29,000 acres of Champion International Paper lands, and acquiring conservation easements on an additional 110,000 acres, we now have access to substantial portions of the Deer, Grass South Branch, Onion, Oswegatchie West Branch, St. Regis main and East branches, and Quebec Brook, including Madawaska Flow.

In 2004, International Paper sold conservation easements to the state on all of its 257,000 acres of park holdings, protecting an additional 9 percent of the park. Despite these recent successes, however, and even though a recent Court of Appeals decision (*Adirondack League Club, Inc., v. Sierra Club, et al.*) has established rights to paddle navigable waterways, many still remain off limits. The salient parts of the decision, allowing portages on private land:

> *[I]n order to circumvent these occasional obstacles, the right to navigate carries with it the incidental privilege to make use, when absolutely necessary, of the bed and banks, including the right to portage on riparian lands. . . . On the other hand, any use of private riverbeds or banks that is not strictly incidental to the right to navigate gives rise to an action for trespass.*

The section that extends navigability to recreational uses:

> *In line with these modern circumstances and our precedents, we are satisfied that recreational use should be part of the navigability analysis.*

However, eight years after the highest New York court decision, we could not gain access to Little Forked Lake from Forked Lake because of a locked gate across the wide connecting waterway. The court decision does not apply to ponds at the upper ends of waterways. However, a bill introduced in the Assembly in February 2006, if passed, would open navigable lakes and ponds, as well as streams and rivers.

Long Island. The Long Island situation differs materially from that in the Adirondacks, in that we have always had access to the best paddling locations on Long Island, but at an increasingly steep price for non-residents. If you did a weeklong tour of Long Island, paddling once on each of the locations in this book, it could cost you hundreds of dollars in access and parking fees. Is it reasonable to charge someone who will paddle a body of water only once in a season $150 for that privilege? We must prod the Department of Environmental Conservation to put in more public accesses on Long Island.

Public Campgrounds. Within Adirondack Park and throughout New York, the state maintains hundreds of campgrounds and camping areas for our enjoyment. Campgrounds charge modest fees, and some camping areas—particularly in Adirondack and Catskill parks—are free. Because fragile vegetation around lakes and ponds can suffer damage easily from heavy use, we recommend camping in designated areas only. For a complete listing, see Appendix A.

Southeastern
New York

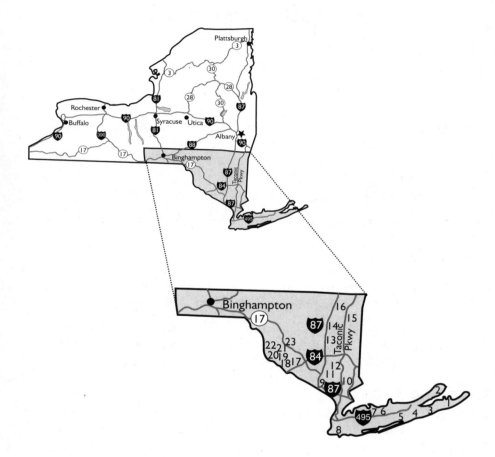

I

Acabonack Harbor

East Hampton

Maps: New York Atlas Map 29:B4, USGS Quadrangle Gardiners Island West

Area: 390 acres (high tide), maximum depth 6 feet

Habitat type: short-grass salt marsh estuary

Fish and shellfish: scallop, whelk, razor clam, bluefish, flounder

Expect to see: osprey, northern harrier, herons, egrets, sea lavender, glasswort

Camping and trails: trails, The Nature Conservancy, www.nature .org, 631-367-3225; camping App. A #31, 117, and 122

Take note: tide tables, www.tidesonline.com; free parking on road shoulder, $100 annual nonresident fee to park at access, www.town .east-hampton.ny.us, 631-324-4142

GETTING THERE

From Route 27 in East Hampton, bear left (north) on North Main Street. Go 0.6 mile, and bear right on Springs Fireplace Road. Go 3.7 miles (4.3 miles), and turn right on Old Stone Highway. Go 0.7 mile (5.0 miles), and turn left to the access on Landing Lane (free parking on road shoulder).

Acabonack Harbor and East Harbor extend roughly 2 miles north-south but offer 8 miles of shoreline to explore, including two principal islands. With limited development, the whole area—rich with fauna and flora and protected by The Nature Conservancy, town and state— exudes wildness.

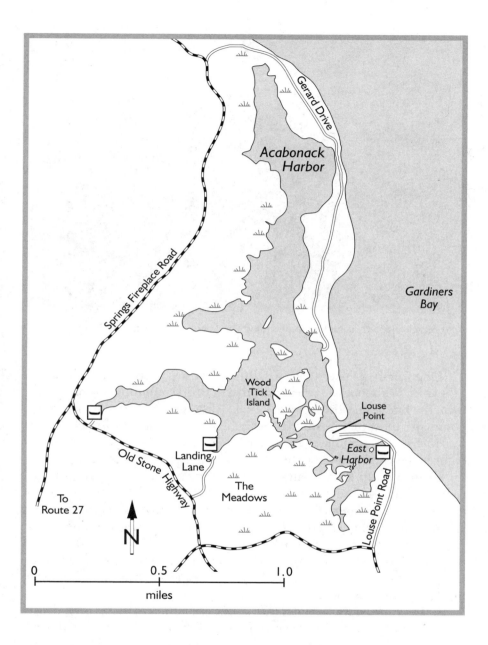

Gerard Drive

Acabonack Harbor

Springs Fireplace Road

Gardiners Bay

Wood
Tick
Island

Louse
Point

Old Stone Highway

Landing
Lane

*East
Harbor*

Louse Point Road

To
Route 27

The
Meadows

N

0   0.5   1.0

miles

Acabonack Harbor at high tide, flooding the *Spartina patens*.

One might suspect that all salt marshes are pretty much the same. Not true. Acabonack Harbor's salt marsh ecosystem differs dramatically from the one at nearby Sebonac Creek. Although tall *Spartina alterniflora* dominates most of the estuaries described in this guide, the much shorter *Spartina patens* dominates Acabonack Harbor. The shorter plants—just eight inches high—endow the marsh with a more diminutive feel.

Even at midtide, you can see out over the marsh for a great distance. At high tide, you literally look down on it. We could see a great egret a mile away, its slender white body prominent against the marsh's greens and browns. Along with dozens of great egrets, we saw great blue heron, snowy egret, herring gull flocks madly picking at some sort of prey in the marsh, osprey, northern harrier, and various sandpipers, including lesser yellowlegs feeding on mud banks. Rare least terns and threatened piping plovers nest here.

In some areas, sea lavender (*Limonium carolinianum*) seems even denser than the ever-present *Spartina patens*. One of the most beautiful salt marsh plants, sea lavender blooms in July with diminutive lavender blossoms. People have removed this plant from vast areas of salt marsh to make dried flower arrangements—please enjoy sea lavender in its natural environment.

Also look for glasswort, an odd plant with no obvious leaves and thick, succulent, jointed stems. In autumn, glasswort turns a deep red, making it noticeable from quite a distance.

White, scarlet, black, and post oaks occupy much of the higher ground, along with pignut hickory, sassafras, and sumac, a lot of it overlain with a tangle of grape, greenbrier, and poison ivy vines. Look for the deep green foliage of aromatic redcedar, *Juniperus virginiana*, readily noticeable among the deciduous trees. Redcedar has small whitish or bluish berrylike cones, ruddy-brown bark, and reddish aromatic wood.

At the harbor's southern end, The Meadows forms the marsh's wildest and most attractive area. From Landing Road, paddle between Wood Tick Island and The Meadows, snaking toward East Harbor. At high tide, the mosquito-control ditches become accessible. Built in the 1930s and 1940s, most of these ditches remain after more than 60 years, showing the permanence of our effects on the salt marsh. People still debate the effectiveness of this past practice.

Development intrudes on East Harbor's eastern side, as well as on much of the main harbor's northern end. For a change of pace, from the north end of East Harbor, cross the dunes, and explore the ocean side. To the south, the quite dramatic Acabonack Cliffs rise from the sea. You could also explore a Nature Conservancy trail between Springs Fireplace Road and Acabonack Harbor.

2

Hallock Bay
(Long Beach Bay)
and Little Bay
Southold

Maps: New York Atlas Map 28:A3, USGS Quadrangle Orient

Area: 680 acres, maximum depth 6 feet

Habitat type: long-grass salt marsh estuary

Fish and shellfish: scallop, whelk, razor clam, striped bass

Expect to see: osprey, northern harrier, herons, egrets, groundsel, eelgrass

Ferry: Orient Point-New London Ferry, www.longislandferry .com, 860-443-5281 (NE), 631-323-2525 (LI)

Camping, trails, and access: Orient Beach State Park, 631-323-2440, entrance fee; Narrow River Road parking permit (nonresident $12 daily, $100 annual), southoldtown.northfork.net, 631-765-1800; camping App. A #32 and 119

Take note: tide tables, www.tidesonline.com

GETTING THERE
Narrow River Road. From the junction of Routes 25 and 48 north of Greenport, go 5.6 miles east on Route 25, and turn right on Narrow River Road. Go 0.9 mile (6.5 miles) to the access on the left (parking permit required).

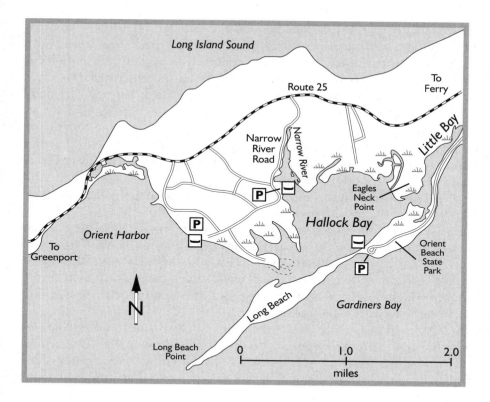

From the Orient Point ferry, go 2.3 miles west on Route 25, turn left on Narrow River Road, and follow as above.

Orient Beach State Park. From the junction of Routes 25 and 48, go 7.6 miles to the entrance on the right (0.3 mile west of the ferry).

Hallock Bay

Located just minutes from the New London–Orient Point Ferry terminus, Hallock Bay offers excellent paddling. Little development intrudes on this area, and currents remain modest (except at the harbor's mouth). On a mid-October paddle, we watched three skeins of migrating snow geese, momentarily distracting us from gazing at the deep reds of oaks, bright orange-reds of sumac, and spots of red glasswort in the salt marsh.

Hallock Bay offers plenty of opportunity for salt marsh exploration. From the access, paddle "upriver" (north), passing through thick stands of salt marsh cordgrass (*Spartina alterniflora*). Though high tide submerges this dominant plant twice daily, it has developed mechanisms to survive high salt concentrations, and it plays a critically important role in this ecosystem, providing habitat for young striped bass and other species.

At the *Spartina* base at low tide, note the thick clusters of ribbed mussel, a species not commercially harvested—perhaps explaining its profusion. Patches of *Phragmites*—a very tall grass displacing *Spartina* in some areas of the Northeast—grow on slightly higher ground. Farther from shore, you will see black locust, sumac, wild cherry, white and scarlet oaks, and Eastern redcedar.

Along the northern shore, you can explore salt marsh inlets, particularly toward the eastern end. At one point, even at midtide, you can paddle a loop. We found the branching inlet just west of Eagles Neck Point especially interesting. As we neared an exposed mud bank, a frenzy of activity broke out as hundreds of critters—appropriately called ghost crabs—skittered along exposed peat banks and scurried down their three-quarter-inch holes. We got our best look through binoculars, sneaking up quietly to within about a dozen feet.

On a calm day, the bay's exceptionally clear water allows views of the bottom nearly throughout. We got a good look at whelks crawling along the sand bottom, while dozens of blue crabs danced along sideways—one that we challenged with a paddle had a foot-long claw span. Just south of the Narrow River mouth, we saw quite a few small striped bass. Eelgrass beds of statewide significance also occur here, along with nesting rare least tern and endangered piping plover.

Little Bay

Little Bay, on the eastern end, extends about a mile to the north-northeast. We saw several northern harriers on this wild shore, along with osprey (more than a dozen nesting platforms dot the bay), Canada goose, great and snowy egrets, greater yellowlegs, cormorant, and common loon. In the fall, notice the groundsel, *Baccharis halimifolia*, near the north end. From a distance, it appears covered with bushy white blooms that are actually cottony tufts (technically, a pappus) that aid in seed dispersal.

Orient Beach State Park

Orient Beach State Park covers the entire 357-acre southeastern shore of Hallock and Little Bays. It has remained in public hands since 1774, when the residents preserved it forever by written agreement. In October 1929, the owners deeded the land to the state for the park, which offers picnicking and swimming, along with hiking among rare plant communities, including prickly pear cactus (*Opuntia humifusa*), blackjack oak (*Quercus marilandica*), and a 69-acre Eastern redcedar forest (*Juniperus virginiana*).

3

Sebonac Creek
Southampton

Maps: New York Atlas Map 28:C2, USGS Quadrangle Southampton

Area: 530 acres, maximum depth 16 feet (Scallop Pond)

Habitat type: long-grass salt marsh estuary

Fish and shellfish: scallop, whelk, razor clam, striped bass

Expect to see: osprey, herons, egrets, ducks, geese

Camping and outfitters: canoe, kayak rentals, transportation, Peconic Paddler, 631-727-9895; camping App. A #31, 32, 117, 119, 120, and 121

Take note: tide tables, www.tidesonline.com; ramp use permit (West Neck Road access), Town of Southampton, 631-287-5740; avoid during duck hunting season

GETTING THERE

West Neck Road Accesses. From the junction of Routes 27 and 52 north of Southampton, go 0.9 mile north on Route 52, and turn left on Route 38. Go immediately left on West Neck Road, and go 1.2 miles (2.1 miles) to the junction with Millstone Brook/Scotts roads. Continue across to one of the three accesses on the map. The farthest south access has a $150 annual nonresident ramp fee.

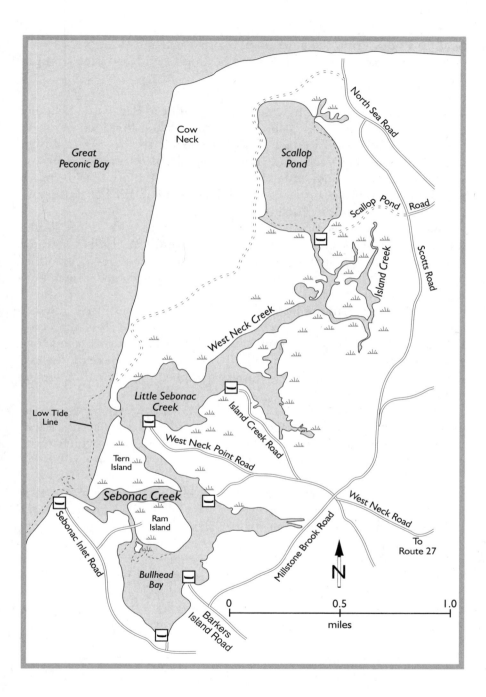

Great
Peconic Bay

Cow
Neck

Scallop
Pond

North Sea Road

Scallop Pond Road

Island Creek

Scotts Road

West Neck Creek

Low Tide
Line

Little Sebonac
Creek

Island Creek Road

West Neck Point Road

Tern
Island

Sebonac Creek

Ram
Island

West Neck Road

To
Route 27

Sebonac Inlet Road

Bullhead
Bay

Millstone Brook Road

N

Barkers Island Road

0   0.5   1.0
miles

Scallop Pond. From the junction of Scotts Road and West Neck Road, go 1.3 miles north on Scotts Road to Scallop Pond Road access on the left (high clearance recommended).

The contiguous waters of Sebonac Creek, Bullhead Bay, Little Sebonac Creek, West Neck Creek, Island Creek, and Scallop Pond may provide the finest paddling on Long Island. Manageable in size, yet extensive enough for lots of exercise, these waters could keep you occupied all day, exploring all of its nooks and crannies. We paddled more than 10 miles and did not explore every last creek, let alone the dozens of mosquito-control ditches, many accessible at high tide.

Salt marsh cordgrass, *Spartina alterniflora*, dominates the entire shoreline of this estuary. One of the few plants able to survive regular saltwater flooding, much of it submerges at high tide and reemerges at low tide. *Spartina alterniflora* evolved to fill an important ecological niche, and it indeed thrives in the salt marsh environment.

On higher ground not flooded by the twice-daily high tides, you will see a much shorter cousin, *Spartina patens*, along with such plants as sea lavender and glasswort. In autumn, the bright red glasswort stands out markedly amid the browns and yellows of other plants. Beneath the salt marsh's raised plain grow thick clusters of ribbed mussel and masses of reddish-brown seaweed.

A thick oak woods stands back from the shore, where white oak dominates, but you will also see scarlet oak and may come across black, post, and scrub oaks. Pignut hickory, beech, black gum (which turns crimson in early fall), sassafras, and black cherry add variety to the tree-species mix.

Bird life fills the estuary, including great blue and green herons, great and snowy egrets, hundreds of black ducks, pied-billed grebe, greater yellowlegs, kingfisher, osprey, northern harrier, and the ever-present herring gull—to mention a few. Note that hunters also know about the many ducks here. Keep your eye out for deer, fox, mink, and otter, as well.

Little development intrudes on the estuary except on Little Sebonac Creek and Bullhead Bay. Many houses there represent architectural statements, and we enjoyed examining them as we paddled along. The estuary's northern sections remain wilder and more remote, though Scallop Pond sports a few houses.

Little Sebonac Creek's eastern extension and Island Creek's extensive winding channels provide a wonderful paddling experience, where

Salt marsh cordgrass in the early morning light.

you can feel truly alone; even on a windy day you can find protected areas to escape rougher water. Along Island Creek, you get a real feel for the marsh—the wide flat plain of grass seems almost like a sea, surrounded by oak forest on higher ground.

On Island Creek's northern extension, you pass a mansion on the right, a colonial-style house set well back from the water. Within a few hours of high tide, you can paddle north, past the house. The channel looks as if it will peter out as you pass a gazebo, but it winds around, passes under a footbridge, and continues at least another quarter mile until the *Spartina* and other vegetation swallows the channel.

Scallop Pond, at the estuary's northern end, is a large oval pond, two-thirds of a mile long. A narrow band of *Spartina alterniflora* surrounds it, too, but trees extend much closer to the water than elsewhere. A very prominent mansion and its associated buildings sit on Scallop Pond, lending a dramatic feel to this area. From a distance, a large boathouse seems to appear on the waterside, but this turns out to be a curving concrete wall with windows that backs up to the water—creating what must be a very unusual space inside.

Just past the mansion, a narrow passageway leads to another, much smaller salt marsh. One might be able to paddle (carefully) through this channel—almost a tunnel of wooden posts—but the wind blew a gale, and we could not get into the channel without being bashed against the sides by the waves.

To go for a walk on a fairly wild section of Peconic Bay shoreline, when you paddle back into Little Sebonac Creek, take out up near the cut at the creek's western end, and cross over the narrow band of dunes. Walking north toward Cow Neck, you will find lots of shells and colorful stones.

You can easily paddle around Ram Island, passing under the island's access road bridge. Though you might explore some marshy islands just south of Ram Island, we found Bullhead Bay less interesting than the marsh north of Ram Island. The bay backs up on a huge golf course with a road right along the western shore.

4

Flanders Bay Tributaries and Peconic River

Riverhead and Southampton

Maps: New York Atlas Maps 27:A7 and 28:C1, USGS Quadrangles Mattituck and Riverhead

Habitat type: tidal estuary below Riverhead, impounded, slow-flowing river above

Expect to see: osprey, herons, egrets, ducks, geese, whitetailed deer, pitch pine

Outfitters: canoe, kayak rentals, transportation, Peconic Paddler, 631-727-9895

Camping and trails: hiking, Suffolk County Parks Department, 631-854-4949; camping App. A #32, 118, 119, 120, and 121

Take note: tide tables, www.tidesonline.com; novice paddlers should avoid Flanders and Peconic Bays under windy conditions; always wear a PFD on the bay

GETTING THERE

Birch Creek. From Route 104, go 4.0 miles east on Route 24, turn left on Birch Creek Road, and go 0.4 mile (4.4 miles) to the access.

Hubbard Creek. From the junction of Routes 24 and 104 in Riverhead, go 5.3 miles east on Route 24, and turn left on Red Creek Road. Go 0.6 mile (5.9 miles), turn left on Upper Red Creek Road, and go

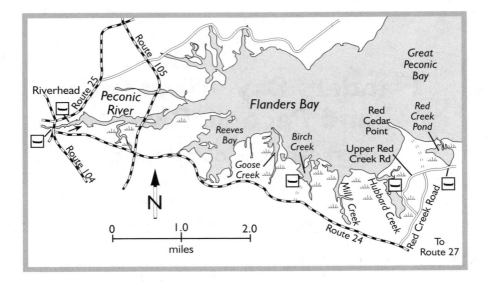

0.4 mile (6.3 miles) to the access on the left by an old building. Carry 175 feet to the water.

Red Creek Pond. From the junction of Routes 24 and Red Creek Road, go 1.7 miles on Red Creek Road to the access on the left.

Riverhead. From I-495, Exit 71, go about 4 miles on Route 24 to Riverhead. Access on Peconic Avenue at Peconic Paddler or just across the river at a public access under development.

Flanders Bay Tributaries

Flanders Bay, large and dangerous on a windy day, offers several tributaries with superb paddling; we recommend three creeks: Hubbard, Mill, and Birch. Hubbard Creek's islands, deep twisting coves, and winding salt marsh channels provide the most interesting paddling. When breezes blow on the bay, sheltered Hubbard Creek provides a quiet retreat from the world—though you have to carry your boat a little way to get to it.

Birch Creek provides the closest access to Mill Creek. Red Creek Pond also has an access, though we would avoid paddling around Redcedar Point under windy conditions. You can also paddle from Riverhead across Reeves Bay to reach these undeveloped areas. We would use sea kayaks with spray skirts when paddling on the bays.

Salt marsh cordgrass, *Spartina alterniflora*, dominates the salt marshes and tidal inlets on Flanders Bay. This grass can survive—and indeed requires—regular flooding by salt water. In centuries past, Long Island settlers harvested this grass as winter feed for livestock.

Paddling here in autumn, we saw lots of black ducks, a half-dozen mute swans, an osprey hovering in search of fish, and an assortment of songbirds preparing for fall migration. In the creeks, the shallow, mucky bottom could leave you high and, unfortunately, not very dry at low tide.

A thick oak–pitch pine woods occurs on higher ground. Early settlers used pitch pine—the only common pine with three-needle clusters—for making charcoal and fence posts, and they tapped the trees for sap, which they made into turpentine and resin. Among the deciduous trees, white and scarlet oaks seem to be most common. Also look for groundsel and bayberry, with its highly scented leaves.

Peconic River—Downstream

Launching in Riverhead, you can explore about 2 miles of river before reaching the bay. A little tributary on the south side, just west of the Route 105 bridge, offers very pleasant salt marsh exploration. The north side of Flanders Bay suffers from quite a bit of development, and we do not recommend paddling there.

Peconic River—Upstream

Paddlers can also enjoy a one-way, 8-mile trip along the Peconic River farther west, from Connecticut Avenue in Manorville to Riverhead, which offers fine paddling. If you are considering paddling the river, be sure to check with the Peconic Paddler about river conditions.

The Peconic River—the longest river on Long Island and one of the most popular paddling locations—flows filled entirely with fresh water west of the dam at Riverhead. Winding through woodlands, farmland, old cranberry bog impoundments, and a few industry backyards, some narrow sections flow with moderate current but no rapids; other sections flow through broad marshes. You must carry over several dams and roads. The Peconic Paddler rents canoes and kayaks, and even if you do not rent a boat, the outfitter will ferry you and your boat to the access in Manorville for a modest fee.

5

Carmans River
Brookhaven

Maps: New York Atlas Map 27:B5, USGS Quadrangle Bellport

Length: 4.5 miles (lower section)

Habitat type: tidal estuary below Route 27, impounded river above; no development

Fish: striped bass, flounder, brown and rainbow trout, pickerel

Expect to see: osprey, herons, egrets, wood and black ducks, deer, muskrat

Outfitters: canoe, kayak rentals, transportation, Carmans River Canoe & Kayak, 631-286-0567

Camping and trails: trails, Wertheim National Wildlife Refuge, 631-286-0485; camping App. A #30, 32, 118, 119, 124, 125, 126, and 127

Take note: tide tables, www.tidesonline.com

GETTING THERE

Squassux Landing. From Route 27, Exit 57, go 0.3 mile west (right) on Montauk Highway (Route 80), and turn left on Old Stump Road. Go 1.4 miles (1.7 miles), turn left on Beaver Dam Road, and go 0.2 mile (1.9 miles) to the access.

Montauk Highway. From I-495, Exit 68, go south on William Floyd Parkway (Route 46) to Montauk Highway (Route 80). Turn right (west),

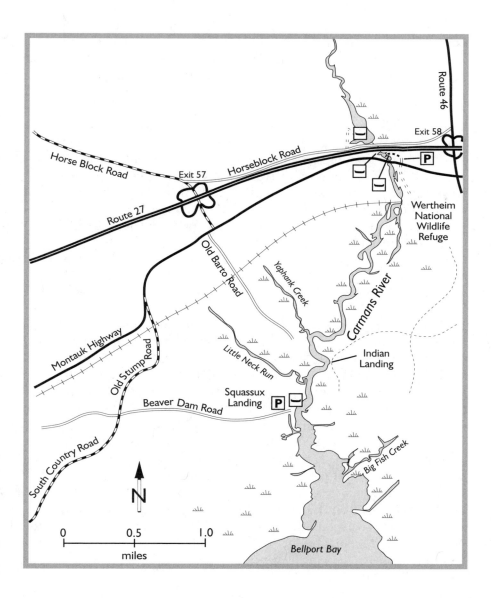

and go 0.9 mile to the access on the right at the traffic light. Carry your boat about 250 yards to the river.

Upper Carmans River. Use Carman's River Canoe & Kayak services; located on Carmans River, just west of the Montauk Highway bridge.

Lower Carmans River

Carmans River and its surrounding marsh represent one of the last undeveloped estuaries on Long Island. The wildest and most pristine of the island's four major rivers—the others are Nissequogue, Connetquot, and Peconic—it offers fantastic paddling and wildlife observing. We include here the lower section, a meandering 4.5-mile tidal flow from Route 27 to Bellport Bay through 2,550-acre Wertheim National Wildlife Refuge.

Phragmites lines the banks in some areas, its tall, plumed stalks swaying in the breeze, along with two species of cordgrass, *Spartina alterniflora* and *S. cynosuroides*. Though not far from major highways and development, you can immerse yourself in wildness here.

The tributary streams Little Neck Run, Yaphank Creek, and Big Fish Creek particularly invite exploration—at least at high tide. On these creeks, you gradually leave the *Phragmites*-dominated marshland, immersing in much more variety: Atlantic white cedar, black gum, and pitch pine, for example. We saw lots of wood duck here, along with herons, osprey, and a snapping turtle.

In the shallow water, crabs skitter along sideways while huge carp wallow in the mud. We spotted two Virginia rails foraging for insects and crustaceans in the mud amid *Phragmites* stems. This elusive, well-camouflaged rail has a fairly long, down-curved bill and very long toes for support on soft mud. We also saw goldeneye, cormorant, mallard, and a loon—perhaps having just returned to the coast from the Adirondacks. Though the loon spends most of its life in salt water, it breeds only in fresh water.

In late summer, look for the dramatic swamp rose mallow, *Hibiscus moscheutos* subspecies *palustris*, a relative of the hollyhock, blooming here. We saw several plants with beautiful, five-petaled, pink, roselike flowers about 5 inches across.

A trail leaves from Indian Landing, on the eastern shore, providing an opportunity to explore the refuge's higher ground on foot. Unless the tide is clearly receding, be sure to tie your boat.

Upper Carmans River

Carman's River Canoe & Kayak operates trips on the upper Carmans River, above the Route 27 dam, which has a very different character from the tidal river below. This 5-mile stretch of fresh water meanders slowly through woodland, as well as marshy areas. For a fee, the outfitter will shuttle you and your boat to the upper end, allowing you to paddle downriver to South Haven Park, just north of Route 27.

Maples and other deciduous trees replace salt marsh vegetation at the north end of the river's tidal portion.

6

Stony Brook Harbor

Smithtown

Maps: New York Atlas Map 26:A3, USGS Quadrangle Saint James

Area: 940 acres (high tide)

Habitat type: tidal estuary, islands and protected coves; mudflats at low tide

Fish: striped bass, flounder

Expect to see: osprey, least tern, herons, egrets

Camping: App. A #30, 32, 123, 124, 126, and 129

Take note: tide tables, www.tidesonline.com; town of Brookhaven, 631-451-6100

GETTING THERE

Stony Brook Village. From I-495, go 3.9 miles north on Route 111 to the junction with Routes 25 and 25A. Go northeast on Route 25A, and when Route 25A goes right at the sign for Stony Brook, go straight on Main Street for 0.5 mile (4.4 miles), then bear left onto Shore Road. Go 0.2 mile (4.6 miles) to the access by the yacht club.

Harbor Road. There seems to be no prohibition against launching from Harbor Road, though parking is limited.

Located along Long Island's north shore on Smithtown Bay, Stony Brook Harbor provides a superb example of tidal estuary. Six-foot tall salt marsh cordgrass, *Spartina alterniflora*, dominates the harbor, including the entire

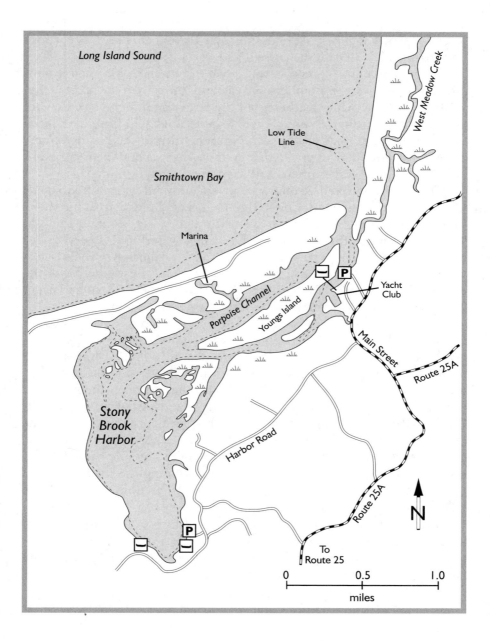

shoreline and numerous islands. Throughout the Atlantic seaboard, thousands of tidal acres contain *S. alterniflora* as almost the only vascular plant. Low tide exposes vast mussel shoals and high peat banks, reducing the open water by about half. At high tide, only the upper cordgrass portions wave back and forth with the current and wakes of passing boats.

Great blue heron, green heron, great egret, and snowy egret congregate here in large numbers. Great and snowy egrets boast a full plumage of snow-white feathers, but the larger great egret's yellow bill distinguishes it from the snowy egret with its black bill. Both have black legs, but the snowy has yellow feet. Near the turn of the century, hunters nearly extirpated them in this country, harvesting their gorgeous breeding-season plumes, then used in women's high fashion.

The double-crested cormorant, an ungainly bird that often stands with outstretched wings drying in the sun, occurs here in great numbers. Its rear-set, webbed feet help it swim through water, hunting for fish. Spending so much time underwater, its wings waterlog and need to dry before the heavy bird takes to the air—quite a laborious process even with dry wings. Watch for least tern, smallest and most graceful of the tern family, particularly along the northeastern end of Youngs Island. The island remains off-limits to protect the nesting colony.

Where the harbor bends south—our favorite section—you can weave through the cordgrass islands, but only at high tide. Beyond the cordgrass, thick deciduous woodlands cling to the hills. Huge white oak and black birch, along with black locust, sassafras, beech, and black walnut, interrupt the manicured lawns of the estates that overlook the water.

Tides can make paddling near the Long Island Sound outlet difficult. Current at the harbor mouth may be so strong that you cannot paddle against it. Starting out on an incoming tide, you can explore the cordgrass islands around high tide, then ride the outgoing tide back through the more southern channel to the access—avoiding the main Porpoise Channel altogether. Only at high tide can you circumnavigate Youngs Island and avoid dealing with strong current on one side or the other. We really had to work to make our way southwest along this channel back to the access with the tide going out. To explore West Meadow Creek without a lot of work, paddle north on the incoming or high tide and back south at high tide or after the tide has turned.

7

Nissequogue River
Smithtown

Maps: New York Atlas Map 26:A3, USGS Quadrangles Central Islip and Saint James

Length: 5 miles one-way

Habitat type: tidal estuary; islands and oxbows; extensive mud flats at low tide

Fish: striped bass; flounder; brook, brown, and rainbow trout above Route 25 bridge

Expect to see: osprey, herons, egrets, ducks, geese

Outfitters: canoe, kayak rentals, transportation, Nissequogue River Canoe & Kayak Rentals, 631-979-8244; Bob's Canoe Rental, 631-269-9761

Camping and access: App. A #30, 32, 123, 124, 126, and 129; Nissequogue State Park, 631-269-4927

Take note: tide tables, www.tidesonline.com

GETTING THERE

Nissequogue State Park. From I-495, Exit 53, go north on Sunken Meadow Parkway to exit SM4E. Go east 3.0 miles on Pulaski Road, which becomes Old Dock Road. At the fourth traffic light, turn right on St. Johnland Road, and go 0.5 mile (3.5 miles) to the entrance on the left. There is also access at the end of Old Dock Road.

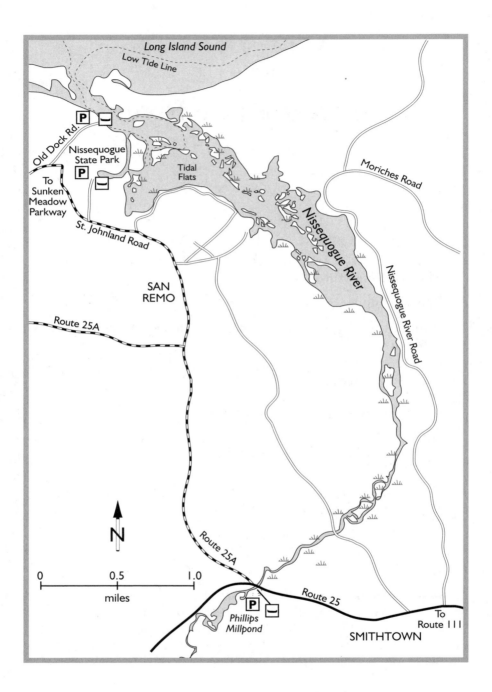

Long Island Sound
Low Tide Line

Old Dock Rd.

P

Nissequogue
State Park

P

To
Sunken
Meadow
Parkway

St. Johnland Road

Tidal
Flats

Nissequogue River

Moriches Road

Nissequogue River Road

SAN
REMO

Route 25A

N

0   0.5   1.0
         miles

Route 25A

Phillips
Millpond

P

Route 25

To
Route 111

SMITHTOWN

Route 25. Access on the south at the junction of Routes 25 and 25A in Smithtown.

New York State designated the Nissequogue a Scenic and Recreational River in 1982, and it remains almost totally undeveloped and one of Long Island's most popular paddling locations. Outfitters rent boats and provide shuttle service, making it easy to paddle both downstream on an outgoing tide or upstream on an incoming tide. Except near the river's mouth, the modest current would not prevent an up-and-back trip, though you might want to shuttle if you have to deal with *both* current and wind.

Nissequogue bristles with salt marsh cordgrass, *Spartina alterniflora*. Among the few tidal salt marsh plants, *Spartina* thrives, using several important adaptations, including maintaining high salt concentrations to counteract salt water's osmotic forces that would otherwise draw water out, dehydrating the plant. *Spartina* also secretes a concentrated salt solution through special pores; as water evaporates, crystals form, giving *Spartina* a whitish sheen until the next tide washes the crystals away.

Early Northeast coastal settlers cut and dried *Spartina alterniflora* as winter livestock feed. The *Spartina* marshes provided spawning habitat for the fish that supplied a livelihood for generations of coastal families. But this environment suffered ecological havoc from the 1940s until the 1970s, caused by intense use of DDT for mosquito control. The osprey you see here provide evidence of the ecosystem's gradual recovery.

The *Spartina* islands and river shoreline offer hours of exploration at high tide—much less at low tide. Passageways may extend around an island or reach a dead end. In places, channels have gradually closed in, leaving narrow, sinewy, mazelike creeks that wind among the islands.

You will see many egrets and herons. In one spot, we saw a group of trees dripping with almost 100 egrets. Even more cormorants covered another tree farther upriver. Kingfishers flew from snag to snag, emitting their rattlelike call. Both common and least terns—the latter a threatened species—nest near the river mouth, the least tern colony supposedly the largest on Long Island.

The river exhibits a pronounced salt-concentration gradient; the farther south you go, the less saline the water. Near the Route 25 bridge, the water runs fresh to brackish, with cattail, arrowhead, sweet flag, alder,

Herring gulls in flight over a *Spartina patens* salt marsh.

winterberry, and sweet pepperbush lining the bank. Trees include red maple, black gum, black walnut, and sassafras. *Spartina cynosuroides*, or big cordgrass, with its much more distinctive, spreading seed heads, also occurs here. *Phragmites* grows here, as well, and then mixes with *Spartina alterniflora* farther north. Near the sound, *S. alterniflora* dominates.

8

Jamaica Bay Wildlife Refuge
Brooklyn and Queens

Maps: New York Atlas Map 25:D5, USGS Quadrangles Brooklyn, Coney Island, Far Rockaway, and Jamaica

Area: 9,155 acres in wildlife refuge

Habitat type: large salt marsh estuary, many islands and protected bays; nature trails; development; motors allowed

Expect to see: osprey, herons, egrets, waterfowl, marsh birds, oystercatcher, Forster's tern, laughing gull

Camping, trails, and organizations: Jamaica Bay Wildlife Refuge—718-318-4340; Sebago Canoe Club—www.sebagocanoeclub.org; Hudson River Watertrail Association—www.hrwa.org; camping App. A #130

Take note: tide tables, www.tidesonline.com; not for novice paddlers, always wear a PFD here

GETTING THERE

Visitors Center. From the north and east, follow signs to JFK Airport. From the Van Wyck Expressway, I-678, go west on Route 27 for about 3 miles to Cross Bay Boulevard. Go south on Cross Bay Boulevard for 3.6 miles to the refuge office on the right.

Cross Bay Boulevard. Just after crossing North Channel Bridge, you can find parking areas on the left and right where you can launch non-motorized boats.

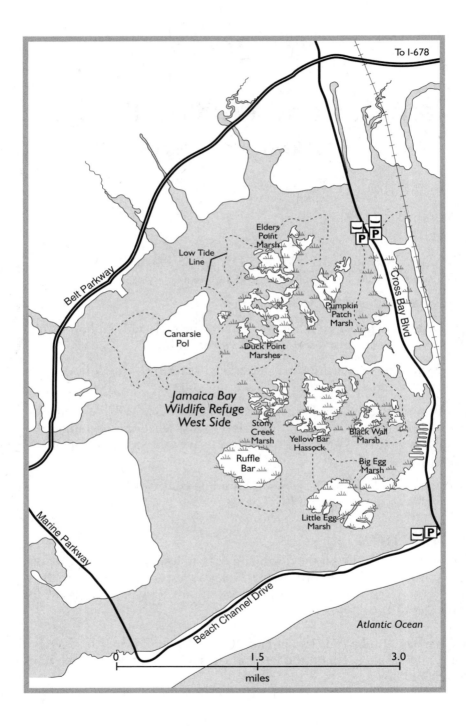

To I-678

Belt Parkway

Cross Bay Blvd

Elders Point Marsh

Low Tide Line

Pumpkin Patch Marsh

Canarsie Pol

Duck Point Marshes

Jamaica Bay Wildlife Refuge West Side

Stony Creek Marsh

Yellow Bar Hassock

Black Wall Marsh

Ruffle Bar

Big Egg Marsh

Little Egg Marsh

Marine Parkway

Beach Channel Drive

Atlantic Ocean

0   1.5   3.0
miles

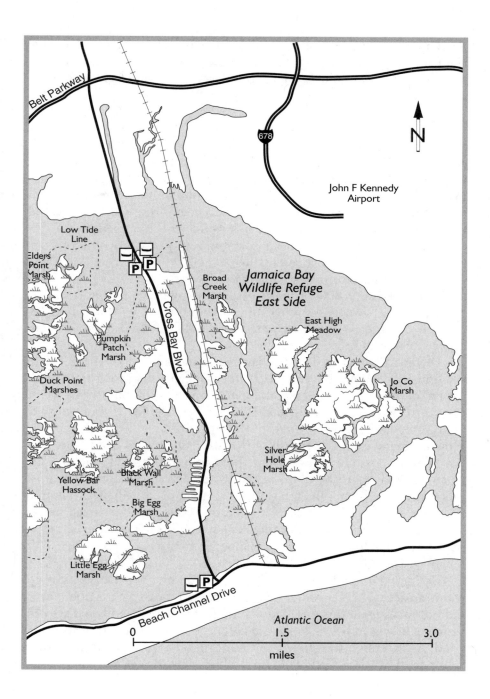

Belt Parkway

678

John F Kennedy
Airport

Low Tide
Line

Elders
Point
Marsh

P P

Broad
Creek
Marsh

Jamaica Bay
Wildlife Refuge
East Side

Pumpkin
Patch
Marsh

East High
Meadow

Duck Point
Marshes

Jo Co
Marsh

Cross Bay Blvd

Yellow Bar
Hassock

Black Wall
Marsh

Silver
Hole
Marsh

Big Egg
Marsh

Little Egg
Marsh

P

Beach Channel Drive

Atlantic Ocean

0   1.5   3.0
miles

Southeastern New York   **31**

Rockaway. Continue past the Visitors' Center; after the tollbooths, go right on Beach Channel Drive, following signs for Riis Park. Access is on the right in 0.5 mile, just after the Beach Channel High School tennis courts.

Huge Jamaica Bay, part of Gateway National Recreation Area, supports an extraordinary number of land, water, and shorebirds that nest, winter, or stopover during migration. At least 325 species have been recorded in the Jamaica Bay environs. The bay supports one of two laughing gull nesting colonies in New York. A diverse group of butterflies, mammals, amphibians, and reptiles—including sea turtles—reside here, as well. It would take several days to explore this wonderful resource fully.

Several islands support nesting colonies of gulls, terns, herons, and egrets. Perhaps the most interesting is 240-acre Canarsie Pol Island, which besides harboring nesting gulls and terns, also hosts a heron rookery with as many as 800 nesting pairs, including green heron, tricolored heron, black-crowned night heron, yellow-crowned night heron, glossy ibis, snowy egret, and great egret. You should not land on any islands, especially during breeding season.

Dozens of islands dot the bay, some natural, some the result of dredging and filling. Because you can easily get lost among the islands, we recommend that you take along a compass and a photocopy of the map in this book. The Visitors' Center also sells maps, can help you get oriented, and has some nature trails to explore. The main question: How does one explore a marsh of this size? One could paddle the eastern section, possibly investigating the common tern and laughing gull nesting colonies on the multi-island Jo Co Marsh. One could also explore the more island-choked western section, eventually heading up to Canarsie Pol Island to look at the heron rookeries. For first-time Jamaica Bay paddlers, we recommend that you go out with experienced hands, perhaps from the Sebago Canoe Club or the Hudson River Watertrail Association.

Besides the Cross Bay and Rockaway access, the DeLorme Atlas shows an access in Negro Bar Channel on the far eastern portion, but we did not investigate this one. Launching from Cross Bay presents an advantage, however, because you can choose the side that suffers from less wind. As you might imagine, wind blowing across several miles of open water and low islands can whip up sizable waves.

9

Harriman State Park Lakes

HAVERSTRAW, TUXEDO, AND WOODBURY

Maps: New York Atlas Map 32:C3, USGS Quadrangles Popolopen Lake, Sloatsburg, and Thiells; good park map, $4.00, Palisades Interstate Park Commission Bookstore, 845-786-5003

Park area: 47,000 acres

Habitat type: nine small ponds and lakes, ranging from 36 to 297 acres; geology, harrimanrocks.rutgers.edu

Fish: brook trout, largemouth and smallmouth bass, pickerel

Expect to see: ducks, geese, deer, beaver

Camping and cabins: App. A #36 and 37 (on-site)

Take note: gasoline motors prohibited; paddling April 1 to November 30; permit and boat inspection required, gate key needed for Tiorati, Welch, Stahahe lakes, Park Office/Tiorati Beach, 845-351-2568

GETTING THERE

From Palisades Interstate Parkway, Exit 18, follow Seven Lakes Drive southwest. From I-87, Exit 15A, turn left (north) on Route 17. Go 2.5 miles, and turn right (northeast) on Seven Lakes Drive.

Situated just north of the New Jersey border and only about 45 minutes from New York City, the lakes of Harriman State Park provided a remarkable surprise with fine paddling close to the city. It takes us two days of exploration to visit the eight bodies of water described here, paddling more than 20 miles, most of it at a very slow pace to maximize wildlife viewing.

Harriman State Park forms the largest parcel of land managed by the Palisades Interstate Park Commission, which owns more than 100,000 acres in New York and New Jersey. In the late 1800s, quarrying began to leave serious scars on the Hudson's scenic west bank; the cliffs and rubble beneath them provided ideal stone for constructing New York's brownstones and for producing concrete aggregate. The New Jersey Federation of Women's Clubs fought for legislation to protect the cliffs, resulting in the establishment of the Palisades Interstate Park Commission in 1900. Andrew H. Green, founder of the American Scenic and Historic Preservation Society, sponsored a similar effort in New York State. Harriman State Park had its beginnings in 1910 with the donation of 10,000 acres of land to New York State from Mrs. Mary Harriman—with the stipulation that the state abandon plans to build Sing Sing Prison on what is now Bear Mountain State Park.

Because 10 million people live within an hour's drive, the park sometimes suffers from extremely heavy recreational use, though most come here for hiking—according to trails.com, Harriman ranked fourth in the country in 2005 for trail use. During a typical summer weekend, hundreds of boats vie for space on some lakes. Annually, the Palisades Interstate Park Commission sells about 3,000 boating permits.

If you can, paddle here before mid-June or after Labor Day. In fact, three of the bodies of water are open to boating only during these times. Also, paddle here on weekdays; on a gorgeous Monday in mid-October—with trees in their full autumn splendor—we had the place to ourselves!

LAKE SEBAGO

Area: 294 acres, maximum depth 37 feet

GETTING THERE

From Palisades Parkway, go 9.6 miles southwest on Seven Lakes Drive to the access on the right. From Route 17, go 4.2 miles northeast on Seven Lakes Drive to the access on the left.

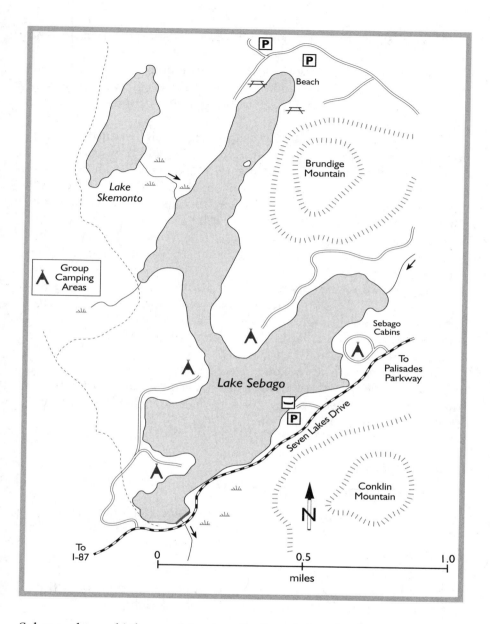

Sebago, the park's largest lake, has 6 miles of shoreline that offer splendid paddling. The widest portion of the lake extends in a northeast-southwest orientation, and a long arm extends to the north from its midpoint.

Massive slabs of granite and gneiss, a metamorphic rock, extend down into the water in places, some carpeted with mosses and polypody fern. Along the banks grow thick stands of mountain laurel, spectacular when in bloom in June. Highbush blueberry also grows in profusion here, so in August, you may want to bring along a container and pick some for your pancakes.

Sebago's surrounding woodlands, comprising almost entirely deciduous trees, include oaks (white, chestnut, scarlet, and red), beech, hickory, black birch, white ash, sugar maple, black locust, witch hazel, and American chestnut. Once one of the most abundant and economically important trees in the Northeast, the chestnut succumbed to the chestnut blight in the early 1900s. Saplings still sprout from rootstock, but these typically die after reaching 20 or 30 feet. We saw clumps of struggling saplings and hope someday a resistant strain will reclaim its place in our eastern forests.

The open woodlands invite exploration. You can explore from shore or hike some of the 200 miles of trails—including the Appalachian Trail—that extend throughout the park. We saw lots of deer browsing along shore, a beaver, mallards, and a loon during a late-afternoon paddle around the lake in mid-October.

Recreational facilities include an extensive swimming beach at the northern tip, along with two picnic areas, playgrounds, ball fields, and rowboat rentals. Several group camping and cabin locations are scattered around the southern section.

LAKE TIORATI

Area: 294 acres, maximum depth 43 feet

Take note: key required for gate; park office at Tiorati Circle

GETTING THERE

From the junction of Seven Lakes Drive and Route 106, go north 3.2 miles on Seven Lakes Drive to Tiorati Circle, and bear right on Tiorati Brook Road. Go 1.1 miles (4.3 miles) to the access on the right.

The second-largest body of water in the park and located near its center, Lake Tiorati perches at the highest elevation of those you can paddle. Also one of the most beautiful, with numerous wooded islands just south of the

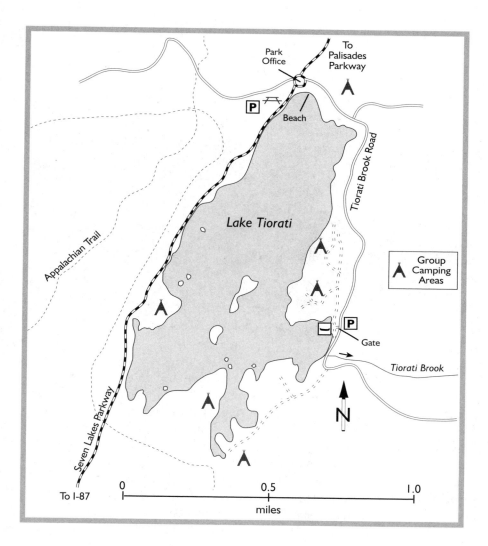

center, Tiorati—which means "skylike"—was created in 1914 by the damming of 40-acre Cedar Pond and 15-acre Little Clear Pond, which raised the water level by 17 feet and flooded 200 acres of swampland.

The southern shore stands out as our favorite part. You will find many coves, inlets, and islands to explore, along with a couple of beaver lodges. Look for beaver early in the morning or at dusk. At dusk, we have sometimes paddled right up to this largest of our rodents, usually hearing a loud slap of the tail as it plunges into the water's depths.

A lone white pine towers over the predominantly oak woods around Lake Tiorati.

In the shallows south of the large islands, notice the extensive beds of underwater vegetation. By midsummer, long bushy tassels of coontail and milfoil reach toward the surface. In the right light, these extraordinary plants—their feathery stems seeming to sparkle in captured light—stand out brightly against the much darker lake bottom. One can easily confuse these native species with the invasive Eurasian watermilfoil, which has taken over some New York lakes and the nearby Hudson River. Fanwort and several species of bladderwort also grow here, providing important habitat for bass and pickerel.

Oak dominates the forests, though you will see more pine and hemlock here than on most other bodies of water in the park. In many places, massive rock outcroppings reach down into the water.

Unfortunately, roads nearly surround the lake—Seven Lakes Drive passes along the entire western shore, and the less-traveled Tiorati Brook Road passes along two-thirds of the eastern shore. Considerable recreational development also encroaches on the lake, including group camping areas, picnic areas, swimming beach, and the park office.

LAKE KANAWAUKE, LAKE SKANNATATI, AND LITTLE LONG POND

Area: Kanawauke, 170 acres; Skannatati, 36 acres; Little Long, 56 acres

Take note: southern part of Lake Kanawauke closed to boating from third Saturday in June through Labor Day; parking fee at Lake Kanawauke

GETTING THERE

Lake Kanawauke. At the junction of Seven Lakes Drive and Route 106, go 0.4 mile west on Route 106 to the access on the left.

Lake Skannatati. From Route 106, go 0.8 mile northeast on Seven Lakes Drive to the access on the left.

Before 1915, only Little Long Pond existed here. Damming Stony Brook at the southern tip of the present lake created Lake Kanawauke—"place of much water." Lake Skannatati, meaning "the other side," was not formed until 1947.

Lake Kanawauke and Little Long Pond

To reach Kanawauke's northern section and Little Long Pond (the only sections accessible during most of the summer), you have to paddle under the arched-stone Route 106 bridge.

A large stand of red pine overlooks Kanawauke's eastern end, alongside the oak-dominated woodland found throughout the park. At the northeastern tip's inlet stream, you can tie your boat up and walk along the creek to Lake Skannatati through a gorgeous section of woodland where gnarled tree trunks rising from massive rock outcroppings lend an almost magical feeling.

Paddling here off-season, you can explore Kanawauke's southern section. About halfway down, just below a cove extending back to the north, you can paddle among an attractive group of islands, but refrain from getting out on them—doing so might harm the vegetation and disturb wildlife.

Despite the group camping areas and the road along Little Long Pond's northern shore, we found this the most interesting of these three connected ponds. A very attractive island cluster greets you as you

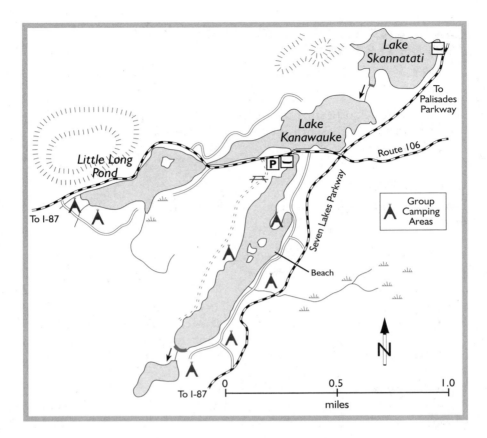

paddle into the pond, and across the way, exposed rock faces provide a delightful vista. Just east of the island, a shallow, stumpy area contains lots of floating vegetation and wildlife. Look for the small purple flowers of aquatic bladderwort here, along with fragrant waterlily, yellow pondlily, and water shield. Also, look for great blue heron, mallard, ring-necked duck, pied-billed grebe, red-tailed hawk, and beaver. As we paddled along the pond's southern shore into a small marshy area, we spooked about a dozen wood ducks getting ready for fall migration.

Lake Skannatati
Despite its small size, we love paddling Skannatati. With no group camping areas, you will find it quieter here. The shallow western end remains our favorite, where the coves and outlet arm take away from the

road. Some spectacular rock outcroppings here drip with ferns, and others sport moss-filled cracks, lending the rock faces a visage like massive road maps.

Igneous granite or metamorphic gneisses and schists form most of the park's exposed bedrock, though Storm King granite—a coarse-grained gray rock highly resistant to weathering—forms Bear Mountain to the east. The Bear Mountain Trailside Museum at the Palisades Interstate Parkway terminus contains information on the area's geology.

Along the western end of Skannatati and the northern cove, look for carnivorous sundews on moss-covered logs by the water's edge and on grassy hummocks and for leatherleaf—a plant frequently associated with bogs and northern fens—with its small, leathery leaves and white, bell-like, early-season flowers.

LAKE STAHAHE

Area and Maximum Depth: 86 acres, 20 feet

Take note: closed to boating from third Saturday in June through Labor Day; key required for gate; park office at Tiorati Circle

GETTING THERE

From the junction of Seven Lakes Drive and Route 106, go 3.9 miles west on Route 106, and turn right on the access road.

The narrow northern end of this mile-long lake has lots of cabins and group camping areas, but these should be mostly empty when you can paddle on Stahahe. Even so, the southern end offers more interesting paddling. Here you'll find lots of islands to explore, along with shallow marshy areas, rich in fauna and flora.

Near dusk on an October day, we watched an otter for about a half hour as it fished—or perhaps just frolicked—in the shallows. We also saw a small flock of Canada geese. Along the shore, deer browsed all over the place—obviously, fairly tame and too used to people. We also saw a beautiful red fox just south of the lake on Route 106.

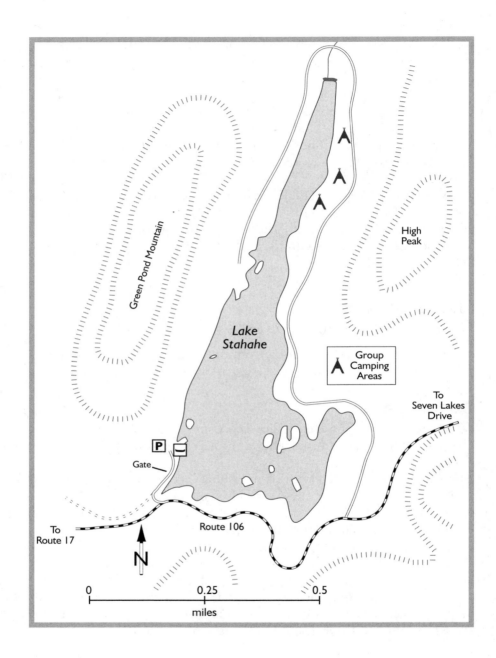

Green Pond Mountain

Lake
Stahahe

High
Peak

Group
Camping
Areas

To
Seven Lakes
Drive

P

Gate

To
Route 17

Route 106

N

0   0.25   0.5

miles

A monarch butterfly sucks nectar from late-season asters in preparation for its long migration to Mexico.

SILVERMINE LAKE

Area: 84 acres, maximum depth 20 feet

GETTING THERE

From Tiorati Circle, go 2.2 miles northeast on Seven Lakes Drive, and turn right into the Silvermine Picnic Area. Cross the small bridge to unload your boat; park in the parking lot.

We get the sense that Silvermine Lake sees somewhat fewer visitors than other Harriman lakes. Created in 1934 by a dam on Bockey Swamp Brook that flooded a beaver swamp, the lake still has a marshy feel and quite different vegetation from that found in and around other park lakes.

A large stand of tamarack grows near the northeastern end, and thick clumps of alder, willow, red maple, red osier dogwood, sweet pepperbush, gray birch, and common reed (*Phragmites*)—all common marsh plants—line the northern shore. A dense oak-beech-maple forest—more typical of the region—rises from the water's southern edge. Submerged

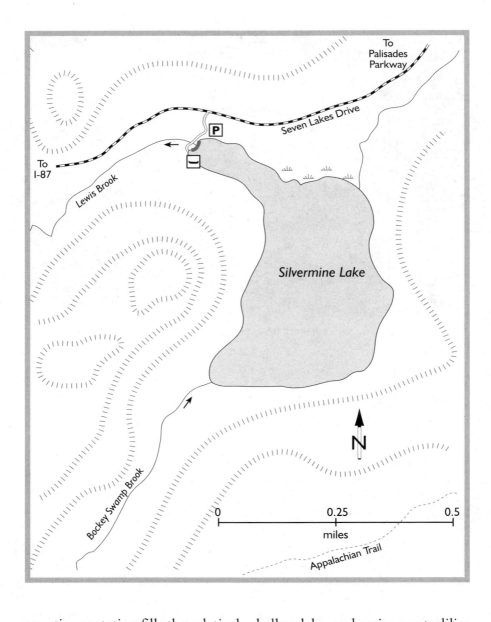

aquatic vegetation fills the relatively shallow lake, and various waterlilies cover the arm to the northwest.

We saw lots of mallards and Canada geese, and turkey vultures and red-tailed hawks soared overhead. Though we didn't climb up the steep slope of the ski area near the access, it looked as if one would get a great view to the north.

LAKE WELCH

Area: 205 acres, maximum depth 33 feet

Take note: key required for gate; park office at Tiorati Circle

GETTING THERE

From Seven Lakes Drive, go 1.7 miles east on Route 106, and turn left on the easy-to-miss access road.

Of all the park's lakes and ponds, Lake Welch remains our favorite. The main lake does not appeal—though we did see a flock of ruddy ducks and several Canada geese during a mid-October paddle—because of its large, oval shape and gigantic swimming beach that dominates the northeast end. But we love the lake's southwest arm and Beaver Pond Brook.

Paddle southeast from the boat access and around the would-be island now connected by Route 106. After crossing under the road, paddle southwest, away from the cacophony of the beach and cars. As the lake narrows and becomes rocky, expect a scratch or two. Ease your way past and into the marshy Beaver Pond Brook inlet, leaving rocks behind, entering a wild, magical area.

True to its name, we quickly came upon a beaver lodge in the brook's broad outlet. Though hard to gauge distance here, we paddled at least a half mile along this highly twisted, slow-flowing brook as it meandered through *Phragmites* and red maple swamp. In places, the channel became so narrow and the curves so tight that it became a challenge to squeak through.

The farther we went, the shallower the water. Eventually, sand replaced mucky bottom, and we found our way blocked by a downed log. Fortunately, we found a place where—with some difficulty—we could turn around. If you paddle a kayak, bring a breakdown paddle; using a two-bladed paddle would be out of the question along this creek.

Beaver Pond Brook teems with wildlife. We saw songbirds galore in the thick shrubs and grasses. Paddling back, after the brook widened out, we noticed movement and spotted a young otter making

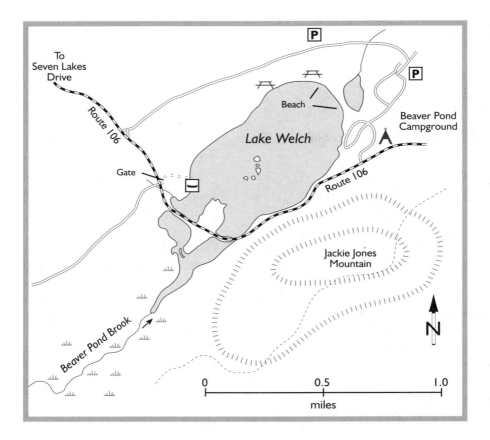

its way along the bank. Obviously hunting, it crawled over, slithered around, and swam under tree roots and grass hummocks hanging out over the water. Watching this otter—with no sign of people anywhere— we reveled in the fact that New York City lay only an hour away.

Paddling back to the north toward the Route 106 bridge, look for a narrow channel heading to the left (northwest) that leads to another part of the lake. Though within view of Route 106, this area felt quite wild. Immediately upon entering the cove, we spotted an osprey that took off with a half-eaten fish in its talons.

Snapping Turtle

Hidden Dweller of the Pond

The snapping turtle—New York's most common turtle species, even more common than the painted turtle—inhabits almost every beaver pond, millpond, lake, marsh, and slow-moving stream. Hundreds live in some bodies of water, but you would not know it. Even if you spend quite a bit of time paddling, you rarely see this large turtle. Unlike its sun-loving cousin, the painted turtle, the snapper prefers pond-bottom depths and rarely basks. (The photo shows an obvious exception to this generality.)

You can easily recognize a snapping turtle, *Chelydra serpentina*, especially out of water. A long, spiny-ridged tail and very large head relative to body size gives it away. The young has a distinct ridge on the top shell (carapace), though on a large adult, the shell may have worn smooth. On the underside, the small bottom shell (plastron) has a crosslike shape.

Mature snapping turtles grow quite large, much larger than any other Northeast turtle. The carapace can reach a length of 20 inches (an overall length, nose to tail, of more than three feet), and a large turtle can weigh more than 60 pounds.

When paddling relatively clear, shallow water, we occasionally see a snapper underwater or on a bank above a pond or slow-moving river— probably en route to a nearby body of water or, perhaps, a female out of water to lay eggs. A snapper may travel a great distance in search of a suitable nesting site—one marked individual traveled 16 kilometers round-trip. Our usual glimpse, though, is just the triangular nose sticking out of the water ahead as we paddle along.

Many people fear the snapping turtle—and we will admit a bit of concern when two large snappers chased one another just inches beneath the boat in a shallow pond—but it really poses no harm *as long as it remains in the water.* Even in the unlikely event that a snapper bites a swimmer's toe, it quickly lets go, realizing that the quarry is more than it can handle. In the water, the shy snapper avoids human contact. Watch out for a snapper on land, though. It lashes out with lightning speed when threatened. With its massive jaw muscles and razor-sharp beak, a large snapper exerts a bite pressure of more than 400 pounds per square inch—enough to sever a finger easily.

The snapping turtle has existed for at least 80 million years, and scientists believe it to be the oldest North American reptile. Like all turtles, its rib cage and vertebrae have evolved into a bony carapace and plastron. Though the carapace provides armored protection, the small plastron offers almost no protection to its underside, making it vulnerable to leeches; it sometimes leaves the water to rid itself of this parasite.

Most turtles hibernate for long periods, but we sometimes see the relatively cold-resistant snapping turtle swimming beneath the ice, though in northern New York, it typically hibernates in the bottom mud for at least a while during the dead of winter. When idle underwater, it typically does not surface for air. Special surfaces in its rear cloacal cavity extract oxygen from water, much like gills. When active, though, it needs more oxygen and must surface for air—providing the quietwater paddler an opportunity to catch a glimpse.

Omnivore and opportunist, the snapping turtle dines on a wide range of animals and plants, including fish, frogs, salamanders, occasional ducklings and loon chicks, dead animals, and aquatic plants. A snapper can kill anything its size or smaller, but it seems to prefer the easy meal. A superb sense of smell helps it to scavenge for dead animals. The snapping turtle literature recounts a story of a Native American who assisted in locating drowning victims using a snapping turtle on a long leash. When released into the water, the turtle unerringly headed for the decomposing corpse, latched onto it with its strong jaws, and its handler slowly reeled it in—corpse and all.

A mature female leaves the water in late spring or early summer to lay eggs. She digs a hole and typically deposits from 20 to 30 (rarely, up to 80) eggs the size of ping-pong balls, then covers the hole. Some lay eggs in two or more holes; some dig several false holes to mislead predators, which take a heavy toll on snapping turtle clutches. The eggs usually hatch in the fall, some 70 to 100 days after laying (depending on temperature), and the inch-long hatchlings make a beeline for the water—often as raccoons, birds, and other predators gobble them up.

As with many turtle species, nest temperature determines snapper sex. Several studies found that at very cool or very warm temperatures, the embryos all developed into females, whereas intermediate temperatures produced males. In most nests, temperature varies with location, so both males and females develop.

The snapper population remains secure in New York—unlike that of most other turtles. It seems to tolerate current levels of environmental pollution and lives in even highly polluted marshy areas in cities. Some regard snapper meat highly, resulting in heavy trapping in certain areas. Roads result in fewer crushed snappers than the toll taken on more terrestrial turtles. If you come across a snapping turtle out of water, avoid the temptation to deliver it to the nearest body of water—chances are pretty good that she knows where to lay her eggs and does not need our assistance in this endeavor.

10

Mohansic Lake and Crom Pond

Yorktown

Maps: New York Atlas Map 33:B5, USGS Quadrangle Mohegan Lake

Mohansic Lake area: 107 acres, maximum depth 27 feet

Habitat type: small, recreational lake and smaller, marshy pond

Fish: largemouth bass, pickerel

Expect to see: ducks, geese, rabbits, deer

Camping and trails: trails, Franklin D. Roosevelt State Park, 914-245-4434; camping App. A #36, 37, and 41

Take note: annual $20 fee provides access to Lake Taghkanic, Rudd Pond, Canopus Lake, John Allen Pond, and Mohansic Lake

GETTING THERE

From I-287, go about 19 miles north on the Taconic Parkway, and exit at Franklin D. Roosevelt State Park. Stay right at each junction to reach the access.

Franklin D. Roosevelt State Park, one of several parks along the scenic Taconic Parkway, contains both Mohansic Lake and connected Crom Pond. When paddling here, you have to contend with road noise from the Taconic—which you can just barely see off through the trees.

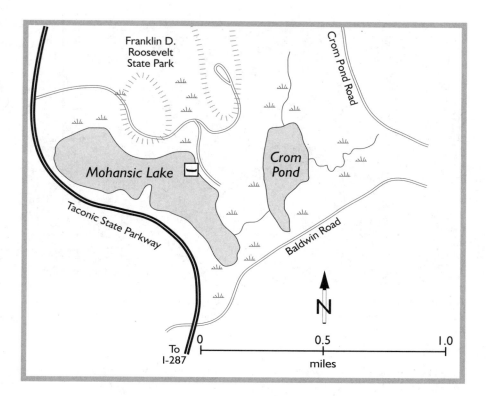

FDR Park has few boaters, especially in the off-season. Most people come for other types of recreation: swimming in one of the largest pools in the United States, hiking on an extensive network of trails, biking in summer, and cross-country skiing and ice-skating in winter. Dubious at first about paddling, given the road noise, we became converted after paddling into Crom Pond, a wilderness retreat, where road noise just barely impinges.

A huge flock of tame Canada geese begged for food at the access, ignoring both signs that say Do Not Feed Wildlife and No Swimming in the Lake. Tame cottontails munched the grass, and pied-billed grebe swam about in thick aquatic vegetation. A flock of coots also worked to keep the abundant aquatic plants in check, seemingly to no avail, while a lone cormorant surveyed the scene from an exposed rock out in the middle.

A female ruddy duck—one of the smallest North American ducks—paddles about the surface of Crom Pond during fall migration.

We left behind the access, with its large beech, weeping willow, sugar maple, big-toothed aspen, and unfed geese, and headed for Crom Pond. As we paddled south to the connector, the sheer volume of white and yellow waterlilies impressed us. Their flat leaves, floating on the water's surface, covered the entire southern cove. The large trees near the access gave way to shrubby shoreline that included dwarfed red maple and black gum.

As we paddled the connector, ducks scurried into the tiny channels back under the shrubbery, and a pied-billed grebe dove for cover. Shrubs and dwarf red maple dominate the connector, with buttonbush, dwarf willow, and purple loosestrife growing in profusion, along with winterberry and lesser amounts of several other shrubs.

Two fishermen in a rowboat tried their luck along the northern shore, casting for bass, while eight ruddy ducks paddled about. As we drew near, we could see that the male ducks already sported winter plumage. These unusually small ducks—also called stiff-tails—have short tails that often point straight up, revealing a bright white rump. Males in breeding plumage have ruddy necks, backs, and sides; a black head with large white face patch; and a bright blue bill—quite a sight to behold! In keeping with their strange visage, in the spring males putt-putt around in little circles and figure eights, using their stiff tails as rudders, trying to attract female attention; this perhaps does not look comical to female ruddy ducks.

Because they usually nest on small ponds, we rarely see these ducks, except in migration. Eventually, this group decided that we had approached too close and dove for cover; they typically dive rather than fly when danger approaches.

Having done all the surveying we could, reluctantly we paddled back to Mohansic Lake where we found the geese panhandling, again without much success. Obviously, given their robust size, they usually find a more responsive crowd. As we left the park near dusk and drove northward on the Taconic heading back to Vermont, the deer that like to dodge cars had emerged. We had not even merged onto the parkway when several deer appeared, browsing roadside shrubs. In gathering darkness, our headlights frequently caught the eyeshine of roadside deer. We had to stop abruptly more than a few times to avoid hitting them, though we did not see any dead along the road. The drivers who travel this road regularly must maintain quite a bit of caution. Frankly, nowhere else in our travels throughout New York can we remember seeing such a large population of deer. What is it about this road and deer?

11

Constitution Marsh
Philipstown

Maps: New York Atlas Map 32:A4, USGS Quadrangle West Point

Area: tidal, 270 acres

Habitat type: tidal marsh

Expect to see: mute swan, ducks, geese

Camping and trails: Constitution Marsh National Audubon Society Sanctuary, 845-265-2601, ny.audubon.org/cmac.htm; camping App. A #36, 37, and 41

Take note: no motors

GETTING THERE

From the south, go north on Route 9 through Peekskill, and turn left on Routes 6 and 202 (Bear Mountain Highway). Turn right off Routes 6 and 202 on Route 9D north.

From I-87, take Route 6, cross the Bear Mountain Bridge, and turn left on Route 9D north.

Train Station. At the junction of Routes 9D and 301, turn left, and go to the end of the street. Turn left on Lunn Terrace, and turn immediately right across a bridge. At the T, turn left, and go through the station parking lot to the end. Lower your boat down over the rocks into the Hudson.

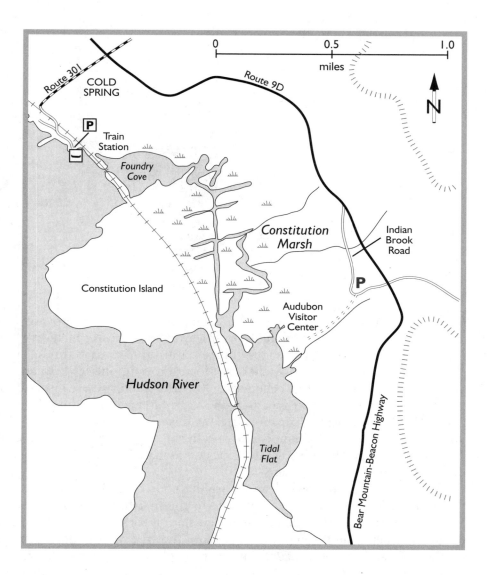

Audubon Society Visitor Center. At the junction of Routes 9D and 301, go south 1.4 miles on Route 9D, and turn diagonally right on easy-to-miss, narrow Indian Brook Road. Go 0.4 mile (1.8 miles) to the parking lot. To avoid being towed, do not park along road. Hike the half mile down to the visitor center.

Cormorants

Constitution Marsh, owned by the National Audubon Society, provides a wonderful location to take children to learn about nature, including forests, streams, and tidal marshes. Three nature trails weave through the 270-acre sanctuary: one teaches tree identification, one leads to an ancient Native American rock shelter, and the third allows close inspection of the marsh by a 700-foot boardwalk. An archaeological dig has dated Native American occupation back at least 5,000 years. Audubon naturalists also run guided canoe trips into the marsh for groups of up to 15 adults; programs for schoolchildren accommodate as many as 25 students, along with adult assistants.

Unfortunately, you really cannot paddle your own boat out from the visitor center. An alternate entrance to the marsh exists, however. You can launch from the Cold Spring train station parking lot and paddle about a half mile through Foundry Cove into the marsh's northern reaches. Because you can paddle the marsh only for about two hours either side of high tide, you should call the visitor center and ask about tides. Note that high tide time will differ significantly from what it is at the George Washington Bridge.

From the Cold Spring station lot, paddle downstream for a few hundred feet, and pass under the railroad bridge. From there, head due east for the very back of Foundry Cove, where outgoing tides drain Constitution Marsh through a wide passageway.

As we entered Foundry Cove, flocks of mallard and black duck and five mute swans greeted us. Three swans spilled out of the EPA Superfund restoration-site at the back of Foundry Cove. We eyeballed them pretty carefully but could discern no extra appendages or other mutations. The ducks and the other two swans had the good sense to stay out of this area.

Up close, the swans—five feet from beak tip to tail end—dwarfed the two-foot-long ducks, especially in bulk. An Old World import, wild populations of mute swan have expanded along the East Coast from Cape Cod to Cape Hatteras.

We paddled back through acres of narrow-leaved cattail. Large deciduous trees line the marsh's eastern edge and populate Constitution Island, which juts out into the Hudson. As we gazed out over the marsh and up the surrounding bluffs and hillsides, we found large, isolated homes overlooking this beautiful area through glorious fall foliage.

The Audubon Society says that the 154-mile tidal stretch of the Hudson from New York City to Troy represents the only major American river still functioning as a complete ecosystem. Despite pollution and development, the Hudson has not lost a single fish species. It produces huge populations of striped bass, shad, blue crabs, and other species, all of which depend on tidal marshes for food.

We recommend that you walk the Conservancy trails and, using their excellent guidebook, study the 39 species of trees and shrubs described. We found interesting information about several tree species. For example, the last Ice Age nearly exterminated the black locust. Early settlers, however, transplanted it from its last holdout in Appalachian valleys to all over the East and Midwest. Settlers used it for many products; today, we still use it to make split-rail fences because of its tremendous durability. Locust also can substitute for pressure-treated wood, which we make rot resistant by impregnating with environmental toxins. We urge you to visit here, to paddle, to walk the trails, and to talk to the staff. We especially urge you to bring children to this wonderful place.

12

Canopus Lake and Stillwater Lake

Kent

Maps: New York Atlas Map 33:A5, USGS Quadrangle Oscawana Lake

Area: 104 acres, maximum depth 15 feet; park area 14,086 acres

Habitat type: small recreational lake

Fish: largemouth bass, pickerel

Expect to see: Canada goose, wild turkey, mountain laurel

Camping: App. A #41 (on-site)

Take note: gasoline motors prohibited; annual $20 fee provides access to Canopus Lake, John Allen Pond, Mohansic Lake, Rudd Pond, and Lake Taghkanic

GETTING THERE
From the Taconic Parkway, go 1.0 mile south on Route 301 to the access on the right. Limited parking across the road.

Canopus Lake
Canopus Lake, within Clarence Fahnestock State Park, offers a wonderful paddling opportunity, especially in the off-season. Although the park prohibits gasoline motors, believe it or not, it can get overrun with rowboats, canoes, and kayaks, especially on sunny summer weekends. Three reasons account for this: the Appalachian Trail, which skirts the

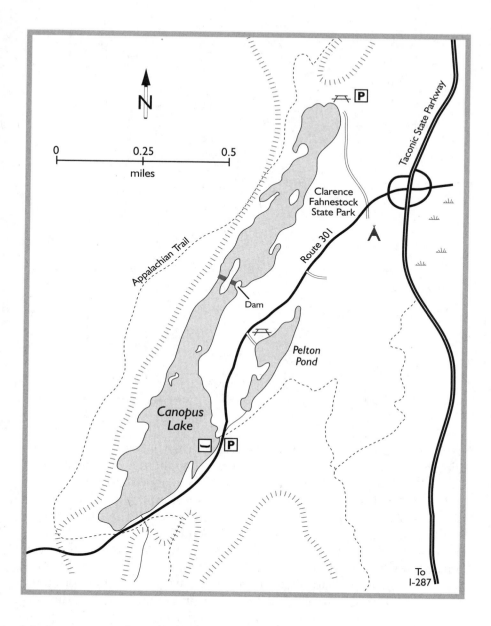

lake's western edge, draws hikers; a popular campground lies within the park; and the Taconic Parkway runs through the park, providing easy accessibility to literally millions of recreation-starved, downstate city dwellers.

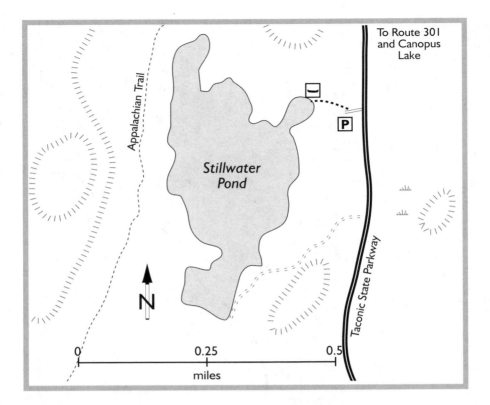

To Route 301
and Canopus
Lake

Appalachian Trail

Stillwater
Pond

Taconic State Parkway

N

| 0 | 0.25 | 0.5 |
miles

Even though we had to share the lake with other boaters, we loved paddling here, given its small, protected nature and incredible beauty. Beautiful tall hemlocks dominate the rocky hillside across from the access,
and their lacy leaves droop out over the shores, especially on the upper
lake, but the real attraction remains the understory's tree-sized mountain laurel. A showy, evergreen member of the heath family—which includes leatherleaf, bog rosemary, sheep laurel, and blueberry—mountain
laurel, like most heaths, prefers acid soil. Blooming in late May, the gorgeous clusters of pink-to-white flowers present a perfect pollen trap for
honeybees. The 10 stamens of each flower press tightly against the petals. When a bee lands on the flower seeking nectar, the stamens spring
out, dusting the bee with pollen to be carried on to the next flower for
cross-pollination.

The twisted tops of oak, beech, and yellow birch dominate the hillsides,
giving cover to the Appalachian Trail. After leaving the park, the trail heads

northeast, eventually entering Connecticut in northern Fairfield County, on its way to its northern terminus in Maine's Baxter State Park.

Many smooth granite boulders dot the lake's surface; unfortunately, the park does not allow swimming on the lower part of the lake. The lake's upper portion is off limits to boating during swimming season; during the off-season, we carried up over the dam that separates the lake's two halves. Stay to the right for the carry.

When we paddled here in April, a pair of Canada geese nested on the south end of a tiny island near the east shore, just where the lower lake starts to narrow down. The bird sitting on the nest hunkered down, trying to look invisible, as we quietly paddled by. Signs tell visitors not to feed the geese, which probably have gotten quite tame over the years. In addition, we saw several other species of birds, all of them newly arrived migrants thinking about nesting: Eastern phoebe, robin, turkey vulture, flicker, and barn swallow. We also saw wild turkey.

Early-season anglers try their luck for smallmouth bass.

Stillwater Pond

To gain access, you need to show your boat permit at the park office.

A huge, three-feet-in-diameter tulip tree grows along the path to the water. This member of the magnolia family—with its large waxy yellow treetop flowers—is at the northern extension of its range here. Smooth gray-barked sweet birch trees (*Betula lenta*) also grow along the path. Scratch off some bark from a branch, and note the sweet aroma of wintergreen. You can use this characteristic odor to distinguish sweet birch from the similar river birch (*Betula nigra*), which lacks this odor.

Along the shore in several places we spotted the heavily serrated nine-inch leaves of American chestnut. This magnificent tree, once a codominant species in the Appalachians and its nuts an important food source for wildlife, has nearly died out because of the inadvertent introduction of the chestnut blight, a fungus that gets under the bark. Stump sprouts such as these rarely live long enough to flower before the disease fells them. The stumps still sprout because the soft, resinous wood resists decay. Used for railroad ties and split-rail fences, many chestnut split-rail fences still survive after many decades.

13

Chodikee Lake
Esopus and Lloyd

Maps: New York Atlas Map 36:B4, USGS Quadrangle Hyde Park

Area: 63 acres, maximum depth 20 feet; river length 2.5 miles

Habitat type: small lake with swampy inlet and outlet streams

Fish: largemouth bass, pickerel

Camping: App. A #43

Expect to see: osprey, kestrel, raven, waterfowl, bluebird, red-bellied woodpecker, muskrat

Take note: gasoline motors prohibited; paddling is better during spring high water

GETTING THERE

From Poughkeepsie, cross the Hudson River on Route 44, and turn right on Route 9W. Go 2.3 miles, and turn left on Route 299. Go 1.3 miles (3.6 miles), and turn right on Chodikee Lake Road. Go 1.0 mile (4.6 miles) to a T, turn left, and go 0.9 mile (5.5 miles) to the access on the right.

From I-87, Exit 18, go 3.8 miles east on Route 299, turn left on Chodikee Lake Road, and proceed as above.

We first paddled Chodikee Lake in spring before the mosquitoes hatched out of the extensive marshes surrounding the lake and before more than an occasional angler plied the waters. We found an idyllic site, an extraordinary wildlife paradise free from insects and people that

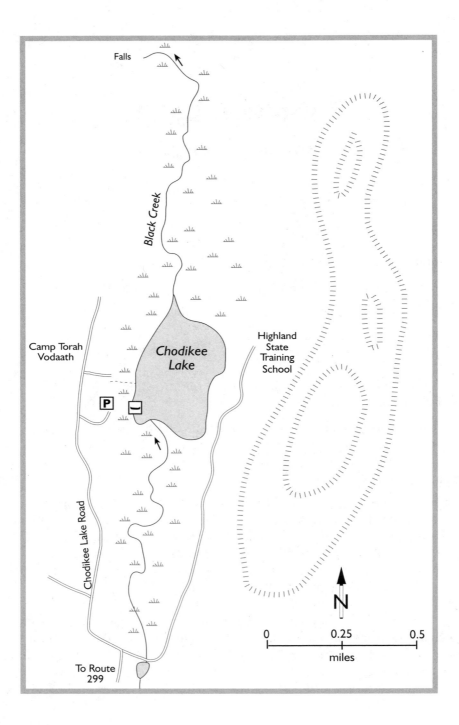

Falls

Black Creek

Camp Torah
Vodaath

Chodikee
Lake

Highland
State
Training
School

P L

Chodikee Lake Road

To Route
299

N

0   0.25   0.5
miles

would later appear in large numbers. We have returned to paddle this lake many times.

The plaintive calls of spring peepers, the chatter of chipmunks, and the mournful cry of doves greeted us at the access, and as we looked out over the lake from the end of the dock, two mute swans drifted slowly by. These Eurasian imports, larger than our native swans at five feet from bill to tip of tail, continue to spread along the eastern seaboard from Cape Cod to Chesapeake Bay. They often swim with their necks carried in a graceful S-shaped curve. We distinguish them from our native swans by their orange-yellow bills with a black knob at the top.

Chodikee Lake overflows with wildlife habitat, with acres of dead and dying trees, meandering streams on the north and south ends, extensive wooded swamps, and stands of cattail and other marsh vegetation. At times of high water, you can paddle the south creek upstream to the road and the north creek downstream to a series of small waterfalls—and encounter a prodigious amount of wildlife along the way.

A Canada goose eyes us as we glide by.

Red-bellied woodpeckers and flickers have carved out holes in hundreds of dead trees, providing nests for themselves and for other cavity nesters, including wood duck, kestrel, bluebird, and tree swallow. Hundreds of tree swallows cruised the water, scooping up early-emerging insects, and we saw several kestrels and many bluebirds. The red-bellied woodpecker used to reach the northern extension of its range in southern New York but has moved north as the climate warms. Distinguish it from the flicker by the large red patch on the back and top of the head and the alternating black and white stripes on the back—a so-called ladder-back.

But the ducks provided the real attraction. We saw many gorgeously colored wood ducks—especially in the northern stream's wooded swamp— and hundreds of green-winged teal, quite a few mallards and black ducks, and many Canada geese. Several pairs of geese, which nest quite early compared with other waterfowl, hunkered down over their nests on rotting stumps, incubating their eggs just a foot or two above the water.

At the outflow stream's northern end, a hemlock canopy draped over beautiful rock formations. Both times we paddled here in spring—six years apart—in the shade of the hemlocks, a phoebe pair nested in a natural cavity in a vertical rock face where the stream narrowed and tumbled gently over rockfalls, the land posted against further travel.

14

Tivoli Marshes—
North Bay
Red Hook

Maps: New York Atlas Map 52:D2, USGS Quadrangle Saugerties

Area: 1,468 acres in the Wildlife Management Area

Habitat type: tidal freshwater marshlands with shrubs; no development

Expect to see: muskrat, waterfowl, marsh birds, aquatic vegetation

Camping: App. A #42, 43, 44, 45, 110, 112, 114, and 116

Take note: no motors; novice paddlers should avoid the railroad bridges and Hudson

GETTING THERE

From I-87, Exit 21, go east on Route 23 across the Hudson, and turn right on Route 9G south. From the junction with Route 78, go south on Route 9G for 0.6 mile, and turn right on Kidd Lane. Go 0.5 mile (1.1 miles) west on Kidd Lane, turn left, and go 0.9 mile downhill (2.0 miles) to the access.

North Bay of Tivoli Marshes, part of the Hudson River National Estuarine Research Reserve, contains one of the most scenic and productive Hudson marshes. Looking out over the broad expanse of marsh with the sun setting over 1,100 foot Indian Head, Overlook, and High Peak

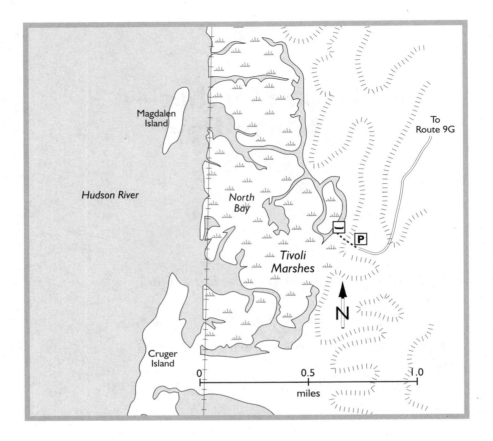

mountains in the Catskills is awe-inspiring. We highly recommend this wonderful paddling destination, especially at mid to high tide. Hundreds of passageways penetrate through all areas of the marsh, but many become inaccessible at lower tide levels.

How we came to be looking out over the marsh at sunset: we got lost—over and over again. We decided to paddle a counterclockwise circuit of the marsh, heading north from the access. After inspecting a few dead-end channels filled with pickerelweed, we had little trouble making our way across the marsh's northern end to the railroad embankment. We just followed the outgoing tide to the more northern of two bridges that connect the marsh with the Hudson. However, after heading south along the railroad embankment—investigating the profuse growth of swamp rose, jewelweed, grape, and Virginia creeper along the way—we tried to complete the circuit by heading inland. Over and over again, what looked like promising passages turned out to be labyrinthine, pickerelweed-filled, carbon copy dead-ends. After several hours of trying—and truly enjoying the sunset—we made our way back to the access. The only two waterways that lead back to the access that we could find occur at the north and at about the midway point. If you do explore the marsh's southern reaches, you should head back north by the embankment before heading back inland.

Besides the dwarf red maple that occupies some of the marsh's higher hummocks, any trees found here hug the eastern shore, hanging out over the channel that runs north from the access. Hemlock interrupts the primarily mixed deciduous woodland. Out in the open swamp, narrow-leaved cattail occurs in profusion, providing nesting habitat for marsh wrens. But red-winged blackbirds rule the marsh. We watched songbirds scatter as a sharp-shinned hawk glided low over the marsh on silent wings. Expect to see waterfowl here, as well, especially during migration. We found large patches of wild rice, yellow pondlily, and arrowhead in and among the abundant pickerelweed.

Though we wanted to explore the Hudson, especially Magdalen and Cruger Islands, squeaking under the bridges just after high tide looked dicey. Though we could have squeezed under the northern bridge, paddling back against the substantial current would not have worked, given the lack of overhead room for hard paddling.

15

Lake Taghkanic and Rudd Pond

Gallatin and Northeast

Maps: New York Atlas Maps 37:A7 and 52:D4, USGS Quadrangles Ancram and Millerton, NY & CT

Area: Lake Taghkanic 168 acres, maximum depth 40 feet; Rudd Pond 66 acres, maximum depth 12 feet; park area, 1,600 acres

Habitat type: small, recreation-oriented ponds

Fish: largemouth bass, pickerel

Expect to see: oaks, pileated woodpecker, beaver, deer

Camping: App. A #42 and #44 (on-site)

Take note: annual $20 fee provides access to Lake Taghkanic, Rudd Pond, Canopus Lake, John Allen Pond, Mohansic Lake; no motors

GETTING THERE

Lake Taghkanic. From I-84, go about 40 miles north on the Taconic Parkway, turn right on Lake Taghkanic Road. Go to East Beach; when the main road goes left, continue straight.

Rudd Pond. From Lake Taghkanic, go southeast on Route 82 to Ancramdale. Turn left on Route 3; when Route 3 goes left, go straight on Over Mountain Road. At the fork, go left downhill, and turn right (south) on Route 22. After crossing Dutchess County line, go 0.9 mile,

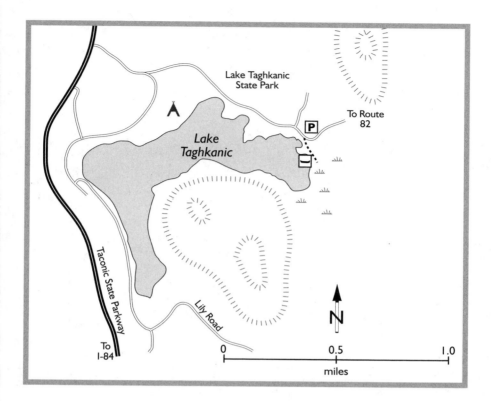

turn left on Route 62, and follow signs to Rudd Pond. Enter the park and pay to use the access, or continue south on Route 22 and put in at the pull-off.

Lake Taghkanic

This small but popular park, located just off the Taconic Parkway in southern Columbia County, draws many recreation-starved downstaters to its shores. A popular picnic and day-use area for swimming, hiking, biking, and boating, it also includes a campground.

We paddled here just before Labor Day as pre-fall colors just started to creep into the hillsides; people crowded the park, trying to get in that last bit of warm, sunny recreation before winter's on-slaught. Still, we paddled alone most of the time. The lake's small size means that even a leisurely paddle will end in about an hour, so this park remains mainly recreation and family oriented. You can

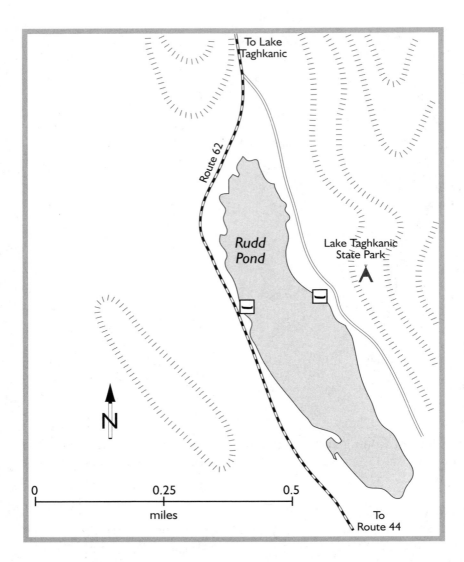

teach your children about plants and wildlife here and, in these protected waters, how to paddle a canoe or kayak.

We especially enjoyed studying the oaks and found 5 of the 12 species that grow in downstate New York: red, white, scarlet, pin, and chestnut oaks. We did not find the other 7—bur, post, swamp white, chinkapin, bear, southern red, and black oaks—but it would be interesting to try to find all of them.

Biologists theorize that oaks evolved millions of years ago in Mexico, which harbors 150 species, and radiated southward and northward from there. The United States has about 50 species, with fewer and fewer species as you approach the Northeast. Oaks fall into two major groups: red and white. The main differences include bristles on red oak leaf tips versus rounded white oak leaf tips, and white oak acorns mature in one year, whereas red oak acorns hang on for two years. Trees usually bear heavy acorn crops on a two- to four-year rotation, and these seeds serve as an important food source for squirrels, wild turkey, grouse, black bear, deer, wood duck, and small mammals.

Shoreside black gum trees had started to turn a brilliant scarlet, which they do before other hardwoods begin to turn. We also found hickory, northern white cedar, red and sugar maples, though not nearly as frequently as oaks.

On the lake's marshy east end, we found large patches of water shield, yellow pondlily, fragrant waterlily, pickerelweed, purple loosestrife, buttonbush, fanwort, and pondweed. On other trips here, we saw pileated woodpecker, Baltimore oriole, and beaver.

Canoes and rowboats share the access on Lake Taghkanic.

Rudd Pond

If Lake Taghkanic is too crowded, you can also camp at Rudd Pond, a much smaller and more out-of-the-way member of the Taconic State Park group near the Connecticut border. Because Route 62 travels down the western shore, paddling here will not be a wilderness experience. But it offers a nice place for camping, picnicking, and relaxing among towering white pine, spreading weeping willow, and tall black locust. Oaks, paper birch, hickory, tamarack, Norway spruce, and red pine round out the tree species. More so than most areas in the vicinity, this area boasts truly huge trees of all the previously mentioned species. The forested hillsides of deciduous trees glowed brightly with fall colors when we returned to this area in mid-October—a month and a half later than our first visit.

The marshy north and south ends of Rudd Pond sport a blanket of aquatic vegetation, including pickerelweed, fragrant waterlily, yellow pondlily, pondweed, cattails, *Phragmites*, purple loosestrife, and more.

16

Catskill Creek and Ramshorn Marsh

Catskill

Maps: New York Atlas Map 52:C3, USGS Quadrangles Cementon and Hudson South

Length: Catskill Creek 4 miles, Ramshorn Creek 1.5 miles, Dubois Creek 1 mile

Habitat type: tidal freshwater rivers, marshlands with trees; little development

Expect to see: muskrat, beaver, waterfowl, marsh birds, aquatic vegetation, varied shrubs and trees

Camping: App. A #42, 45, 110, 112, 114, and 116

Take note: motors at mouth of Catskill Creek; Ramshorn Creek access from Hudson River; novice paddlers should avoid the Hudson and always wear PFD

GETTING THERE

From I-87, Exit 21, go 1.4 miles east on Route 23, and turn right on Route 9W. Go 0.8 mile (2.2 miles) south, and turn left on West Main Street. Go 0.3 mile (2.5 miles) to the far end of the Catskill Elementary School parking lot on the left.

We found three wonderful places to paddle. Paddling left up Catskill Creek, after 1.5 miles you come to a beautiful falls, with water cascading

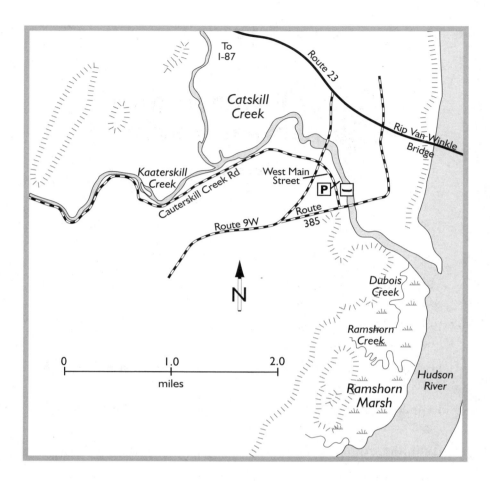

down over a series of broken ledges. We saw flocks of Canada geese here during migration in this broad waterway with tree-lined shores. By carrying up through the middle, you can paddle beyond, up Catskill Creek or up Kaaterskill Creek. At the start, we noticed many Norway maples along the banks.

Paddling downstream, you pass through a boat basin. In less than a mile, after clearing the last boat dock on the right, turn right into the mouth of Dubois Creek, which penetrates Ramshorn Marsh for about a mile. Paddling back in here, we saw beaver during the day, iris in bloom, arrowhead, alder, dogwood, and myriad other shrubs and dwarf red maple. The creek starts out wide and gradually narrows; near the end, we had to pull ourselves under overhanging branches as we winched our boats around tight turns.

Back out on the Catskill, you can paddle to its mouth and head downstream on the Hudson, noting the *Phragmites* and cattail growing along the marshy right-hand shore. About three-quarters of a mile south of Catskill Creek, turn into Ramshorn Creek, which starts out 50 feet wide and narrows as it proceeds inland. The 436-acre RamsHorn-Livingston Sanctuary, operated by the Scenic Hudson Land Trust and National Audubon Society, protects this whole marsh. The habitat here mimics that of Dubois Creek, though with a wider and longer waterway. We saw lots of beaver sign; we expect it would be easy to see them here in the evening. Paddling back into the marsh's far reaches, exploring the many side channels, wood ducks erupted from the water as we emerged around tight turns. We also saw red-bellied woodpecker, cedar waxwing, bluebird, song sparrow, chickadee, tufted titmouse, kingfisher, and great blue heron.

We saw several flocks of yellow-rumped warbler, though other warbler species had already migrated south. It winters farther north—as far as coastal Maine—than any other warbler; indeed, most warblers winter in the Caribbean or Mexico. The yellow-rumped remains one of the most abundant warblers because it has adapted to a wide array of food sources. Most warblers eat mainly insects and spiders; some either just glean insects from main branches, such as the black-and-white warbler, or engage in active flycatching, such as the American redstart. The yellow-rumped does both, but more importantly, it readily switches diet in winter to abundant bayberries that grow along the coast. It also eats other berries, including poison ivy, viburnum, mountain ash, honeysuckle, redcedar, and probably lots more.

17

Basher Kill
Mamkating

Maps: New York Atlas Map 35:D6, USGS Quadrangle Yankee Lake

Area: 2,213 acres (entire wetland)

Habitat type: large, shallow marsh; meandering open channel; no development

Fish: largemouth bass, chain pickerel

Expect to see: osprey, bald eagle, northern harrier, Canada goose, wood duck, wild turkey, deer, muskrat, beaver

Camping and trails: Bashakill Wildlife Management Area, 845-256-3000; camping App. A #36, 37, 113, and 115

Take note: gasoline motors prohibited

GETTING THERE
Northern Access. From Route 17, Exit 113, go south on Route 209 for 1.2 miles to the access on the left. We prefer the bisecting bridge or southern accesses.

Haven Road Bridge. From Route 17, Exit 113, go south on Route 209 for 1.9 miles, and turn left on Haven Road. Go 0.3 mile (2.2 miles) to the parking area on the left; launch across the road. Alternatively, go 0.2 mile (2.4 miles) to the bridge (room for two small cars).

Southern Access. From the bridge, continue for 0.4 mile (2.8 miles) to South Road. Turn right, and go 1.7 miles (4.5 miles) to the access on the right.

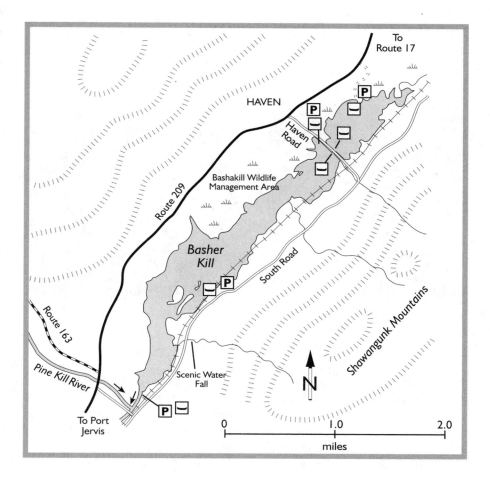

Waterfall. From the southern access, continue south for 0.5 mile (5.0 miles) to the waterfall on the left. There is also an access 0.9 mile (5.9 miles) south of the waterfall, where Pine Kill enters.

For observing wildlife near New York City, nothing beats Sullivan County's Bashakill Wildlife Management Area. The largest freshwater wetland in southeastern New York, the Bashakill's 2,213 acres protect the habitat of deer, grouse, wild turkey, fox, beaver, muskrat, raccoon, rabbit, skunk, mink, opossum, and waterfowl, particularly wood duck.

The middle section of the Shawangunk Mountains—the northern "Gunks" are famous with rock climbers and hikers—parallels Basher Kill's

Rising early-morning mists reveal clumps of purple loosestrife—an alien species—as it invades the marsh.

eastern shore, providing a scenic backdrop for paddlers and hikers alike. The western shore's beautiful hillsides dripped with fall colors in late October, the first time we paddled here. We have since returned in spring with dogwood in bloom and in summer to watch osprey dive for fish. We have seen many deer, muskrat, and wild turkey, along with a few beaver. We recommend the perimeter trails hikes: one follows the historic Delaware and Hudson (D & H) Canal along the west shore, and the other proceeds over a long-abandoned railroad grade along the east shore.

In the absence of gasoline motors, you can paddle here for hours in peace, among the islands and drowned timber. The Department of Environmental Conservation enhances nesting success of three species in particular by erecting nesting platforms for osprey and nesting boxes for wood duck and bluebird.

In addition to nesting populations, migrating wood ducks stop here to fatten up on acorns and aquatic plants, and flocks of Canada geese from the far north honk from the marsh. In October at the tail end of songbird migration, in one mixed foraging flock, we saw chipping, white-throated, song, and fox sparrows, junco, yellow-rumped warbler, a tail-bobbing palm warbler, and ruby-crowned kinglet. We also spotted hermit thrush, tufted titmouse, and Eastern phoebe.

Red and white oaks dominate the surrounding high ground, their leaves turning a burnished red in the fall air. Occasional sugar and red maples add orange and red accents, and aspen and birch lend a vibrant yellow against a backdrop of dark green conifers. Besides providing food for wood ducks, oaks and beeches nourish wild turkey and abundant gray squirrels. Waterlilies and other aquatic plants cover the reservoir's shallow surface, and alien invader purple loosestrife vies with buttonbush and arrowhead to dominate the shallows. Muskrat homes—small vegetation piles—dot the marsh. Along streams, they burrow under roots in soft banks; in an area with abundant food but no banks, they use an alternate strategy.

If recent rains have fallen and in the spring, a beautiful waterfall tumbles down out of the Shawangunks, cascading over ledges in three drops, through an overhanging canopy of lacy hemlock boughs, flowing into the reservoir's south end. You can easily see it from South Road as you approach.

18

Rio Reservoir
Forestburg, Deer Park,
and Lumberland

Maps: New York Atlas Maps 35:D5 and 31:A5, USGS Quad-rangles Highland Lake and Pond Eddy

Area: 435 acres, maximum depth 85 feet

Habitat type: deep, narrow reservoir

Fish: brown trout, largemouth and smallmouth bass

Expect to see: bald eagle, Canada goose, great blue heron, bryozoa

Camping: App. A #113 and 115

Take note: gasoline motors prohibited; on windy days, the gorge funnels wind; open April 1 to November 30

GETTING THERE

From I-84, Exit 1, go north on Route 97 for a few miles, and turn right on Route 42. Go 6.0 miles, and turn left on Plank Road. Go 0.8 mile (6.8 miles), and turn left on Rio Dam Road. Go 1.3 miles (8.1 miles), and cross the dam to the access. Or put in at the northern access on Plank Road, 2.6 miles (9.4 miles) north of Rio Dam Road.

From Route 17, Exit 105A, go 9.6 miles south on Route 42, cross Route 43, and immediately turn right on Mill Road. Go 0.5 mile (10.1 miles), and turn left on Plank Road. Go 1.9 miles (12.0 miles) to the northern access on the right, or go 2.6 miles (14.6 miles) farther to Rio Dam Road.

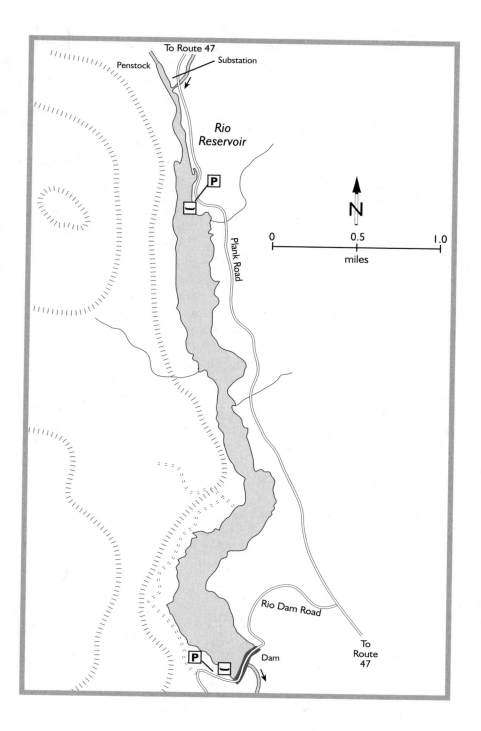

Rio Reservoir (rhymes with "bio"), the southernmost of three paddle-able reservoirs on the Mongaup River near Monticello, New York, lies within the Mongaup Valley Wildlife Management Area, which provides protection for wintering bald eagles (see Mongaup Falls Reservoir).

Rio Reservoir extends roughly 3.6 miles north-south, with several sweeping S-curves in the southern half. Maximum width reaches about a third of a mile. On a morning paddle on a sunny Labor Day weekend, only about a half dozen boats plied the water. On spring visits, we saw fewer visitors.

Rio's exposed outcroppings and fairly uniform rocky shoreline, rising steeply from the water, preclude marshy areas. Though hemlock dominates the banks, the hillsides support white pine, beech, black birch, ironwood, sassafras, shagbark hickory, red and sugar maples, and at least four oaks (red, white, chestnut, and scarlet). Though not as dense as those on nearby Lake Superior, rhododendron grows in profusion along the shore and should be gorgeous during the late June or early July flowering season. A few weeks earlier, paddlers will be treated to blooming mountain laurel—a shorter, smaller-leaved member of the same heath family.

Look for roundish blobs growing on submerged branches—these bryozoa, an animal phylum, grow in associated colonies like coral. Most bryozoa live in salt water, but a few freshwater species—such as *Pectinatella magnifica* growing here—occur in New York. Each knob on the globular mass represents an individual animal. Hairlike appendages filter food particles out of the water.

We saw common merganser, Canada goose, and great blue heron, among other bird species, and we saw some evidence of beaver but not the critters themselves.

From the northern access, you can paddle a little ways north, passing the remains of an old wooded structure for a gas pipeline that used to cross the reservoir. Beyond, the reservoir narrows into a rocky river section with quickwater.

19

Mongaup Falls Reservoir
Forestburg and Lumberland

Maps: New York Atlas Map 35:D4, USGS Quadrangle Highland Lake

Area: 130 acres, maximum depth 20 feet

Habitat type: small, shallow reservoir with some marshy areas

Fish: brown trout, largemouth and smallmouth bass

Expect to see: bald eagle

Camping: App. A #113 and 115

Take note: gasoline motors prohibited; open April 1 through November 30; novice paddlers should avoid the inlet river

GETTING THERE

From I-84, Exit 1, go north on Route 97 for a few miles, and turn right on Route 42. Go north on Route 42 for 10.9 miles, and turn left on Route 43. Go 2.0 miles (12.9 miles) to the access on the left.

From Route 17, Exit 105A, go 9.6 miles south on Route 42, turn right on Route 43, and follow previous directions.

Winter Eagle-Watching Area. Go 0.3 mile past the access to the viewing area on the left.

Mongaup Falls Reservoir—a 2-mile-long, dammed-up section of the Mongaup River, upstream from Rio Reservoir (see previous section)—feels much different compared with its southern neighbor. Smaller and

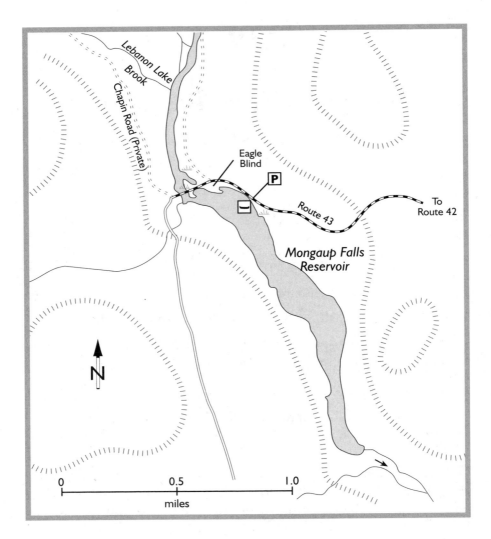

shallower than Rio, we prefer paddling here on windy days because surrounding hills seem to do a better job of shielding it from wind.

At the reservoir's north end, you can paddle upstream for another
half mile on a usually quiet Mongaup River section. Caution: the river
can rise suddenly, carrying vastly more water, turning a relaxing paddle
into a more exciting quickwater adventure. When both turbines generate power, the flow increases from about 100 cubic feet per second

(cfs) to 1,600 cfs. We paddled up to the inlet brook from Lebanon Lake; above there, exposed rocks and rapids blocked our way.

Mongaup Falls offers quite a bit of variety. Marshy areas contain all sorts of wetland plants (pickerelweed, bulrush, and sedges, for example). In the marsh just below the Route 43 bridge, we studied a well-camouflaged green heron before it flew. A few small patches of cattail marsh occur north of the bridge.

On the reservoir's eastern side—heavily wooded, except for a few stretches of marsh—white pine predominates, with oaks, maples, beech, and birch mixed in. A few, small, well-hidden cabins do not intrude on the wild feeling here.

Along the western shore's powerline right-of-way, open fields extend down to the water's edge. Some fields consist mostly of hay-scented fern, which turns a golden brown in early September. Where their feet can remain moist, closed gentian, cardinal flower, turtlehead, and false dragonhead grow along here. When a dropping water level exposes new ground during summer, gorgeous cardinal flower often springs up.

We saw bryozoa colonies on most submerged branches, indicating fairly pure water. If you reach down into the water and touch a globular bryozoa colony, it will feel gelatinous.

In winter, Mongaup Falls draws as many as 150 bald eagles from the Northeast and Canada because the dam keeps water from freezing and the turbines kill some fish. An eagle-watching blind at the reservoir's north end allows visitors to watch these majestic creatures without disturbing them. Eagles had historically wintered here, but by the 1960s, the population had fallen drastically because of DDT poisoning. New York eagles have made a dramatic comeback, largely the result of a bald eagle reintroduction program begun in the Adirondacks in 1976.

You might also see eagles here during the rest of the year. Several pairs of eagles nest in the Mongaup Valley and along the Upper Delaware River. We saw pairs on both Cliff Lake and Toronto Reservoir.

Bald Eagle

Our National Bird Back from the Brink

The bald eagle—with its unmistakable white head and tail—soars over the nation's waterways on powerful wings. In flight, its large size stands out, with wings that span as much as 8 feet. From beak to tip of tail, the eagle measures from 34 to 43 inches; males weigh 8 to 9 pounds, whereas the larger females weigh 10 to 14 pounds. Bringing new meaning to "light as a feather," the feathers can contribute up to 15 percent of the bird's body weight.

The bald eagle attains its distinctive plumage only after attaining an age of four or five years. Until then, it resembles the dark brown golden eagle, except with some white mottling on the underside and tail. As it matures, the bald eagle's head and tail become progressively whiter. At close range, the adult's large yellow beak and piercing yellow eyes convey a fierce strength. Our country's founders evidently felt this image symbolized what our young nation stood for, selecting *Haliaeetus leucocephalus,* the only eagle found exclusively in North America, as our national symbol.

Ranging throughout New York, eagles generally locate their nests in trees at the water's edge. Pairs return to the same nest for years, adding to it annually. An old eagle nest may measure 6 feet in diameter and 8 feet deep and weigh more than a ton. The largest nest ever found was 9.5 feet in diameter and 20 feet deep. Because eagles often build nests in dead trees, the huge mass eventually topples the tree.

Bald eagles usually lay two eggs several days apart. Incubation lasts 30 to 36 days, during which the male and female share nesting duties. The young hatch several days apart, a strategy that improves the chances of fledging at least one chick. In times of food scarcity, the earlier-born chick may outcompete its younger sibling for food, and the younger chick will die. Because eagles live long lives—as long as 30 years in captivity but usually much less in the wild—they really only need to fledge a few chicks to replace themselves, thus maintaining a stable population.

After 10 to 12 weeks of a diet consisting mostly of fish, chicks fledge and begin to fly. For the next 7 or 8 weeks, they increasingly gain independence, eventually migrating to coastal areas and to outfalls below dams where the water does not freeze. In years past, they congregated in great numbers off both coasts and in the Mississippi drainage each fall. Eagles still congregate by the thousands in mid-November along a 10-mile stretch of the Chilkat River in Alaska to feed on hordes of dead and dying salmon.

Although bald eagles occur frequently in New York today—thanks to efforts by the Endangered Species Unit of the Department of Environmental Conservation (DEC)—just a few years ago only a few remained. In the late 1960s and early 1970s, long-lasting chlorinated hydrocarbons—such as DDT and its breakdown product DDE, left over from mosquito control projects—reached high concentrations in osprey, eagle, peregrine falcon, and other top-of-the-food-chain species, causing thinned eggshells to break during incubation. The eagle population plummeted to just one nesting pair in western New York that doggedly nested in the same tree for more than 20 years. Only once during that time—in 1973—did they successfully hatch and raise a chick, but they served as successful foster parents for captive-born chicks over several years, starting in 1978, in the DEC's fledgling reintroduction program.

Eagle populations have rebounded to about 7,000 nesting pairs (up from 4,000 in 1995) in the United States outside Alaska, with 92 in 2005 in New York, up from 25 in 1995—with the greatest concentration around remote lakes in the far western, far northern, and southeastern regions. In 2005, New York eagles fledged 112 young, up from 30 in 1995, 20 in 1994, 15 in 1990, and 3 in 1987. In addition to the increasing number of young produced in New York, another satisfying statistic has occurred: nest success rates remain relatively high, averaging 1.2 chicks fledged per breeding pair, the same number that occurred from 1990 to 1995. This stands in contrast with less than 1 chick fledged per breeding pair in Maine with 300 nests. Possibly, eagles in New York suffer from less contamination by DDT, DDE, dioxins, mercury, and PCBs.

Because eagle populations rose during the 23 years after DDT's ban, aided by reintroductions in many areas in the country, the U.S. Fish and

Wildlife Service removed the bald eagle from the Endangered Species List in 1995, placing it on the Threatened List.

We feel privileged to paddle on lakes with resident bald eagles. Some accuse them of opportunism, and indeed, we have watched a few chase smaller osprey, laboring with heavy fish, circling to gain altitude before flying off to their aeries. In one sighting, after the osprey dropped its hard-won catch, a bald eagle snatched it and flew off. This represents the triumph of bald eagle adaptation, ensuring its survival, not a case of good and evil.

Humans still shoot eagles on occasion and build high-voltage lines that electrocute them—although designs and devices exist that reduce eagle mortality—and many eagles die flying into human-made structures (towers, smokestacks, power lines, and buildings). But the biggest threat to the eagle's continued survival comes from an expanding human population, one that spews toxic chemicals and continues to develop shorelines. If we wish to enjoy this majestic creature as it patrols America's waterways—and to keep it from returning to the Endangered Species List—we must take steps to keep some of its habitat undeveloped and unadulterated by the toxic wastes of a consumer society. The eagle represents an enduring wildness that we must protect for future generations to enjoy.

20

Cliff Lake
Bethel, Highland, and Lumberland

Maps: New York Atlas Map 35:D4, USGS Quadrangle Highland Lake

Area: 200 acres

Habitat type: small reservoir

Fish: largemouth and smallmouth bass, pickerel

Expect to see: bald eagle

Camping: App. A #113 and 115

Take note: gasoline motors prohibited; open May 1 to November 30

GETTING THERE

From the Mongaup Falls Reservoir access, continue 0.3 mile west on Route 43, turn right, and go 2.0 miles (2.3 miles) to the access.

Cliff Lake and the surrounding upland belong to Mirant, but the company allows public access from May 1 though the end of November. We love paddling on this out-of-the-way lake, as it receives little recreational pressure.

The lake extends roughly 2 miles in a north-south orientation, with a maximum width of about a quarter mile. When we visited in early September, the markedly low water level detracted significantly from the feel of the place. The level can be down several feet in very dry years, exposing quite a bit of shoreline. The utility company usually keeps the water level higher—within 5 feet of 1,070 feet in elevation. Interestingly, Cliff Lake

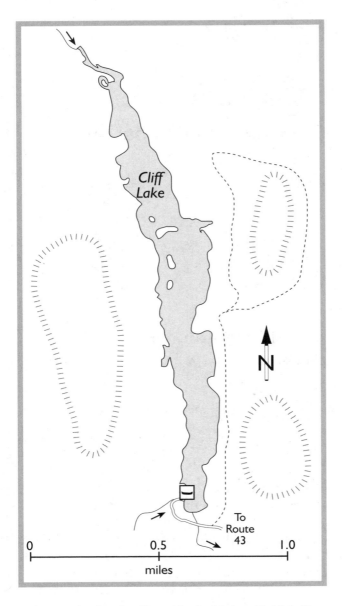

Cliff
Lake

N

To
Route
43

0   0.5   1.0

miles

connects hydraulically with Swinging Bridge Reservoir through an underground aqueduct, so the two water levels remain the same. We recommend visiting before fall to improve chances of finding the reservoir full. The sandy or pebbly shore suffers from erosion in some places.

A large lodge that the resident beaver extended downward as the lake level dropped.

We saw a curious beaver lodge where the ever-industrious animals worked hard to keep "growing" the beaver lodge downward, trying to keep it underwater as the lake's level dropped. Given the age of some of the lodge's material, it appeared that the lodge, built into a fallen tree, holds firm through the seasonal water level fluctuation—beaver must have weighted the sticks down with stones to keep the lodge from floating away.

When we hiked up to Cliff Lake and around the reservoir, the open meadows—some carpeted with ferns, some filled with shade-loving grasses or sedges—struck us as particularly gorgeous. They give the woods a very open, inviting feel. Sugar maple and white pine seem to be the dominant trees here, with beech scattered throughout. We noted a few groves of red pine.

Several islands appear just above the midpoint. At the north end, we watched a number of plovers and sandpipers scurry over exposed mudflats, hunting for insects and crustaceans. Wilson's plover, looking somewhat like a killdeer but shorter and with only one neckband, was most common.

Also at the north end, we saw three bald eagles: two adults and a three- or four-year-old juvenile. Several eagle pairs now nest in the Mongaup Valley (see section on Mongaup Falls Reservoir).

21

Toronto Reservoir
Bethel

Maps: New York Atlas Map 34:C4, USGS Quadrangles White Lake and Highland Lake

Area: 834 acres, maximum depth 50 feet

Habitat type: reservoir

Fish: largemouth bass, pickerel

Expect to see: bald eagle, Canada goose, common merganser, deer, wild turkey

Camping: App. A #113 and 115

Take note: maximum boat size 20 ft; personal watercraft prohibited; reservoir section off limits

GETTING THERE

From Route 17 in Monticello, go west on Route 17B for 7.5 miles, and turn left on Route 55 south. Go 1.8 miles (9.3 miles), turn left onto Moscoe Road, and go 0.8 mile (10.1 miles) to the access.

Alternately, at times of low water, you can launch at the Toronto Reservoir dam, reached via Pine Grove Road from the hamlet of Smallwood.

Visit Toronto Reservoir early in the season. The reservoir typically gets drawn down late in the season, exposing hundreds of feet of ugly muddy shoreline. Under provisions of recent federal relicensing of the dams now owned by Mirant, summer drawdown has become less extreme.

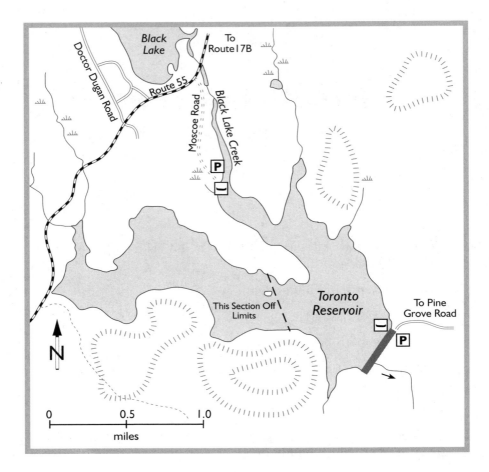

People use the reservoir primarily for fishing. The state-record chain pickerel was caught on Toronto Reservoir in 1965 and remains one of the longest-standing records.

The Iroquois Hunting & Fishing Club owns roughly half of Toronto Reservoir's fairly large surface area and has posted it off-limits to the public. Large shoreline signs and several floating buoys mark this division. The club controls surface water access under an agreement with Rockland Light & Power, the utility that built the dam in the late 1920s. Because the reservoir inundated land owned by the club, the utility granted the club exclusive hunting and fishing rights on that portion of the reservoir.

A common merganser casts a wary eye in our direction.

Toronto's rocky shoreline sports exposed outcroppings of a sedimentary, shalelike rock. Grasses and small shrubs prevail along most of the immediate shoreline, with woodland extending away from the shore. Some tall white pines emerge above the beech-maple forest canopy. Dense groves of hemlock occur here and there, along with scattered rhododendrons in the understory.

Half a dozen deer fed on grasses along the higher banks when we visited in early morning, as mist still swirled above the reservoir. In the water, a small flock of Canada geese and several families of common merganser hunted for food. On other trips here, we saw flocks of wild turkey.

Near the reservoir's midpoint, we heard a distinctive raptor call and spotted a bald eagle pair sitting side by side on an oak branch. A little further scanning with binoculars turned up a juvenile in a tree nearby. We watched these majestic birds for some time and witnessed a rare treat. After a while the immature eagle took off and began flying above the water in search of fish. Shortly, one of the adults joined it for what was almost certainly a fishing lesson. As we watched, the two birds made dozens of passes over the same section of water, each time dropping down and dipping feet into the water. Several times they landed on the nearby shore. Eventually, the adult caught a small fish, and the two flew off to tell stories about the big one that got away.

Bald eagles, which have long wintered near the Mongaup River dams, recently resumed nesting, as well. To protect bald eagle wintering grounds, in 1986 the state purchased 6,000 acres along the Mongaup River from Orange and Rockland Utilities and protected another 6,000 acres through easements. For more on bald eagles, see the section on Mongaup Falls Reservoir and the nature essay on page 88.

22

Lake Superior
Bethel

Maps: New York Atlas Map 34:C4, USGS Quadrangles White Lake and Lake Huntington

Area: 188 acres, maximum depth 27 feet

Habitat type: small, shallow, weedy pond

Fish: largemouth bass, pickerel

Expect to see: aquatic plants, marsh areas

Camping and recreation: Lake Superior State Park, 845-794-3000; camping App. A #113 and 115

Take note: gasoline motors prohibited; small entrance fee; free between Labor Day and Memorial Day

GETTING THERE

From Route 17 in Monticello, go west on Route 17B for 9.2 miles, and turn left on Doctor Duggan Road. Go 1.5 miles (10.7 miles) south to the access at Lake Superior State Park.

The bucolic, rolling countryside of Bethel rocked to a different tune in the summer of 1969. The Woodstock Music Festival, held just a mile from Lake Superior on Max Yasgur's farm, drew several hundred thousand participants. We could find only one hint at the park of this historic event—which no doubt bore a heavy impact from the overflow crowd: reference to the festival on wrappers of locally made ice-cream bars at the concession stand.

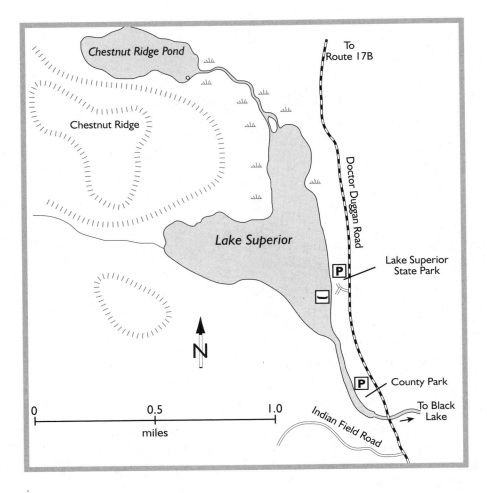

Lake Superior offers a very pleasant spot for a half-day paddle, mainly because of gasoline motor prohibition. Thick mats of aquatic plants populate the extensive marshy areas at the north and south ends of this highly productive pond. At the south end, a long outlet channel extends almost a half mile toward Black Lake. In the spring, you should be able to paddle this without difficulty, but by late summer, it becomes nearly impenetrable, choked with pickerelweed, bulrush, waterlilies, and sedges.

The marshy north end, very different ecologically, harbors typical swamp vegetation: red maple, buttonbush, leatherleaf, blueberry, royal

Look for buttonbush, with its spherical flowers and seed heads, at the lake's marshy north end.

fern, swamp rose, and swamp loosestrife. We had hoped to paddle up into Chestnut Ridge Pond, about a half mile north, but try as we might, we could not get through the dense growth. It might be possible—though unlikely—to wend your way through in the spring with a bit higher water level.

Even in late summer, however, we would explore a little way into the swamp. After a number of false starts, we managed to squeeze in 50 or 100 yards, where we sighted a sora rail, a small, elusive, sometimes heard but rarely seen, marsh bird. We sat still for about a half hour as it darted in and out of view, a mere 10 feet away. We recognize this brownish bird by its short bill; its short, triangular cocked tail; and its greenish legs with striations above and very long toes below. We also saw evidence of beaver up here.

At the pond's northeastern tip, look for a large stand of tamarack, with delicate, feathery needles that turn yellow and then drop in autumn. More common in northern New York, this species typifies the northern fen because it can become established in saturated soils—even on floating peat mats.

Waterlilies—fragrant waterlily, yellow pondlily, and water shield—abound. Typically, emergent plants occur along shore, including bur-reed and pickerelweed, then a fringe of floating waterlilies lies slightly farther out. You can pretty well judge the water depth by the plants; most aquatic plants cannot grow in more than four feet of water. In contrast with the mucky-bottomed marshy areas, much of the lake has a sandy bottom, providing good habitat for freshwater mussels, which occur here in abundance.

The fairly open woods abounds with ferns, clubmosses, and wildflowers beneath a canopy of sugar maple, yellow birch, cherry, beech, red oak, hemlock, and white pine. Rhododendron grows in abundance, thicker here than we have seen on any other lake in the state. Visit in late June or early July, and you should be treated to rhododendron in bloom. It is thickest along the eastern shore, just north of the access, and directly across from the access along the southwestern shore. At one spot on the eastern shore, a network of tunnels through the tall rhododendron groves extends away from the lake.

23

Morningside Lake
Fallsburg

Maps: New York Atlas Map 35:C5, USGS Quadrangles Liberty East and Monticello

Area: 126 acres, maximum depth 12 feet

Habitat type: small, shallow, marshy pond

Fish: largemouth bass, pickerel

Expect to see: Canada goose

Camping: on-site, Morningside Park, 845-434-5877

GETTING THERE

From Route 17, Exit 100, go east on Route 52 for 4.3 miles, and turn right on Route 104 south. Go 1.1 miles (5.4 miles), turn left on County Route 52, and go 0.6 mile (6.0 miles) to the access on the left (0.1 mile past the park entrance).

Morningside Lake really surprised us. Though surrounded by relatively developed areas and dominated by Fallsburg's town park, the lake offers very pleasant paddling. Except for summer weekends, you should paddle this small lake in peace.

Morningside Lake extends for less than three-quarters of a mile, but numerous small islands provide opportunity to explore for hours and to feel a bit of solitude. These islands, with their delicate tamarack, remind us of bogs and fens in the Adirondacks and northern New England.

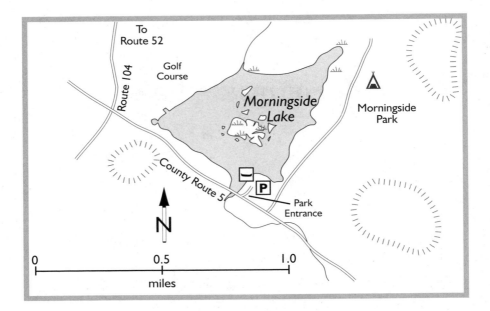

Morningside's shallow, 2- to 4-foot depth in most places provides great wildlife habitat. In the extensive marshy areas at the northeast tip and around the islands, we saw dozens of wood duck, along with great blue heron, cormorant, and lots of painted turtles. In one section, masses of uprooted waterlily tubers floated on the surface, looking from a distance like huge dead carp, the leaf scars reminding us of scales. Paddling closer, turtles skittered from their floating platforms into the murky water.

The pea green, quite eutrophic water suffers from overfertilization—probably from the many Canada geese that call this home and possibly from fertilizer applied to the golf course that adjoins the lake's northwestern side. Golf courses often provide substantial amounts of chemical runoff; we should demand that golf course managers use chemicals wisely.

Stands of bur-reed, cattail, arrowhead, pickerelweed, sedges, grasses, blueberry, winterberry, and leatherleaf dominate much of the shoreline. Fragrant waterlily, yellow pondlily, and water shield float in the water. Buttonbush, tamarack, and swamp loosestrife—a native cousin of the introduced purple loosestrife that continues to take over many wetlands—dominate the islands. Be careful paddling around these islands: when

Feathery tamarack on the boggy islands of Morningside Lake.

swamp loosestrife dies back, the woody stems rot away at about the water's surface, leaving sharp spikes that could puncture a delicate fiberglass boat.

Much more activity takes place at the southern end. The park concession does a good business renting rowboats. A fairly thin row of trees and shrubs along the eastern shore buffers 144 campsites; expect to hear activity from the campground, ball fields, tennis courts, playground, swimming pools, and camp store that figure prominently in this park.

Central New York

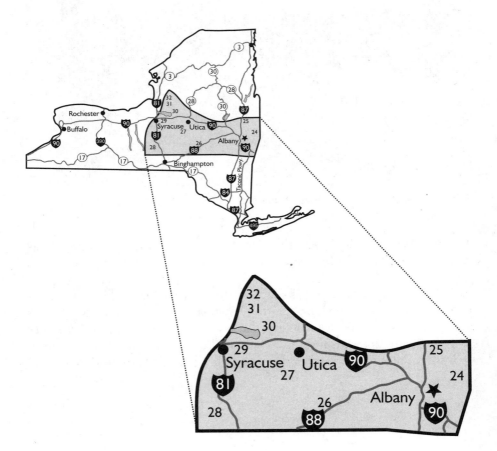

24

Grafton Lakes and Dunham Reservoir
Grafton

Maps: New York Atlas Map 67:B6, USGS Quadrangles Grafton and Berlin

Area: Long Pond 113 acres, Second Pond 29 acres, Mill Pond 19 acres, Shaver Pond 45 acres, Dunham Reservoir 98 acres

Habitat type: small, shallow ponds

Fish: largemouth and smallmouth bass (Second and Mill ponds, Dunham Reservoir), rainbow and brown trout (Long and Second ponds), brook trout (Shaver Pond)

Expect to see: osprey, mallard, Canada goose, beaver

Camping and trails: Grafton Lakes State Park, 518-279-1155, trail map available; camping App. A #40

Take note: no gasoline motors

GETTING THERE

Dunham Reservoir. From Troy, go east on Route 2. From the junction with Route 278, continue on Route 2 for 5.1 miles, and turn right on Dunham Road. Go 0.6 mile (5.7 miles) to a gate. Park and carry down to the reservoir's western end. To reach the east end, go back to Route 2, and take three right turns to the access, just before the inlet stream.

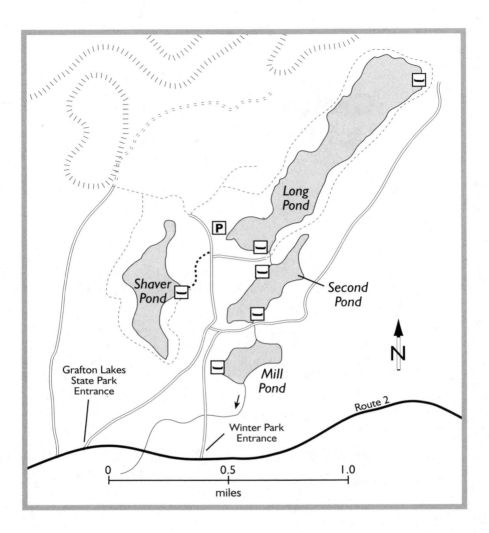

Long, Second, Mill, and Shaver Ponds. Continue east on Route 2 to the park entrance on the left. Follow signs to the access to Long and Second ponds. For Shaver Pond, park in the main parking area, and take the trail from the southwest end of the parking lot.

We enjoy paddling here very much, and the park's close proximity to Albany and Troy draws many hikers and boaters. The large beach area

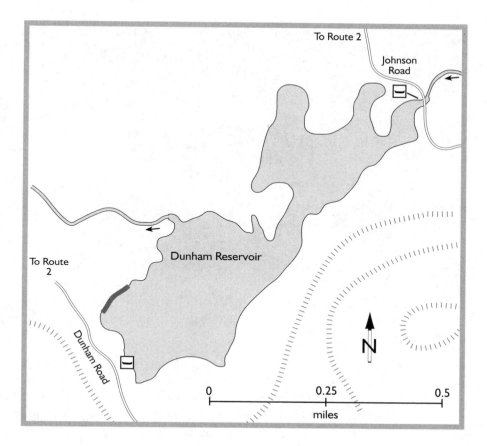

To Route 2

Johnson Road

To Route 2

Dunham Reservoir

Dunham Road

N

0   0.25   0.5

miles

on Long Pond gets crowded on nice summer weekends, so we recommend visiting midweek or outside of the summer season.

We found the less-accessible Shaver Pond and Dunham Reservoir the most enjoyable to paddle. The easy half-mile carry into Shaver Pond follows a nature trail, suitable for a portage cart. Pick up a nature guide to the trees and other natural features of the Shaver Pond trail. Dunham Reservoir, with extensive berming and a dam on the western end, supplied Troy's drinking water until the 1960s when the reservoir area became a state park.

Explore the eastern end of Dunham Reservoir and the winding inlet stream, which you can paddle for nearly a half mile before reaching

Getting ready to head out on our first paddle of the season in late April.

quickwater and rocks. Paddling under the bridge, you enter an area thick with grasses, sedges, and other marsh plants. In late April as dusk approached, spring peepers regaled us and potential mates with their high-pitched peeping. Mallards paddled about the shallows, Canada geese eyed us warily from a likely nesting site, kingfishers announced their presence with rattlelike calls as they flew ahead, and beaver swam about, harvesting the new growth of spring.

Several different species of clubmoss, *Lycopodium*, carpet extensive stretches of shoreline around most ponds. Among the most primitive vascular plants (those with xylem and phloem to conduct water and nutrients), several species look like tiny trees, thus the common names "ground pine" and "ground cedar." Other species creep along the ground on long stems with short leaves extending from all sides. The soft, branching stems of staghorn clubmoss resemble the velvet of deer antlers in spring. In the age of dinosaurs, clubmoss relatives grew as large as trees.

Deciduous woods surround these undeveloped ponds and include red oak, beech, four different birches—paper, gray, black, and yellow—black cherry, and red and sugar maples. Along the shore, blueberry bushes grow alongside taller shadbush, both providing edible berries in summer. We watched an osprey ply the water for its next meal, hovering, body tilted up slightly, wings flapping quickly to maintain a stationary position, peering into the water for fish.

A great place for families that enjoy both paddling and hiking, the park boasts easy trails extending around Long and Shaver ponds and several others that head off in various directions.

25

Fish Creek
(Saratoga Lake)
Saratoga and Saratoga Springs

Maps: New York Atlas Maps 80:D4 and 81:D5, USGS Quadrangles Quaker Springs and Schuylerville

Length: 11 miles

Habitat type: meandering, slow-flowing stream

Fish: largemouth and smallmouth bass, northern pike, walleye

Expect to see: great blue heron, waterfowl

Camping: App. A #38, 68, 69, 70, and 71

Take note: motorboats near Saratoga Lake; access fee at Saratoga Lake

GETTING THERE

Saratoga Lake. From I-87, Exit 14, go 2.0 miles east on Route 9P, and turn left into the access, just across the iron bridge.

Victory. From Schuylerville, go south on Route 4, and turn right on Route 32. Go 1.2 miles, turn left on Mennen Road, cross the bridge, and park on the right (southwest corner).

A huge stand of willows and an RV park greet you at the northern outlet of Saratoga Lake as it forms Fish Creek. Because of water-ski and personal watercraft traffic, we recommend that you paddle Fish Creek

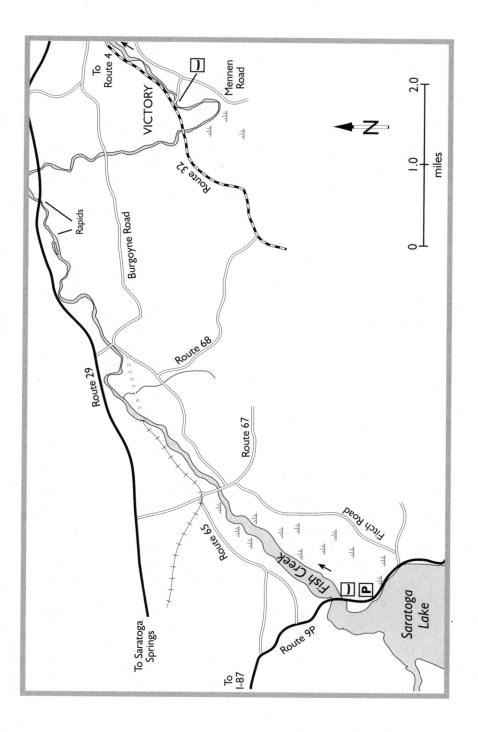

away from Saratoga Lake, meandering toward the Hudson. Because of dams and occasional shallow rapids in a few spots, you cannot paddle the whole way. We include two sections here, separated by a short section of rapids, dams, and falls. When faced with a lot of creek traffic, we put in at Victory, instead of at Saratoga Lake.

We have paddled here in spring and in summer. Paddling out from Saratoga Lake in midspring, a bass fishing tournament had just begun, so we had to contend with dozens of 150-horsepower bass boats roaring up and down the creek, rushing to the next hot spot, of course putting the fish down from the commotion. Because these boats hydroplane at high speeds, displacing little water, they leave very little wake. To avoid being run over, we stayed along the edges and did not see much wildlife in the heavily traveled portions of Fish Creek.

With springtime high water, however, we could paddle back into narrow creeks and coves where we saw numerous basking turtles and surprised a male wood duck in full breeding plumage right beneath a nesting box. We also saw mallard and black duck—which sure beat the drowned tires, plastic buckets, and broken-up docks that mar Fish Creek's first few miles.

About 3.5 miles from Saratoga Lake, a nice little creek goes off to the right. Vines hang out over the water, and you have to thread your way through the narrow passageway. We found many ducks feeding and an Eastern phoebe pair nesting under a low bridge. Cardinals called "bir-dy, bir-dy, bir-dy" from the thickets, and red-winged blackbirds sang "cong-ka-ree" from the reeds. Once we got this far from Saratoga Lake, the number of boats dwindled to zero.

The lower portion of Fish Creek, closer to the Hudson, also receives much less boat traffic. We put in at Victory in midsummer and paddled upstream to the more western of two Route 29 bridges, where rapids block further passage upstream.

In contrast with Fish Creek's spilling over into broad marshes as it flows out of Saratoga Lake, low banks contain the lower section. Dense grapevines drape over streamside willows and silver maples all along the creek, closing in much of the canopy. Great blue heron, as many as three at a time, stood poised over the water on downed trees, taking flight as we passed. We threaded our way upstream through this maze, listening to cardinal, Eastern phoebe, gray catbird, brown thrasher, and mockingbird songs from the undergrowth. Barn and tree swallows dipped

Serviceberry blooms in early spring along the banks of Fish Creek.

to drink the water, a spotted sandpiper bobbed along the shore, and a belted kingfisher paced us up the waterway.

We had no trouble negotiating the current of midsummer, until we reached the first Route 29 bridge. Here, a small falls and rapids blocked our way upstream. We suppose that with two cars, you could paddle from Saratoga Lake to Victory, walking your boat through the shallows and around dams. As we drifted lazily back down to Victory, listening to the haunting song of the mourning dove and the high-pitched "pee-o-wee" of the Eastern wood-pewee, we reveled in the solitude so close to crowded Saratoga Lake.

26

Susquehanna River
Milford

Maps: New York Atlas Map 64:D1, USGS Quadrangle Milford

Goodyear Lake area: 366 acres, river length 10 miles

Habitat type: meandering, slow-flowing river through farmland and woodlot

Fish: largemouth and smallmouth bass, walleye

Expect to see: osprey, harrier, ducks, great blue heron

Camping: App. A #8, 9, and 11

Take note: books—to run downstream sections, use Ehling, *Canoeing Central New York* (Backcountry Publications, 1982) or Freeman, *Canoe Guide to Western and Central New York State* (Adirondack Mountain Club, 1993)

GETTING THERE

Route 166 Bridge. From Cooperstown, at the junction of Routes 28 and 80, go 8.1 miles south on Route 28, and turn left on Route 166. Go 0.7 mile (8.8 miles) to the access on the left.

Crumhorn Landing (better access). From the Route 166 bridge, continue east on Route 166 for 0.3 mile (9.1 miles), and turn right on Route 35C. Go 0.2 mile (9.3 miles), turn right on Route 35 south, and go 2.7 miles (12.0 miles) to the access on the right.

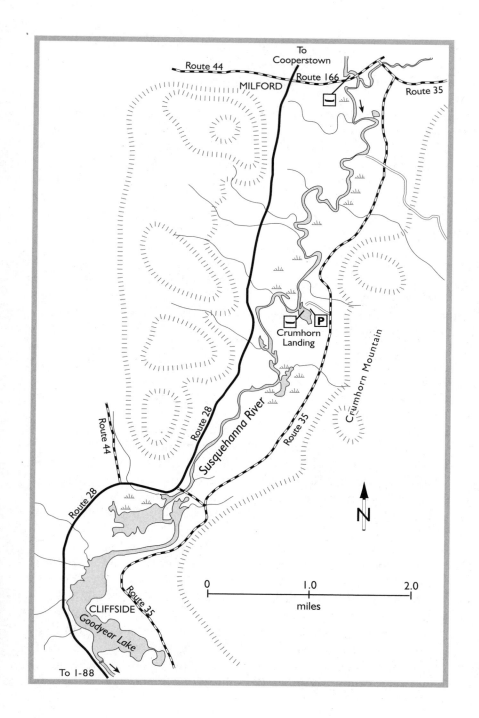

From I-88, Exit 17, go 4.5 miles north on Route 28, and turn right on Route 35A. Go 0.3 mile (4.8 miles), turn left on Route 35, and go north 2.4 miles (7.2 miles) to Crumhorn Landing on the left.

From modest beginnings in Otsego Lake—the famed "Glimmerglass" of James Fenimore Cooper—the Susquehanna River meanders quietly southward, gathering hundreds of feeder streams and rivers along the way. Draining much of south central New York, by the time the river exits the state about 30 miles west of Binghamton, it transforms into the major river that eventually forms Chesapeake Bay estuary. The Susquehanna, more than 400 miles in length, remains second in drainage size only to the St. Lawrence among East Coast rivers.

The General Clinton Canoe Regatta over Memorial Day weekend includes a race on the Susquehanna that begins on Otsego Lake, ending 70 miles later at Bainbridge. In August 1779, General James Clinton and his forces floated a handmade fleet of 220 boats down the Susquehanna for 170 miles to join forces with General John Sullivan at Tioga Point in Pennsylvania, in a campaign to subdue the Finger Lakes Iroquois tribes loyal to the British. Because the upper Susquehanna had little water, Clinton's troops built a three-foot-high dam across Otsego Lake's outlet. With his newly constructed fleet loaded and ready, he ordered the dam breached, and they floated on a human-made crest down into Pennsylvania.

We chose a 10-mile section of the Susquehanna near its beginnings—just below Cooperstown—where it meanders slowly through farmlands, meadows, and woodlots, where at times of low water you can hardly tell which way the river flows. Because of muddy banks at the Route 166 access, we prefer to put in at Crumhorn Landing, where you can paddle upstream to the Route 166 bridge or downstream to Goodyear Lake.

A rather tame osprey greeted us with its piercing cries as we put in at Crumhorn Landing, foreshadowing our close look at many more birds along the way. The river's tight meanders and high banks deliver you to a new section of water with little commotion, making for good wildlife viewing. Coming out of a curve, we came right up on a bittern—a reclusive, brown-streaked marsh heron that would rather hide than fly—causing it to bolt skyward with a great thrashing of wings.

We also saw mallard dabbling for underwater plants, rear end pointing skyward; spotted sandpiper bobbing along the shoreline, aiming

A northern harrier—formerly known as marsh hawk—hovers low over a field, searching for rodents.

for a better look at rock-clinging insects; northern harrier swooping over fields with an uptilted dihedral, searching for rodents without the good sense to stay under cover; chickadee foraging in small, loosely knit flocks, "chipping" to maintain contact; the spring's first yellow-rumped warbler, darting over the water, feeding on the first insect hatch; ruffed grouse drumming, attracting females to begin the rites of spring; and flicker, tapping out holes in dead streamside trees, providing nest cavities for itself and wood duck, hooded merganser, kestrel, tree swallow, and bluebird. We also saw or heard mourning dove, song sparrow, robin, crow, flicker, killdeer, red-winged blackbird, white-throated sparrow, and grackle.

Beaver have cut down many streamside willows that reach out over the water, and we paddled right up to one beaver before it dove for cover. We rescued a meadow vole, thrashing in the water, returning it to dry ground. A warm southern breeze reminded us that a meandering river provides a great place to paddle when early- and late-season winds have turned large bodies of water to a foamy froth.

Though occasional road noise intruded as a meander neared a road, most of the time we paddled peacefully, with great views of forested hillsides, a few with layered fields retreating into the distance. We paddled by farms with fields edging on the water and occasional cottages, but most of the time we enjoyed in solitude the sounds, sights, and smells of spring.

27

Ninemile Swamp (Sangerfield River)

Brookfield and Hamilton

Maps: New York Atlas Maps 62:B4 and 63:B4, USGS Quadrangle Hubbardsville

Length: 8 miles round-trip, Wickwire Road bridge to Swamp Road bridge

Habitat type: meandering, swampy stream

Fish: largemouth bass, northern pike

Expect to see: red-tailed hawk, ducks, great blue heron, pileated woodpecker, deer, beaver, aquatic plants

Camping and books: we found out about this wonderful creek and the Loomis Gang from Ehling, *Canoeing Central New York* (Backcountry Publications, 1982); see also Walter, *The Loomis Gang* (North Country Books, 1985); camping App. A #6 and 11

Take note: you may have to portage over and around beaver dams and downed trees

GETTING THERE

From Utica, at the junction of Routes 12 and 20, go 8.3 miles south on Route 12, and turn right on Green Road. Go 0.1 mile (8.4 miles), and turn right on Wickwire Road. Go 0.6 mile (9.0 miles) to the access on the right. Do not block the drive down to the water.

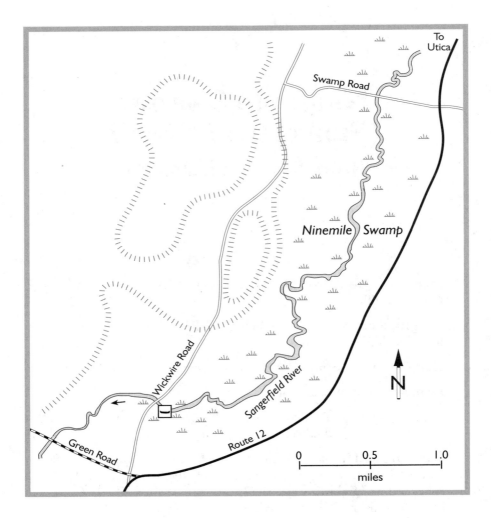

This creek's rich history includes the escapades of the notorious Loomis Gang that operated in the swamp from the time of patriarch George Washington Loomis's arrival in 1802 until nearly 1900. Supposedly, shortly before his arrival, he had run stolen horses in Vermont and fled before a posse, ending up in Sangerfield where he married and raised a gang of outlaw children. This family of horse thieves, arsonists, highway robbers, and murderers lived on nearby Loomis Hill, overlooking the swamp from the west. Loomis Road crosses the swamp in the sec-

The Sangerfield River alternately narrows and broadens as it meanders south through Ninemile Swamp.

tion above the one included here, and the gang used the swamp to hide themselves and their ill-gotten horses from local vigilantes.

From the access, you begin an easy paddle up to Swamp Road. Even during drought years, plenty of water should carry you over the shallows and through the abundant aquatic vegetation. The snowmelt and winter rains funnel down off the surrounding hillsides, percolate through the ground around the swamp, and slowly release into the creek. When other area water levels drop in midsummer, the Sangerfield usually still has plenty. Local anglers, who fish for largemouth bass and 30-inch northern pike, told us that during high water, if you did not mind getting out of your boat on occasion, you could paddle past Swamp Road, all the way to Loomis Road and beyond.

When we checked out the bridge over the creek at Loomis Road in September, the water—what there was of it—did not look at all inviting. You can still paddle up to the Swamp Road bridge, however, even though willow, alder, and other branches drape over the meandering waterway.

Paddling up this beautiful valley, with layered fields on the lower hills followed by timbered mountaintops, one can easily forget time. We never tire of paddling through this wildlife paradise, with deer crossing the stream in the morning mists; crow-sized pileated woodpecker in undulating flight, looking for a dead tree full of carpenter ants; and red-tailed hawk circling lazily above, wary eyes cast for rodents.

Alders and huge overhanging willows dominate this wooded swamp, along with occasional box elder, sugar and red maples, oak, ash, cherry, big-toothed and quaking aspens, tall white pine, northern white cedar, and other conifers. In late September, the swamp's red maples turn brilliant scarlet. Red maple has red on it at all times: buds in winter, flowers in spring, leaf stems in summer, and leaves in fall.

Tree leaves remain green because the dominant pigment, chlorophyll, reflects mainly green light, absorbing other colors of the visual spectrum to do photosynthetic work. When chlorophyll disappears in fall, brilliant reds, yellows, and oranges emerge from the leaf's surface, reflected back by other selectively absorbing pigments. Against the brilliant blue sky of an arctic high-pressure cell, the river's fall foliage burned brightly when we paddled here.

Early in the year, look for turtles and frogs out sunning, along with swirling lily pads caused by bass and northerns chasing bait fish in these productive waters. In the spring, mating calls of birds sound throughout the swamp.

In the fall, wood duck fatten up on acorns and aquatic vegetation and jump to the air at your approach, some blasting out from streamside branches. What a pleasure to paddle amidst the glorious foliage of fall, a season free from swamp-bred biting insects, though we would be back in spring, fighting the bugs, just glad to be out there again.

28

Dryden Lake
Dryden

Maps: New York Atlas Map 47:A4, USGS Quadrangle Dryden

Area: 106 acres, maximum depth12 feet

Habitat type: small, shallow, weed-filled pond

Fish: largemouth bass, pickerel

Expect to see: osprey, Canada goose, great blue heron, turtle, beaver, aquatic vegetation

Camping: App. A #16 and 24

Take note: no gasoline motors; Chaffee Road crosses an abandoned railroad grade, turned into a hiking/biking path.

GETTING THERE

From Ithaca, go east on Route 13 or Route 366. From the junction of Routes 13 and 366, go 5.9 miles east to Dryden, and turn right on Route 38. Go 2.1 miles (8.0 miles), and turn left on Chaffee Road. Go 0.2 mile (8.2 miles), turn left on West Lake Road, and go 0.1 mile (8.3 miles) to the access on the right, just across the outlet stream bridge.

Recreational opportunities abound in the Ithaca region. One can enjoy spectacular Taughannock and Buttermilk Falls, the Rim and Gorge Trails at Taughannock Point, bike and foot trails—including the abandoned railroad grade near Dryden Park—several vineyards, state parks and forests, beaches, and cruises on Cayuga Lake. However, Dryden Lake presents one of the few quietwater paddling opportunities.

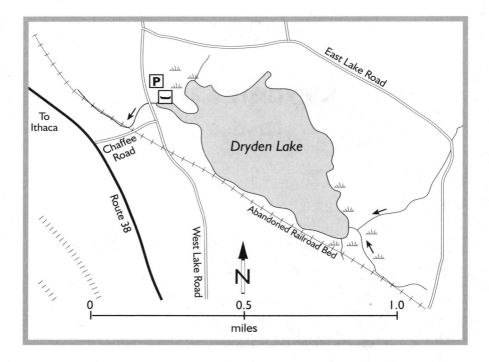

The state and town of Dryden, through farsighted efforts, set aside Dryden Lake as a town park and a state Wildlife Management Area. A picnic area hugs the western shore, and a golf course covers a hillside on the east. Scenic farms layer the hillsides, and fields march down to the lake's east shore. The cows, along with the abundant Canada geese—real feces factories—fertilize these waters, ensuring abundant plant life. Neither cows nor geese move quickly, and that should serve as a metaphor for our approach to these waters: enjoy them slowly, study the plants, and watch the wildlife.

Usually on heavily vegetated bodies of water, frogs use the fronds as furniture. In this lake, the vegetation supports turtles. A great blue heron even stood on it, trying with some difficulty to spot passing fish. Besides the usual waterlilies, when we first paddled here, we found an aquatic member of the buttercup family in bloom, along with waterweed, a type of *Elodea*, with unusual underwater leaves one-quarter inch long by one-sixteenth inch wide, whorled in threes on slender stalks. It also bears the tiniest, barely visible purple flowers borne on tendrils; some flowers occur underwater, and others float in the surface film. In the intervening years, invasive Eurasian watermilfoil has become the dominant aquatic plant species. Experiments with biological control have occurred here, and we can only hope that those efforts will successfully control this noxious weed.

Narrow-leaved cattail covers much of the shore. In the marsh at the south end, along with the usual basking turtles, we spotted a young red-winged blackbird sitting on an exposed branch, a few inches above the water's surface. The male parent resented our proximity and flitted about the cattails, scolding us constantly. We hurried away, so as not to disturb the nest.

The inlet creek at the southeast corner meanders through a cattail swamp, past a large beaver lodge with massive amounts of cuttings in the water. After a short distance, a beaver dam blocks the entrance to a broad meadow. As we paddled up, a green heron family bolted skyward, accompanied by more loud squawking.

After things quieted, we listened to the metallic chip note of a swamp sparrow among the streamside vegetation of *Rumex*, jewelweed, bur-reed, and much more. Eventually, one appeared in the brush, with its bright rufous cap and wings, pumping its tail as it flitted about. The melodious marsh wren song wafted by as tree swallows and cedar waxwings snatched insects on the wing.

Paddling back out onto the main lake and around to the southwestern shore, we surprised a few wood duck families that scurried into the surrounding marsh. You can paddle the entire circumference of this small lake and explore the inlet thoroughly in about two hours. We highly recommend a paddle here for those not in a hurry who want to study plants and animals.

29

Old Erie Canal
De Witt and Manlius

Maps: New York Atlas Map 75:D7, USGS Quadrangles Manlius and Syracuse East

Length: 2.5 miles from De Witt to Manlius Center, 5.5 miles to North Kirkville Road

Habitat type: shallow former canal

Fish: largemouth bass, northern pike

Expect to see: hikers, bikers, ducks, painted turtles, muskrat

Camping and recreation: Old Erie Canal State Historic Park, 315-687-7821; camping App. A #6, 10, and 15

GETTING THERE

Cedar Bay Road. From Syracuse, go east on Erie Boulevard (Route 5) or East Genesee Street (Route 92). From the I-481 bridge, go 0.9 mile to where Routes 5 and 92 split, and turn sharply left onto Lyndon Street. Go 0.7 mile (1.6 miles) to the T. Across the road is the beginning of the Old Erie Canal.

Burdick Road. From the T, go 1.3 miles (2.9 miles) east on Cedar Bay Road, and turn left on Burdick Road. Park immediately on either side.

Manlius Center. Go 1.1 miles (4.0 miles) north on Burdick Road, and turn right on Route 290. Go 1.3 miles (5.3 miles), and turn left on Minoa Road. The access is immediately on the right.

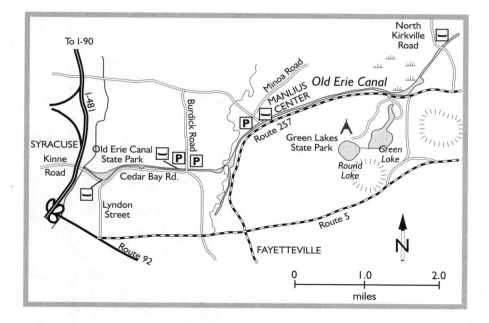

North Kirkville Road. Continue 2.7 miles (8.0 miles) east on Route 290 (pass Green Lakes State Park at 1.5 miles [6.8 miles]), turn left on North Kirkville Road, and go 0.7 mile (8.7 miles) to the access on the right.

Perched on the edge of Syracuse, Old Erie Canal State Historic Park draws hundreds of visitors on warm summer days. People hike, run, and bike along the towpath, while paddlers ply the canal's shallow, still waters. Because of disuse, the canal suffers from siltation and deadfalls and eventually will fill in.

Work began on the 363-mile Erie Canal in 1817. When completed eight years later, it stood as an engineering marvel and a tribute to human genius. Think about trying to dig a wide, deep, 363-mile-long ditch with parallel road today . . . *with* bulldozers, draglines, and dump trucks.

In 1817, we knew little about canal construction. Fortuitously, a surveyor named Canvass White (1790–1834) perfected a waterproof hydraulic cement made from limestone that hardened underwater. Without motorized machines, workers felled and removed trees and pulled stumps; hand dug through soil, rock, and swamp; and built towpaths, culverts, aqueducts, locks, gates, and bridges. When finished, they

Paddlers cause the only ripples on leaf-strewn water in the fall.

had accomplished the foremost engineering feat of their time. Western New York flourished as goods moved cheaply from New York, up to Albany, and west over the canal to Lake Erie and the hinterlands, hastening Midwest development.

A modern system of canals replaced the Old Erie Canal in 1918. The new Erie, Cayuga-Seneca, Champlain, and Oswego barge canals tamed the Mohawk and Seneca with dams and locks and used diesel-power to cross Oneida, Ontario, and Erie. In many places—now criss-crossed with roads, farms, and development—we cannot find any trace of the original canal. Thankfully, we have preserved some parts of it in state parks. We wonder if the joggers, bikers, and paddlers appreciate the significance of the Old Erie Canal in, appropriately, De Witt, named for De Witt Clinton, the former 10-term New York mayor (1803–1815) and two-time governor (1817–1821; 1825–1828), who sponsored building the canal.

Paddling out from the canal's beginning in De Witt, we found a tree-covered south bank and a path-covered north bank. In between, the canal's murky water hid much of civilization's detritus—except for the elusive *Goodyearis submergicus*; though many populate these waters, its bottom-dwelling habit frequently hides it from view. Tree species lining the south bank include black locust, lots of ash, black walnut, cottonwood, and box elder and other maples, including one large silver maple whose grapevine-covered branches draped way out over the water, lending a closed-in, intimate feeling.

Smaller trees and shrubs cover the north banks down to Burdick Road. The wide, rounded crown of sumac had turned brilliant red in the crisp, early morning October air. Clumps of clematis clung to streamside shrubs as the first joggers made their way down the towpath. By midmorning, vultures started to ride the thermals, painted turtles climbed out onto sun-facing logs, more people trod and biked the path, and a few paddlers appeared, as well.

An osprey fished a wide spot—how it could see fish in the cloudy water remains a mystery. Gray squirrels appeared frequently along the ground, harvesting seeds for winter stores. Nine wood ducks fattening up for fall migration bolted skyward as we approached. A cormorant fished for its morning meal, and black ducks and mallards dabbled along the edge. Muskrats pruned the canal-side grass, as more turtles climbed out into the midday sun.

We saw many bird species, which surprised us, given the level of recreational use. Expect to say "Hi!" constantly to cheerful passersby. Past tiny Manlius Center, the crowds thin out, trees crowd in, and wildlife abounds.

We prefer to put in at the beginning and to paddle down and back on the nonexistent current. Though no longer serving as a vital transportation corridor, the Old Erie Canal still holds immense historical significance—and provides a relaxing place to paddle to boot.

30

Fish Creek to Oneida Lake
Vienna

Maps: New York Atlas Map 76:C2, USGS Quadrangle Sylvan Beach

Length: 9 miles one way, Route 49 bridge to Sylvan

Habitat type: wide, shallow, slow-flowing stream

Fish: largemouth and smallmouth bass, northern pike

Expect to see: ducks, great blue heron, osprey, river otter

Camping: App. A #7 and 15

Take note: can paddle both directions at low water

GETTING THERE

From Sylvan Beach, go 2.3 miles north on Route 13, and turn right on Route 49. Go 5.1 miles (7.4 miles) to the unmarked access on either side, just before the bridge.

To paddle in one direction, leave a vehicle in Sylvan Beach at the lakefront public parking area. Take-out on the right, just downstream from Route 13 bridge. You can also pay to take out at one of the private campgrounds at Fish Creek Landing.

We did not expect much when we put into Fish Creek in early October, even though a local kayaker told us we would enjoy paddling here. Sylvan Beach and its environs serve as a summer vacation mecca, drawing

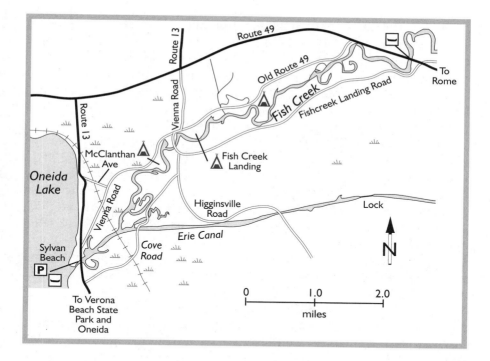

people from far and wide to Oneida Lake's crowded shores. We found a wildlife haven on nearby Fish Creek, standing in sharp contrast with people-packed Sylvan Beach. Try to get to the river at sunrise to maximize wildlife viewing. Do not rush down the river—paddle the shoreline quietly, looking for wildlife, trying to remain unobtrusive.

This section cuts a wide swath through a broad plain. More than 100 feet in width, Fish Creek's shallow, clear water reveals either a sand- or dead-tree-covered bottom. Grapevine and Virginia creeper drape over streamside vegetation among the aspen, cottonwood, box elder, large flowing willow, sumac, and more. The layered canopy stretches for every available light ray to maximize photosynthesis; in one area an undergrowth of dwarf willow, a midstory of river birch, and an overstory of big-toothed aspen placed leaf surfaces in the sun from bank top to treetop. A beaver had nearly gnawed through the base of some aspen, a favorite food.

As we paddled out at sunrise, the sun's early rays burned off the morning mist as white-tailed deer came down for an early morning drink. We listened to robins singing and blue jays squawking, and two black ducks leapt from the water at our approach. Rounding the first bend on the inside of the curve, we spied movement on the bank downstream. We quit paddling, drifting in the lazy current. A red fox pounced from tuft to tuft along the bank, looking for mice, too intent on its pursuit to see us drifting toward a rendezvous. As it placed its forepaws on a log jammed against the bank, we arrived. It looked at us from 10 feet only for a moment before bounding up and over the bank in alarm.

As we curved to the left, wood ducks blasted out of the coves—in all we counted 10 taking off in this short stretch. The first of three great blue heron took wing, as well. A flock of about 40 Canada geese flew over, honking noisily as they began their southward migration to water remaining open all winter. We stopped to watch a mixed foraging flock of more than 40 birds in an extensive grapevine thicket: we found song and white-throated sparrows near the ground, yellow-rumped warbler— the last warbler to migrate south—in the midstory, and chickadee and white-breasted nuthatch overhead, all trying to glean late-season insects and berries from the foliage.

As we drifted back into the current, the first of two sharp-shinned hawks drifted across the waterway, and all became still in the grapevines. How could so many birds vanish so quickly? Evolution obviously favors those that become scarce when a major bird predator such as the sharpie appears. Across the way in an overgrazed field, a flock of red-winged blackbirds—the males' red epaulets barely visible in their fall plumage— foraged on the ground, along with a herd of fat cows. Up in the sun-bleached branches of a dead tree, crows mobbed a red-tailed hawk as another hawk circled on gathering thermals overhead. As we paddled to the other side to get a closer look, two killdeer took to noisy flight. A greater yellowlegs, calling a descending "tew-tew-tew-tew-tew," ran along the shore as Eastern bluebirds stood on fence posts, watching for insects aroused by the rising sun.

Just after passing a row of bank swallow holes in the soft steep bank—the swallows had long ago left for warmer climes, still abuzz with insects—we heard a noisy chomping among the branches of a deadfall. As we drifted closer, a young river otter munched away on a fish. Such manners! After a few minutes, deciding that we would not leave, it dove with its fish into the water behind the snag. A few moments later, it and its mother and two siblings tried to sneak away upstream. After swimming about 15 feet, the mother poked her head skyward, neck fully extended, to get a better look. With head and neck a foot above the water and no shoulder in view, she uttered a muffled snort, clearing her nose of water. Perhaps this is not a comical sight to other otters.

While mourning doves perched on bare branches, a belted kingfisher dove headlong into the water after a fish, emerging quickly to fly off to its perch. We spent some time identifying a flycatcher out on a limb. After a few puzzling moments, we decided that it was one we usually identify by song: the Eastern wood-pewee. We also saw the similar Eastern phoebe.

As we neared Fish Creek Landing, a large flock of common merganser rested on stumps, logs, rocks, and water in a protected cove. We counted 48 birds in our binoculars and turned around to avoid forcing them to fly off. Down here, closer to the lake, ring-billed gulls flew over frequently.

We paddled back at a faster pace and saw only one new species, a rather tame green heron that let us get within 20 feet before taking flight. As we paddled by a rope swing suspended from a willow branch, we reflected on the prodigious amount of wildlife we had seen and wondered about the protection of this wildlife paradise. The rope swing dangles from a fragile branch—willow branches shatter easily—but no more fragile than the habitat that harbors this wildlife. Clearly, shoreline development and tree clearing threaten this habitat.

Judging from the amount of downed timber, spring runoff frequently topples streamside trees. Roots of standing trees stabilize the banks, keeping the river from broadening and getting too shallow, and also provide habitat for fish, otter, mink, muskrat, and beaver. The narrow woods bordering houses and fields provide this stream's only protection. We hope that people who enjoy nature's bounty will seek shoreline protection. They might ask farmers not to cut trees within 100 feet of the shore. They might convince residents not to subdivide their land and to plant trees along the bank. A cooperative effort could help ensure that this fragile habitat remains for future generations to enjoy.

The Playful River Otter

If you paddle New York's remote lakes, especially in early morning or at dusk, sooner or later you will see a river otter—or perhaps a family of these sleek mammals. We have seen dozens throughout New York, mostly in the Adirondacks but some much farther south and even in the highly visited waters of Harriman State Park. The otter's playful antics and masterful swimming make it one of our favorite species to observe.

The river otter, *Lutra canadensis,* once inhabited virtually every U.S. watercourse, from sun-warmed southwestern rivers to icy far-northern lakes and streams. Today, because of 250 years of trapping, water pollution, and encroaching development, the otter has retreated to the far corners of its former range. Because it eats at the top of the food chain, the otter also suffers from pollution and toxic chemicals in the environment, such as heavy metals, DDT derivatives, dioxin, and PCBs.

In 1936, New York passed legislation to protect the otter. Though subject to a limited trapping season, the otter has returned to New York's waterways and might be seen anywhere east of I-81. In recent years, it has been sighted on Long Island and in western New York, where River Otter Project volunteers released over 200 from 1995 to 2001.

With its long, thin body and relatively thick, sharply tapered tail, it can reach 4 feet in length and weigh up to 25 pounds. Long prized by trappers, its dense dark-brown fur above gives way to lighter colors on the belly and throat.

The otter has adapted well to the aquatic environment. Nose and ears close when underwater, and webbed toes aid in swimming. Though it swims fast enough to catch trout, it usually preys on slower-moving suckers, minnows, crayfish, tadpoles, and salamanders. It often thrusts its head way above the surface, exhaling loudly and looking around.

Though adapted for water, the otter does well on land, as well, with its typical weasel-family undulating gait. Clocked at as fast as 18 miles per hour, it can travel as much as 100 miles overland in search of new territory. It generally places dens—natural cavities under tree roots or abandoned beaver lodges—at the water's edge, with an underwater entrance.

The otter consumes smaller fish and crayfish in the water and larger prey on shore or on a protruding rock. An ingenious hunter, the otter sometimes herds fish into shallows or punches a hole in a beaver dam—allowing water to escape—then wades in and feasts on fish flopping in shallow water. Because it hunts so successfully, it has plenty of time to play—a famous otter trait.

The young of many mammal species play. Animal behaviorists believe such play provides practice for future hunting, territorial interactions, and courtship. But the otter does not stop playing when it reaches adulthood. It rolls in the water, chasing one another, or climbs repeatedly up a snow- or mudbank and slides down into the water.

The otter mates in late winter or early spring, but birth follows almost a year later. As with many weasel-family members, embryo implantation is delayed, and development stops until the following fall or winter, followed by birth of two to four cubs in a well-protected den, anytime between November and April. Cubs emerge fully furred, but with eyes closed and no teeth. They venture outside the den after about three months, remaining completely dependent on their mother for at least six months. Though the mother provides initial care for the young, the father may rejoin the family to help out after the cubs reach about six months.

Though the otter is curious and relatively bold, keep your distance. Interference from humans may cause it to move away and search for more-remote locations.

31

Gifford Lake/
West Branch Fish Creek
Amboy and Camden

Maps: New York Atlas Map 76:A1, USGS Quadrangle Westdale

Length: 6 miles

Habitat type: marshy, slow-flowing creek

Fish: brown trout, smallmouth bass

Expect to see: great blue heron, marsh birds, muskrat, beaver

Camping: App. A #15

Take note: to run other East or West Branch sections, use Ehling, *Canoeing Central New York* (Backcountry Publications, 1982); Freeman, *Canoe Guide to Western and Central New York State* (Adirondack Mountain Club, 1993); Proskine, *Adirondack Canoe Waters: South & West Flow*, 2nd edition (Adirondack Mountain Club, 1989)

GETTING THERE

From Rome, go northwest on Route 69 to the Camden stoplight, and turn right on Route 13. Go 5.0 miles, turn right on Cemetery Road, and go 0.1 mile (5.1 miles) to the access on the right.

From I-81, Exit 34, go east on Route 104 to Williamstown, turn right on Route 13 east, and go 7.9 miles to Cemetery Road on the left.

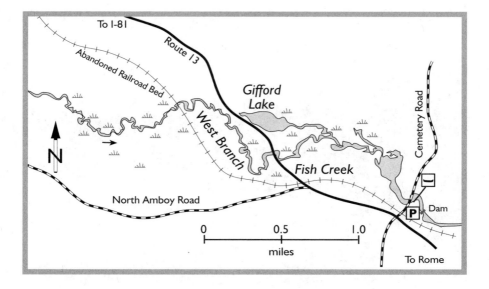

A popular one-way canoe route begins at the access on the downstream side of the dam on the Fish Creek West Branch. Except for a few kayakers and local anglers, few people take advantage of the beautiful upstream paddling available here. Above the dam, the West Branch meanders through forest and marsh, passes by the Gifford Lake outlet, skims unobtrusively under Route 13, and heads upstream through brushy, wooded banks. Water celery and pondweed undulate back and forth, trailing in the lazy current.

Heading upstream, you pass by a cluster of houses on the right. Quite a way upstream, a fishing camp on the right marks the entrance to Gifford Lake. An old railroad grade several miles upstream where we turned around—although we could have gone farther—alludes to a time when civilization encroached more extensively on this wild little creek that meanders through an extensive marsh.

Although hemlock and silver maple line the right-hand shore occasionally, marshes and shrubs generally own the banks. The first side channel on the right penetrates well back into the woods, and tons of pondweed, pickerelweed, yellow pondlily, and underwater vegetation grow in the stagnant water. The great blue heron patrols the shallows, ever watchful for the next frog or fish meal, while the kingfisher hovers in the air, waiting to dive headlong on unwary fish.

Marshy areas abound at the entrance to Gifford Lake and in the many coves along the West Branch of Fish Creek.

In most places, grasses, ferns, long-leaved *Rumex*, and shrubbery dominate the shoreline, while extensive marshes lead off in all directions. Clumps of arrowhead grow out from the bank, while pickerel-weed—growing singly—occurs in slightly deeper water. A large patch of iris, in and among the cattails, caught our eye, but in other places we noted that alder covers the banks.

The high biological productivity of this area makes it a paradise for bird-watchers and others interested in wildlife. We saw or heard great blue heron, kingfisher, robin, mourning dove, yellow-rumped warbler, yellow warbler, common yellowthroat, Eastern phoebe, barn swallow, red-winged blackbird, grackle, osprey, Eastern kingbird, song sparrow, rose-breasted grosbeak, and cedar waxwing. Although we did not see beaver, we did see lodges and lots of fresh alder cuttings. A muskrat, seemingly unconcerned by our presence, harvested grasses by the shore, and we witnessed a rarity: a mink furtively fishing the shore, working stealthily along the bank, waiting to pounce on anything that moved.

The mink—like most other weasel family members—has an elongated body with high surface-area-to-volume ratio, causing high heat loss for its size, a high metabolic rate, and a voracious appetite. It kills

Mink

just about anything: fish, rodents, frogs, crayfish, birds, eggs, and your prized hen in the henhouse. Even though it usually weighs about two pounds, it easily slays larger animals. The mink ranges widely, from Key West to arctic Alaska, from Labrador to central California. Given its huge appetite, and the need to kill a lot to fulfill it, the mink never appears in large numbers in any habitat. So you're fortunate to see one, especially because it usually remains nocturnal.

To reach Gifford Lake, take the right-hand fork at the fishing camp on the right, about a mile upstream from the access. Although the lake sports a beautiful hardwood stand along its shores, we prefer the scenic creek that connects the lake with Fish Creek. A very narrow, meandering passageway leads through a wide expanse of marsh. Beaver cuttings along the way suggest that an early evening paddle here would be rewarding. Arrowhead crowds the channel, and you have to weave your way through fragrant waterlily and yellow pondlily.

As we paddled back to the access in the waning afternoon sun, we marveled at the beauty of recently emerged, iridescent green damselflies with jet-black wings that hovered over the drooping tips of streamside grasses.

32

Salmon River Reservoir
Orwell and Redfield

Maps: New York Atlas Maps 83:D7 and 84:D1, USGS Quadrangles Orwell and Redfield

Area: 2,660 acres

Habitat type: large reservoir

Fish: brown and rainbow trout, largemouth and smallmouth bass

Expect to see: bald eagle, osprey, waterfowl, deer

Camping: on-site, campsites scattered about the lakeshore

Take note: main lake dangerous under windy conditions, novices should always wear personal flotation devices (PFDs)

GETTING THERE

Jackson Road. From I-81, Exit 36, go 10.3 miles east on Route 2, and turn right on Jackson Road. Go 0.4 mile (10.7 miles) to the access.

CCC Road. From Jackson Road, continue 0.9 mile (11.2 miles), and turn right on CCC Road. Go 0.9 mile (12.1 miles) to the access.

Redfield Bridge. From CCC Road, continue 4.0 miles (15.2 miles), and turn right on Route 17. Go 1.3 miles (16.5 miles), cross the bridge, and park on the right.

From Rome, go west on Route 69 to Camden. Go west on Route 13, and turn right (north) on Route 17. Go 8.6 miles to the access on the left, just before the Redfield bridge.

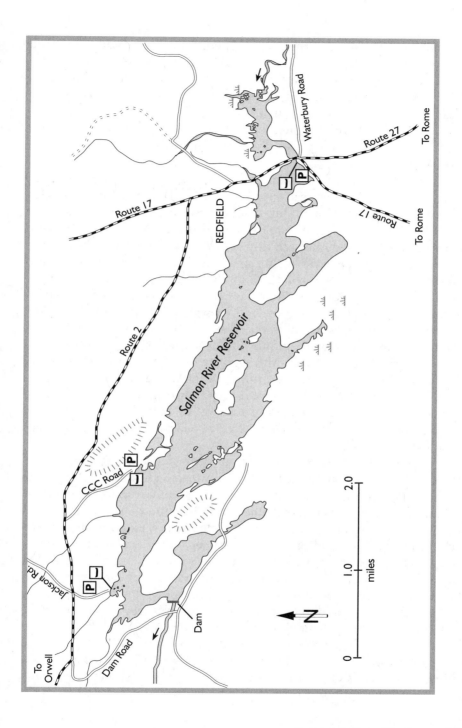

Our two favorite areas of this state-owned, little-used reservoir include the far west end, down through the cove southeast of the dam, and the far east end where the Salmon River flows through extensive marshes. When paddling the west end, we use the Jackson Road access, mainly because of wind problems. When we paddled out at sunup in late August, the surface barely rippled, but on our return at midmorning, the wind had started to roll waves down the lake in preparation for afternoon whitecaps.

This daily cycle of calm and wind happens because the land mass heats up during the day, causing warm air to rise, drawing in cooler, denser air off nearby Lake Ontario. Because of its generally east-west orientation, the reservoir suffers from wind-driven waves from the west. By threading your way through the willow-clad islands near the Jackson Road access, then down the western shore to the southern cove, you can avoid the large waves that roll through the main lake.

As we paddled down to the cove below Hall Island—really a peninsula—we watched gulls, loons, and crows and listened to chickadees and Eastern wood-pewees off in the woods. A belted kingfisher flew before us, leading us through stump-filled shallows, under a culvert, and out into a magnificent marsh. Although we found a few campsites along Hall Island, we found none past the culvert. Aquatic plants—including Eurasian watermilfoil, yellow pondlily, pondweed, and water shield—choked the whole cove, dampening any swells from the freshening wind. As we paddled the shoreline, we noticed two large, but apparently inactive, beaver lodges.

Three great blue herons flew off at our approach, but a kingfisher stood its ground among dead tree limbs out in the water. Paddling back up the shore through the clear water, as a common merganser brood rushed out of harm's way, we studied the shoreline trees, including red and white pine, ash, elm, sugar and red maples, box elder, Eastern hemlock, birch, quaking and big-toothed aspens, cottonwood, apple, black and pin cherries, beech, yellow birch, and willow. Except for the Hall Island hump, the flat western landscape allows the water to creep up to the plateau's edge, then spill through cataracts down to Lake Ontario.

We also enjoy paddling the lake's eastern end where the Route 17 bridge and a twisting channel through wooded shores block much of the wind. We passed under the Route 17 bridge and into a wildlife paradise. The entire northern shore—honeycombed with channels through small, willow-clad islands and patches of aquatic vegetation—provides habitat for myriad fauna and flora. As we paddled the channel, a river otter paced us, periodically bobbing up with a snort to look around, head held high above the water, then diving in typical undulating otter fashion.

Feeding flocks of common merganser, black duck, and wood duck scurried into the *Equisetum* and grasses as we approached. Two wood ducks bolted from a streamside tree as we rounded a bend, and a sharp-shinned hawk alternately flapped and glided across in front of us. This small member of the accipiter group—along with Cooper's hawk and goshawk—preys mainly on other birds, which it chases down and plucks from the sky. The sharpie's small size, short rounded wings, and long tail give it agility not shared with other hawks when flying through woods.

A much, much larger raptor soared on wide wings overhead: an immature bald eagle, dark brown with white flecks on its tail and belly, cast its eagle eye on dead and dying suckers that littered the water. Our nation's symbol catches live fish, snaring them from the water's surface with powerful claws, but it more typically eats carrion, including dead suckers.

As we paddled by bushy basswood, through islands of grass and willow, water celery indicated current direction. Reaching a shallow riffle, we drifted back down the Salmon River, following its flow, marveling at how close the pebbly bottom seemed in the crystal-clear water. Reentering the marsh, we found brilliant red cardinal flower in bloom near a beaver impoundment on a side channel. Smartweed, a member of the buckwheat family, leaves prostrate upon the water's surface, had sent up short bloom pikes with bright pink flowers measuring maybe an inch long. We spent hours looking at plants, animals, and birds in this huge wetland.

We paddled here alone until near the end, when a lone personal watercraft flew up the river from under the bridge, took one look around, and zoomed back down the reservoir. We who use this area should try to preserve the section upstream from the Redfield bridge as a motorless area. Given the huge concentration of wildlife—including bald eagle, sharp-shinned hawk, river otter, and many more less exotic species—we should try to protect their habitat from noisy, disruptive incursions.

Although the lake remains popular with local anglers, the Salmon River downstream attracts thousands of anglers to fish the salmon runs. To accommodate river fishing, starting in late August, the power company starts to draw the reservoir down, eventually several feet, to maintain stream levels for the salmon run, making the reservoir a less pleasant place to paddle.

Adirondack Park and Environs

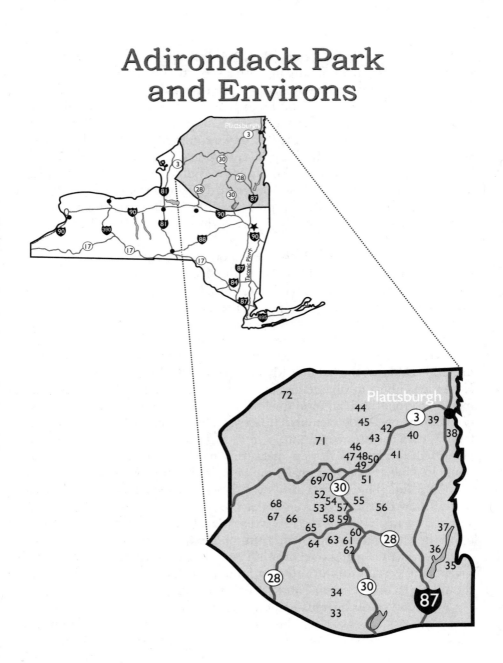

33

Canada Lake and West Lake
Caroga

Maps: New York Atlas Map 79:C4, USGS Quadrangles Canada Lake and Caroga Lake

Canada Lake area: 554 acres, maximum depth 150 feet

Habitat type: deep lakes

Fish: lake trout, smallmouth bass, pickerel

Expect to see: osprey, loon, waterfowl, great blue heron, muskrat

Camping: App. A #102

Take note: main lakes treacherous under windy conditions

GETTING THERE

From Gloversville, go west on Route 29A to Caroga Lake. At the junction with Route 10, continue 4.3 miles on Route 29A, and turn left on Point Breeze Road. Turn immediately right on West Lake Road, and go 0.3 mile (4.6 miles) to the access on the left.

Alternatively, from Route 119, go north on Stewart Landing Road to the end.

Canada and West lakes mark Adirondack Park's southern end, and although the state owns huge tracts of forest all around these connected waterways, it does not own any significant amount of shoreline. Private inholdings abound, and with them wall-to-wall shoreline

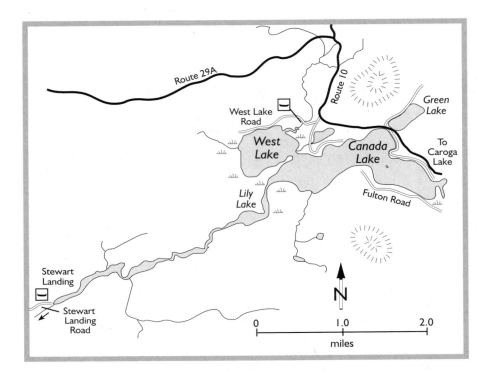

camps, bringing substantial motorboat and personal watercraft traffic. Consequently, we would avoid Canada Lake's heavily developed eastern arm and concentrate on its southern shore and West and Lily lakes. If you do not mind paddling by an occasional summer home—particularly when you near Stewart Landing—you can still have a wonderful paddling experience through scenic waterways chock-full of interesting plants and wildlife.

Paddling out through the winding, twisting waterway leading to West Lake, with grasses and alder lining the banks, you wonder if any large bodies of water actually exist in this area. Muskrats break from harvesting streamside grasses, song sparrows sing from the undergrowth, and red-winged blackbirds flutter from the water's edge as you paddle by. Eventually, you emerge in West Lake's northeast corner. Although some houses appear on the northwestern shore, the picturesque southern shore remains unblighted. Paddle the shoreline counterclockwise, wind permitting, to get to the pine-covered peninsula marking the entrance to Canada Lake.

Adirondack peaks hover over the north end of Canada Lake on the southern end of the park.

Although hemlock and white pine appear in good numbers along the shoreline, oak, sugar maple, yellow birch, cherry, and other deciduous trees dominate the surrounding hillsides. In places, a dense understory of balsam fir competes for light, stretching for the canopy. When you round the point into Canada Lake, notice the extensive marsh along the southern shore. We saw deer here, taking a morning drink, as we headed for Lily Lake, and several loons plied the waters.

As we entered long, narrow Lily Lake, a chorus of songbirds serenaded us, announcing their breeding territories; white-throated sparrows with their "Old Sam Peabody, Peabody, Peabody" called from the undergrowth. Flickers drummed out holes for themselves and other cavity nesters, including wood duck, hooded merganser, and tree swallow, all of which we saw as we paddled down to Stewart Landing. Ducks appeared in profusion, some just migrating through, others looking to nest: hooded and common merganser, wood duck, ring-necked duck, mallard, and black duck. We watched an osprey swoop down and snatch a fish, carrying it off to its aerie in a dead tree. Other prominent birds included blue jay, kingfisher, great blue heron, and killdeer.

After a few hours of paddling down to Stewart Landing, mostly without other boats, we picked our way back to West Lake with care. Stick to the center of these shallow waterways at times of low water to avoid rocks.

34

West Branch Sacandaga River
Arietta

Maps: New York Atlas Map 79:B4, USGS Quadrangles Canada Lake and Morehouse Lake

Length: 8 miles

Habitat type: meandering stream and connected small ponds

Fish: brook, brown, and rainbow trout

Expect to see: bald eagle, otter, beaver, deer

Camping: App. A #102 and on-site wilderness camping

Take note: may need to carry around an occasional logjam or beaver dam

GETTING THERE

Second Bridge. From I-90, Exit 29, go north on Route 10. From the junction of Routes 10 and 29A west, go 6.0 miles north on Route 10 to the access on the right, just past the bridge.

Northern Access. From Second Bridge, go 6.4 miles (12.4 miles) north on Route 10 to a wide shoulder; carry 100 feet down to the water.

The Sacandaga West Branch provides spectacular paddling—our favorite place in the Adirondack Forest Preserve's southern reaches. The clear, quick-flowing river meanders generally south to north through

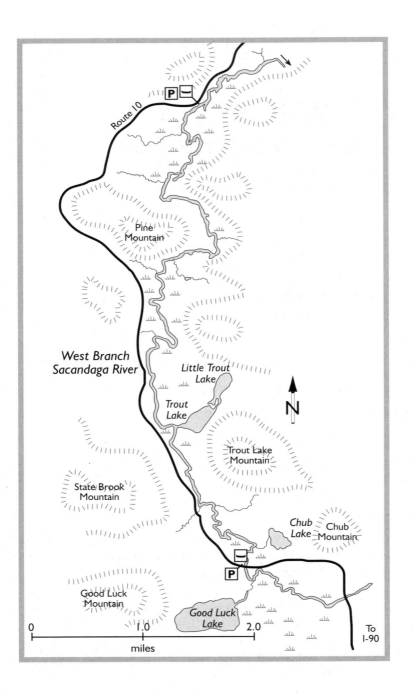

Route 10

Pine Mountain

West Branch Sacandaga River

Little Trout Lake

Trout Lake

N

Trout Lake Mountain

State Brook Mountain

Chub Lake

Chub Mountain

Good Luck Mountain

Good Luck Lake

0   1.0   2.0

miles

To I-90

undeveloped, wild country, though often within earshot of roughly parallel Route 10.

The river's sinewy channel passes through grassy marshland, with alder lining the banks in places, thick masses of pickerelweed at the river bends, and underwater grasses carpeting the river-bottom, undulating rhythmically in the quick flow. Mixed hardwoods, hemlock, and white pine rise from the valley floor on higher ground, and steeply rising hills gird the narrow valley. We saw some huge yellow birch here.

The river, just a dozen feet across in places, can jam up with logs and beaver dams. We had to slide over a few shallow dams, and one substantial logjam required carrying across a grassy, hummocky bank—a challenging proposition with a long-haired dog that we preferred not to have shaking off water in the boat.

From the main river channel, you can make wonderful side-explorations into Good Luck, Chub, Trout, and Little Trout lakes—none of which can rightly claim title to "lake." Good Luck and Chub lakes' narrow outlet streams—in places just 5 or 6 feet across—make maneuvering a longer canoe or kayak a challenge. Depending on water level, gaining access to these lakes may prove difficult. To reach Good Luck from Second Bridge, paddle upstream a couple hundred yards to the small inlet stream on the right. Steeply rising hills bound the roundish lake.

Look for the tiny inlet stream from Chub Lake about a quarter mile downstream from Second Bridge. Boggy streambanks and the lake abound with sphagnum, pitcher-plant, tamarack, bog rosemary, and tiny-leafed cranberry. In late summer, if you can get through the inlet creek, you should find large red cranberries that dwarf the plant's leaves. Entering Chub Lake, look directly across for a large boulder, a great place for a picnic and camping (state-designated primitive campsite).

Close by and fairly easy to spot, Trout and Little Trout lakes also enter on the right a couple miles downstream from Chub Lake. When we paddled here, we had no difficulty paddling into both, but during dry years and midsummer, access might be difficult. We spotted one state campsite on Trout Lake's southern shore.

As we returned from Little Trout into Trout Lake one late afternoon, we heard some commotion and drifted quietly toward a group of four otter, one of which munched noisily on a bullhead. Once they spotted us, they slid from a sandy island and, in typical otter fashion, watched us from deeper water, popping their heads up with distinctive snorts to investigate our intrusion into their solitude.

Paddling from Second Bridge down to Trout Lake and back to the put-in makes a good day trip. If planning an out-and-back trip all the way to the northern Route 10 access near Shaker Road, leave early enough in the morning, and remember that current will slow your return.

35

South Bay
Dresden, Fort Ann,
and Whitehall

Maps: New York Atlas Map 89:D6, USGS Quadrangle Whitehall NY/VT

Area: 1,100 acres

Habitat type: large, shallow lake with marshy bays and inlets

Fish: largemouth and smallmouth bass, northern pike, walleye

Expect to see: great blue heron, aquatic plants

Camping: App. A #68, 69, 70, 72, and 84

Take note: avoid when windy

GETTING THERE

From Whitehall, go 2.8 miles north on Route 22, cross the bridge over South Bay, and take the second right.

South Bay lies along Champlain Canal's western edge at the southern terminus of Lake Champlain. A pleasant surprise awaits you. Gaze down the waterway at gorgeous cliffs and hillsides receding into the distance, beckoning you to paddle south.

Note the warning at the access about picking up "hitchhikers," referring to three serious aquatic pests: Eurasian watermilfoil, water chestnut, and zebra mussel. All three hitch rides on boat trailers, in bilges, and even on canoe and kayak hulls, to be deposited later in the next

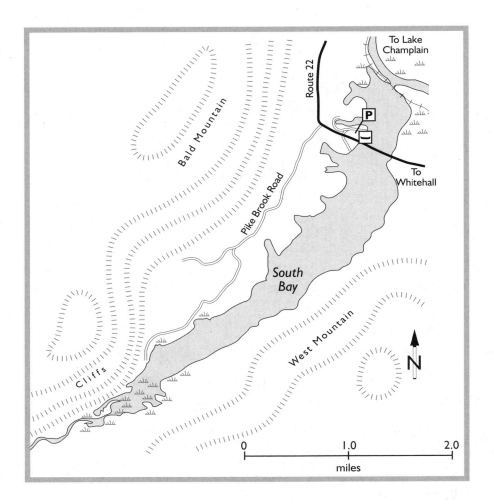

waterway. Biologists worry that these alien species, introduced from Europe and Asia to the East Coast, will eventually infect most bodies of water in the East and Midwest. They arrived without natural predators and now crowd out native species.

The first time we paddled here, in the first bay on the right, we found a huge beaver lodge, a great blue heron patrolling the shallows, and a waterway choked with water chestnut, *Trapa natans*. Its rosettes eventually grow so thick that they push up over other aquatic vegetation, limiting access to light, smothering it. We tried to paddle through the sea of water chestnut—as we have done countless times before with

Steep cliffs and layered hillsides line the shores on the bay's south end.

stands of waterlily—but it was like trying to paddle over dew-covered grass.

Another invasive, Eurasian watermilfoil, *Myriophyllum spicatum*, already had made its way to the south end and, indeed, all the way up the inlet creeks. This underwater plant with its slender, lacy foliage also crowds out native vegetation. Experiments with biological control of watermilfoil seem to be working in some locations, and mechanical harvesting of water chestnut can rid waterways of this scourge.

We did not see zebra mussel when we paddled here, although it has likely made it to South Bay. It sticks to underwater structures in many layers and clogs intake pipes. Unless we can find an effective control mechanism that does not harm native species, zebra mussel will infest most waterways in the United States. This tiny mussel filters out microscopic plankton and other organisms, clarifying the water, but it may filter so effectively that the food chain gets depleted, ultimately reducing fish populations.

Although concern about alien pests continues unabated, they should not spoil your paddle here, where you can enjoy the stately great blue

Dense rosettes of water chestnut have clogged many waterways in the Northeast.

heron standing knee-deep in every bay. Near Route 22, fields march down to the water's edge, but farther down the bay, they give way to layered, forested hillsides and high cliffs. If the peregrine falcon nests here, it would have a spectacular view from its cliff-side aerie.

A great horned owl startled us as it flew off with powerful wing beats from a bankside willow. We explored all the deep inlets that dot the western shore, paddling back into the cattails, bur-reed, pickerelweed, yellow pondlily, and tuberous waterlily. Rufous-sided towhees called from the undergrowth, and barn swallows dipped low over the water.

We paddled up the creek on the south end, with its gorgeous cliffs, in among the waterlilies, pondweed, water celery, and grasses. We paddled through thick stands of pickerelweed into a swamp with alder and cattail, cardinal flower and purple loosestrife. Two aquatic plants emerged in great mats: yellow-flowered bladderwort and one of the small yellow pondlilies—*Nuphar rubrodiscum*. Silver maple continued as the dominant tree species. We watched large schools of fish swim in the creek's clear water, in sharp contrast with the bay's milky water.

As we paddled back to the access, hugging the picturesque western shore, we wondered what we would find here next time. With its huge expanse of water, South Bay often suffers from strong winds, the same winds that carry nuisance aquatic plants to the waterway's far reaches.

36

Northwest Bay of Lake George

Bolton

Maps: New York Atlas Map 89:D5, USGS Quadrangles Shelving Rock and Silver Bay

Habitat type: shallow, marshy creek with side bays

Fish: landlocked salmon, lake and rainbow trout, largemouth and smallmouth bass, northern pike

Expect to see: waterfowl

Camping: App. A #67, 68, 69, 70, 72, and 84

Take note: always wear personal flotation devices (PFDs) on main lake; avoid main lake under windy conditions

GETTING THERE

From I-87, Exit 24, go 4.6 miles east, and turn left (north) on Route 9N. Go 4.3 miles (8.9 miles) to the access on the right.

Layered hills and forested islands—grand vistas of the North Country—contribute to Lake George's scenic setting and help attract multitudes of vacationers to its beautiful shores. The largest lake in Adirondack Park, Lake George draws many large boats to its deep, clear waters. We recommend that you stay off the main lake, with its personal watercraft, water-skiers, speedboats, and wind, which can cause huge swells to build up over miles of lake, creating treacherous paddling conditions.

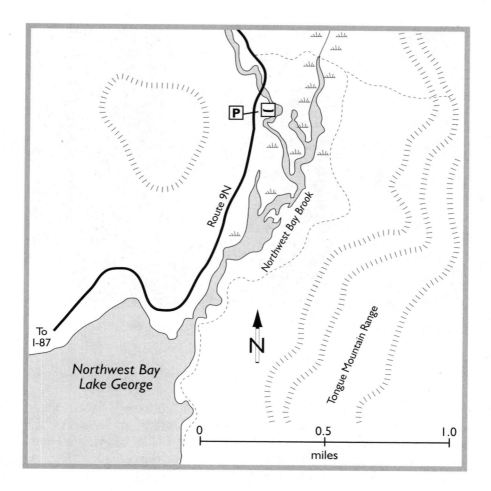

From the access, you can paddle to the left up the creek for about a tenth of a mile where you will encounter lots of beaver activity, and you can paddle down Northwest Bay Brook into Northwest Bay. Take time to explore the sinuous channel of the brook's east fork. You will have to elbow your way through pondweed, water celery, bur-reed, and other aquatic vegetation, but you should find a lot more solitude here than downstream.

Yellow pondlily covers the channel in places, and grasses and ferns carpet the banks where alder has not elbowed everything out of the way. Tall red and silver maples hang over the alder and grassy banks. Farther

Yellow pondlily grows in the shallow waters of Northwest Bay.

down the lake, after the marshes disappear, tall white pine and hemlock grace the shores.

In several places along the creek, you will see large beaver lodges, along with downed trees and many cuttings. Dragonflies mated on the wing along the protected, placid waters of the brook as we paddled here, and a large snapping turtle cruised by just under the water's surface. As we rounded a little island on the western shore just before the bay, we saw a sign on a dying white pine that said, "Caution, Rattlesnakes. Unlawful to Disturb or Take." The land belongs to The Nature Conservancy to protect a rare northern population of the timber rattlesnake that dens in the rockfall on this hillside.

Species become rare on the edges of their range. Because Lake George and Champlain Valley represent the northern extension of the timber rattlesnake's range, we find very few in isolated populations. The rattlesnake probably arose in the southwestern United States and northern Mexico, where it speciated and radiated outward, ranging as far as southern Argentina and southern Canada. About 30 species occur in a wide variety of habitats from sea level to over 10,000 feet. As you go

Forested hillsides surround Northwest Bay.

north, its preferred habitat gets closer and closer to sea level, probably in response to colder temperatures at higher elevations.

Two species occur in New York: the timber rattler (*Crotalus horridus*) occurs in isolated populations over much of the state's southern half, while the massasauga (*Sistrurus catenatus*) occurs in two isolated populations near Lake Erie. As you move southwest, toward its evolutionary beginnings, more species appear. Three species occur in Missouri, 8 in Texas, and 11 in Arizona. A total of 15 species—half of all rattlesnake species—occur in the United States.

People fear the rattlesnake, probably because of its famed hypodermic venom injection system, the most highly developed poison delivery system among snakes. Indeed, some rattlesnakes stand their ground when aroused and vigorously defend themselves. People have eliminated them from much of their range through a combination of habitat destruction and direct killing. However, rarely do rattlesnakes kill humans. Many more people die from lightning strikes or allergic reactions to bee stings.

As a member of the pit viper family, the rattler has two small pits about midway between the nostrils and eyes. (If you can see these pits, you have definitely gotten too close; look at them with binoculars.) These pits sense infrared energy and allow the snake to distinguish between warm organisms and the cooler environment. The rattler dines mainly on rodents but will also take birds, frogs, and lizards.

Snakes grow throughout their lives, rapidly at first and slowing later. As the snake grows, it sheds its stretched skin, composed of dead cells. Each time it sheds, the rattlesnake adds a segment to its rattle. Young snakes may shed twice or more per year, whereas older snakes shed once, or not at all. Because rattle segments often break off, the number may not reliably indicate the snake's age.

Most people shun snakes of any stripe, and we understand if you choose to ignore this hillside. The Nature Conservancy does not want people traipsing all over this habitat, either; please stick to the trails.

37

Putnam Pond
Ticonderoga

Maps: New York Atlas Map 89:B5, USGS Quadrangle Graphite

Area: 185 acres, maximum depth 35 feet

Habitat type: shallow pond with marshy coves

Fish: smallmouth and largemouth bass, pickerel

Expect to see: loon, red-breasted merganser, great blue heron, beaver

Camping: App. A #84 (on-site)

Take note: watch for barely submerged boulders

GETTING THERE

From Ticonderoga. At the junction with Route 9N, go 4.8 miles west on Route 74 to Chilson, and turn left at the sign for Putnam Pond. Go 3.9 miles (8.7 miles) to the access at Putnam Pond Campground.

From I-87. From Exit 28, go 12.4 miles east on Route 74 to the right turn for Putnam Pond.

Nestled in the Pharaoh Lake Wilderness—with high Adirondack peaks all around—Putnam Pond sports a scenic campground and many hiking trails—some accessible only by water. Because the surrounding wilderness attracts hundreds of hikers all summer long, try to visit in spring or fall; if you must visit in summer, avoid weekends. When we paddled here mid-September, we shared the water with three other canoes.

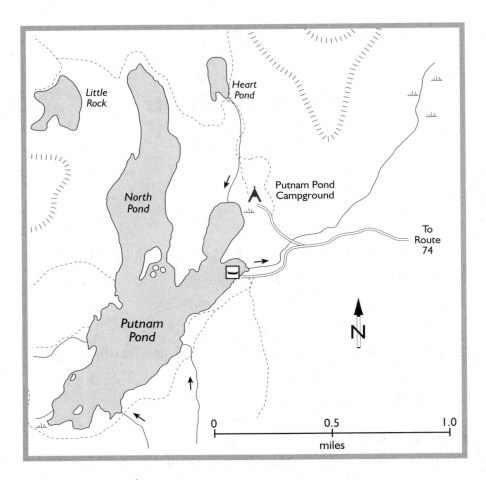

Putnam Pond contains many beautiful features. Smooth granite boulders rise from the pond's surface and protrude from shore. About a dozen widely separated, water-accessible, scenic campsites spread along the shore, seemingly wherever one of the few flat places occurs. Most include fire grate, picnic table, and outhouse. From the grassy boat-launch, the point on the right harbors a wonderful picnic area. The cove around to the right, filled with pickerelweed and other aquatic vegetation, leads to the main campground.

Towering hemlock line the roadway to the water; around the pond, occasional dense hemlock stands include considerably smaller trees. Red

The boggy south end of Putnam Pond.

maple, northern white cedar, and paper birch line the shore, interrupted by dense red pine stands. Large white pine stand farther back from shore. Large areas of aquatic vegetation accumulate in late summer—mostly water shield, along with fragrant waterlily, yellow pondlily, pickerelweed, and water celery. Marshy coves occur in several places, and way down on the southwest shore, a nearly pure stand of tamarack covers a boggy island. Larger islands have more diverse tree species, along with groups of flat granite boulders, perfect for picnics. Be careful when paddling near shore: the jagged surfaces of barely submerged boulders seem incompatible with smooth boat hulls.

In places, mussel shells litter the pond bottom, probably left by foraging otter or raccoon. Heavy visitation has not driven out the healthy beaver population. Along the western shore, we paddled by numbers of downed trees, floating and submerged, felled by these industrious waterway engineers. In the early evening, two beaver swimming along slapped the water's surface with their broad, flat tails to show their annoyance at our intrusion before diving for cover, only to surface a short distance away to repeat the ritual. Besides the tail-slapping beaver, several red squirrels and a kingfisher scolded us as we paddled by their pond-side perches.

Two loons cruised the lower pond's center, and several flocks of ducks, including wood duck, fed in the shallows. A red-breasted merganser family watched us warily from close range as we glided by, in stark contrast to the chaotic fluttering across the water's surface that occurs with younger broods.

38

Ausable Marsh
Ausable and Peru

Maps: New York Atlas Map 103:D6, USGS Quadrangle Keeseville

Area: 580 acres in Wildlife Management Area

Habitat type: marshes and slow-flowing river

Fish: largemouth and smallmouth bass, northern pike, walleye

Expect to see: osprey, waterfowl, great blue heron

Camping: App. A #73 (on-site)

Take note: launch from campground under windy conditions; always wear PFD on Lake Champlain; no motors from March 1 to October 1

GETTING THERE

From I-87, Exit 35, go 2.7 miles east on Bear Swamp Road (Route 442), and turn left on Route 9. Go 0.4 mile (3.1 miles) north to the park entrance on the right. Go 0.4 mile (3.5 miles) to the Lake Champlain access on the left. Go 0.3 mile (3.8 miles) farther to the Dead Creek access at the culvert. Campers may launch from their campsites, as well.

Three separate paddling areas await you at Ausable Marsh: Dead Creek, Ausable River, and the marsh between the river's mouths, all part of a broad delta formed from silt carried by the Ausable as it tumbles down out of the Adirondack High Peaks—including the state's tallest, Mt. Marcy—to the Champlain Valley.

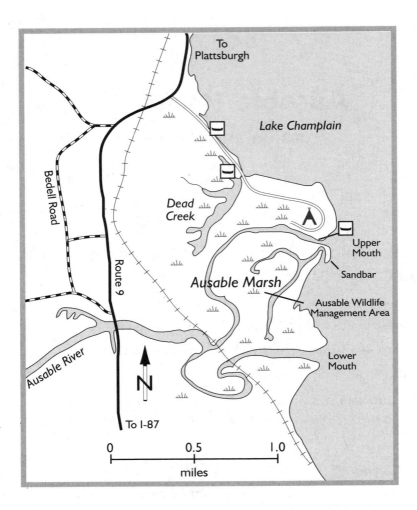

Under calm conditions, paddle south on Lake Champlain from the first access to take advantage of panoramic views of Vermont. Initially, you paddle through *Equisetum*—or horsetail, a fern relative with segmented stalk—growing near shore. Look for ducks feeding among the rushes in deeper water. We saw many, including a female mallard herding her brood. The sand bottom, easily visible in the clear water, harbors hordes of freshwater mussels. Looking to the shore, silver maples stand shoulder to shoulder along the bank all the way down to the campground.

Belted kingfishers paced us as we paddled upriver from the sandbar at the Ausable's Upper Mouth. A ground-dwelling warbler, the northern waterthrush, patrolled the shore, bobbing its tail constantly. This 5-inch bird, with its streaked breast and white eye stripe, has a loud song, thought to be an adaptation to attracting mates and announcing its territory over the streamside roar of rushing water.

A sea of underwater vegetation undulated over rippled sand in the clear current as we passed by gravel bars, eroded banks, and tree trunks waiting to be washed out into the lake. Even at very low water levels, you will have to work paddling against the current, particularly after passing under the railroad bridge. Nearing the Route 9 bridge, we worked harder than we wanted to and turned around to drift back downstream with the current, enjoying ostrich fern towering over the banks, beautiful iridescent green damselflies mating on the wing, and a fat groundhog munching on lush streamside grass.

Paddling downstream, before reaching the railroad bridge, look for a channel cutting back to the right (south), leading to the Lower Mouth. A catch-22: at high water, strong current may preclude making this a loop trip (it might be easier going clockwise); at low water, the channel leading to the Lower Mouth may have insufficient water.

Drifting back into the lake at the Upper Mouth, we turned right to clear the quarter-mile-long sandbar and to paddle back up into the Ausable Wildlife Management Area sloughs. In retrospect, we should have carried over the 30-foot-wide sand spit, rather than paddled around it, especially given that we continually ran aground trying to stay in an elusive channel.

However, taking the long way around got us a close-up sight of a very rare bird in full breeding plumage: a ruff, a Eurasian shorebird slightly larger than the killdeer with which it shared the sand spit. The ruff appears only occasionally along the East Coast and rarely this far inland. The male's breeding plumage includes long feather tufts (ruff) that stream for several inches from the head and neck down either side of the breast. The highly variable ruff color ranges from steel gray to red to white. We watched this bird—with its striking reddish orange head, snow-white ruff, and bright orange legs—run and fly over the sand for at least 10 minutes, so close we did not need binoculars. Other than seeing a bald eagle nest with young or an otter noisily chomping on fish, this provided perhaps the biggest treat of the paddling season.

Abundant deadfalls occur in the clear waters of the Ausable River.

The wildlife management sloughs provided our most enjoyable paddling. Except for the occasional angler, you likely will find yourself paddling alone in this marshy wilderness, not very far from the bustling lake. Immediately upon entering the marsh you have to choose a direction—west or south—and neither channel goes far.

We paddled the whole area because of abundant wildlife—especially wood duck, Eastern kingbird, flicker, and muskrat—and opportunity to study the huge variety of marsh plants. According to some plant keys, more than 30 species of pondweed (genus *Potamogeton*) occur in the Northeast. We saw several species here, all with two things in common: floating leaves with parallel veins, all running the same direction as the midvein, and small, knobby flowers looking like a pale raspberry, extending a few inches above the water on a stout stalk. These serve as aerial landing pads for the diminutive blue damselfly that leaps to the air as you glide by.

We also studied bladderwort, with its yellow snapdragon-like flowers borne on short stalks above the water. Most of the plant lives underwater in dense, feathery mats, bearing hundreds of tiny (0.02 to 0.1 inch long), bulbous traps that catch and digest microscopic animals. In most ponds, mosquito larvae form the bulk of the diet, but the plants also ingest other insect larvae, rotifers, protozoans, small crustaceans, and even tiny tadpoles (for more on carnivorous plants, see page 341).

You can enter Dead Creek in two ways: paddle in from Lake Champlain through a culvert (portage over the top during high water) or launch from the Dead Creek access. Surprisingly, on occasion we have found water flowing from the lake into Dead Creek, filling the culvert to the top, with the road surface just a foot or two above the water's surface. One of our largest bodies of water not controlled by a dam, Lake Champlain's water level can vary dramatically, depending on rainfall.

We enjoyed paddling this placid water while the setting sun drew pastel colors across the western sky. Although we did not see anything new, we had to marvel at the sheer abundance of ducks, great blue heron, muskrat, and the insect-eating tree swallow, barn swallow, and purple martin, doing their best to keep down the ubiquitous deerflies.

We left this wildlife paradise knowing that we would return. Habitats such as these have become increasingly rare, as urban sprawl, strip development, and consumptive land practices have gnawed away at these priceless habitats. We thank the farsighted individuals who set aside this marshland for us and for future generations to enjoy.

39

Davis Lake and Salmon River
Peru and Schuyler Falls

Maps: New York Atlas Map 103:D5, USGS Quadrangles Peasleeville and Peru

Area: 60 acres, stream length about 1 mile

Habitat type: small, shallow lake; narrow, slow-flowing stream

Fish: brown trout

Expect to see: beaver, muskrat

Camping: App. A #60 (on-site)

Take note: no motors allowed

GETTING THERE

From I-87, Exit 35, go 1.1 miles west on Route 442, and turn right on Route 22. Go 0.2 mile (1.3 miles), and turn left (north) on Route 22B in Peru. Go 4.5 miles (5.8 miles), and turn left on Norrisville Road. Go 2.6 miles (8.4 miles), and turn left on Campsite Road at the Macomb Park sign. Go 0.1 mile (8.5 miles), and turn right to the beach and north shore access (fee), or continue straight and launch at the bridge (free).

We really enjoy paddling this small lake and the Salmon River that flows into its west end. Surrounded by hills and wilderness, Macomb Reservation has a wild feel to it. We should rename it "Salmon Creek," in keep-

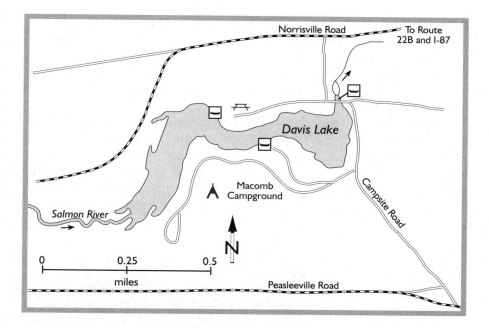

ing with its size and to avoid confusing it with the other North Country Salmon Rivers.

Traverse small Davis Lake slowly to savor its beauty. Vegetation layers back from the water's edge, starting with ferns or cattails and various shrubs, giving way to birch and other small trees, ending with large red pine and a few scattered white pine. Near the stream entrance, narrowleaved cattail gives way to wooded shores. Where alder has not crowded everything else out, a fine grove of walnut grows. Look for feather-like leaves resembling ash and deeply furrowed bark on straight trunks in older trees.

We did not get out of the boat to check to see whether the grove contained butternut or black walnut. Butternut ranges over the entire state, whereas black walnut occurs primarily in the southeast and in isolated populations in the central region. Because horticulturists have planted them widely—mainly because of their very valuable dark wood—these could be black walnut nonetheless. Butternut has lighter bark and 11 to 17 leaflets per leaf; black walnut's bark can get almost black in older trees and has 15 to 23 leaflets per leaf.

Black walnut (and butternut to a lesser extent) has adopted an interesting strategy to limit competition for light and space from other trees. Established trees exude a chemical, juglone, into the surrounding soil that inhibits germination of walnut and many other seeds, which also limits plant growth. So when we looked at the grove of even-aged walnut on Davis Lake, we thought black walnut. In retrospect, we should have checked them out more thoroughly to make sure they were not butternut.

As we paddled the Salmon River upstream, trout rose from their underwater haunts, deftly sucking in the evening hatch's floating insects. Beaver own this stream. We turned around after carrying over three dams, one with a two-foot drop and jewelweed sprouting from its bulwarks. In contrast with the muskrat that slipped quietly under the water's surface at our approach, three beaver on separate occasions slapped the

A well-kept beaver dam provides a momentary impediment to paddling up the Salmon River.

water with their tails, splashing water bank to bank, showing annoyance at our intrusion.

We only wished the beaver had done a better job of pruning back the alder that converges on the channel, leaving only a few feet of passageway in spots. As we worked our way back down the meandering stream in the fading light, veeries called from the undergrowth. A mallard hen reenacted its broken wing trick, leading us away from its brood. Grapevines draped over the streamside vegetation, giving sanctuary to song sparrow, yellowthroat, yellow warbler, brown thrasher, cardinal, and catbird. The strains of the night—cicada, barred owl, frog, veery, white-throated sparrow—flooded the summer air as we paddled across Davis Lake, back to the campground in the semidark. We strongly recommend an evening paddle into this wilderness.

40

Taylor Pond
Black Brook

Maps: New York Atlas Map 96:A3, USGS Quadrangle Wilmington

Area: 803 acres, maximum depth 95 feet

Habitat type: deep oligotrophic lake

Fish: lake, brown, and rainbow trout; salmon

Expect to see: loon, bald eagle, osprey, great blue heron

Camping: App. A #88 (on-site)

Take note: *nearby peaks funnel wind, making paddling treacherous in windy conditions*

GETTING THERE

From Saranac Lake, go north on Route 3 to Bloomingdale. Turn right, go 0.2 mile on Route 3, and turn right on River Road (County 18; becomes County 48). Go 8.9 miles (9.1 miles), and bear left on Plank Road/ Forrestdale Road where County 48 curves right. Go 8.4 miles (17.5 miles), and turn sharply left on Nelson Road. Go 0.9 mile (18.4 miles), and turn left on Silver Lake Road at the T. Go 0.6 mile (19.0 miles), and turn left to Taylor Pond Campground.

From I-87, Exit 34, go about 10 miles west on Route 9N to Au Sable Forks, and turn right on Palmer Street/Silver Lake Road. Go about 9 miles (about 19 miles), and turn left to Taylor Pond Campground.

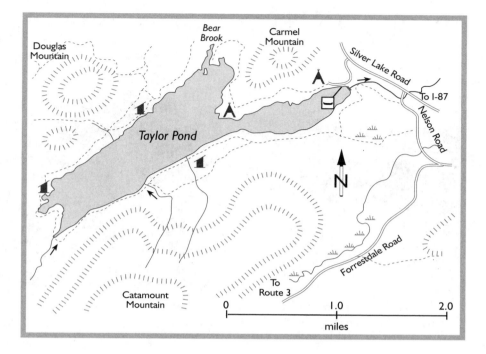

Surrounded by 8,000 acres of wild forest, Taylor Pond exudes wilderness. Because of its out-of-the-way location and the campground's rustic character, the pond does not draw large numbers to its shores. We appreciate the 25 well-separated, wooded campsites but prefer those accessible only by boat. Campsites I-1 and I-2 on the peninsula tip separating the eastern arm from the main lake appeal to us most. Each nestles in a grove of hemlock, birch, and pine, with an outhouse, picnic table, and fire grate.

Most of the lake sports a sandy bottom, but watch out near shore for barely submerged granite boulders. Very narrow-leaved water celery floats on the surface in shallow areas, but the pond's depths do not support an abundance of aquatic vegetation. We found cranberry growing among the shoreside shrubbery, under a canopy of stunted birch and red maple. A wide array of deciduous trees dominates the hillsides, and conifers cling to the Catamount Mountain crest.

Paddling up Bear Brook mouth, with large, lichen-covered, pink granite boulders lining the shore, we glided by a large beaver lodge that

A beaver lodge in the mouth of Bear Brook as it flows into Taylor Pond, with Catamount Mountain looming large over the pond.

nearly obliterated a small island. We could not find the underwater entrance; it seemed pretty rocky for digging.

Paddling back to the main lake, we gazed out over the water to the wooded peaks and extensive shoulders of Catamount Mountain that seem to guard the entire southern shore, providing a picturesque backdrop for a leisurely cruise down the pond. Though the mountain lion no longer patrols the mountain shadows, we did see another species that has recently retreated from the Endangered Species List: a mature bald eagle. As we approached the peninsula, it took flight from a tall pine and soared ever higher on Catamount's thermals, becoming barely visible among the billowing white clouds. Given the midfall season, we suspect that it had just started its migration to the coast or other body of water that does not freeze over.

We also saw wood duck and great blue heron in quieter coves, along with the usual array of songbirds back in the woods. Hiking trails ring the pond and extend into the nearby hills, adding an extra dimension to this beautiful location.

41

Moose Pond
St. Armand

Maps: New York Atlas Map 96:B1, USGS Quadrangles Blooming-dale and Saranac Lake

Area: 140 acres, maximum depth 70 feet

Habitat type: small, deep pond

Fish: brook, rainbow, and lake trout; landlocked salmon; small-mouth bass

Expect to see: northern white cedar; scenic mountains and unbroken forest

Camping: App. A #81, 86, 88, and 89

Take note: wind may cause hazardous paddling conditions

GETTING THERE

From Saranac Lake, go north on Route 3 to Bloomingdale. Turn right, go 0.2 mile on Route 3, and turn right on River Road (County 18). Go 1.6 miles (1.8 miles), and turn right on Moose Pond Road. Go 1.5 miles (3.3 miles) to the access.

With its 70-foot depth, Moose Pond differs from most of the area's shallow, boggy ponds, and because of its depth, supports a cold-water trout fishery. Trout succumb readily to acidified water. Bogs, especially those with sphagnum—which secretes hydrogen ions that acidify its environment—do not support trout well. Decaying bog

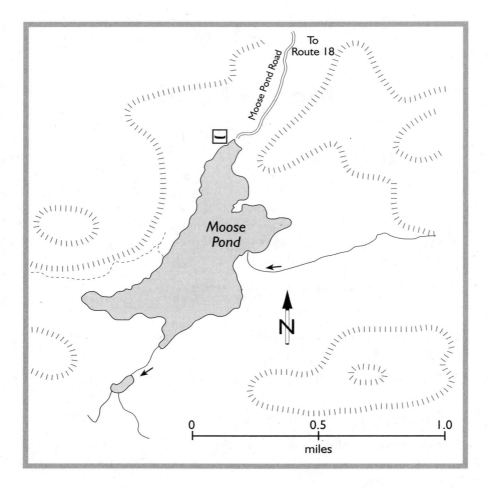

vegetation also gives off tannic and other acids during oxidation that add further acidity. Although trout might survive, barely, under such conditions, they certainly cannot survive the added import of acid rain from the Midwest. Sulfur dioxide—eventually converted to sulfurous and sulfuric acids in the atmosphere—along with hydrochloric and nitric acids, emanating from unscrubbed, coal-fired power plants, toll a death knell for high Adirondack lakes. Hundreds of them no longer support trout. Thankfully, such environmental insults have not ruined this body of water.

High Adirondack peaks overlook the placid waters of Moose Pond.

Precambrian rock—mostly granite and gneiss (pronounced "nice")—pokes up through sedimentary rock to form the Adirondacks High Peaks. Although a relatively new upthrust, and evidence suggests it is ongoing, the high peak rocks date to about a billion years ago. These rocks do not react with acids and, therefore, do not buffer (reduce acidity of) acid rain or high-altitude bogs. Most low-elevation lakes in the Adirondacks lie over marble, a type of calcium carbonate, just like limestone. Acids readily react with calcium carbonate, liberating carbon dioxide and water, effectively neutralizing acid rain. So fish have not disappeared from low-elevation lakes as they have from higher elevations.

Surrounded by scenic, forested Adirondack peaks, Moose Pond nestles in a deep, pristine valley. These same peaks funnel north-south winds, making this small pond's waters treacherous during windy periods. Large, smooth granite boulders line the shore in places, adding to its scenic character, and offer easy egress for picnicking and camping at designated sites. In the fall, deer hunters use them for base camps as they foray off into the huge, roadless McKenzie Mountain Wilderness—home of 2 of the 100 tallest Adirondack peaks.

A hemlock stand grows near the access, and northern white cedar ring the pond. Thick stands of birch reflect off the clear water, standing in stark contrast to the evergreen conifers. Occasional yellow birch blend in with the hemlock and tall white pine. Although it does not take long to paddle the complete shoreline of Moose Pond, one could camp here for days, relaxing, reading, philosophizing, and, of course, paddling in relative isolation, surrounded by clear, trout-filled waters and scenic mountains.

42

Lake Kushaqua and Rainbow Lake
Brighton and Franklin

Maps: New York Atlas Maps 95:A7, 101:D7, 102:D1; USGS Quadrangles Loon Lake, Debar Mountain, Bloomingdale

Area: Rainbow Lake 588 acres, maximum depth 60 feet; Lake Kushaqua 377 acres, maximum depth 90 feet; Buck Pond 128 acres; river length 3 miles

Habitat type: extensive interconnected lakes and river

Fish: kokanee salmon, lake trout, largemouth and smallmouth bass, northern pike, walleye

Expect to see: osprey, great blue heron, waterfowl, deer

Camping: App. A #74 (on-site)

Take note: to paddle from Jones Pond to Rainbow Lake or to run Saranac River North Branch, use Jamieson and Morris, *Adirondack Canoe Waters: North Flow*, 3rd edition (Adirondack Mountain Club, 1988)

GETTING THERE

Kushaqua Narrows. From Paul Smith's College, go 3.7 miles east on Route 86, and turn left on Route 60. Go 6.1 miles (9.8 miles), and go straight on Kushaqua-Mud Pond Road where Route 60 goes right. Go 0.7 mile (10.5 miles) to the access at the bridge over Kushaqua Narrows.

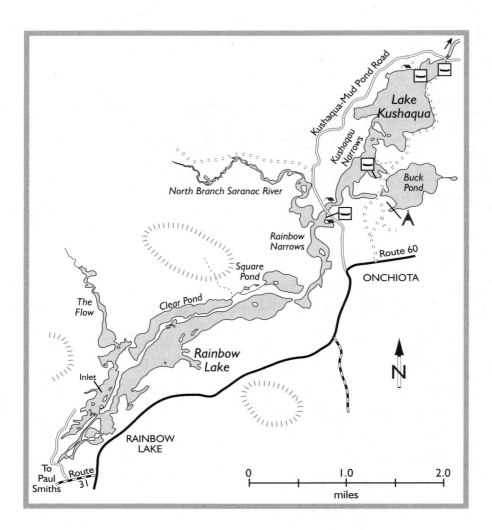

Lake Kushaqua. Continue north for 0.5 mile (11.0 miles) on Kushaqua-Mud Pond Road, and fork right. Go 1.9 miles (12.9 miles) to the access on the right (high clearance required). Or go 0.4 mile (11.4 miles) to the bridge over the outlet.

Buck Pond Campground. From the junction of Route 60 and Kushaqua-Mud Pond Road, go 0.3 mile (10.1 miles) east on Route 60 to the campground on the left.

The Kushaqua Lake area contains several different types of water; you could spend several days exploring it all. To keep you oriented, we start descriptions on the north and move south.

Lake Kushaqua

Kushaqua offers picturesque scenery with forested hillsides and wonderful lakeside camping, but the relatively round lake offers few inlets and marshes to explore. The delicate branches of gray birch, suspended over the water, add to the scenic beauty. Fall foliage—crimson and orange from many red and sugar maples, coupled with vibrant yellow of striped maple and big-toothed aspen, viewed against a dark green backdrop of white and red pine—makes fall camping here a colorful experience.

Kushaqua Narrows

Explore the Narrows' interesting coves and islands. Buck Pond Campground and boat ramp do not intrude significantly. A rope swing dangled from a red pine bough, and deer nonchalantly browsed the shoreside brush and drank from the cool waters as we cruised by. A great blue heron took flight at our approach. Sweet gale and sheep laurel draped the shores, and bracken fern stretched for filtered light from the pine canopy. Mussel shells littered the bottom in the clear water.

If you paddle back through the narrow cove that goes off southeast near the base of the narrows—a quiet, idyllic spot with ducks swimming and lacy green hemlock branches draping out over the water—you can reach Buck Pond . . . eventually, by carrying up over a steep bank and road.

North Branch of the Saranac River

The North Branch, entering the narrows from the west—beginning with a maze of drowned timber, floating vegetation, and a large, thickly forested island—provides a haven for wildlife and quietwater paddlers. We saw one other canoe at the mouth and nary a soul in the upper reaches. If you have limited time, make this your prime destination. It avoids the lakes' congestion and noise and provides hours of solitude in pristine and varied wildlife habitat.

We felt transported back to a distant time as we paddled among the towering tamarack, spruce, white pine, and balsam fir at the river's mouth. The primeval forested swamp funneled down to a narrow, boulder-strewn passageway, then opened into a series of wide beaver

Conifers line the shore in many places on Lake Kushaqua, Rainbow Lake, and the North Branch of the Saranac River.

meadows. We wondered how the aquatic plants divide the habitat as we paddled, first through acres of pondweed, followed by acres of water shield, and then several acres of yellow pondlily. Water celery undulated in the light current, as alder began to appear along with rafts of beaver cuttings, beaver dams, and lodges. Large birds appeared: turkey vulture, northern raven, and great blue heron.

An alder flycatcher cried a buzzy "fee-bee-o" from, appropriately enough, the alder swamp. This uncommon, inconspicuous, and very drab warbler-sized bird has an olive brown back and pale yellow belly, with two white wing bars and a small white eye ring. Like the nine other, similarly drab *Empidonax* species found throughout the United States and Canada, it sits upright on exposed branches, waiting to pounce on juicy insects that fly by. Listen for its song near alder stands in the spring and early summer.

As we gazed into the distance, the tall, cathedral-like spires of balsam fir provided a mesmerizing effect—we did not mind carrying up over beaver dams to penetrate farther back into the wilderness. The metallic chip of the swamp sparrow, followed by a musical trill, made us want to locate the furtive little bird. A painted turtle swam up to greet

Pine seeking light over open water

us in the clear water. Reluctantly, we paddled back down the river, not wanting to leave this wildlife paradise.

Rainbow Narrows
Rainbow Narrows, really just a continuation of Kushaqua Narrows, has much the same beauty of the latter but with slightly more boat traffic. A waterways crossroads of great beauty, with spirelike spruce, balsam fir, and other conifers, it transports boaters between Rainbow and Kushaqua lakes and the mouth of the Saranac River North Branch. The exceedingly narrow concrete passageway keeps the bigger boats in Rainbow Lake from polluting Lake Kushaqua.

Rainbow Lake
Rainbow Lake's development started with an inn and a few rustic camps back in 1856; it now gets too much attention from personal watercraft, water-skiers, and motorboats. Cottages and houses line the banks in places. We had hoped to spend a short time on Rainbow Lake by carrying up over the mile-long esker that separates it from Clear Pond, but we decided that it was too brushy and steep. For a fascinating discussion

of eskers, see the Rainbow Lake section of Jamieson and Morris's *Adirondack Canoe Waters: North Flow.*

Clear Pond and The Flow

To reach Clear Pond and The Flow, paddle southwest on Rainbow Lake about 2.5 miles to a developed area known as Inlet. Paddle through the narrow break in the esker into The Flow. Paddling north here, you leave the lake traffic behind and return to the peace and quiet you expect in the northern Adirondacks. About two-thirds of a mile north from the opening, a narrow channel to the right (east) leads into Clear Pond.

As we paddled back through the narrows—listening to calls of white-throated sparrow, hermit thrush, ovenbird, white-breasted nuthatch, red-eyed vireo, and several species of warbler—the nesting barn swallows under the bridge once again exploded into the air at our passage. We knew we would be back for further explorations.

Adirondack Park

Sweeping mountain vistas, sparkling waterfalls, the loon's haunting cry, the river otter's playful antics, clear mountain lakes in steep glaciated terrain, broad expanses of untrammeled wilderness—all these identify the remarkable Adirondack Park. Located less than a half-day's drive for more than 30 million people and covering an area larger than either Massachusetts or New Hampshire, Adirondack Park has a fascinating history.

History

Before the Industrial Age and the resource consumption that fueled it, we knew little about the Adirondack Park region. Native Americans traversed the mountains and traveled the region's rivers, linking with lands as far away as Maine. High northerly elevations, where winter lingered long and cold, relegated humans to a transient existence. Early adventurers explored the Pacific Northwest and Rockies long before mapping the Adirondacks.

During the 1800s, the area fell victim to greed and waste. Loggers penetrated nearly every corner of the park, mainly to remove tall white pine—some towering 150 feet or more—standing well above other forest trees. Logs floated down the Hudson and every other river of consequence. Hemlock, cut and stripped of its bark, provided tannic acid for the tanning industry. When the logging boom ended in the late 1800s, only 1 percent of the original six million acres remained untouched. Hunters killed the last moose in the 1860s; extirpated the cougar, wolf, lynx, and wolverine by 1900; and relentlessly trapped beaver until only a handful remained in 1904.

Ironically, though, wealthy industrialists—whose mills and factories depleted the region's forests and despoiled its air and water—finally led the charge to protect the Adirondacks. The wealthy literally fled to the mountains for its clean air and water. Recreational visitation mushroomed in 1869 when Boston preacher William H. H. "Adirondack" Murray wrote the widely read book *Adventures in the Wilderness; or, Camp-Life in the Adirondacks.* He likened the "magnificent scenery" to that of Switzerland. In the 1880s, George Washington Sears, under the pen name Nessmuk, wrote in *Forest and Stream* exciting accounts of his adventures paddling the *Sairy Gamp,* a 10-pound canoe built by J. Henry Rushton, through the Adirondack wildlands.

Little Long Pond, Adirondack Park.

People came in droves for the pure mountain air that might cure tuberculosis or offer relief from New York or Boston's polluted air. Intellectuals, including Ralph Waldo Emerson, James Russell Lowell, and Louis Agassiz, came to "rough it" at the "Philosophers' Camp" on Follensby Pond. They used waterway corridors to explore the remote wilderness in famed Adirondack guide boats. Entrepreneurs catered to the wealthy with dozens of grand hotels—the hotel at Blue Mountain Lake, the first in the world to have electric lighting in every room—and luxurious fishing and hunting camps. The guide industry flourished, and many of the carry trails we use today were in use long before roads. While enjoying the out-of-doors, these industrialists also witnessed the destruction of the Adirondacks around them, including their own rampant overfishing and overhunting.

They heard the message from Vermont lawyer George Perkins Marsh in his 1864 book *Man and Nature*. Marsh convinced many powerful New Yorkers that denuded slopes would hold neither soil nor water, that floods and droughts would increase, that the prized artery of commerce, the Erie Canal, might go dry.

A young, well-to-do Albany lawyer, Verplanck Colvin, reinforced Marsh's message. Colvin gave up lawyering to survey the Adirondacks for more than 20 years, climbing its peaks and mapping its valleys, taking every opportunity to write and to speak about the threats to this glorious land. Colvin and his powerful allies convinced the state legislature in 1872 to set up a commission to study the Adirondacks, eventually leading to the Forest Preserve Law of 1885: the Adirondacks and Catskills would be "forever kept as wild forest lands."

But because of continuing abuses, Governor David Hill asked the Forest Commission to draw a line around those lands most worthy of protection, resulting in 1892 in the first "blue line" around two million acres of the Adirondack Forest Preserve. A state constitutional convention in 1894 gave constitutional protection to these lands with the passage of Article 14:

> The lands of the State, now owned or hereafter acquired, constituting the forest preserve, as now fixed by law, shall be forever kept as wild forest lands. They shall not be leased, sold, or exchanged or taken by any corporation, public or private, nor shall the timber thereon be sold, removed, or destroyed.

The publicly owned lands within the Adirondack Park blue line are among the most fully protected lands in the nation. To open these lands for logging or development would require not just the passage of a new law but amending the state constitution. Over the years, the blue line has expanded to its present boundaries, encompassing approximately six million acres.

Adirondack Park includes a mix of public and private land. The Forest Preserve founders hoped to acquire all of the land within the blue line eventually, but that will not occur. The state has acquired about 45 percent of the land within the park, and that fraction is expected to creep upward gradually as the state purchases additional lands.

Unprecedented massive land ownership changes all across the northern forest, from New York to Maine, have occurred since the first edition of this book. Timber companies have sold vast parcels of land to other timber companies, investment companies, private developers, states, and The Nature Conservancy. Sales started in Maine where 5.5 million acres or nearly 30 percent of northern Maine changed hands between 1998 and 2003; to put this into perspective, the 8,600 square miles sold is 2.5 times the size of Yellowstone National Park and equals the area of New Hampshire and of the Adirondack Forest Preserve. Although timber companies sold some lands to The Nature Conservancy or included conservation easements, the vastness of the sales from one timber company to another, to investment companies, or to land developers galvanized the conservation community.

The Northern Forest Alliance (www.northernforestalliance.org), currently a consortium of 47 organizations, brought forth the importance of the Northern Forest and developed strategies to conserve the most valuable tracts through outright purchase or conservation easements.

New York, with leadership from conservation organizations such as the Adirondack Mountain Club, The Nature Conservancy, and Governor George Pataki, has added tens of thousands of acres to public ownership. The first efforts, which resulted in taking formerly private holdings off the tax roles, resulted in some public resistance. More recent acquisitions include purchases that provide replacement taxes and conservation easements that provide access to some parcels for the first time.

Geology

The Adirondacks' unique character stems in large part from its geological history. The Canadian Shield inexplicably pushed up through overlying sedimentary rock, exposing ancient Precambrian metamorphic rock. A distinct dome, extending generally northeast to southwest, covers an area of roughly 120 miles by 80 miles. Although much of the rock formed a billion years ago, the mountains themselves formed much more recently—only about 15 million years ago—making them far younger than the weathered, 350-million-year-old Appalachian Mountains of neighboring Vermont. Some geologists believe that the Adirondacks continue to rise. Because no active tectonic plates collide beneath the Adirondacks, the usual mountain-building mechanism does not explain the mountains' recent, and possibly continuing, uplift.

The Adirondacks' high mountain granite, quartz, and gneiss (pronounced "nice") do not react with acid. Thus, airborne acids from coal-fired power plants in the Ohio River Valley—deposited on the peaks as acid rain, dew, frost, and snow—acidify high-elevation waterways. Native brook trout and other game fish cannot reproduce under moderately acidic conditions, so many Adirondack lakes and ponds have become depleted of fish. In contrast, lower elevations' underlying marble—made up of calcium carbonate, just like limestone—neutralizes acidity. Consequently, lower-elevation lakes have not suffered the drastic declines in fish populations that have occurred at higher elevations.

Looking toward the Future

Adirondack Park contains the largest wilderness area and the vast majority of remaining virgin old-growth forest in the eastern United States. The region offers a tremendous resource for learning about forest ecosystems and wildlife habitat, and it could serve as the site for reintroduction of species long extirpated from the Northeast. The Adirondacks, part of 26 million acres of the Northern Forest, stretching from northern New York to northern Maine, should serve as a model for preserving these magnificent forests for future generations. But major conflicts have arisen over management—as one might expect when 10 million visitors per year descend on an area that just 130,000 residents call home. Most residents depend on visitors for their livelihoods, but many resent regulatory controls from "downstate."

Ultimately, the goals of residents and visitors coincide. Both want scenic vistas, deep forests, and pristine waterways that support hiking, canoeing, camping, hunting, and fishing. But keeping privately owned portions of the park attractive to visitors, upon whom the residents depend, means some controls on development. No one wants to see the cheek-to-jowl vacation homes, such as those dotting the Fulton lakeshores, expand to the rest of the park, a very real risk for much of the 55 percent in private ownership.

The state and conservation organizations seem to have arrived at a workable solution by purchasing available paper lands—while continuing to pay taxes on those lands—and by purchasing conservation easements on other lands. This effort's ultimate success hinges on state residents' willingness to continue to support setting aside the necessary funds for these purchases. So far, that willingness remains intact.

Among the highest priorities for Adirondack Park, in our estimation, are the following:

1. Control shoreline development. Current zoning requires that single-family homes sit on parcels of at least several acres, except along shorelines with a minimum lot size of only 1.2 acres. This carving up of private land around our waterways introduces pollutants from high population densities. We should place a moratorium on shoreline development until we can agree on a master plan that adequately protects river and lake shores.

2. Purchase all 400,000-acres of the Bob Marshall Great Wilderness in the park's core. Link the Oswegatchie wildlands into one wilderness

corridor. When the New York legislature agreed to the original blue line that enclosed the most significant natural features on the Adirondacks, it intended to purchase all lands inside. Many of those lands still remain in private hands more than a hundred years later.

3. Use voluntary check-offs on tax returns, the sale of vanity license plates, funds from nonprofit organizations such as The Nature Conservancy, designated surcharges on recreational equipment (including binoculars, canoes, and fishing gear), and renewed emphasis on bond issues to fund land acquisition within the park's core. Pay year-round residents for conservation easements, which provide a way for residents to receive money for their land, yet keep the land intact—as most would choose to do.

4. Support sustainable, nonpolluting businesses that strengthen the local Adirondack economy. Look for products labeled as "Made in the Adirondacks," for example. If residents have a dependable source of year-round income, the pressure to develop or sell land will decrease.

Those of us who love the Adirondacks—residents and visitors, loggers and birders, anglers and paddlers—must work together to guarantee its continued splendor for future generations to know and enjoy. Get to know this most remarkable of parks. Paddle its lakes and rivers, climb its mountains, hike its trails, explore its history, study its wildlife and geology.

43

Osgood Pond, Jones Pond, and Osgood River
Brighton

Maps: New York Atlas Map 95:A7, USGS Quadrangles Bloomingdale and St. Regis Mountain

Area: Osgood Pond 508 acres, Jones Pond 170 acres

Habitat type: marshy ponds and stream surrounded by boreal forest

Fish: brook trout, largemouth and smallmouth bass, northern pike

Expect to see: ducks, muskrat, carnivorous plants, bog shrubs

Camping: App. A #74, 76, 80, 85, and 86

Take note: to run other Osgood River sections, use Jamieson and Morris, *Adirondack Canoe Waters: North Flow*, 3rd edition (Adirondack Mountain Club, 1988)

GETTING THERE

Osgood Pond. From the junction of Routes 30 and 86 at Paul Smith's College, go 0.6 mile east on Route 86, and turn left on White Pine Road. Go 0.2 mile (0.8 mile), and turn left to the access.

Jones Pond. From Paul Smith's College, go 0.9 mile east on Route 86 east, and turn left on County Route 31. Go 2.6 miles (3.5 miles) to the access on the right.

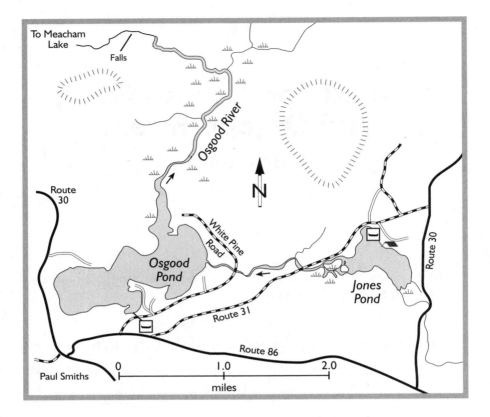

Tall white pine ring the cove at the Osgood Pond access. Occasional tamarack and red maple and a few birch appear, as well. The shoreline surrounding the rest of the pond also contains large numbers of pine. Despite the forested shores, noise from Route 30 and summer cabins intrude on the pond's solitude. Fortunately, solitude begins just about a mile from the access, as you paddle north down the Osgood River outlet.

Tamarack, spruce, northern white cedar, and balsam fir dominate the river's western bank, and pine covers the eastern side's higher ground. In and amongst these trees—many actually red pines—lies White Pine Camp, the home of Calvin Coolidge's 1926 summer White House. With its 20 buildings and walkways surrounded by rhododendron, the restored camp opens to visitors from 10:00 A.M. to 5:00 P.M., mid-May through mid-October. One of the great rustic estates of the Adirondacks, the

camp boasts 3,900 feet of shoreline and 35 acres and is featured on the cover of this book.

As the camp gives way to state-owned land along the river, note the stunted, spirelike black spruce of the sphagnum bog, the only spruce species that tolerates partially submerged roots. We paddled down-river about 3 miles, until reaching a series of waterfalls. If you want an adventure and intend to continue on, refer to Jamieson and Morris's *Adirondack Canoe Waters: North Flow*. In places, the river disappears under marsh vegetation, making the trek down to Meacham Lake a real challenge.

We saw only a handful of deciduous trees along the river. Conifers completely dominate the boggy northern boreal forest here. A wide va-riety of shrubs perch on the sphagnum hummocks, including sweet gale, leatherleaf, sheep laurel, bog laurel, and bog rosemary. Large clumps of pitcher-plant line the shore in spots, and diminutive sundew rosettes glisten in the sun, awaiting insects drawn to the sticky "dew" of their traps. Yellow pondlily, fragrant waterlily, pondweed, and water celery crowd the channel, while bur-reed and pickerelweed compete for space along the shore.

As we rounded each bend, through early morning autumn mists drift-ing slowly across the water, small flocks of black duck leapt to the air, beat-ing their wings furiously. Many groups of three to a dozen wood ducks,

Tamarack and balsam fir line the shores of the Osgood River as it flows out of Osgood Pond.

some all males in bright plumage, erupted from the water while sounding out their mournful, unducklike cries. They circled around behind us, only to be disturbed once again on our return trip. This beautiful duck, driven to the verge of extinction around the turn of the century by unregulated hunting and clearing of forests, has rebounded nicely. Prompted by the newly formed National Audubon Society, the government passed legislation in the early 1900s that protected the wood duck and other migratory species. Bird-watchers and wildlife management officials began erecting wood duck nesting boxes in the 1940s, leading to greatly increased populations of this beautiful bird, one of our few cavity-nesting ducks.

A logjam followed by a series of falls indicated the end of the line. Lichens festooning some spruces provided a primeval look as the bog gave way to forest. Reluctantly, we turned around to retrace our way back to the pond.

Reaching the pond, we paddled southeast to the Jones Pond outlet. We paddled this small creek all the way up to Jones Pond, carrying over a few beaver dams and one road. Water had breached some abandoned dams, and we eased our way through the narrow channels. Most alders that formerly lined the banks had disappeared, leaving only stumps and conifers, which beaver rarely eat. Apparently, the beaver had eaten itself out of house and home, leaving only grasses to feed the muskrats that we saw occasionally.

On Jones Pond, a pleasant, informal camping area extends along a dirt road from the access. Ovenbirds call from the midstory level in an extensive red pine grove. Camping here on several occasions, we never tired of the nighttime sounds of whip-poor-will, barred owl, and great horned owl.

44

Deer River Flow and Horseshoe Pond

Duane

Maps: New York Atlas Map 101:C6, USGS Quadrangle Large Titus

Area: 500 acres

Habitat type: shallow, marshy pond surrounded by boreal forest

Fish: largemouth and smallmouth bass, northern pike

Expect to see: bald eagle, harrier, deer, beaver, muskrat

Camping: App. A #74 and 80

Take note: to run other Deer River sections, use Jamieson and Morris, *Adirondack Canoe Waters: North Flow*, 3rd edition (Adirondack Mountain Club, 1988)

GETTING THERE

From Paul Smith's College, go 15.3 miles north on Route 30, and turn left on Cold Brook Road. Go 0.1 mile (15.4 miles) to the access on the right.

From Malone, go south on Route 30 to the junction with Red Tavern Road (Route 14) and Route 26. Continue south for 2.2 miles to Cold Brook Road on the right.

Paddling out in the shallow, tea-colored water, we felt transported to the time of nineteenth-century Adirondack guides. Ringed with spire-like conifers—tall tamarack, balsam fir, black and red spruce, northern white cedar, white pine—and gorgeous mountain views to the south and west,

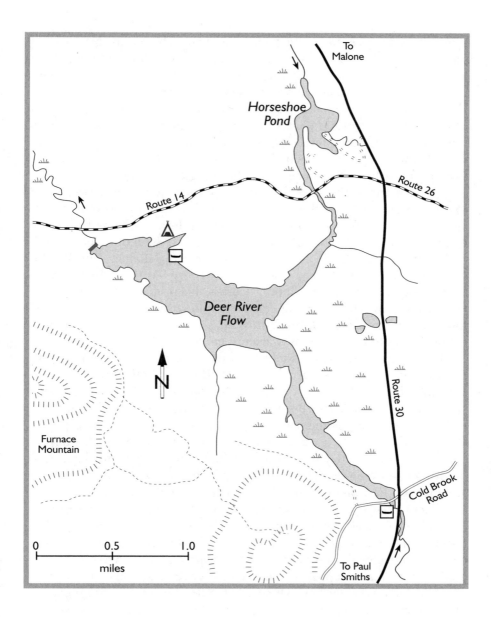

To Malone

Horseshoe Pond

Route 26

Route 14

Deer River Flow

N

Furnace Mountain

Route 30

Cold Brook Road

0   0.5   1.0
miles

To Paul Smiths

Deer River Flow retains a magical aura, even though Route 30 intrudes a little on its southern arm.

The magic increased dramatically when we spotted a bald eagle nest with two nearly grown fledglings perched on side branches. Seeing four eagles at once made our paddle here superbly enjoyable. Bald eagles nested widely in the Adirondacks until done in by DDT poisoning and habitat destruction. Beginning in the late 1980s, they resumed nesting—the result of a massive reintroduction program that began in 1976. Even though we have seen many bald eagles in our intensive exploration of the state's quiet waters, we still marvel at the grace and power of this remarkable bird. Awe inspiring is the only way to describe seeing one swoop down on powerful wing beats to snatch with its talons a fish from the water's surface. For more on the bald eagle, see page 88.

As we scanned the skies for more raptors, a northern harrier glided low over the marsh, on the watch for rodents. But the shoreline habitat along both Deer River Flow and Horseshoe Pond belongs to the redwinged blackbird. The territories must be worth defending, because the males sing from cattails every few feet along the marsh. The shrubby shoreline, lined with sweet gale, bog rosemary—with its long, narrow leaves, green on top, white underneath—sheep laurel, and more, provides excellent habitat for the common yellowthroat, a diminutive yellow warbler with a black mask through its eyes, looking rather like a robber ready to pounce on unwary insects.

Out on the flow, mussel shells litter the bottom near the boggy shore. Although tamarack has started to invade the peat bog, and will eventually fill it in, it still supports tons of bog specialists, including sundew and pitcher-plant. Because pitcher-plant and sundew live in nutrient-poor soils, they supplement the meager nitrogen available by capturing and digesting insects. Pitchers fill with rainwater, into which the plant secretes digestive enzymes. When unlucky insects fall in, downward-pointing hairs keep them from crawling back out. Eventually they drown and give up their precious nutrient stores to the plant.

The sundew operates in a similar manner. Glistening dewlike secretions on stalks emanating from the sundew pad attract insects, which become entrapped on the sticky secretion. The plant rolls the insect inward slightly to come in contact with shorter stalks that contain digestive enzymes. The degraded insect material provides needed nitrogen to the plant.

The shallow water harbors acres of yellow pondlily, fragrant waterlily, and water celery, with its long narrow leaves floating on the surface, especially on the long connecting stream into Horseshoe Pond. As you enter Horseshoe Pond, an occasional house intrudes on the right-hand shore, while sphagnum, black spruce, tamarack, and carnivorous plants cover the opposite shore.

We loved paddling here and found it hard to leave. We spent quite a bit of time trying to photograph iridescent green damselflies. Besides interruptions by the eagles and harrier, we watched deer come down to the water's edge for a drink and numerous muskrats harvesting aquatic vegetation. We saw one beaver and evidence of many more.

We highly recommend paddling here, especially in early morning or late afternoon, to see wildlife and to study myriad bog and aquatic plants. But please keep your distance from wildlife, especially eagle nests.

45

Meacham Lake and Osgood River

Brighton and Duane

Maps: New York Atlas Map 101:D6, USGS Quadrangle Meacham Lake

Area: 1,185 acres, maximum depth 63 feet

Habitat type: large lake, marshy stream, boreal forest

Fish: brown trout, splake, landlocked salmon, smallmouth bass, northern pike

Expect to see: beaver, a diminutive yellow waterlily, sundew, pitcher-plant

Camping: App. A #80 (on-site)

Take note: to run other Osgood River or St. Regis River East Branch sections, use Jamieson and Morris, *Adirondack Canoe Waters: North Flow*, 3rd edition (Adirondack Mountain Club, 1988)

GETTING THERE

Dam access. From Paul Smith's College, go 9.3 miles north on Route 30, and turn right to the dam, just past the bridge.

Upper access. From the dam, go 2.6 miles (11.9 miles) north on Route 30, and turn right on State Camp Road, which leads to the access and campground.

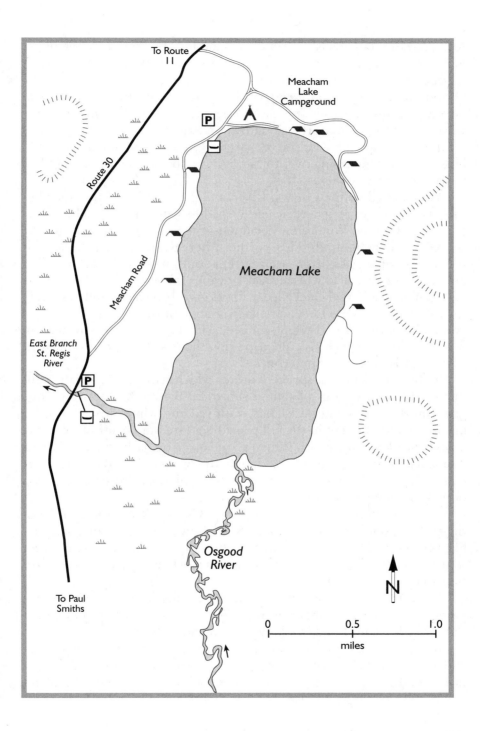

To Route 11

Meacham Lake Campground

P

Route 30

Meacham Road

Meacham Lake

East Branch St. Regis River

P

Osgood River

To Paul Smiths

N

0   0.5   1.0
        miles

Although the state owns the land surrounding Meacham Lake, it allows motorboats and personal watercraft. On summer weekends, the lake's surface crawls with noise and wakes. We vastly prefer paddling up the Osgood River on the south end, easily reached by putting in at the dam on the outflow and paddling east along the shoreline. Even when the wind blows from the north, abundant aquatic vegetation on the lake's south end damps the wind-driven swells. On a very windy day, we had little difficulty traversing over to the river and back, even though we had to paddle in wave troughs.

We paddled up the Osgood River, and the same scene unfolded before us that we experienced when we paddled the upper reaches flowing out of Osgood Pond. Few deciduous trees appear along the marshy shores; conifers abound. This northern boreal forest supports an unusual array of species rarely seen farther south in New York, including gray jay—the so-called whiskey jack or camp robber—that exhibits little fear of humans; boreal chickadee, with its gray-brown cap and nasal call; spruce grouse, a quite tame, chunkier relative of the ruffed grouse; and crossbills, both red and white-winged, with bills that cross instead of meet together when closed, an adaptation they use to good advantage in prying seeds loose from pinecones.

Tamarack and black spruce, both of which withstand partially submerged roots, grow on sphagnum substrate. Balsam fir and white pine grow on the banks and on islands, with red and white spruce on drier ground. Paddling here in the fall provides a rare but beautiful treat: the golden-needled tamarack against a backdrop of dark green conifers. Tamarack drops all of its needles in fall, the only conifer to do so. Other conifers drop only two- or three-year-old needles, leaving a healthy crop of new green needles growing at twig ends.

Another interesting plant grows in the Osgood River, the smallest of the yellow pondlilies, *Nuphar microphyllum*, which as its name suggests has very small leaves—less than 5 inches long—compared with larger waterlilies. Its diminutive flower measures less than an inch across when fully open

You can paddle up the Osgood for many miles before it becomes impassable, disappearing under swamp vegetation. To paddle from Osgood Pond to Meacham Pond would be quite an adventure.

Reluctantly, after a few miles of slow progress on this endlessly meandering stream, carrying over downed logs and halfhearted beaver dams, we had to contemplate paddling back to the access. The dams,

The smallest yellow pondlily—*Nuphar microphyllum*—grows amid pondweed leaves on the Osgood River.

beaver lodges, and abundant cuttings reminded us that beaver generally do not forage on conifers' resinous bark, thereby limiting numbers on the Osgood River. As it hacks down streamside alders, it literally eats itself out of house and home. As the fast-growing alder returns, so do beaver to start the cycle once again.

Trappers extirpated the beaver in New York in the late 1800s. In 1904, conservation officials released 6 beaver near Old Forge, and in 1906, they released 25 more from Yellowstone Park. From this nucleus, the prolific rodents reached a population of nearly 20,000 by 1915. Amazingly, the beaver now covers the state, numbering about 100,000 individuals. You will see them on the Osgood River in early evening . . . unless they decimate the alders again.

Paddling back to the river's mouth on calm water, we had almost forgotten the north wind-driven swells on Meacham Lake, but after a short sprint to the outlet channel, we again met calm waters.

The outlet channel leading to and from the dam differs significantly from the Osgood River. Its rounded boulders poke up above the water's surface, and the boggy areas contain sundew and pitcherplant in profusion. Deciduous trees—a rare commodity in the boreal forest—grow along the bank. And instead of the exotic bird species of the coniferous forest, here red-winged blackbird, black-throated green warbler, and white-throated sparrow serenaded us from streamside perches. Dwarf gray birch graced the shores, along with alder, sheep laurel, and other shrubs; *Equisetum*, floating heart, pickerelweed, and pondweed covered patches of water.

46

St. Regis Lakes and Spitfire Lake

Brighton and Harrietstown

Maps: New York Atlas Map 95:A6, USGS Quadrangles St. Regis Mountain and Bloomingdale

Area: Lower St. Regis Lake 365 acres, Spitfire Lake 254 acres, Upper St. Regis Lake 711 acres

Habitat type: lakes with many islands and coves

Fish: splake and lake trout, landlocked salmon, largemouth and smallmouth bass, northern pike

Expect to see: loon, spectacular Adirondack architecture

Outfitters: St. Regis Canoe Outfitters, canoe rental, 518-891-1838

Camping: on-site wilderness camping

Take note: provides access to St. Regis Canoe Area

GETTING THERE

Lower St. Regis Lake. From the junction of Routes 86 and 186 north of Saranac Lake, go 7.2 miles on Route 86 to Route 30. Go straight across into Paul Smith's College, and bear right to two parking areas behind Franklin and Essex residence halls. Carry 200 yards between the halls to the access. If leaving your vehicle overnight, check with campus security.

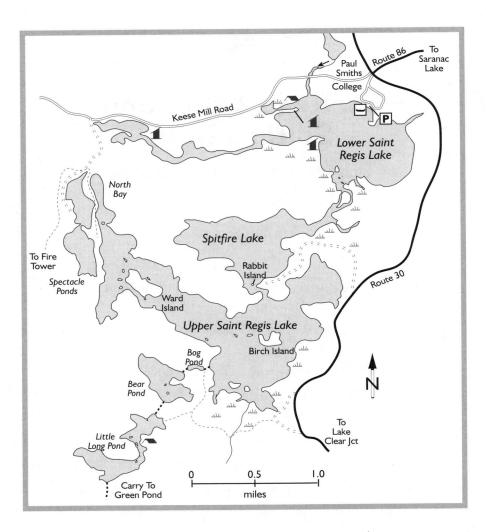

Upper St. Regis Lake. From the junction of Routes 30 and 86, go 3.0 miles south on Route 30, turn right on St. Regis Carry, and go 0.4 mile (3.4 miles) to the access.

From Lake Clear Junction, go 2.9 miles north on Route 30, and turn left on St. Regis Carry.

Lower St. Regis Lake

Lower St. Regis, the northernmost of these lakes, suffers much less from development and sports a more varied habitat, including extensive marshy areas, and several lean-tos for camping. While Paul Smith's College dominates its environs, most of the shoreline remains undeveloped. Botanists will find the small inlet west of the college particularly interesting. Its boggy perimeter harbors a classic northern fen ecosystem, thick with leatherleaf, sheep laurel, bog rosemary, cranberry, sweet gale, sphagnum, pitcher-plant, rose pogonia, and tamarack.

The college gets its name from Paul Smith, who owned thousands of acres in this area. In 1859, Paul Smith opened the Saint Regis House on Lower St. Regis, and it quickly became a playground for the rich and famous, including three U.S. presidents and P. T. Barnum. The original Saint Regis House—commonly known as Paul Smith's—had a modest 17 rooms, but the building mushroomed to a sprawling 225-unit complex by the early 1900s, with gardens, casino, bowling alley, and—for visiting financiers—even a direct line to the New York Stock Exchange.

Much more important than the luxury accommodations of ages past, this area played a role in awakening interest in the environment. In *An Adirondack Passage: The Cruise of the Canoe Sairy Gamp*, Christine Jerome described how the region cemented a young Theodore Roosevelt's interest in natural history into a lifelong commitment that helped usher in this nation's conservation movement. During several visits here as a boy and during a June 1877 visit as a Harvard student, Roosevelt published his observations of the area's bird life in what became his first natural history contribution: *The Summer Birds of the Adirondacks in Franklin County, N.Y.*

Not far from here, 24 years later as vice president of the United States, Teddy Roosevelt climbed the state's highest peak, Mt. Marcy. On the hike back down, he learned that President McKinley had been shot and lay gravely wounded. By the time he reached North Creek by horse, McKinley had died, and Roosevelt became president. Appreciation of the outdoors gained in the Adirondacks no doubt played an important role in his determination to protect the nation's natural treasures—which he did with the creation of the National Park Service and the National Forest System.

A beautiful lean-to perches on Peters Rock, across from Paul Smith's College; several others, all built by college students, occur along the wide, 2-mile-long outlet channel toward Keese Mill. The marshy south end of Lower St. Regis Lake and the channel into Spitfire Lake abound with thick floating vegetation by early summer. Depending on water level, you can explore several navigable channels and islands in the marsh.

Spitfire and Upper St. Regis Lakes

Rabbit Island at Spitfire's south end played a role in important medical research; in 1886, Dr. Edward Livingston Trudeau studied how the environment influenced the spread of tuberculosis within a rabbit colony. The island kept the rabbits—and presumably the disease—isolated, according to the plaque.

Normally, we would not include lakes such as Upper St. Regis and Spitfire because of development, but here you will find classic old Adirondack vacation homes, many dating from the late 1800s, a wilderness retreat for New York's aristocracy, which traveled here by train from Albany and New York City. Architecturally spectacular homes adorn the shoreline, many with large three- or four-bay boathouses that store classic wooden motorboats from the early 1900s. One could spend a day paddling the 11-mile shoreline of these two lakes, gazing at the buildings, whose rustic architecture became known as the Adirondack style.

Summering New York Yacht Club members founded a sailing club on Upper St. Regis in 1897 and designed their own sailboat—the Idem class. With all boats identical, races tested participants' skills, not differences in their boats.

Looking across Upper St. Regis Lake from the carry into Bog Pond and the St. Regis Canoe Area.

Camp Topridge, most grandiose of the estates on Upper St. Regis, occurs on the western arm extending to the north. Marjorie Merriweather Post, heiress of the cereal company that later became General Foods, built the scattered 60 or so buildings in the early 1900s. At one time, the "camp" employed 85 staff. When the mistress of Topridge died in 1973, the heirs gave the property to the state, which then sold it in 1985 for less than $1 million to New Jerseyite Roger Jakubowski, who went bankrupt in 1993. It has since sold to another private owner.

From the end of North Bay, a trail extends around Spectacle Ponds, up to the top of St. Regis Mountain at 2,874 feet. It looks as if the peak's fire lookout tower would provide tremendous views out over the St. Regis Canoe Wilderness Area.

Despite the development, loons nest successfully, as evidenced by the parent with two chicks we watched on our paddle through. To enjoy your time on these lakes, paddle early in the morning, midweek, or before or after the main vacation season.

Gateway to the St. Regis Canoe Area
Near the south end of Upper St. Regis Lake, a carry into Bog Pond and the St. Regis Canoe Wilderness Area begins (see following section). Even when not doing a backcountry trip, we carry into Bear Pond and Little Long Pond to get a sense of the wild, remote country in this spectacular region.

The carries to Bog Pond and Bear Pond—only 50 to 60 yards each— provide a taste of canoe carrying, but not enough to wear you out. Aptly named tiny Bog Pond, with its mucky bottom and shores thick with sheep laurel and other shrubs, also harbors pitcher-plant and other bog vegetation.

By contrast, deeper Bear Pond sparkles with clear water and sections of sandy shore. Huge white pine grows here, along with hemlock, spruce, and balsam fir. We saw a loon and several great blue heron.

47

St. Regis Canoe Area
Santa Clara

Maps: New York Atlas Map 95:B6, USGS Quadrangles St. Regis Mountain and Upper Saranac Lake

Area: St. Regis Pond 383 acres, Hoel Pond 455 acres, Rollins Pond 445 acres, Polliwog Pond 185 acres, Ledge Pond 43 acres

Habitat type: small- to medium-sized ponds connected by short carries, surrounded by boreal forest

Fish: brook, brown, and lake trout; splake; kokanee salmon; largemouth and smallmouth bass; northern pike

Expect to see: osprey, loon, great blue heron, wood duck, muskrat, beaver, deer

Outfitters: St. Regis Canoe Outfitters, canoe rental, 518-891-1838

Camping: on-site wilderness camping

Take note: dozens of ponds in 18,000-acre St. Regis Canoe Wilderness Area covered here

GETTING THERE
Five primary access locations:

Lower St. Regis Lake at Paul Smith's College. See previous section.

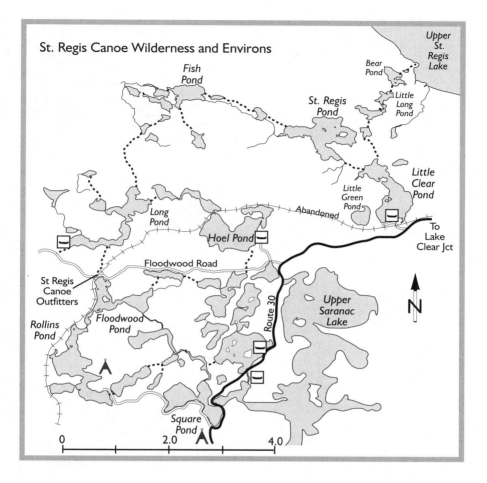

St. Regis Canoe Wilderness and Environs

Upper St. Regis Lake. From the junction of Routes 186 and 30 at Lake Clear Junction, go 2.9 miles north on Route 30, and bear left on access road. Go 0.4 mile (3.3 miles) to access.

Little Clear Pond. From Lake Clear Junction, go 2.5 miles west on Route 30, and turn right at fish hatchery. Follow signs to access.

Hoel Pond. From Lake Clear Junction, go 5.3 miles west on Route 30, and turn right on Floodwood Road. Go 0.3 mile (5.6 miles), and turn right on Hoel Pond Road. Turn left on the access road at the golf course's northern edge.

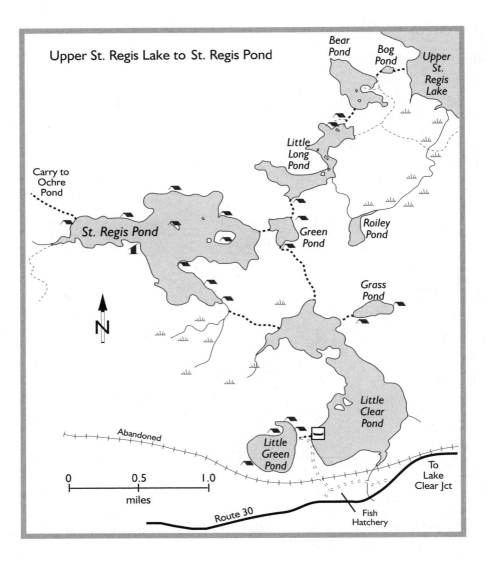

Upper St. Regis Lake to St. Regis Pond

Bear Pond

Bog Pond

Upper St. Regis Lake

Little Long Pond

Carry to Ochre Pond

St. Regis Pond

Green Pond

Roiley Pond

N

Grass Pond

Little Clear Pond

Abandoned

Little Green Pond

0   0.5   1.0
miles

To Lake Clear Jct

Route 30

Fish Hatchery

Long Pond. From Route 30, go 5.0 miles west on Floodwood Road (pass St. Regis Canoe Outfitters on left), and turn right to access. (Carry trail to Long Pond suitable for portage cart; most carries not suitable.)

Wild. Remote. Gorgeous. Pristine. The St. Regis Canoe Area offers the finest backcountry paddling in New York. Fifty-eight lakes and ponds—most accessible by water or short carries—dot the landscape throughout

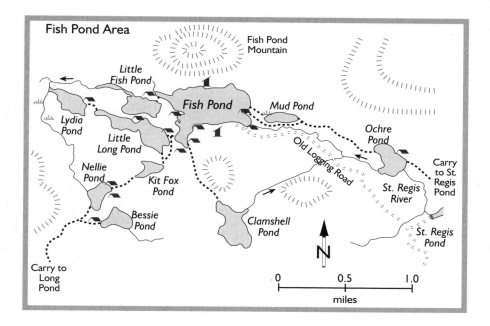

Fish Pond Area

this 18,000-acre wilderness. In the 1970s, the state set aside this part of Adirondack Park for nonmotorized use and temporary (rather than seasonal) camping. The state banned all motorboats, motorized vehicles, airplanes, and snowmobiles from the canoe area.

For the paddler, several excellent trips wend their way through the Canoe Area. You can take a multiday loop or in-and-out trip, but we prefer a through-trip—put in at one location and take out at another. You can use two vehicles or hire an outfitter to shuttle you and your gear.

The most common loop trip winds through Hoel, Turtle, Slang, and Long canoe-area ponds, then through Floodwood, Middle, and Polliwog ponds just to the south. For a through-trip, you can put in or take out on Lower or Upper St. Regis lakes or on Little Clear, Hoel, or Long ponds. For an even more extended trip, you can put in on Rainbow Lake to the northeast or on a number of southern bodies of water, such as Rollins Pond, Fish Creek Pond, or the Saranac Lakes. We describe several routes here.

Upper St. Regis Lake to St. Regis Pond

Though a fairly easy trip, Upper St. Regis Lake into St. Regis Pond involves five relatively short carries. Near St. Regis Lake's south end (see

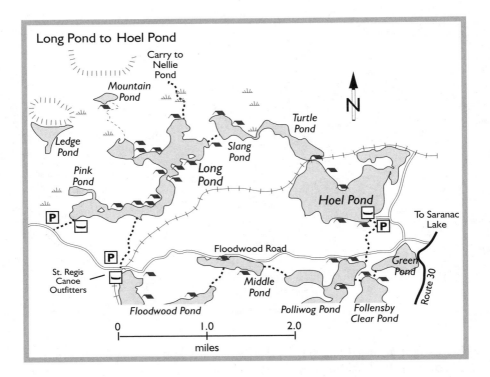

Long Pond to Hoel Pond

previous section), a short carry of about 50 yards leads to Bog Pond, which marks the Canoe Area's northeast end.

Entering tiny Bog Pond, just a few hundred yards long, you initially paddle along a winding channel amid leatherleaf, sheep laurel, pitcher-plant, and other typical bog vegetation. The large number of frogs here—as on most of the area's ponds—surprised us. A quick paddle (longer if you study the plants) brings you to the pond's western end; look for the rectangular white sign marking the carry into Bear Pond.

A short carry brings you into a very different pond, with deep, clear water and sandy shoreline sections. Tall, ancient white pines rise from Bear Pond's picturesque shores. We watched loons dive for fish and great blue herons stalk the shallows. Even if paddling the shoreline and around all the islands, you will quickly reach the next carry—into Little Long Pond.

Though a little longer than the first two—with a bit of up and down—the carry into Little Long Pond remains very manageable (warming you up for more strenuous carries to come). Little Long Pond, with

Small creeks flow between many of the lakes in the St. Regis Canoe Area.

an S-shape about a mile in length, has the highest elevation of any pond in this section. Little Long, Bear, and Bog ponds drain into the St. Regis River Middle Branch, whereas other ponds covered here drain into the St. Regis West Branch or Saranac River.

Conifers, including hemlock, spruce, fir, tamarack, and some towering, wind-sculpted white pine, dominate the Little Long Pond shoreline. Most paddlers choose to push on into St. Regis Pond to camp, rather than take advantage of the several great campsites here. Look for the carry to Green Pond at the pond's southernmost tip. Abundant wildflowers border the carry—we saw pink lady's slipper, trillium, and Indian cucumber root, for example, nestled among the thick clubmoss and hobblebush. The 125-yard trail winds through deep yellow birch-sugar maple-beech woods. On tiny Green Pond—as with quite a few others— you can see the carry sign around to the right before getting in your boat (the trail at the southern tip leads to Little Clear Pond in about three-fifths of a mile).

One of the finest Adirondack camping spots, St. Regis Pond looks a bit like a flying duck, with the bill at the far west end by the dam. From bill tip to tail, the pond ranges for about 1.5 miles. A well-kept shelter perches on the south shore where the pond narrows to the west. The su-perb campsite across from the shelter features a massive slab of granite that extends down into the water, perfect for swimming. To the north, you can see St. Regis Mountain, which rises to 2,874 feet, with a fire lookout tower on top.

Many people know that St. Regis Pond—though a true wilderness pond—provides a wonderful place to camp, with most of the dozen or so campsites frequently in use. For more solitude here, visit after Labor Day, when most summer vacationers (and mosquitoes) have fled.

From St. Regis Pond's southern arm, you can paddle for several hundred yards up the winding inlet creek, an area rich with aquatic veg-etation, including pickerelweed, yellow bladderwort, sundew, pitcher-plant, wild calla or water arum—with heart-shaped leaves somewhat rounder than those of pickerelweed—and yellow pondlily. Sweet gale lines the banks, and feathery spires of tamarack rise from the ground farther back. Paddling up this creek a few hundred yards, you reach a boardwalk extending across the boggy shore from the left—the carry to Little Clear Pond.

Little Clear Pond

Some paddlers reach St. Regis Pond from the access on Little Clear Pond; for others, Little Clear Pond makes a great day trip from St. Regis Pond. The nearly two-thirds-mile carry starts out some-what steeply, with lots of exposed tree roots, then levels out for most of the distance.

From the end of the carry, you can paddle to the right (southwest) into a shallow cattail marsh leading to a small inlet creek. By midsum-mer, dense mats of water shield and other floating vegetation cover the cove's surface. We saw wood ducks here, watched great blue herons hunt methodically, spooked a few painted turtles, and noticed a sizable beaver lodge. Though impossible in summer, it might be possible to paddle up the inlet creek in spring.

Because the fish hatchery uses water from Little Clear Pond, the state prohibits camping and fishing to ensure water quality and to prevent introduction of unwanted fish species, which suits the resident osprey just fine, assuring plenty of fish. Along with osprey, we saw as many as a half-dozen loons here, including one adult with two chicks near the small islands. We were troubled, though, to see one loon with a deformed bill—possible evidence of dioxin or PCB poisoning.

At the north end of Little Clear Pond, a short carry leads to Grass Pond. When we visited, low water levels had exposed a rather unappealing muddy shoreline. If you get a chance, visit the State Fish Hatchery at the south end. The southeast end remains off-limits, so you have to visit from Route 30. You will see mammoth landlocked salmon and brook trout breeding stock, some about two feet long. They even had pails of fish food at some of the tanks for you to feed the fish. The visitor center is a great place to take kids.

Fish Pond Loop

Getting to Fish Pond requires effort, which helps make it such a wonderful spot. You can carry to Fish Pond from Hoel, Long, or St. Regis ponds, each including a somewhat rugged carry of a mile or more. You could use a portage cart along much smoother abandoned logging roads from the dam at St. Regis Pond to Fish Pond—a distance of about 2 miles—but carts are useless elsewhere in the canoe wilderness. Though not possible at times of low water, in the spring it may be possible to paddle or pole a canoe from the dam on St. Regis Pond down the St. Regis West Branch to Ochre Pond.

We describe the carry from St. Regis Pond here. The half-mile carry trail begins near St. Regis Pond's western end, northeast of the dam and involves some up and down, with lots of exposed rocks and roots.

Upon arriving at small Ochre Pond, you can see the next carry sign on the other side. The pond gets its name from the color ochre. Rust-colored deposits form in some mountain lakes when just the right conditions provide a food source for iron-loving bacteria. Acidic bogwater dissolves iron out of rock and soils, putting it in solution as ferrous ion (Fe^{++}). Iron-rich—but oxygen-poor—springwater welling up into oxygen-rich surface water creates just the right environment to support a type of "iron bacterium" that obtains energy by converting ferrous ion and oxygen to ferric oxide (Fe^{+++}) and uses the energy to fix carbon dioxide into organic matter, just as plants convert carbon dioxide and water into organic matter, driven by the sun's energy through photosynthesis. The bacterium-catalyzed reactions precipitate ferric oxide in flocculate orange masses in some areas—including Ochre Pond. Over time, the ferric oxide gradually changes into less hydrated forms, with earthy colors ranging from yellow to red and brown.

Going from Ochre Pond to Fish Pond entails traversing a one and a quarter-mile carry, but over a gorgeous trail, passing along a ridge studded with mammoth old-growth white pine and hemlock. You can carry to Fish Pond or turn off to the right after about two-thirds of a mile into tiny Mud Pond. We carried our gear on to Fish Pond but paddled Mud Pond anyway—and were glad we did.

Alex at the St. Regis Pond end of the carry between Little Clear Pond and St. Regis Pond. The boardwalk protects fragile bog vegetation.

Surrounded by cathedral-like white pine, the shallow pond's rich bog life includes floating logs festooned with fascinating plants: delicate rose pogonia orchid; upright nodding spikes and long, cuplike leaves of carnivorous pitcher-plant; terrestrial horned bladderwort, with small yellow flowers with long drooping spurs (most bladderworts are aquatic); and a low, reddish carpet of sundew, which uses sticky droplets to entrap tiny insects. This floating-log ecosystem really showcases plant adaptation to nutrient-poor environments.

From Mud Pond's western end, a short carry leads to Fish Pond, a spectacular place, less than a mile across, nestled beneath Fish Pond Mountain. Because you will work hard to get here, plan to spend a few days—if you can find an available campsite. We counted two lean-tos and another eight campsites. Enjoy the excellent brook trout and lake trout fishing, as well.

The northwestern cove—by the outlet into Little Fish Pond—offers a great spot to watch beaver. Paddle up here in the evening, and you'll likely see (and hear) this industrious rodent hard at work. On some large boulders extending out of the water here, we watched two large snapping turtles soak up the late afternoon sun. Rarely have we seen snappers

Alex and family on Fish Pond.

sunning—as painted turtles do all the time—yet references in the journal at the Blagden Lean-to lead us to believe that these particular turtles sun themselves frequently. They may be sunning to rid themselves of leeches that attach to their fleshy underparts.

From Fish Pond, you can take wonderful day trips into nearby ponds, including Little Fish, Little Long (a different Little Long Pond from the one described earlier), Lydia, Kit Fox, Nellie, Bessie, and Clamshell.

Reach Little Fish Pond—tranquil and pristine—from near the end of the outlet cove on Fish Pond's northwest end. During an evening paddle on Little Fish Pond, the still air scarcely rippled the water's surface. Leatherleaf, sheep laurel, and bracken and royal ferns line the shrubby shoreline.

Along the southern shore, we saw several freshwater sponge colonies. Though we find sponges (phylum Porifera, loosely aggregated colonies of primitive animals) far more commonly in the ocean, a few freshwater species exist in very pure water. We probably saw *Spongilla lacustris*, which looks more plantlike than animal. Bright green and branching, sponges attach to submerged sticks and rocks. The green color comes from single-celled algae, *Zoochlorellae*, that live symbiotically with the sponge colony. We have seen branching colonies more than a foot in height.

Along Little Fish Pond's southern shore, in a few spots you can walk up and over the steep ridge into Little Long Pond. You can get your boat into Little Long Pond from Fish Pond's southern arm—watch your footing on this short up-and-down carry. Little Long Pond, deep and oligotrophic, had an odd milky-blue color when we visited—quite different from the color of other area ponds. We saw one campsite, roughly centered on the northern shore. A retreating glacier left a deposit of sand and rock there, an esker that now separates Little Long and Little Fish ponds.

The sand suits the snapping turtle very well, as it uses the steep exposed sand banks for building nests. When we visited in mid-July, we saw hundreds of curled pieces of leathery eggshell, likely the remains of nests dug up by raccoon, fox, otter, or some other predator. Very few snapping turtle offspring make it to the water, but the species does well because, once in the water, it may live for 30 or more years, reproducing many times.

Lydia Pond, accessible by carrying from Little Long Pond's western end, lies along the same esker. As on Little Long, we saw evidence of

The conifer canopy and heath-family shrub understory on Little Long Pond is typical of the St. Regis Canoe Area.

snapping turtle nests on the sandy northern shore. Although whitened drift logs blocked further exploration of the marshy outlet at Lydia's west end, we did see rose pogonia, pitcher-plant, sundew, and muskrat here. A lone loon swam about the pond when we visited. The lone campsite on Lydia lies at the end of the carry from Little Long Pond.

A hike into Clamshell Pond makes another pleasant day trip from Fish Pond—with or without canoe. The carry heads south from near the tip of Fish Pond's southern arm (across from the carry into Little Long Pond). The six-tenths of a mile hike has significant ups and downs but winds through beautiful old-growth hemlock and yellow birch—some the largest we have seen.

Occasional boulders dot Clamshell Pond's shoreline and generally sandy bottom, and a mixed hardwood-conifer forest surrounds the pond with white pine, hemlock, northern white cedar, spruce, sugar maple, and yellow birch. Through-paddlers can carry from here down to Turtle and Hoel Ponds, though the Clamshell to Turtle carry is quite long and steep.

The third route out of (or into) Fish Pond, via Kit Fox, Nellie, and Long ponds, proceeds from Fish Pond's south arm. Carry to Little Long, as described earlier, then paddle to Little Long's southern tip to the carry to Kit Fox. Alternatively, from Fish Pond, you can carry all the way to Kit Fox, avoiding a steep trail down into Little Long. The alternate trail to Kit Fox branches off from the trail between Fish and Little Long ponds.

Tiny Kit Fox Pond, an easy carry from Little Long Pond, is well worth exploring. Slowly skirting the perimeter, we happened on a bullfrog bedded down in a soft (sticky) mat of sundew beneath a healthy clump of pitcher-plant atop a floating log. Many ancient logs extended out from shore or floated in the shallow water and muck. The significantly longer carry to Nellie Pond can be quite wet in spring but should be dry in summer. A couple of campsites greet you right as you reach the pond.

The carry you have built up for traverses from Nellie to Long Pond. Only 1.5 miles long, beaver have flooded parts of it. About a tenth of a mile from Nellie, a trail bears sharply left to Bessie Pond, which has a gorgeous campsite on a thick pine-needle carpet. A huge floating log extends 60 or 70 feet into the water from shore, providing a great swimming or fishing platform. If you make two trips at the Long Pond carry, Bessie Pond offers a great midpoint break. One trail section passes through a beautiful pitch pine forest, a very unusual sight in this part of New York. The trail section that passed through a beaver-flooded swamp near the south end provided the greatest surprise, however. You can easily paddle this well-signed, 100-yard section.

Long Pond to Hoel Pond
Reaching 2-mile-long Long Pond by carrying a quarter mile from Floodwood Road requires just enough effort to give one a feeling of accomplishment—but nothing like the achievement of reaching it from Fish Pond! The dozen or so campsites that dot the shoreline spread out enough so that you can find solitude here.

From Long Pond, you can take a pleasant evening or early morning paddle up to Pink Pond, where you should see beaver and other wildlife. Near Long Pond's western end, paddle up the entering creek's narrow channel. When we visited, we carried over a beaver dam almost immediately, then quietly wended our way up into the small pond. The channel banks grow thick with leatherleaf, sheep laurel, sweet gale, royal fern, pickerelweed, wild calla, and grasses and sedges on the many sphagnum hummocks. In the late afternoon, sunlight filters through feathery tamarack branches. The water harbors yellow pondlily, fragrant waterlily, water shield, and long floating leaves of bur-reed.

We had the good fortune to watch a beaver family lazily munching on yellow pondlily stems. Although the adult disappeared as our canoe drifted close, we got a great look at the young, who seemed oblivious to our presence. As evening settled in, we spotted a deer drinking from shore and listened to a white-throated sparrow's melodious song.

From Long Pond's eastern end, you can make a short carry into Slang Pond, where you will find a few campsites. From Slang, you can usually paddle through to Turtle Pond, but at low water, you may have to wade through the shallow passage. The one campsite on Turtle Pond occurs east of the carry to Hoel Pond.

At Turtle Pond's eastern end, you have to carry up over abandoned railroad tracks to get to Hoel Pond. About a mile long and a half mile across, Hoel offers an alternate put-in point for a Canoe Area trip. Because it lies outside the Canoe Wilderness, you will see development and powerboats here. Avoid Hoel Pond under windy conditions, as waves build up very quickly across its broad expanse, and the shoreline affords little protection on most of the pond.

48

Fish Creek Loops
Santa Clara

Maps: New York Atlas Map 95:B5, USGS Quadrangle Upper Saranac Lake

Area: Follensby Clear Pond 491 acres, Rollins Pond 445 acres, Polliwog Pond 185 acres, Ledge Pond 43 acres, Whey Pond 108 acres

Habitat type: small ponds, some connected by streams, surrounded by forest

Fish: brook, brown, and rainbow trout; landlocked and kokanee salmon; largemouth and smallmouth bass; northern pike

Expect to see: great blue heron, loon, beaver

Outfitters: St. Regis Canoe Outfitters, canoe rental and shuttle service, 518-891-1838, www.canoeoutfitters.com

Camping: App. A #76, 85, and on-site wilderness camping

GETTING THERE

Floodwood Pond. From Lake Clear Junction, go 5.3 miles west on Route 30, and turn right on Floodwood Road. Go 4.0 miles (9.3 miles) to the access just short of the canoe outfitter.

Follensby Clear Pond. From Floodwood Road, go south on Route 30 1.6 miles (6.9 miles) or 2.4 miles (7.7 miles) to either of two accesses on the right.

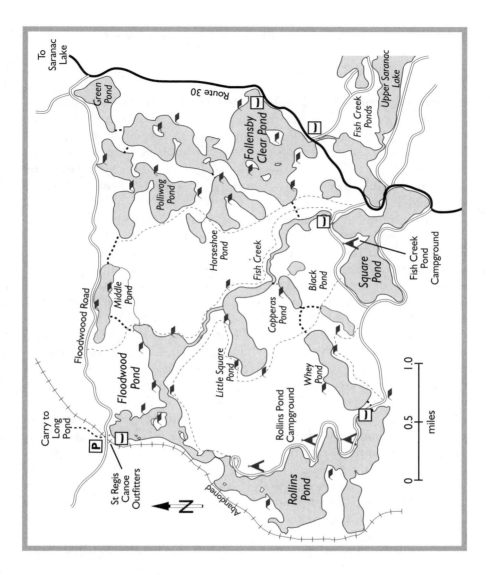

Rollins Pond Campground. Go south on Route 30 from Floodwood Road 4.2 miles (9.5 miles) to the campground entrance on the right.

Fish Creek Loops allow you to paddle a string of ponds with minimal carrying, ending at the starting point. The compact scale of these trips, with just a few short carries, makes them ideal first trips for young paddlers. Our five- and eight-year-old girls did a half-dozen carries superbly and explored nine different ponds during three days and two nights here.

Floodwood Pond—Fish Creek—Whey Pond—Rollins Pond Loop

Several points provide access for this loop trip, as shown on the map. One could camp at Rollins Pond Campground and paddle this loop as a day trip from a lakeside campsite. On a visit in early May, we launched from Floodwood Pond's northern tip, paddled to the large island, and set up base camp from which we explored this loop, as well as the loop described below.

We recommend traveling clockwise, which permits paddling downstream on Fish Creek, rather than against the light current between Floodwood and Little Square ponds. Starting on Rollins Pond, paddle north from the campground (or from one of the primitive campsites along the western shore). At the northern end, paddle to the east (right). The pond narrows to a small stream, which connects to Floodwood. In May, the stream floated our boat, though we had to lie down to maneuver under a fallen birch tree and had to drag our canoe over a small beaver dam. Later in the season, you usually need to carry along a small portage trail on the left bank. Look for a path leading off to the left as the pond narrows to a stream. If you paddle through, watch for rocks.

Floodwood's narrow western end, with an abandoned railway bed on the north, also has a few vacation houses along the shore—the only ones you will encounter on this trip. As with most ponds here, it has a fairly sandy bottom and not too many rocks. The shoreline's thick understory makes landing a canoe just anywhere out of the question, though the woods opens up as it rises from the water. Hemlock, white pine, yellow birch, white birch, beech, and sugar maple predominate. Because the area has not been logged for more than 100 years, some hemlock has grown to huge size.

Red pine and hemlock—both providing an open, accessible forest floor—dominate Floodwood's large island, with campsites and outhouses scattered about. When we camped here, merlins nested in one of the island's tall pines. Their cries advertised their presence many times during our two-night stay. This relatively rare falcon looks very much like a peregrine, but about half the size—just slightly larger than a more common falcon, the kestrel. We watched with binoculars as one devoured a small rodent 50 feet up on a dead snag.

Floodwood resembles a butterfly, with Fish Creek flowing out the eastern wing's bottom lobe toward Little Square, Copperas, and Fish Creek ponds. Fish Creek's first section—between Floodwood and Little Square ponds—flows shallow and quick, though without rapids. Rocks and many logs provide an obstacle course of sorts. In times of low water, passage may be difficult. Shortly after leaving Floodwood, pass under a wooden hiking-snowmobile bridge. In several places, kind souls have notched out large submerged logs to provide passage. We had to squeeze over a couple of tiny beaver dams when we visited.

Be sure not to rush through too fast. Beautiful Fish Creek winds through quite varied vegetation. In some sections, the streambed meanders through shaded woodland, with trees overhanging the channel. In other places, it winds through marsh thick with grasses, sedges, and cattails, where you can expect to startle a great blue heron from its patient fishing. Everywhere in the gently flowing stream you will see yellow pond-lilies and various other floating and emergent aquatic plants. Leatherleaf—with its small leathery leaves and drooping clusters of small white, inconspicuous bell-like flowers—dominates most of the shoreline.

About a half mile below Floodwood, Fish Creek flows into Little Square Pond's eastern end. If west winds do not blow too strongly, you may want to explore this pond, but each time we paddled here the waves coming off Little Square Pond discouraged us from more thorough exploration.

Below Little Square Pond, Fish Creek widens, and the vegetation becomes more fenlike, with feathery tamarack, particularly along the western shore. On the sphagnum tussocks, watch for carnivorous pitcher-plants. As the channel begins to narrow again, keep an eye out for the narrow stream heading off right to Copperas Pond. You can easily miss this turn in the summer when thick pond vegetation covers the surface. Paddle southwest through Copperas to the carry into Whey Pond. Conspicuous rectangular white signs and yellow trail markers point the way to and down all the carries. The trail to Whey Pond heads due west from the takeout; another trail from the same point leads south into Black Pond.

Like most carries on park lands, the Whey Pond carry traverses the terrain gently, through thick beds of wildflowers, ferns, and clubmosses. Although paddling your boat is distinctly easier than carrying it, the carries provide a chance to stretch your legs, to exercise your sore buns, to enjoy the woods from a distinctly different perspective, and to study

A portage cart makes light work on a carry, as Lillian and Francis demonstrate.

wildflowers—particularly when bugs do not patrol the woods. During an early visit, with huge velvety buds of hobblebush just beginning to unfurl, the yellow bell-like flowers of trout lily bloomed fully.

Whey Pond, just less than 1 mile long, runs in a northeast-southwest orientation. At the southwest end, look for the carry sign to Rollins Pond. Of the two carries there, the southern one is shorter and ends at a boat launch on Rollins, whereas the other empties onto the campground road.

Rollins Pond, much larger than the other ponds on this loop, can become quite choppy on a windy day, so use caution. Do not expect solitude, as 288 campsites line the eastern shore. The campground offers an attractive setting, with ample room between sites. To get the most out of a paddle on Rollins Pond, though, stick to the western shore, where you can escape into several deep coves—or paddle here early in the season before it opens.

Follensby Clear Pond—Polliwog Pond—
Floodwood Pond—Fish Creek Loop

This trip covers six ponds connected by Fish Creek and by four relatively short carries. The carries, though somewhat longer and a bit steeper than those in the preceding section, still allow you to do the loop as a day trip. Camping opportunities abound on Follensby Clear Pond, and several campsites nestle along the shores of most other ponds. Or you can camp at Fish Creek Pond Campground and paddle north into Follensby Clear Pond, via the Spider Creek Passage.

Starting at Floodwood, paddle southeast into Fish Creek. Pass through Little Square Pond's eastern end, and continue in a generally southeastern direction, keeping an eye out for the carry to Follensby Clear Pond on the left. A wooden boardwalk extends out into the water, but vegetation may hide it by early summer. Ferns, clubmosses, and wildflowers line the quarter-mile trail to perhaps the prettiest pond in this area, Follensby Clear Pond, which remains our favorite.

Seven islands, most with campsites, dot the 2-mile-long pond's surface. Several sites sport sandy beaches, topping off the wilderness splendor. Hemlock, its shade providing an open, inviting woodland and its needles leaving a soft, footstep-quieting carpet, dominates the forest. We paddled alone here, sharing the water only with loon and merganser.

After paddling north through the pond's narrowest part, you can get to Horseshoe Pond by paddling into the cove on the left. A well-marked and very short carry over a slight rise brings you to true-to-its-name Horseshoe Pond. Several campsites cluster near the portage trail, and one lies directly across.

Near Follensby Clear Pond's northwest end, look for a somewhat hidden carry to Polliwog Pond. The beautiful trail passes through old-growth hemlock forest. Although timber companies clear-cut much of the Adirondacks in the mid-1800s, about 60,000 acres remain as virgin forest, some of those acres right here. Since 1892, no logging has occurred on public lands in the park, thus returning much more of the forest to old-growth. The carry into Polliwog Pond will give you a sense of what virgin forest looks and feels like. Note the standing dead trees, the moss-covered logs slowly rotting into the ground, the tremendous variation in tree age, and the high plant-species diversity.

Polliwog Pond has a sandy bottom, and several campsites offer beautiful sand beaches. Depending on water level, the point of land to the left

A northern water snake suns on a dense patch of aquatic vegetation. It swims underwater to catch small fish.

after you enter the pond will either be a peninsula or an island. Another peninsula comes in from the west across the pond. To paddle through to Middle Pond, pass through a narrow section of Polliwog into the pond's western extension. At the western end, you will see the sign marking the carry to Middle Pond. The exception that proves the rule about gentle carries, this trail goes up and down somewhat steeply for a third of a mile—again, passing through gorgeous, deep woods.

A westerly breeze can generate surprisingly large waves on Middle Pond, with its long, narrow, east-west orientation. One campsite perches along Floodwood Road, with another on the south side. Tree swallows patrolled the air, swooping for flying insects, then returning to dead trees that no doubt provide nesting sites. A solitary loon, clearly oblivious to the cold wind and choppy waves, dove for fish near the pond's center. Watch for the carry to Floodwood Pond along the south shore about three-quarters of the way up this pond. This final carry in the loop starts out steeply but then becomes an easy walk.

49

Middle Saranac Lake
Harrietstown and Santa Clara

Maps: New York Atlas Map 95:B6, USGS Quadrangles Saranac Lake, Tupper Lake, Upper Saranac Lake

Area: 1,393 acres, maximum depth 20 feet

Habitat type: large lake with marshy coves and outlet stream

Fish: largemouth and smallmouth bass, northern pike

Expect to see: osprey, loon, waterfowl, great blue heron

Camping: App. A #86 (wilderness on-site camping)

Take note: treacherous paddling under windy conditions

GETTING THERE

From the stoplight in Saranac Lake, go 9.7 miles west on Route 3 to the South Creek access on the left.

From Tupper Lake, go east on Routes 3 and 30; when the roads divide, go 5.4 miles on Route 3 to the South Creek access on the right.

The middle of three Saranac lakes remains the least heavily traveled because of more difficult access. You can launch from the South Creek hand-carry access on Route 3, or carry the half mile through Bartlett Carry from Upper Saranac Lake, or pass through the lock that connects Middle and Lower Saranac lakes. Middle Saranac lies along two popular long-distance canoe routes. One comes down from the hamlet of Saranac Inn, traversing the length of Upper Saranac to Bartlett Carry, east to Middle Saranac, through the outlet stream into Lower Saranac,

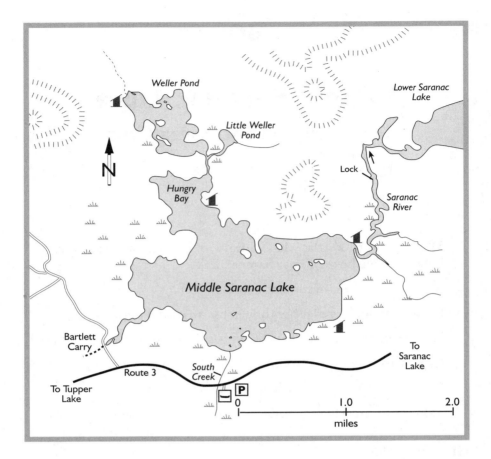

and then either directly to Saranac Lake town or through Ossetah Lake to the town site. The second route travels the length of Long Lake to Axton Landing, up through Stony Creek Ponds, with a three-quarter-mile carry to Upper Saranac, a 2-mile paddle to Bartlett Carry, finishing as previously.

Launching from the South Creek access, we could not resist paddling up South Creek through a cedar-lined beaver swamp. We carried over a few beaver dams but decided not to clamber over the downed timber that clogs the waterway.

Resist the temptation to bolt out onto the lake. Take the time to study the South Creek channel. We found huge pitcher-plant clumps perched precariously on sphagnum hummocks, trying to elbow the ubiquitous leatherleaf out of the way. In all of our travels throughout New York, this may be the easiest place to view pitcher-plants from a boat.

Tamarack, northern white cedar, and black spruce have invaded the sphagnum bog as it makes the gradual transition from wetland to upland. Eventually, trees crowd out the sheep laurel, leatherleaf, bog rosemary, sweet gale, winterberry, and pitcher-plant, and decaying vegetation builds up an overlying soil.

Even though traversing the lock from Lower Saranac into Middle Saranac remains a popular pastime for motorboaters, Middle Saranac retains a wilderness character, mostly because of lack of development along the shore. The state owns about three-quarters of the shoreline, starting at the southwest corner of Hungry Bay, moving clockwise up through Weller and Little Weller Ponds, down along the northern shore through the lock into Lower Saranac, down the eastern shore of Middle Saranac, and around the southern shore, stopping just short of the South Creek entrance.

Paddling clockwise around the lake, note the many conifer species lining the shore, the few, small birches fast disappearing as beaver cut them down to drag to their lakeside lodges for winter food. We wonder whether the preponderance of white pine, northern white cedar, tamarack, hemlock, and spruce along the shore results from selective cutting by beaver. We also noted the conspicuous browse line on the shoreline cedars, where deer sliding along the ice gnawed on low-hanging branches.

As you paddle the lake's western end—most of its cedar-clad shore owned by the Bartlett Carry Company—look back east and savor the view of saw-toothed peaks in the McKenzie Mountain Wilderness. The protected coves contain patches of pickerelweed, pondweed, and water celery, as well as feeding ducks. Paddling here in fall, we found many loons in twos and threes and hundreds of ducks feeding furiously in protected coves, trying to gain a few last ounces of fat to fuel their migratory flight.

Weller and Little Weller ponds—the most interesting, secluded, and scenic portions of the lake—harbor a sea of aquatic vegetation among the many side channels, coves, and islands. Tamarack, a deciduous conifer with golden needles in the fall, has invaded the marsh, and leatherleaf lines the waterways. Cedar and scrub birch along shore give way to conifer-clad hillsides. Wildlife abounds—from frogs to great blue heron, from red-winged blackbird to beaver, from yellow-rumped warbler to belted kingfisher—and one can enjoy it in quiet seclusion. As you paddle back to the main lake, Stony Creek and Ampersand mountains dominate the skyline, but you can also see several other peaks, including a few in the distant High Peaks Wilderness.

A marshy area also exists along the narrow connecting river between Middle and Lower Saranac lakes. The channel rules include a 5-mile-per-hour speed limit, so you should keep your speed down when passing motorboats. You can explore side channels during high water, carrying up over beaver dams, where you will see lots of wildlife, including wood, black, mallard, teal, and ring-necked ducks. We listened to the strange American bittern call ("woooom-pah-pah") as we paddled back in and saw yellowlegs and spotted sandpipers.

When you get to the lock, you have four choices: turn around, go through the lock, carry around, or run the river to the right at medium to high water. Scout it first because of boulders and a sharp left turn at the bottom of the run. The lock intrigued us because of its counter-weighted wood construction and hand operation. In the off-season, you can operate it yourself, following posted instructions.

View of Adirondack High Peaks from the lock that separates Middle and Lower Saranac lakes.

50

Lower Saranac Lake
Harrietstown

Maps: New York Atlas Map 95:B7, USGS Quadrangle Saranac Lake

Area: 2,214 acres, maximum depth 60 feet

Habitat type: large, island-filled lake with deep coves

Fish: largemouth and smallmouth bass, northern pike

Expect to see: osprey, loon, waterfowl, great blue heron

Camping: App. A #86 (wilderness on-site camping)

Take note: treacherous paddling under windy conditions

GETTING THERE

From the stoplight in Saranac Lake, go 5.0 miles west on Route 3 to the Second Pond access on the left. Paddle under the Route 3 bridge to the left.

From Tupper Lake, go east on Routes 3 and 30; when the roads divide, go 11.0 miles on Route 3 to the Second Pond access on the right.

You will encounter more boat traffic here than on Middle Saranac. Trailers often jam the large Second Pond fishing access parking lot. You can also launch at the much-less-used South Creek access on Middle Saranac Lake, then paddle into the lower lake. Despite the motorboat traffic, Lower Saranac presents a wonderful, historic place to paddle, especially because the state owns the vast majority of shoreline surrounding it and First and Second ponds.

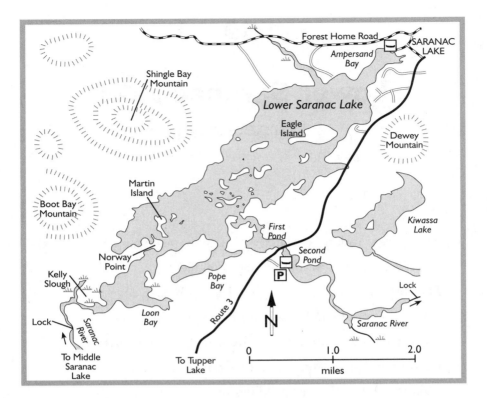

Much of the early guide lore and its literature took place on the Saranac lakes, which served as a gateway to all northern Adirondack drainages. This should not be surprising, given the area's central location, its linkages to other river and lake systems, and its beauty. The surrounding Adirondack peaks form a dramatic backdrop, providing many hiking trails for those seeking a wilderness experience.

Many islands dot Lower Saranac's surface, breaking up the view, making it seem much smaller than its large area would indicate. These same islands provide many beautiful campsites and block the wind—indeed, winds can pose more of a problem on smaller, but less protected, Middle Saranac.

Because development on Lower Saranac concentrates at the northeast end, we focused on the southern half and the winding coves and bays to the southwest. It takes quite a while to explore fully the lake's 17 miles of shoreline and many islands—making this a great location for a several-day vacation, especially off-season.

Views of the Adirondack tall peaks lend scenic character to Lower Saranac Lake.

At the Second Pond access, note the many towering hemlock; on the pond, northern white cedar dominates the shoreline, joined by an occasional birch and a few very tall white pine. From here, paddle northwest onto First Pond and work your way out onto Lower Saranac. Continuing left, you eventually reach the Saranac River lock leading to Middle Saranac. As the lake narrows into the Saranac River inlet, quite a contrast unfolds: sheer, cedar-clad cliffs stand guard on the left, while flat, bird-filled marshes spread out on the right. When we paddled here, red-winged blackbird, Eastern kingbird, and ducks filled the marsh with their spring songs. Ring-billed ducks scattered into the emerging marsh vegetation in Kelly Slough.

We heard or saw Eastern phoebe, chickadee, crow, winter wren, hermit thrush, spotted sandpiper, grackle, yellow-rumped and black-throated green warblers, black and ring-billed ducks, robin, red-eyed vireo, and white-throated and song sparrows.

When we paddled here, negligible winds allowed us to meander around the islands, enjoying the emerging spring plants and the gorgeous mountainside scenery.

51

Raquette River
Harrietstown

Maps: New York Atlas Map 95:C6, USGS Quadrangle Tupper Lake

Length: 10 miles

Habitat type: slow-flowing, marshy river

Fish: smallmouth bass, walleye, northern pike

Expect to see: waterfowl, great blue heron, beaver, deer

Outfitters: Raquette River Outfitters, canoe/kayak rental and shuttle service, 518-359-3228, www.raquetteriveroutfitters.com

Camping: on-site wilderness camping

Take note: to run Raquette River, use Jamieson and Morris, *Adirondack Canoe Waters: North Flow*, 3rd edition (Adirondack Mountain Club, 1988)

GETTING THERE

Routes 3. From the stoplight in Tupper Lake, go 3.9 miles east to the access on the right.

Axton Landing. From the junction of Routes 3 and 30 east of Tupper Lake, go 2.4 miles east on Route 3, and turn right on Coreys Road. Go 2.2 miles (4.6 miles) on a rough road to the access.

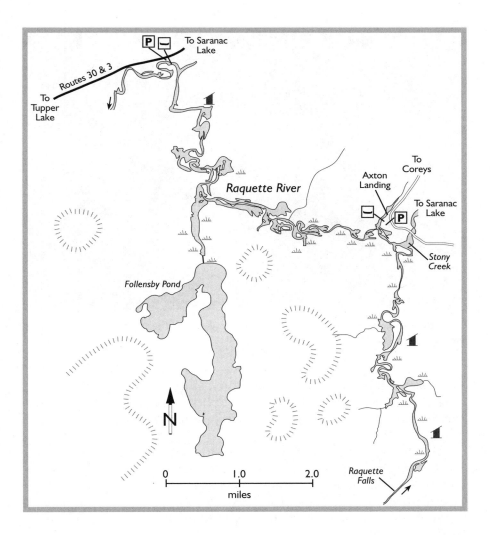

Long Lake. Long-distance paddlers can paddle from Long Lake, carrying around Raquette Falls, taking out at either access, or continuing through Stony Ponds to Upper Saranac Lake.

The Raquette ("rocket"), second longest river in New York, features prominently in early Adirondack lore, from Ralph Waldo Emerson's poem "The Adirondacs" about his explorations in 1858, to Nessmuk's (George Washington Sears) voyages in J. Henry Rushton's 10-pound

Black ducks, along with many other species, nest and feed in the marshes along the Raquette River.

Sairy Gamp in the late nineteenth century, to the Old Forge-to-Saranac-Lake guide-boat race of this century. Still very popular today, the Raquette accommodates many paddlers in July and August.

We chose the section between Raquette Falls and the Route 3 access east of Tupper Lake because of its slowly meandering wilderness character, where one sometimes questions current direction. Jamieson and Morris in *Adirondack Canoe Waters: North Flow* say that a dam only 10 feet high constructed in Piercefield in 1870 flooded the valley for nearly 30 miles, all the way back to Raquette Falls near Long Lake. Fifteen years later, after many protests, they lowered the dam to where it stands today. During times of high water, much of the formerly flooded marshland becomes accessible by boat again for a short time.

The state owns both sides of the river between Route 3 and a mile or so upstream of Follensby Pond outlet. After that, up to Raquette Rapids, the state owns only the eastern shore. The High Peaks Wilderness Area borders the river's eastern shore upstream from Axton Landing.

One could spend days here, exploring the oxbows and inlets, the braided channels and side streams, watching the professorial great blue heron preside over the marsh, stealthily hunting fish, frogs, and indeed anything that moves. The channel turns back on itself over and over, occasionally doubling or even tripling the water distance between two points. Ducks erupt from the water's surface as you round the bend, startling you as much as you startle them.

Flooding of more than a century ago killed the large trees that lined the banks, although some tall white pine and relatively large northern white cedar have grown back. Today, streamside silver maple provides forage for many beaver. Watch for the large number of beaver dams on inflows and side channels. Carry up over and explore in quiet seclusion, away from motorboats that occasionally roar around the bend. We found anglers to be quite courteous toward paddlers . . . if they see you!

We particularly enjoyed, as did Emerson nearly 150 years ago in a guide boat, paddling up the expansive marshy connector to Follensby Pond, where he camped for a few weeks in August 1858, under some huge pine and maple.

> *Next morn, we swept with oars the Saranac,*
> *With skies of benediction, to Round Lake [Middle Saranac],*
> *Tahawus, Seward, MacIntyre, Baldhead,*
> *And other titans without muse or name.*
> *Pleased with these grand companions, we glide on,*
> *Instead of flowers, crowned with a wreath of hills,*
> *And made our distance wider, boat from boat,*
> *As each would hear the oracle alone.*
> *By the bright morn the gay flotilla slid*
> *Through files of flags that gleamed like bayonets,*
> *Through gold-moth-haunted beds of pickerel-flower,*
> *Through scented banks of lilies white and gold,*
> *Where the deer feeds at night, the teal by day,*
> *On through Upper Saranac, and up*
> *Pere Raquette stream, to a small tortuous pass*
> *Winding through grassy shallows in and out,*
> *Two creeping miles of rushes, pads, and sponge,*
> *To Follansbee Water, and the Lake of Loons.*

EMERSON, POEMS (Houghton Mifflin, 1904)

Although Follensby Pond remains off-limits, one can explore the outflow creek. You will need a map and compass to find it; if you succeed, you will not regret it. Paddling upstream, look for a broad, marshy expanse to the right as the river curves left. As you enter, paddle over barely submerged posts of a long-abandoned bridge, back into a broad expanse of pickerelweed and other aquatic vegetation. Grasses line the banks, and many ducks raise their broods, fattening them up for fall migration. Paddling here in fall, we saw many black duck—the smaller wood duck and teal having migrated earlier. The biggest flock numbered about 30.

Two shelters perch on the bank where indicated on the map. Several other obvious camping spots—flat, grassy, needle-carpeted—beckon from under hemlock and pine. We saw little other evidence of human activity, save two rope swings hanging from birches.

52

Lows Lake
(Bog River Flow)
Clifton, Colton, Long Lake, and Piercefield

Maps: New York Atlas Map 94:D3, USGS Quadrangles Little Tupper Lake and Wolf Mountain

Area: 2,845 acres, maximum depth 55 feet, average depth 5.2 feet

Habitat type: long, narrow, shallow, marshy pond

Fish: brook trout, largemouth bass

Expect to see: osprey, loon, waterfowl, spruce grouse, raven, beaver, deer

Camping: on-site wilderness camping

Take note: west winds can make paddling hazardous; to run the Bog River down to Tupper Lake, use Jamieson and Morris, *Adirondack Canoe Waters: North Flow*, 3rd edition (Adirondack Mountain Club, 1988)

GETTING THERE

From Route 30 north of Long Lake or south of Tupper Lake, go 5.8 miles west on Route 421, and turn left on the Lows Lower Dam access road. Go 0.7 mile (6.5 miles) to the access.

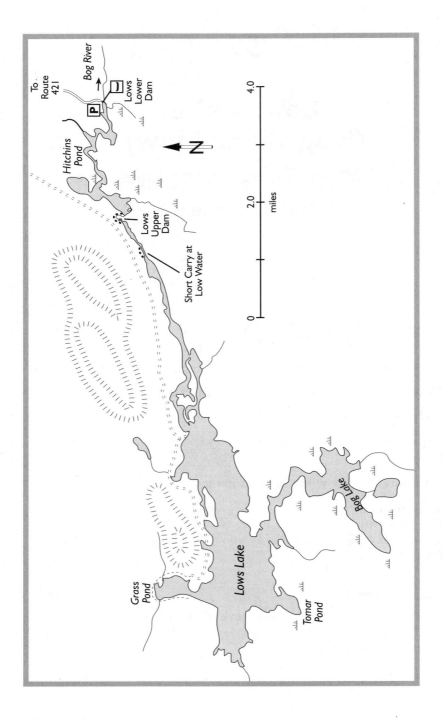

Bog River Flow and its lakes and ponds, islands and shores, floating bogs and surrounding forests represent an extraordinary paddling resource. Two dams built by A. A. Low in 1903 and 1907 provide sufficient water to allow a 14.5 mile paddle from the lower dam to the main lake's west end. A 3-plus mile trail through the woods connects the far western end with the upper reaches of the Oswegatchie River East Branch. The violent windstorm that swept through the Adirondacks in mid-July 1995 downed thousands of trees, since removed, that blocked the trail.

Thirty-nine numbered campsites, available on a first-come basis, provide wonderful camping opportunities. Check the bulletin board at the access for campsite locations. If required, you may camp at non-designated sites, but only on state land, which increased by 1,000 acres in 2006. The state restricts parties to nine but encourages six or fewer to reduce impact on fragile bog habitat. This popular recreation destination suffers from too many paddlers in summer. We recommend paddling here on weekdays during summer or in spring or fall.

Tall spruce and pine perch precariously on huge granite boulders that line the narrow passageway leading out from Lows Lower Dam at the flow's east end. Mosses, lichens, and ferns cling to rock faces, and pine needles carpet the forest floor.

Bears patrol the shores and islands, looking for an invitation to destroy food bags and coolers left carelessly lying about. Searching dense conifer stands might turn up a spruce grouse, the ruffed grouse's increasingly rare northern cousin. Spruce grouse often stand out in plain view, allowing humans to approach closely, which probably explains a lot about their reduced numbers. Ravens appear in pairs, croaking out their hoarse cries. When we paddled here, we saw lots of deer, as well. In the not-too-distant past, one might have seen a rare golden eagle soaring overhead, along with much more common osprey.

Perhaps most impressive, however, is the loon population—the state's largest—that inhabits the far reaches of the flowage's ponds. Loons suffer from human disturbance: boat wakes drown their nests, lead sinkers poison them, and repeated encounters with humans drive them away. Fortunately, the Department of Environmental Conservation excludes motors between Lows Lower and Upper Dams. The upper lake borders the Five Ponds Wilderness Area, and we hope the state will include it in the wilderness someday, which would eliminate all motors.

We saw many other species in our all-too-brief stay in this wildlife paradise. We noted a large number of beaver lodges, along with

The common loon, *Gavia immer*, inhabits most large lakes in the Adirondacks.

mounds of fresh cuttings set aside as winter food. One enterprising beaver had just downed a large paper birch. Given that beaver prefer deciduous trees, probably because of the resins in conifers, one wonders why they eat so much resinous paper birch. Firewood users know that unsplit paper birch logs rot from the inside out in short order, because the resinous bark does not allow moisture to escape. Beaver also trim the leaves and twigs from branch ends to lessen drag as they swim, sometimes for long distances, back to their lodges.

After a short carry around Lows Upper Dam and about a mile paddle, we reached a floating bog blocking the narrow channel leading to the main lake. In high water, you can probably paddle over or around it, but we had to carry around it on the north, taking care not to harm the fragile sphagnum mat with its few dwarf tamarack, along with sundew, pitcher-plant, leatherleaf, sweet gale, and other bog specialists.

Spirelike spruce and balsam fir ring the main lake's shore, providing habitat for spruce grouse and many other species. Appropriately enough, an extensive sphagnum bog guards the entrance to Bog Lake. Scattered tamarack and a carpet of leatherleaf cover the bog, along with sweet gale and grasses around the edges. A great blue heron watched warily as we paddled by, and an osprey wheeled overhead. This extraordinarily rich and varied habitat, filled with myriad plants and wildlife, offers one of the finest paddling experiences in the Adirondacks.

A tall beaver dam holds back the water on a tributary just upstream from the access.

The St. Lawrence County Historical Association, in January 1974, chronicled the enterprises of A. A. Low. Built in 1903 and 1907 by Low, the dams generated electricity for the small enclave and for Low's residence on nearby Lake Marian and provided water for log drives. Low owned 40,000 acres, which he used to produce timber and maple syrup. He tapped more than 10,000 maple trees and produced 20,000 gallons of maple syrup in the peak year of 1907. An innovator, Low used tubs, pipes, and troughs to bring sap to railcars to transport to his huge evaporator. He held more than 200 patents, several on sap-boiling devices. He also held a patent on a square bottle used to package virgin Adirondack forest springwater that he sent off to New York City. His company, the Horseshoe Forestry Company, met its demise in the devastating fire of 1908. Low died in 1912.

The historical association's account of this amazingly accomplished man ended with these words: "In life his aim had been to develop, improve, and utilize the fruits of his mountain empire without despoiling it. His spirit roams the Bog River Valley. Today it must be pleased that two monuments to his enterprise still stand tall and proud after more than 60 [now 100] years. They are the two dams. . . ."

The Loon

Voice of the Northern Wilderness

No animal better symbolizes wilderness than the loon, whose haunting cry resonates through the night air on many northern New York ponds. The bird seems almost mystical, with its distinctive black-and-white plumage, daggerlike bill, and piercing red eyes. But like our remaining wilderness, the loon is threatened over much of its range. As recreational pressures on lakes and ponds increase, the loon gets pushed father away. We who share its waters bear responsibility for protecting this wonderful bird.

A northern wilderness symbol, the common loon, *Gavia immer,* is one of the most extraordinary birds you will ever encounter. A large diving bird that lives almost its entire life in water, it visits land only to mate and to lay and incubate eggs. The loon has adapted remarkably well to water. Unlike most birds, it has solid bones, enabling it to dive to great depths. It also has an internal air sac that controls how high it floats. By compressing this sac, a loon can submerge gradually, with barely a ripple, or swim along with just its head above water.

Its heavy body and rearward legs make takeoff difficult. A loon may require a quarter mile of open water to build up enough speed to lift off, and it may have to circle a small lake several times to gain enough altitude to clear nearby hills. When migrating, a loon flies rapidly—as fast as 90 miles per hour—but cannot soar.

The loon generally mates for life and can live for 30 years. The female lays two eggs in early May, and both male and female—indistinguishable to the casual observer—take turns incubating the oblong, moss-green eggs. Because the loon's rearward legs preclude walking, it always builds its nest very close to shore—where a passing paddler can scare birds away and a motorboat wake can flood the nest with cold water. The loon most often nests on islands to hide the eggs from predators, such as raccoons and skunks. On some lakes, you will see floating platforms constructed to improve nesting success. On reservoirs with varying water levels, these platforms take on special importance because they rise and fall with water level, reducing the likelihood of flooding or stranding a nest.

Loon chicks hatch fully covered in black down and usually enter the water a day after hatching. Young chicks often ride on a parent's back to conserve heat and to avoid predators. They grow quickly on a diet of small fish and crustaceans; by two weeks of age, they have grown to half the size of the adult and can dive to relatively deep lake bottoms, covering more than 30 yards underwater. Loon chicks remain totally dependent on their parents, however, for about 8 weeks and do not fly until 10 to 12 weeks of age. After leaving the nest a day after hatching, loons do not return to land for three or four years—until they reach breeding age. Young mature on the sea, having followed their elders to saltwater wintering areas.

Though New York lists the species as one of "special concern," the loon remains fairly plentiful in parts of the Adirondacks. The last statewide survey in 1984–1985 found more than 700 loons on 518 surveyed lakes, including 157 breeding pairs with 197 chicks. Of those lakes with breeding loons, 95 percent had only one pair, though a few lakes had more—notably Stillwater Reservoir with 15 pairs and Lows Lake with 6. By extrapolating the results to unsurveyed lakes, the state estimated a total population of as many as 1,000 adults and 270 breeding pairs. Though no statewide survey has been conducted since then, loon biologists believe that the population has increased somewhat. Despite this generally good news, we should remain concerned about the loon. As development encroaches on our lakes and as recreational use increases, recent population trends could well reverse.

Because paddlers can easily disturb loons when nesting, watch for warning displays during nesting season, early May though mid-July. If a nest fails, loons may try up to two more times, though the later a chick hatches, the lower its chances of survival. Keep away from loons and nest sites to help ensure their survival.

The loon has lived in this area longer than any other bird—an estimated 60 million years. Let's make sure this wonderful species remains protected so future generations may listen to its enchanting music on a still, moonlit night. For more information, visit the website of the Adirondack Cooperative Loon Program at www.adkscience.org/loons.

53

Lake Lila
Long Lake

Maps: New York Atlas Maps 86:A2 and 94:D3, USGS Quadrangles Beaver River, Forked Lake, Little Tupper Lake, Wolf Mountain

Area: 1,490 acres, maximum depth 64 feet

Habitat type: shallow wilderness lake

Fish: brook and lake trout, landlocked salmon, smallmouth bass

Expect to see: osprey, loon, beaver

Camping: 24 on-site wilderness campsites

Take note: suffers from overuse in midsummer

GETTING THERE

From the junction of Routes 3 and 30 in Tupper Lake, go 11.3 miles south on Route 30, and turn right on Sabbatis Circle Road. Go 3.0 miles (14.3 miles), and bear right on Sabbatis Road. Go 4.8 miles (19.1 miles), turn left, and go 5.9 miles (25.0 miles) to the access.

From Long Lake at the junction of Routes 30 and 28N, go 7.2 miles north on Route 30, and turn left on Sabbatis Road. Go 3.0 miles (10.2 miles), bear left on Sabbatis Road, and follow as earlier.

Autumn-hued foliage of beech, sugar and red maples, paper and yellow birches reflected off the glasslike surface of Lake Lila. Wisps of mist rose gently into a cloudless sky, burned off the lake's surface by the rising

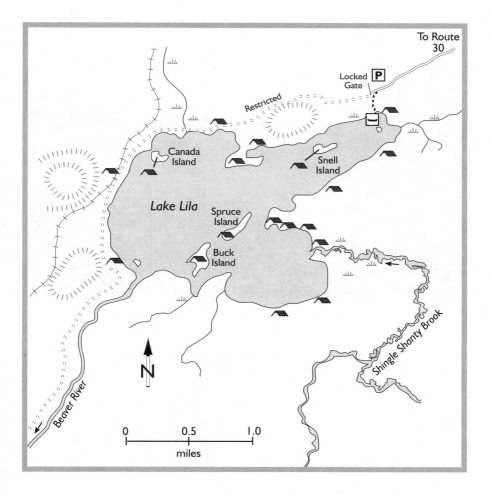

sun, as we paddled out early one October morning. We paddled alone—not surprising this late in the season.

The state owns the entire shoreline of this wonderful place and prohibits motors in the William C. Whitney Wilderness Area, which encompasses the entire lake. Great campsites exist all around the lake's perimeter and on some islands. Shingle Shanty Brook offers hours of pleasant diversion, and Beaver River can be paddled down to the falls, about halfway to Nehasane Lake, which lies about 2 miles to the southwest. Intrepid explorers can paddle through Nehasane

Mists lift from the waters of Lake Lila near the access at sunrise.

all the way to Stillwater Reservoir, at least during high water. Clear water makes it possible to avoid barely submerged boulders that rush up to greet your hull.

Rocks, shrubs, and tall white pine dominate Lake Lila's shoreline, along with occasional stands of red pine, spruce, northern white cedar, red maple, and a few mountain maple. Pine and paper birch cover the islands. In contrast to the lakeshore, deciduous trees dominate the hillsides, along with some dense conifer patches.

Yellow-rumped warblers searched for insects, still fattening up for their fall migration. Of the 52 nesting U.S. warbler species, 31 nest in New York, and 2 more pass through during migration. The yellow-rumped arrives first in spring, leaves last in fall, and winters farther north than any other warbler—as far north as coastal Massachusetts. Given that warblers feed nearly exclusively on insects, the yellow-rumped warbler has had to adapt to insectless conditions in the fall and winter by eating berries. Even though insects remain its preferred food, it commonly eats poison ivy berries, bayberries, and others during cold weather. This adaptation has served the yellow-rumped well, as it remains one of our most abundant warblers. Another late migrant, an osprey, hovered over Lake Lila's placid waters, waiting to crash-dive onto unsuspecting fish.

Shingle Shanty Brook, Beaver River, and the lake all showed evidence of extensive beaver activity. We saw them foraging in the middle of the day. Beaver naturally forage during daylight hours, but in the presence of human disturbance, they become crepuscular (out in twilight), if not completely nocturnal.

We very much enjoyed our three-hour paddle on Shingle Shanty Brook, one of the most meandering bodies of water we have ever paddled. Grasses, clematis, sweet gale, alder, swamp rose, and other shrubs line the banks, with the pointed spires of golden-needled tamarack, spruce, and balsam fir providing contrasting habitat. Bur-reed and water celery, our constant companions, had little trouble in the light current. With a combination of paddling and portaging, intrepid explorers can now travel from Round Lake, through Little Tupper Lake, to Rock Pond, to Hardigan Pond, to Lily Pad Lake, to Shingle Shanty Brook, to Lake Lila and on beyond to Lows Lake or to Stillwater Reservoir (see Lows Lake and Little Tupper Lake sections).

The Beaver River flowing out of Lake Lila cuts a broad, shallow, scenic swath through coniferous forest, connecting Lake Lila with Nehasane Lake and eventually Stillwater Reservoir. About halfway to Nehasane Lake, a short falls bars your way. To avoid walking your boat through miles of shallows, attempt the trek down to Stillwater only during high water.

54

Little Tupper Lake, Round Lake, and Rock Pond

Long Lake

Maps: New York Atlas Maps 86:A4 and 94:D4, USGS Quadrangles Little Tupper Lake and Forked Lake

Area: Little Tupper Lake 2,300 acres, Round Lake 800 acres, Rock Pond 282 acres

Habitat type: interconnected lakes with marshy inlets and coves

Fish: Little Tupper strain of brook trout unique to these lakes

Expect to see: bald eagle, loon, merlin, otter, beaver

Outfitters: through paddler shuttle service, Raquette River Outfitters, 518-359-3228, www.raquetteriveroutfitters.com; St. Regis Canoe Outfitters, 518-891-1838, www.canoeoutfitters.com

Camping: on-site wilderness camping

Take note: hazardous paddling during windy conditions

GETTING THERE

Little Tupper Lake. From the junction of Routes 3 and 30 in Tupper Lake, go 11.3 miles south on Route 30, and turn right on Sabbatis Circle Road. Go 3.0 miles (14.3 miles), and bear right on Sabbatis Road. Go 1.3 miles (15.6 miles) to the access on the left.

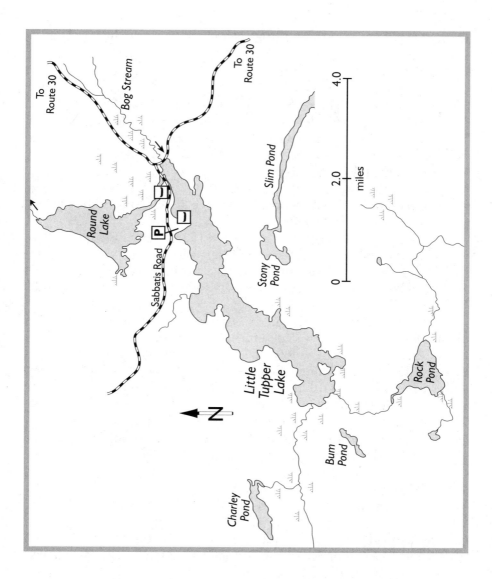

From Long Lake at the junction of Routes 30 and 28N, go 7.0 miles north on Route 30, turn left on Sabbatis Road, go 3.0 miles (10.0 miles), bear left on Sabbatis Road, and follow as above.

Round Lake. Access from Little Tupper or park at the junction of Sabbatis and Circle roads and carry to the right as you walk southwest toward the overpass over Little Tupper outlet.

Since its purchase by the State, Little Tupper Lake and associated waterways have joined New York's best quietwater paddling locations. William C. Whitney and a partner purchased 68,000 acres of land through several acquisitions between 1896 and 1898 that eventually Whitney named Whitney Park. An ardent conservationist, Whitney hired forester Henry Graves, a protégé of Gifford Pinchot, to manage the property, and early forest operations here became one of the first applications of scientifically based forest management.

In December 1997, the state purchased 15,000 acres of Whitney Park for inclusion in the Adirondack Forest Preserve. In March 2000, the Adirondack Park Agency combined this purchase with a portion of the Lake Lila Primitive Area (see Lake Lila section), and designated it the William C. Whitney Wilderness Area.

In January 2001, The Nature Conservancy purchased 26,500 acres of land from International Paper, including three parcels of great interest to paddlers: 9,926-acre Round Lake tract at Little Tupper's northeast end; 15,536-acre Shingle Shanty Pond tract that links Little Tupper with Lake Lila; and 1,100-acre Bog Lake–Clear Pond tract that links Lows Lake/Bog River Flow area with Lake Lila (see respective sections). The Conservancy subsequently transferred a portion to the state to provide a publicly accessible waterway corridor from Round Lake through Little Tupper, into Lake Lila, and then to Lows Lake.

Little Tupper Lake

We paddled Little Tupper Lake three times since the 1997 purchase. In 1999, we saw much evidence of the intense microburst of July 15, 1995 (we had camped in two different locations not far away). Winds in excess of 100 miles per hour felled thousands of trees around Little Tupper, including more than half the trees in some western sections. By August 2006, we saw far fewer signs of the 1995 microburst.

As called for by the wilderness management plan for Adirondack Forest Preserve, the state established 22 well-separated campsites. More heavily used sites have pit-privies, and all have fire circles (the only allowable fire locations), but no grills and no picnic tables. From Short Island campsite 14, we watched three otter fishing on an early mid-September morning. From campsite 18, we saw a merlin (a small falcon) and a bald eagle. On another trip, we watched a bald eagle swoop low over the lake; loons seem ever-present.

Development intrudes on the shoreline only at the access, where the former Whitney Industries headquarters now serves as Little Tupper headquarters, and at two private dwellings retained by the Whitney family: Camp Francis and Camp on the Point. Hemlock, some huge yellow birch, balsam fir, beech, red maple, red spruce, and scattered white pine—including a few huge vestiges of the ancient forest that once stood here—occur along the shoreline.

Typical northern shrubs, including sweet gale, blueberry, huckleberry, and a variety of ferns, grow along Little Tupper's 20 miles of rocky shoreline. At the half-dozen inlets, shallow waters grow thick with floating and emergent wetland plants: fragrant and yellow waterlilies, water shield, pickerelweed, water celery, and bulrush, with thick mats of bladderwort beneath the surface.

At the far western tip, we paddled up the Charley Pond outlet in an early August evening's waning light—after winds had died down. The gently meandering stream leaves an open channel in an otherwise vegetation-covered surface. Dozens of beaver lodges occur along here. In about a mile, we passed under a steel I-beam bridge, and in another mile, we came by the remains of on old crib dam or bridge. Beyond that, the stream narrowed, with progress eventually blocked—first by beaver dams, then by fallen trees.

Rock Pond

At the southwestern tip, about two-thirds of a mile west of Short Island, you can make a great day trip up the easy 3-mile outlet from 282-acre Rock Pond. Floating vegetation, pickerelweed, wetland shrubs, royal fern, alder, and tamarack line the wide meandering stream. We saw a few dozen clumps of pitcher-plant here, along with tiny sundew on exposed logs. Expect to see beaver along here—or at least evidence of their work. We also watched two otter frolic on our most recent visit.

In 2006, we carried over two beaver dams and over another portage (150 yards, crossing an old logging road). Along the carry trail, note the huge white pine, measuring more than 4 feet in diameter at breast height. In mid-August in wet years, raspberries grow in abundance here.

Some sizable granite outcroppings in Rock Pond make excellent picnic stops. The five campsites that occur along the shoreline, plus one on the island and two along the outlet stream, see much less use than those on Little Tupper. On an August weekend in 2006, with most of the Little Tupper campsites occupied, only one party camped on Rock Pond; one site had seedlings growing in the fire pit.

At the southwestern tip, we explored some marshy sphagnum islands but could not paddle far up the inlet creek. Near here, the carry trail leading to Hardigan Pond and Lake Lila takes off to the west. At the eastern tip, we explored quite a distance up the inlet creek, winding through alder, where we watched a young beaver in a hidden recess as its mother paced back-and-forth just upstream, until she finally slapped her tail in warning. Beaver dams eventually blocked our upstream progress. We also watched a merlin here.

Round Lake

To reach Round Lake, paddle under Sabbatis Road to the left, 300 yards short of Little Tupper's east end. The inlet stream immediately opens up and remains a wide, shallow, slow-flowing, serpentine channel, thick with waterlilies and other floating vegetation, for the mile-and-a-half downstream paddle to Round Lake.

On a mid-August twilight paddle, several duck families skittered into thick shoreline vegetation, and we surprised several beaver beginning their nocturnal forays. We also saw deer, great blue heron, and kingfisher. The inlet stream gradually opens up into roughly triangular Round Lake. From a far northern campsite, close to the outlet, we watched three young otter in first light, and saw them again farther down the western shore.

Cliffs extend down into the water along the spectacular western shore, with huge lichen-encrusted boulders capped with polypody fern, clumps of interrupted and royal fern, wild sarsaparilla, steeplebush, bottle gentian, and a variety of shrubs. You will see the same trees here as on Little Tupper Lake: yellow birch, hemlock, balsam fir, red maple, red spruce, and white pine. Watch for an occasional striped maple and mountain ash—whose berries turn bright orange in fall. Looking inland from the western shoreline, the land rises steeply, with large outcroppings and cliffs.

At the southwestern tip, you can explore the mucky shallows to some extent, though by early summer, floating vegetation restricts paddling. Note the feathery tamarack set back from the water's edge. Coves and a handful of islands along the deeply folded southern shoreline beg to be explored.

55

Long Lake

Long Lake

Maps: New York Atlas Maps 87:A5 and 95:D5, USGS Quad-rangles Deerland and Kempshall Mountain

Area: 3,904 acres, maximum depth 50 feet

Habitat type: long wide lake with coves, islands, and inlet streams

Fish: brook trout, largemouth and smallmouth bass, northern pike

Expect to see: loon, scenic vistas

Camping: on-site wilderness camping

Take note: windy conditions cause hazardous paddling conditions; to run the Raquette River, use Jamieson and Morris, *Adirondack Canoe Waters: North Flow* (Adirondack Mountain Club, 1988)

GETTING THERE

From the junction of Routes 28N and 30 in Long Lake, go 0.4 mile north on Route 30, turn right, and go 0.4 mile (0.8 mile) to the access on the left.

The 4,000-foot mountains of the High Peaks Wilderness dominate the view to the northeast from Long Lake, which lies in the glaciated Raquette River valley. The view alone makes the northern stretch of Long Lake worth paddling. Long-distance paddlers traverse Long Lake on their way to Tupper Lake or to Saranac lakes via Stony Creek Ponds.

Long Lake's 14-mile southwest to northeast length funnels winds. We have paddled here with two-foot waves crashing over the bow and under

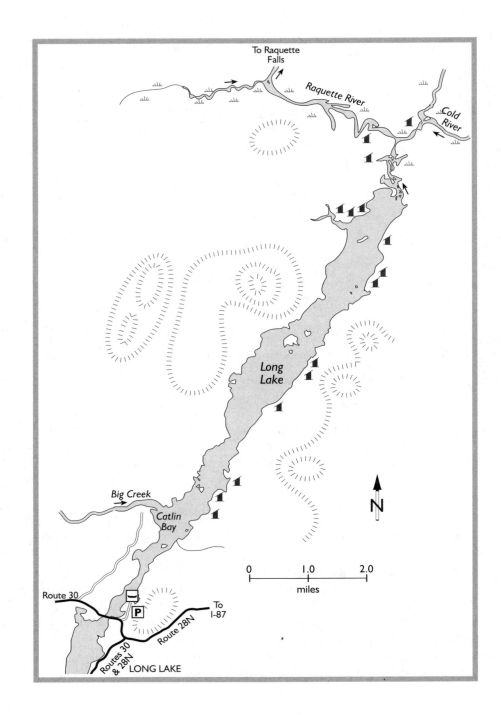

dead-calm conditions. Although well worth paddling, we advise that you paddle smaller, more protected bodies of water during strong winds.

Do not let the personal watercraft, floatplanes, and motorboats hovering about Long Lake village intimidate you. The lake stretches for many miles and includes several small paddlable streams where you can escape the noise and congestion. At the lake's north end where it narrows, and continuing on the 6 miles to Raquette Falls carry, the Raquette has earned a scenic river designation, which keeps out motorboats and personal watercraft.

The lake's high elevation (1,627 feet) and considerable depth keep the water quite cool until midsummer, making early season swimming a brisk experience. Twenty shelters dot the shoreline, providing wonderful camping spots, especially those with a view down the scenic valley toward the High Peaks Wilderness. The state owns much of the eastern shore but not the western until far down the lake. A grove of large red pine helps conceal the eastern shore's first shelter, announcing the beginning of state-owned land.

Hikers along the 133-mile-long Northville-Placid Trail that follows the right side compete for shelter use on the southern shore. Near the lake's northeastern end, several shelters occur on the opposite shore, away from the trail. We suggest taking a tent along in July and August, as the shelters may be in use.

Northern white cedar, paper birch, and hemlock line the shore, along with a wide assortment of pine and deciduous trees. We saw few ducks when we paddled here, but loons appeared in good numbers. We watched several crows chase a Cooper's hawk. Like the other accipiters—the larger goshawk and smaller sharp-shinned hawk—Cooper's hawk preys on birds. We delighted in watching this increasingly rare bird's agile flight on short, rounded wings, using its long tail as a rudder. Although we have not witnessed a Cooper's hawk kill, we have witnessed several by the similar, but smaller, sharp-shinned hawk. Agility allows it to take songbirds on the wing, leaving nothing but a puff of feathers drifting slowly to the ground.

Take time to explore the two creeks that flow into Long Lake: Big Creek and Cold River. Big Creek flows into Catlin Bay on the northern shore. Pickerelweed, bulrush, and grasses greet you at the outlet, along with lots of beaver activity. We paddled through two breached beaver dams and carried up over a third. About a half mile upstream, we passed

Beautiful views await paddlers on Long Lake.

under an unusual bridge with four, 8-inch-wide by 3-feet-deep, laminated, wooden support beams.

About 0.2 mile after the bridge, a rock fall blocked the way, the rounded boulders forming a sizable rapids flanked by a large stand of tall, pointed balsam firs. Yellow birch dominates the southern shore, with some alder along the bank. Occasional red maple and paper birch occur, as well, in this beautiful and peaceful setting. We noted lots of open mussel shells in the clear water and many species of aquatic plants, including fragrant waterlily, yellow pondlily, and pondweed.

Cold River flows into the Raquette about a mile downstream from the lake's north end. You can paddle back up its marshy wilderness for nearly 2 miles during high water. Other coves and inlets on Long Lake harbor marshes and their assorted plants and animals. And the river's myriad channels at the north end down to Raquette Falls provide many more exploration opportunities. One has to paddle here for a few days to explore it all, the whole time under the magnificent High Peaks Wilderness backdrop.

56

Harris Lake and Rich Lake

Newcomb

Maps: New York Atlas Map 87:A7, USGS Quadrangle Newcomb

Area: Harris Lake 310 acres, Rich Lake 342 acres, maximum depth 65 feet

Habitat type: small lakes with extensive marshes and access to upper Hudson

Fish: smallmouth bass, northern pike

Expect to see: osprey, loon, wood and ring-necked ducks, otter, beaver

Camping: App. A #78 (on-site)

Take note: avoid Hudson River Class III rapids downstream; Newcomb Visitor Center, between Harris and Rich lakes, offers trails and an interpretive center.

GETTING THERE

Harris Lake. From Long Lake, at the junction of Routes 28N and 30, go 14.8 miles east on Route 28N, and turn left at the sign for Newcomb Town Beach.

From I-87, Exit 29, go about 19 miles west on Route 84/Boreas Road, and turn right on Route 28N. Go 4.4 miles (about 23.4 miles) to the access on the right, 0.9 mile after crossing the Hudson River.

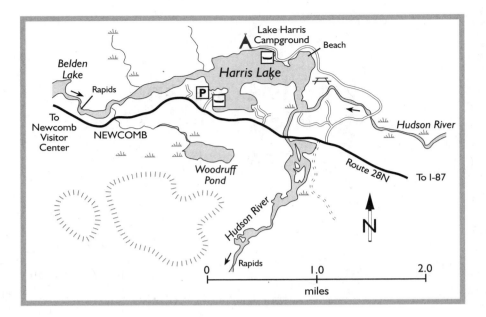

Rich Lake. From Long Lake, at the junction of Routes 28N and 30, go 12.1 miles east on Route 28N, and turn left on Rich Lake Road (SUNY Syracuse research center). Carry 120 yards to the water. Access is 2.7 miles west of Harris Lake.

Harris Lake

Though Harris Lake lies adjacent to Route 28N, we enjoy paddling here for the gorgeous scenery on the nearby Hudson and because three cavorting river otter thought it remote enough for them. The otter, a weasel family member with 30-inch body length and 25-pound weight, ranges from northern Alaska to Labrador, south to Florida's tip, and across to Yuma, Arizona. Despite this huge range, people rarely encounter this magnificent creature that has grown increasingly rare as development and commotion drive it away.

Scattered development along the southern and western shores did not seem to bother the resident loons, either. Crows searched the shoreline for washed-up food, and a kingfisher eyed the water, looking for those last few fish to eat before migrating on to warmer climes. Northern white cedar grows along the shore, along with patches of

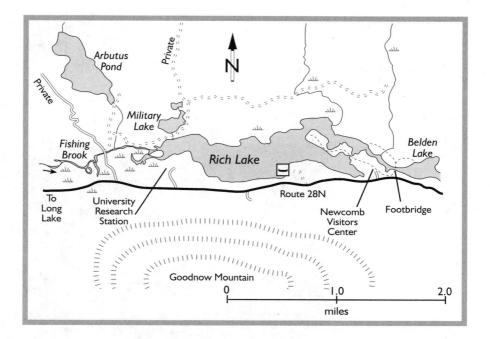

tall, pointed fir, occasional white pine, and sugar and red maples. Note the conspicuous browse line, carved by white-tailed deer reaching up from winter ice.

Rushes inhabit the shallows, along with pondweed, pickerelweed, water celery, and yellow and fragrant waterlilies. Bur-reed also occurs in places, and royal fern graces the banks. Water shield, a member of the waterlily family, with stems entering the center of a floating oval leaf, occurs in large patches. Notice the slimy, gelatinous coating on its stems.

Paddling east, you enter the mighty Hudson, the state's longest river, near the beginning of its almost 300-mile sojourn from Lake Tear of the Clouds on Mt. Marcy to Verrazano Narrows Bridge and the Atlantic Ocean. You can paddle upstream a short distance before meeting quick-water or a mile downstream, passing under the Route 28N bridge. Note the warning signs for impending rapids that lead to the Hudson River Gorge. Use caution; avoid getting swept into these Class III rapids, not usually run in open boats. Only really serious whitewater paddlers traverse the gorge's Class V water farther downstream.

A handicapped-accessible board-walk and observation platform make the beauty of Rich Lake accessible to all.

Rich Lake

Paddling out one early fall morning, mist swirled slowly down this shallow, sandy-bottomed lake. Mussel shells lay in piles near shore where raccoons feasted on nightly forays. Looking out from the sand beach at the access, we could see a marsh across the way . . . and no development. This wild place offers hours of exploration.

Rich Lake allegedly got its name when early settlers discovered graphite flakes in the surrounding rocks and thought it silver ore. Miners later extracted graphite, a form of carbon, from the deposits near Ticonderoga for the "lead" in lead pencils.

Paddling around to the right, you reach the eastern tip, which narrows to a rocky stream with definite current. A footbridge on one of three nature trails crosses overhead; after this, a short rapids leads to Belden Lake and eventually Harris Lake. At low water, you would have to walk your boat down these rapids.

On the main lake, we saw loon, kingfisher, and osprey, all three fishing in different ways: the loon gliding underwater, snaring fish in its bill; the kingfisher folding its wings at the last moment, diving headlong into the water, catching a fish in its beak; and the osprey hovering overhead, swooping down, crashing into the water, grabbing a fish with its talons.

Fishing Brook enters on the northwest end, but you can also paddle through an extensive beaver swamp on the south that extends back quite a way through encroaching pickerelweed to a few-hundred-acre marsh. At various places, if you carry up over a few well-kept beaver dams, some surprisingly high, you enter Fishing Brook. Many more dams occur on the brook's myriad channels.

Grasses grow on banks, along with thick stands of sweet gale, leatherleaf, swamp milkweed, sheep laurel, bur-reed, and many more swamp specialists. Northern white cedar, with a few towering white pine, occasional hemlock and balsam fir, some paper and yellow birches, and lots of red, sugar, and silver maples occur on higher ground.

We paddled back up the alder-lined brook, with occasional dogwood and viburnum interspersed, for about three-quarters of a mile, until we reached a large area flooded by a beaver dam. Having carried over many beaver dams already, we turned around and paddled back to the lake.

On our travels through the marsh, several small flocks of wood and ring-necked ducks sprang to air as we interrupted their fattening up for fall migration. But the wildlife highlight came as we left the lake. Right in front of us, a female black bear with two young cubs bounded across the road, with mom woofing copious instructions. Black bear populations have increased significantly in Adirondack Park in recent years. In dry summers, bears seem to move around often, undoubtedly because of less-plentiful traditional food sources. If you spend time in wild areas, you stand a good chance of seeing them.

57

South Pond

Indian Lake and Long Lake

Maps: New York Atlas Map 87:A5, USGS Quadrangle Deerland

Area: 428 acres, maximum depth 55 feet

Habitat type: round lake with islands

Fish: splake (unless the otter ate them all)

Expect to see: osprey, raven, loon, otter, deer

Camping: App. A #77, 95, 96, 98, and 101

Take note: difficult to find, follow directions closely

GETTING THERE

From the junction of Routes 28N and 30 in Long Lake, go 4.9 miles south on Routes 28N and 30, and turn right into the pullout, a few hundred feet past the trailhead. The steep 300-foot trail down to the water is slippery when wet.

From the junction of Routes 28, 28N, and 30 in Blue Mountain Lake, go 5.7 miles north on Routes 28N and 30 to the pull-out on the left.

We loved paddling South Pond . . . after we finally found it. You cannot see this large, scenic pond from the road. The steep trail to the shore passes through a grove of massive hemlock, punctuated with large yellow birch, and a needle-carpeted floor; the path waxes slippery when wet and represents a bit of challenge getting back up.

Because of difficult access, the pond receives only modest attention, primarily from anglers. The state owns more than three-quarters of the

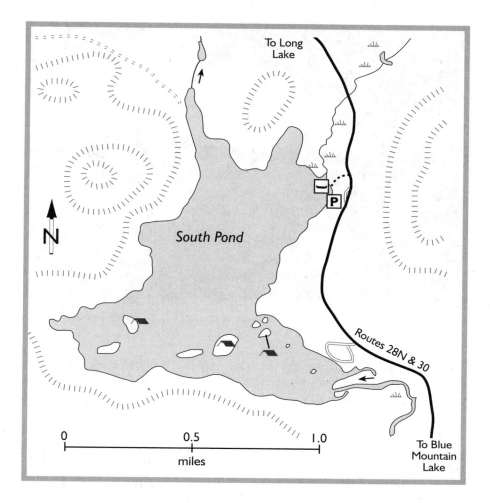

shoreline and all of the beautifully forested islands; we found campsites on three south-end islands. Superb views—of 3,600-foot Blue Mountain, a member of the tallest 100 Adirondack High Peaks club, and sister peaks to the south and of Inlet Mountain Ridge, ending in 2,900-foot Mt. Sabbatis to the northeast—kept us from casting a wary eye for barely submerged granite boulders.

The sheer numbers of these boulders—lining the banks, submerged, and emerged, some standing taller than a person—greatly impressed us, and impressed *upon* us the need to go carefully. Generally, you can see submerged boulders in the clear water; most of those poking up through

Sunlight filters through hemlock branches at the access on South Pond.

the surface, particularly on the pond's south end, had fish skeleton adornments. After viewing the many picked-clean carcasses, we decided that the local otter population probably needs to go on a diet-and-exercise routine. Look for them in the early morning or evening hours.

Cruising the eastern shore, we spotted a doe and spotted fawn at the water's edge, down for an afternoon drink. Ravens—almost always traveling in pairs, compared with the flocking behavior of the closely related crow—croaked out their hoarse cries. A colony of ring-billed gulls, opportunists of the first order, no doubt also pleased by the otter presence, patrolled the rocks, looking for partially eaten rotting fish carcasses. A brood of common mergansers headed off into the reeds as we approached, and two northern divers, the common loon, dove for fish as the sun started to dip down over the western horizon.

Reluctantly, we paddled back to the awaiting hill, past the rows of northern white cedar and other conifers that line the bank, gazing off at the distant hillsides of intermingled conifers and hardwoods. We look forward to our return to enjoy the splendid beauty of this wild place—and to look once again for those big furry guys with fish breath.

58

Forked Lake
Long Lake and Arietta

Maps: New York Atlas Maps 86:A4 and 87:A4, USGS Quadrangle Forked Lake

Area: 1,248 acres, maximum depth 74 feet

Habitat type: long, large lake

Fish: brook and lake trout, landlocked salmon, largemouth and smallmouth bass

Expect to see: osprey, loon, deer

Camping: App. A #95 (on-site, including some island campsites accessible only by boat)

Take note: treacherous paddling in windy conditions

GETTING THERE

From the junction of Routes 28N and 30 in Long Lake, go 3.0 miles south on Routes 28N and 30, and turn right on North Point Road. Go 2.9 miles (5.9 miles), and turn right to the access at Forked Lake Campground (fee), or continue 5.6 miles (11.5 miles) to Canoe Carry Road on the Whitney Park access (free).

On a calm day, Forked Lake (pronounced with two syllables: *fork*-ed) offers miles of wonderful shoreline paddling and exploration. The lake stretches over 4 miles east to west, with a 2-mile section extending to the north.

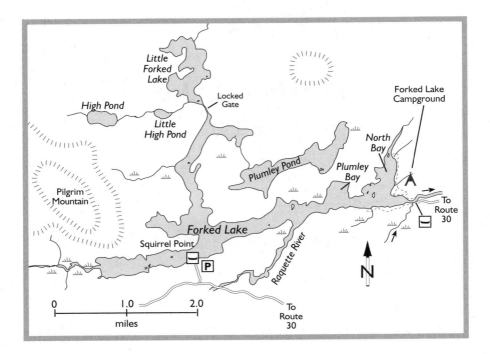

Northern white cedars line much of Forked Lake's shoreline. White-tailed deer love cedar twigs, resulting in a conspicuous browse line marking the height deer can reach above the ice. White pine, red spruce, balsam fir, hemlock, red and sugar maples, yellow and paper birches, and beech round out the diverse mixed-hardwood-conifer forest surrounding the lake. Notice the dense stands of hobblebush that dominate the understory with its symmetrical pairs of large, heart-shaped leaves. A variety of heaths—principally leatherleaf, blueberry, and sheep laurel—create a thick, generally impenetrable shoreline.

Where the lake's west end narrows to a meandering inlet channel from Brandreth Lake, the shoreline becomes much boggier. Tamarack grows on sphagnum hillocks, along with bog rosemary, pitcher-plant, leatherleaf, and broad expanses of marsh grass. Thick vegetation clogs the shallow inlet, but you can work your way west for quite a way. After paddling through the marsh for a mile or so, the channel narrows, hills gradually close in, a sandy bottom replaces the muck, and current quickens. We carried above one beaver dam and stopped at quickwater.

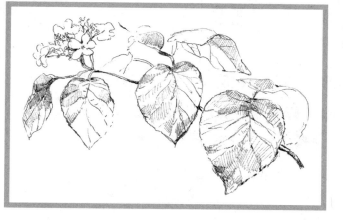

Hobblebush
(*Viburnum lantanoides*)

Towering white pine, some to 150 feet, on the creek's northern hillsides rise up toward Pilgrim Mountain—at 2,785 feet, the area's tallest peak. The bog and steep slopes probably protected this stand from logging in the 1800s, leaving an old-growth forest remnant for future generations to enjoy.

A fence and locked gate still block access to Little Forked Lake, part of Whitney Park. The state acquired other Whitney lands to the north that now comprise the William C. Whitney Wilderness Area, which contains Little Tupper Lake.

We saw quite a few loons on Forked Lake, including one pair with a chick, great blue heron, common merganser, kingfisher, and a great horned owl. On the lake's south side, you can paddle up the Raquette River a ways toward Raquette Lake, but you will reach quickwater and rapids in less than a mile.

59

Blue Mountain, Eagle, and Utowana Lakes and Marion River

Indian Lake

Maps: New York Atlas Map 87:B5, USGS Quadrangles Blue Mountain Lake and Raquette Lake

Blue Mountain Lake area: 1,220 acres, maximum depth 100 feet

Habitat type: large, deep lake connected to smaller lakes and a river

Fish: lake trout, landlocked salmon, largemouth and smallmouth bass, northern pike

Expect to see: loon, waterfowl, deer, scenic vistas

Camping: App. A #96, 98, 101, and on-site wilderness camping

Take note: Blue Mountain Lake treacherous under windy conditions

GETTING THERE

From the junction of Routes 28, 28N, and 30 in Blue Mountain Lake, go 0.3 mile west on Route 28 to the access on the right.

Blue Mountain Lake

A sign at the Blue Mountain Lake public access area says, "Boat Speed Limit 45 MPH," not very encouraging and probably a good reason to

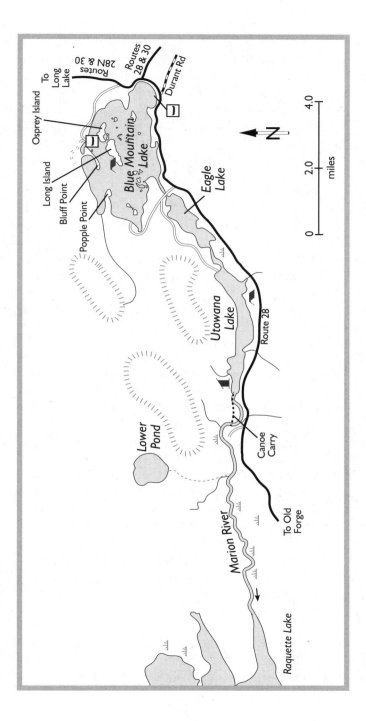

Osprey Island
To Long Lake
Routes 28N & 30
Routes 28 & 30
Durant Rd
Long Island
Bluff Point
Blue Mountain Lake
Popple Point
Eagle Lake
Utowana Lake
Route 28
Canoe Carry
Lower Pond
Marion River
To Old Forge
Raquette Lake

N

0   2.0   4.0
miles

avoid this lake on busy summer weekends. When we paddled here in September, few high-speed boats plied these waters, and we enjoyed the beauty of one of the most scenic locations in the Adirondacks.

Blue Mountain Lake, at an elevation of 1,790 feet, nestles among the High Peaks of the central Adirondacks, with Blue Mountain on the east stretching to more than 3,600 feet. Looking back from the lake's west end, we see how the mountain got its name: ringed with high-altitude conifers, the peak's upper reaches look dark, even blue.

Scenic granite boulders and islands dot the lake. One cannot help but notice, especially on the lake's western end, a conspicuous browse line on the northern white cedars that hang out over the water. Deer often yard up in cedar stands; here, they browse the shoreline cedars up to head height as they walk along the ice.

Holding a special place in Adirondack history, Blue Mountain Lake's environs served as the heart of the Adirondacks during its first wave of popularity. Luxury hotels and a full range of amenities greeted the rich and famous in the 1880s, as they completed railroad and stagecoach excursions from cities to the east and south.

Prospect House here became the first hotel in the world to have electric lighting in every room! At this hotel in August 1883, Verplanck Colvin first outlined his vision of protecting the Adirondacks as a state park. Colvin, a lawyer by training, starting in 1872 spent several decades mapping and describing the Adirondack region. Thanks largely to Colvin's efforts and vision, the legislature created a state Forest Preserve two years later, and in 1892, Adirondack Park came into being. Sadly, all of the grand hotels burned to the ground over the years.

Except near Blue Mountain Lake village and on the northeast, little development intrudes on the shoreline. But despite the gorgeous setting and even with a huge expanse of boat-free water, we prefer to paddle on Eagle and Utowana Lakes—the rest of what some refer to as the Eckford Chain—and the Marion River. These latter waterways include more habitat diversity, including a small waterfall on Utowana Lake, extensive marshes, more aquatic plants, and a lot more wildlife. And they do not suffer nearly as much from wind.

Eagle Lake

As you paddle into Eagle Lake, stay to the right, passing under the north bridge. The stone bulwarks date to 1891, when William West Durant built the Pioneer Bridge in memory of his father, Dr. Thomas Clark

The Thomas Clark Durant Bridge at the entrance to Eagle Lake.

Durant, conceiver, builder, vice president, and general manager of the first transcontinental railroad, the Union Pacific. The elder Mr. Durant also served as president and builder of the Adirondack Railroad.

Little development mars Eagle Lake. Eagle Nest Park owns the surrounding lands and most of Utowana Lake, preserving them from development. The north shore houses a summer artist colony. On one morning excursion, we paddled along with someone heading from Blue Mountain Lake to the colony. A kingfisher also accompanied us down the connecting waterway, as black ducks dabbled for aquatic plants and crows called off in the distance. Common mergansers fled before us as we glided through a canopy of cedar, hemlock, balsam fir, spruce, and very tall white pine, along with occasional sugar and red maples, paper and yellow birches. As we neared the end of Eagle Lake, towering hemlock appeared.

Utowana Lake
Resist the temptation to hurry through into Utowana Lake. The long connector contains an extensive swamp with many side channels to explore. Along with bog rosemary, sweet gale, alder, and other typical bog

vegetation, tall white pine and many large spruce cover the islands. Red and sugar maples and yellow birch grow here, as well. Ferns line the banks, and pickerelweed, water celery—with its long, narrow leaves floating on the water's surface—and fragrant waterlilies grow in profusion in the shallows.

Stick to Utowana's southern shore. Watch for a small creek flowing into the lake, the entrance guarded by large patches of pickerelweed and a grove of tamarack that give way to balsam fir, yellow birch, striped and red maples, and alder. Paddle back up this creek to a small waterfall that tumbles down over moss-covered granite boulders. Hemlock drapes out over the water to shade the falls, and ferns grow in clumps under the canopy. Look for pitcher-plant in the marshy areas.

Eagle Nest Park maintains a campsite on a point on Utowana's southern shore, just down from the creek. Mussel shells litter the shore near the campsite, probably the work of foraging raccoons. Farther down the lake on the north shore, near the outlet, the state maintains a lean-to shelter. The marshy area right in front of the shelter provides habitat for an extensive patch of small pitcher-plants.

Conifers dominate the shore and surrounding hills. Great, feathery tamarack mix with red maple at the west end, along with tall hemlock, a few white pine, spruce, yellow birch, and lots of balsam fir. A few mountain ash—not an ash at all but actually a member of the rose family—drip with large clusters of bright red berries in fall. The marshes contain acres of fragrant waterlily, along with cattails and some pickerelweed.

These lakes provide excellent views of ring-billed gull, loon, kingfisher, black duck, common merganser, and crow, and marshes treat you to the sounds and sights of wood duck, common yellowthroat, white-throated sparrow, yellow-rumped warbler, and great blue heron.

Marion River

A carry around the first few hundred feet of the Marion River begins at the end of Utowana, taking you through a dense stand of balsam fir, interspersed with a few tall white pine and hemlock. In contrast to raucous calls of a group of flickers, white-breasted nuthatch called softly while we carried, fighting off the few remaining—but determined—mosquitoes.

At its beginnings at the small dam on Utowana, the clear, shallow Marion River carves out a narrow, meandering channel, lined with alder, ferns, cattails, and grasses, affording a relatively unobstructed view of surrounding hillsides. Aquatic vegetation, including bur-reed, pickerelweed, water celery, yellow pondlily, and fragrant waterlily, chokes the marshy stream. Milkweed, sweet gale, swamp rose, and viburnum—with large clusters of dark purple berries—appear in clusters. We paddled over a couple of beaver dams, marked with fresh cuttings.

Extensive marshes keep the conifers at bay as they sink their roots into higher ground back from the water's edge. The pointed spires of tamarack and balsam fir, along with tall white pine and northern white cedar, mark the inexorable advancement of higher ground as the marsh slowly fills in.

Many side channels lead off through the marsh, a wonderland filled with plants and wildlife, including many beautifully hued wood duck, red-breasted merganser, and several great blue heron. We watched a northern harrier as it hunted the marsh, tilting back and forth on motionless wings, ready to pounce on hapless rodents.

Spoiled by the wonders of the marsh, "civilization" intruded on our wilderness experience as we passed out of the river's mouth into Raquette Lake, with its noisy personal watercraft and shoreline development. Disappointed by the proximity of such threats to the marsh, we immediately turned around to retrace our steps back through nature's glory. The river's negligible current did not impede our progress, and the entire round-trip of 20 miles took one very long day. You might want to arrange a pickup to make this a one-way trip, or camp en route.

The hardest part of the journey awaited us back at Blue Mountain Lake where the late afternoon wind had whipped the surface to a froth, providing a wet ride through ever-deepening troughs of whitecapped waves. With our cameras, binoculars, and field guides safely tucked away in watertight bags and with the knowledge that our life jackets would keep us afloat if we tipped, we plunged on through darkening skies that only enhanced the eerie beauty of the surrounding dark blue peaks. A long—but absolutely extraordinary—day, to be sure.

60

Lake Durant and Rock Pond

Indian Lake

Maps: New York Atlas Map 87:B5, USGS Quadrangle Blue Mountain Lake

Lake Durant area: 289 acres, maximum depth 20 feet

Habitat type: long, shallow, marshy lake and pond

Fish: largemouth bass, tiger muskellunge

Expect to see: wood, ring-necked, and black ducks; Canada goose

Camping: App. A. #98 (on-site)

Take note: east-west winds can cause treacherous conditions

GETTING THERE

Durant Road. From Blue Mountain Lake, go 0.8 mile east on Routes 28 and 30, and turn right on Durant Road. Go 0.2 mile (1.0 mile), and turn left at the Cascade Pond Trailhead sign. Go 0.2 mile (1.2 miles) to the access.

Campground. Go another 2.0 miles (2.8 miles) on Routes 28 and 30, and turn right to Lake Durant Campground.

Although the highway parallels the shore for about a mile, we include Lake Durant and connected Rock Pond because of their scenic beauty, productivity, and lowered susceptibility to windy conditions—at least

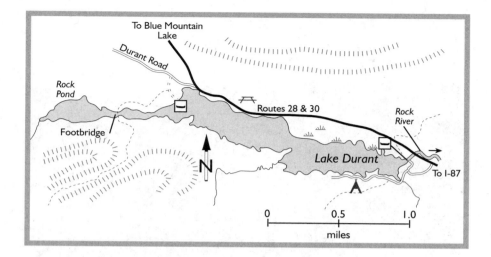

compared with nearby Blue Mountain Lake. To get an appreciation of Durant's beauty, stop at the roadside rest area, and gaze out over the water at the distant hillsides. Hemlock at the water's edge gives way to mixed hardwoods that cover the hillsides, with patches of darker conifers adding to their multihued beauty. When we paddled here in early fall, it looked like a dark-green canvas splashed with red, yellow, and orange.

The lake's productivity draws people to its waters. Anglers come to catch trophy tiger muskies and smallmouth bass, their success attested to by the many photographs on the campground bulletin board. This stands in stark contrast to events occurring in many other lakes. Airborne acid rain spewed from tall smokestacks in the Ohio River Valley rains down on Adirondack lakes, causing the slow death of many. Sulfuric, hydrochloric, and nitric acids acidify them, lowering pH to the point where aquatic organisms no longer reproduce, resulting in barren, lifeless lakes. We should enjoy the primordial productivity of Lake Durant and do what we can to protect it from the continued airborne assault from midwestern pollution.

Carpets of aquatic vegetation cover the coves and shallows of Lake Durant and Rock Pond. Fragrant waterlily, pickerelweed, floating heart, water celery, smartweed, water shield, cattails, and yellow pondlily seemingly compete for every inch of surface space in the shallows. In many areas around the lakes, hobblebush dominates the understory.

Adirondack Park and Environs 287

Many types of aquatic vegetation crowd the surface of the shallows in Lake Durant. In the fall, surrounding hillsides glow with red, yellow, and orange leaves.

Paddling west by a stand of beautiful balsam fir—pointed spires and upright purple cones pointing skyward—into the connector between Lake Durant and Rock Pond, many flat topped granite boulders greet you, clearly identifying how Rock Pond got its name. A low footbridge separates the two bodies of water. Part of the Blue Ridge Wilderness Area, Rock Pond enjoys a prohibition on motors. Two large islands add character and varied habitat to Rock Pond, a superb place to view wildlife early or late in the day among the rafts of aquatic vegetation.

We listened to the whistling wings of wood ducks as they leapt into the air upon our approach, black ducks bobbed nervously for aquatic plants, and several great blue herons stalked fish and frogs in the shallows, while kingfishers dove for minnows. White-throated sparrows called from the underbrush as we paddled here completely alone.

61

Cedar River Flow
Lake Pleasant

Maps: New York Atlas Map 87:C5, USGS Quadrangle Indian Lake

Area: 710 acres

Habitat type: shallow, weed-filled lake and slow-flowing river

Fish: brook trout

Expect to see: loon, ruffed grouse, deer, beaver

Camping: on-site wilderness camping

Take note: lots of barely submerged boulders

GETTING THERE

From Indian Lake village, go 2.1 miles north on Routes 28 and 30, and turn left on Cedar River Road. Go 11.8 miles (13.9 miles) to the access on the left.

A long, rough road from Inlet village on Fourth Lake, traveling southeast on Limekiln Road, also leads here.

Cedar River Flow remains one of south-central Adirondacks' little-known treasures. Fed by cool, clear, mountain water flowing out of Cedar Lakes in the West Canada Lake Wilderness Area, the flow provides wilderness camping, paddling, and hiking opportunities, all of it above 2,100 feet elevation. The flow will impress you with its wild, spectacular character. Although it extends only 3 miles south-southwest from Wakely Dam, many more miles of meandering streams and beaver meadows offer hours, or even days, of paddling pleasure.

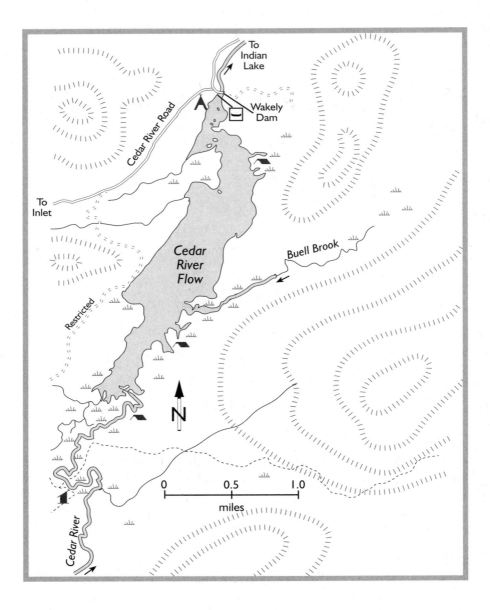

To
Indian
Lake

Cedar River Road

Wakely
Dam

To
Inlet

Cedar
River
Flow

Buell Brook

Restricted

N

Cedar River

0   0.5   1.0

miles

An aspen grove guards the entrance to the first cove on the right; farther back, spirelike balsam fir ring the shore. The shallow waters harbor, in addition to submerged rocks, tons of water shield, water celery, and a beaver lodge with its stash of cuttings stored for the coming winter.

On the main lake, we encountered piles of mussel shells, lots of paper birch, balsam fir, sugar maple, and masses of water shield, pond-weed, bulrush, and submerged rocks. Difficult to see in the dark water, rocks made frequent contact with our hulls—a small price to pay for the privilege of paddling such pristine waters.

Buell Brook enters from the opposite (eastern) shore, about two-thirds of the way up the flow. The creek's mouth hides from view amid a sea of bulrush. We paddled back up the shallow, sinewy, sandy-bottomed brook for about a mile, its depth varying from more than eight feet to just a few inches where sand and gravel deposits collect. Initially, the creek passes through a grassy marsh with Christmas-tree-perfect balsam fir spires scattered here and there. We expected instead to see tamarack and black spruce, given the marshy conditions. Fallen red maple leaves swirled in the undulating, crystal-clear current during an early October visit. Huge mats collected in the eddies, reminding us, sadly, that we neared the end of paddling season.

Reaching the lake's south tip, we paddled up over several beaver dams to explore the marsh. Alder abounds, along with typical marsh shrubbery, including sweet gale, leatherleaf, bur-reed, and much more. Occasional stands of tamarack foreshadow the filling in of the marsh. This area does not connect with Cedar River, which enters the flow on the southeast corner. Shortcuts will not get you to the river, as we found out after several attempts. Look for a thick line of alders and some trees, and head for where they end out in the lake. Follow the deep, broad channel, guarded by bulrush, with downward-pointing underwater veg-etation indicating the current's direction.

The meandering Cedar River flows clearly, the sun illuminating its sandy bottom. We paddled back up to the lean-to on the right shore; as we paddled a few hundred yards past the lean-to, the formerly barely noticeable current started to pick up, and we turned around reluctantly. As we paddled back under darkening skies, a beaver swam before us. After several meanders, it finally realized that we had paddled mere feet from its tail. It got even for the intrusion by splashing us with its flat, broad tail as it dove for cover.

We recommend early spring or late summer or fall paddling because of mosquito hatches from the swamps and black flies from the river.

Black Flies and Mosquitoes

Scourges of the North

Anyone who has spent any time at all in the Adirondacks knows these insects all too well. They can detract from outdoor fun throughout the summer and can make most of June virtually off-limits to outdoor recreation in the state's northern reaches. So what are these little beasts that hover in annoying clouds around your head as you portage your canoe or tie a fly on your line? Though it will not take away any of the itch, understanding these insects may help us accept them as part of the ecosystem we enjoy.

Black Flies

Black flies belong to the family Simuliidae ("little snub-nosed beings"), and most species of concern to us belong to the genus *Simulium*. Scientists have identified more than 1,500 species of black flies worldwide, 300 in North America. Only 10 to 15 percent of black fly species suck blood from humans or domestic animals.

In parts of northern North America, black flies cause considerable livestock losses—mostly weight loss because cattle do not eat well when tormented by flies, but they actually can kill cattle. In parts of Alberta, mortality rates from black flies range from 1 to 4 percent. Researchers have collected as many as 10,000 feeding black flies from a single cow. Black fly problems in North America, however, pale compared with problems in Africa and Central America, where the aptly named species *Simulium damnosum* has infected an estimated 20 million people with onchocerciasis, or river blindness (a disease caused by roundworms transmitted by the fly).

Black flies begin their lifecycle in streams. Adult females deposit eggs in the water, and emerging larvae attach to rocks, plants, and other surfaces in the current. Two tiny, fanlike structures sweep food particles into their mouths. Black fly larvae can become so dense that they form a slippery, mosslike mat. A several-hundred-foot stretch of a narrow stream can support more than a million larvae. In a river, the population can number in the multibillions per mile.

After a period of days or weeks, each larva builds a pupal case in which it metamorphoses into an adult black fly. When ready to emerge, it splits the case open and rides to the water's surface in a bubble of oxygen that had collected in the case.

Adult black flies have one primary goal: to make more black flies. Trouble begins when females seek a blood meal to nourish their eggs. Only females bite (actually puncture and suck); pacifist males sip nectar from flowers and may be important blueberry pollinators. Black flies rely heavily on eyesight to find prey, so they remain active mostly during daylight—and at temperatures above 50 degrees Fahrenheit. Some black flies fly more than 50 miles in search of blood meals.

No black fly species preys exclusively on humans. We are too new on the evolutionary chain to be a specific host to black flies, which arose during the Jurassic period 180 million years ago. An estimated 30 to 45 black fly species in North America feed on humans. One species (*Simulium euryadminiculum*) feeds only on loons.

Mosquitoes

Another insect nemesis is the ubiquitous mosquito. Mosquitoes, members of the Culicidae family, number more than 3,400 species worldwide, with 170 in North America. Three-quarters of the mosquito species in the United States and Canada belong to three genera: *Aedes* (78 species), *Culex* (29 species), and *Anopheles* (16 species).

As with black flies, mosquito larvae live an aquatic life; unlike black flies, most mosquitoes have adapted to *still* water. In any quiet bog or salt marsh, you can find mosquito larvae wriggling about, eating algae and other organic matter they filter out of the water with brushlike appendages. Larvae molt several times as they grow and develop into pupae. Both larvae and pupae breathe through air tubes at the water's surface.

Adult mosquitoes live short lives: females about a month and males about a week. The high-pitched buzz comes from beating their wings at about 1,000 beats per second. Females generate a higher-pitched whine that helps males locate mates. You can recognize males with a hand lens; look for their bushier antennae, used to locate females.

Both males and females feed on plant nectar as their primary energy source, but females of most species also require a blood meal to fuel egg production. As with the black fly, a mosquito does not really bite. Rather, she stabs through the victim's skin with six sharp *stylets* that form the proboscis center. Saliva flows into the puncture to keep the blood from coagulating. Most people have an allergic reaction to the saliva, comprising itching and swelling. Upon repeated exposure to mosquito bites, one gradually builds immunity.

Although really just a nuisance in New York, mosquitoes cause more deaths in the tropics than any other animal. They carry more than 100 diseases, including malaria, yellow fever, encephalitis, filariasis, dengue, and West Nile virus. The most destructive of these, malaria, kills about 1 million people a year, mostly children, and as many as 200 million people carry the disease.

Southern latitudes have far greater mosquito-species diversity (tropical areas can harbor as many as 150 different species in a square mile), but the numbers of individuals generally increase farther north. In the Arctic, with fewer than a dozen species, adults can be so thick they literally blacken the skies. In one experiment, several rugged Canadian researchers bared their torsos, arms, and legs to Arctic mosquitoes and reported as many as 9,000 bites per minute! At this rate, an unprotected person could lose half of his or her blood in two hours.

So, you see, we really don't have it so bad in New York. Most mosquitoes do not carry deadly disease (despite occasional cases of mosquito-borne encephalitis and West Nile virus), and even in the Adirondacks in June, we have found it rare to get more than a thousand bites a minute. . . .

Black Fly and Mosquito Control

Humans have tried many different control strategies. For mosquito control, we drained thousands of square miles of salt marsh during the 1930s and 1940s by building long, straight drainage ditches—many still visible. As much as half of the wetland area in the United States has been lost during the last 200 years—partly for mosquito control and partly for development and agriculture. Along with eliminating habitat, we have used thousands of tons of pesticides in the battle against mosquitoes. DDT remained the chemical of choice for decades because of its supposed safety to the environment—a claim that proved tragically untrue. Since the banning of DDT and other deadly chlorinated-hydrocarbon pesticides in 1973, osprey, bald eagle, peregrine falcon, and other important bird species have made a comeback in the Northeast.

Today, most attention focuses on biological control of these insects, relying on natural enemies of the pest: viruses, protozoa, bacteria, fungi, and parasites. A bacterium, *Bacillus thuringiensis* variety *israelensis,* generally known as Bti, discovered in 1977 in Negev Desert sand, has exhibited the most successful control. Gardeners use another variety of this bacterium for controlling cabbage loopers, corn borers, and other garden pests, and foresters use it for gypsy moth control. Bti bacteria produce protein crystals that react with other chemicals in the insects' stomachs, producing a poison that kills the larvae.

Although Bti currently enjoys high success rates, hidden problems could arise, just as with DDT, especially as bioengineers incorporate Bti genes into plants. This widespread and indiscriminate spreading of the Bti protein could easily lead to pest resistance. Conservation biologists also worry that monarch butterflies, on their 1,000-mile-plus migrations to their Mexico wintering grounds, will suffer huge mortality from Bti-engineered corn.

Protecting Yourself from Biting Insects
One option: stay out of the woods—buy a good book on paddling and read it in the comfort of your home. This might be a good choice in June when clouds of black flies and mosquitoes could stick in your mind as the most memorable part of an outing. Largely because of biting insects, autumn and May—during that narrow window between ice-out and the black fly hatch—remain our favorite times for paddling the North Country. During all but the height of the black fly season in June, however, these insects should not spoil your trip. Out on the water where breezes often blow, paddlers can usually escape insects.

Proper clothing forms the most important line of defense. During black fly season, wear long-sleeved, tight-knit shirts and pants with elastic cuffs, or tuck your pant legs into oversize socks. Black flies land on your clothing and search for openings, such as wrists, ankles, and necks. A mosquito-cloth head-net works well, but with a collared shirt, black flies will usually find a route in. Cotton gloves can help, too.

Mosquitoes can penetrate soft clothing better than black flies, so more rugged materials work well for shirts and pants. Wearing two light shirts also works. Tight cuffs are not as important because mosquitoes usually fly directly to their dining table.

Insect repellents generally repel mosquitoes better than black flies. DEET (N, N-diethyl-meta-toluamide) remains the chemical of choice in the Adirondacks. Fortunately, one of our coauthors, a chemist, can actually pronounce this name. Unfortunately, he also knows enough about its chemical structure to be concerned about potential long-term toxicity to humans. Most repellents outdoors people swear by have DEET as the primary active ingredient. Because DEET works by evaporating into the nearby air to clog insects' odor receptors, you have to keep slathering it on. Although we admit to keeping some high-test DEET around when the bugs get really bad, we recommend clothing as the primary defensive strategy.

Some new, more natural repellents, such as Bite Blocker, Buggspray Vanilla, and Avon Skin-So-Soft Bug Guard Plus, may work for you. Eventually, natural-products chemists will find very effective, totally nontoxic alternatives to DEET. Applying a nontoxic skin softener sounds really great. We would be even more excited if it kept black flies away. Maybe it does have some effect, maybe it even provides ironclad protection for some people, but we remain unconvinced.

In northern Maine, some locals use smoke as a repellent. Lots of it. Build a fire in a bucket, then stuff green leaves in so it spews forth thick smoke. And you stand in that smoke. It seems to work beautifully, but after seeing these in use (and enjoying their protection a few times), we wonder about the incidence of emphysema and other respiratory ills among users. Also, we find they don't work well in canoes and kayaks.

Is There Anything Good about Black Flies and Mosquitoes?

In reviewing all the problems with black flies and mosquitoes, one wonders what might possibly be good about the little beasts. The answer lies in the role they play in aquatic ecosystems, where they provide a vital food source for a wide variety of animals. Many game fish rely on black fly and mosquito larvae for part of their diets. One study found that black fly larvae constitute as much as 25 percent of the brook trout diet. Even if black fly and mosquito larvae do not provide a *direct* food source for our favorite game fish and waterfowl, chances are pretty good that they form a vital part of the food chain upon which these animals rely. If we appreciate angling for brook trout, listening to the call of the loon, or watching the stately great blue heron, we should recognize that these species might not be here without black flies and mosquitoes.

Without these insect pests, vacation homes long ago might have sprouted up on every pond, and the solitude we so appreciate might not exist. Even though we slap the little devils with a vengeance, occasionally slather on the DEET, and do everything in our power to prevent getting bitten, we should recognize that, yes, even black flies and mosquitoes have an important place in the aquatic ecosystem.

62

Indian Lake
Indian Lake and Lake Pleasant

Maps: New York Atlas Map 87:C6, USGS Quadrangles Blue Mountain Lake, Indian Lake, Page Mountain

Area: 4,255 acres, maximum depth 85 feet

Habitat type: huge deep lake

Fish: lake and brown trout, landlocked salmon, smallmouth bass, northern pike

Expect to see: peregrine falcon, osprey, loon, barred owl, deer

Camping: App. A #99 and 97 (on-site wilderness camping)

Take note: strong winds, funneled by nearby mountains, can cause treacherous conditions; novice paddlers should avoid this lake

GETTING THERE
From Indian Lake village, go 11.5 miles south on Route 30, and turn left into Indian Lake Islands State Campground and access.

Tired of camping cheek-to-jowl in noisy, crowded campgrounds? Indian Lake offers a peaceful alternative with widely separated campsites where you can listen to loons, barred owls, and whip-poor-wills calling at night, instead of to neighbors' televisions.

At 14 miles long, narrow and scenic, Indian Lake nestles among the sculpted cliffs and forested hillsides of the Adirondack peaks. Many people come to Indian Lake for weeklong camping. Consequently, we avoid

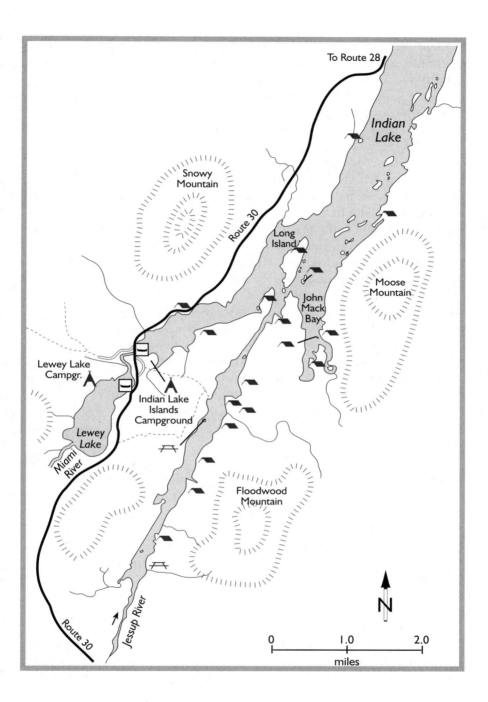

To Route 28

Indian Lake

Snowy Mountain

Route 30

Long Island

Moose Mountain

John Mack Bay

Lewey Lake Campgr.

Indian Lake Islands Campground

Lewey Lake

Miami River

Floodwood Mountain

Route 30

Jessup River

N

| 0 | 1.0 | 2.0 |

miles

Adirondack Park and Environs   **299**

the lake on the busiest holiday weekends, even though the lake's great size can accommodate a lot of boat traffic. Under calm or modest wind conditions, the lake offers wonderful paddling opportunities, with many bays, inlets, protected coves, and islands to explore. However, when the wind blows strongly from any direction, the surrounding hillsides funnel the wind, raising whitecaps and two- to four-foot swells, making paddling extremely hazardous.

We prefer paddling the lake's southern half, because the northern half suffers much more from weather, development, and motorboat traffic. The southern half harbors most campsites, almost all accessible only by water. Each site has a picnic table and a fire grate.

Paddling out from the access on the western arm, note the bare cliffs of Snowy Mountain off to the north, looking like a good spot for nesting peregrine falcons. Led by New York's Cornell Ornithology Laboratory, the peregrine falcon has made a miraculous comeback from the brink of extinction. Peregrines eat high on the food chain, where biocides get concentrated. Insects eat leaves sprayed with pesticides, concentrating the poisons. Insectivorous birds, in turn, concentrate the poisons even more. When the peregrine eats bird after poison-laden bird, it gets a much higher dose than that intended for those original insects. Now that we no longer use the most deleterious pesticides—at least in this country (we still export these lethal poisons to the rest of the world to poison their avifauna)—peregrine falcons no longer suffer from disastrous eggshell thinning, which nearly wiped them out.

We saw one of these incredible birds over the entrance to the lake's southwestern arm. The peregrine soars high in the sky, swooping down on ducks and other birds at speeds as great as an incredible 180 miles per hour. As it careens by its target, its talons rip open the bird, leaving a puff of feathers to drift slowly to the ground. We have seen this bird take waterfowl on the wing (its name in the time of Audubon was "duck hawk"), but its preferred prey in the cities is the ubiquitous pigeon.

Peregrine now nest on the large bridges leading to Manhattan and the other islands and on skyscrapers, as well as on cliffs in upstate New York. In 1994, 22 pairs fledged 35 young, and in 1998, 36 pairs fledged 69 young, showing that the peregrine continues on its recovery path.

As you paddle up the western arm, note the size of the deciduous trees lining the shore. Mature yellow and paper birches, sugar and red maples, beech, and aspen, along with hemlock, balsam fir (particularly in

Sea kayaks offer a great way to explore New York's larger lakes, as John demonstrates on a cool October morning.

wetter areas), spruce, and white and red pines cover the shoreline. Look for tall, conical balsam fir and hefty hemlock lining the narrow channel at the southern arm entrance. The usually quite-clear water in this 85-foot-maximum-depth lake indicates low biological productivity.

In selecting a campsite, particularly in the early season, choose an exposed one, trading off some tent flapping at night with an insect-reducing breeze during the day. The following campsites fill this need: 39 at the point separating the western and southwestern arms; 32 on the northern point of the small island on the east side of Long Island (lots of large boulders sloping to the water for lounging around; nice view up the lake, as well); 34 on the northern tip of Long Island; 28 on an island in John Mack Bay; 45 on a peninsula jutting out from the eastern shore about one-third of the way down the southern arm.

A nice picnic area perches on an island along the right-hand shore, about two-fifths (2 miles) of the way down. A second, larger one at the very end of the arm has three picnic tables, a grate, and an outhouse. Although it nestles back into a protected area that can suffer from mosquitoes, it boasts a beautiful series of cascading waterfalls flowing down a brook into a nice swimming area. This picturesque spot makes traveling all the way down the arm well worthwhile.

At the end of the long southern arm, the meandering Jessup River flows into the lake. In the spring, if you are willing to get out of your boat occasionally in shallow riffles and at beaver dams, you can paddle upstream all the way to the Route 30 bridge. This great wildlife-viewing area remains totally free of motorboat traffic.

63

Eighth Lake
(Fulton Chain)
Inlet

Maps: New York Atlas Map 86:B3, USGS Quadrangle Raquette Lake

Area: 320 acres

Habitat type: small lake in a scenic valley

Fish: smallmouth bass

Expect to see: loon, black duck, deer

Camping: App. A #94 (on-site)

Take note: part of the historic guide boat watertrail

GETTING THERE

From Blue Mountain Lake, go 17.8 miles west on Route 28 to the Eighth Lake Campground on the right.

From Inlet, go east on Route 28 past the Seventh Lake access for 1.9 miles to the campground on the left.

The Fulton Chain of eight lakes figures prominently in early Adirondack guide lore. Although intrepid mid-nineteenth-century explorers plied these waters in elegant wooden guide boats, taking downstaters out into the wilds to fish and hunt, some modern explorers prefer floatplanes, high-speed boats, and personal watercraft (PWC), all of which dominate the chain's first seven lakes.

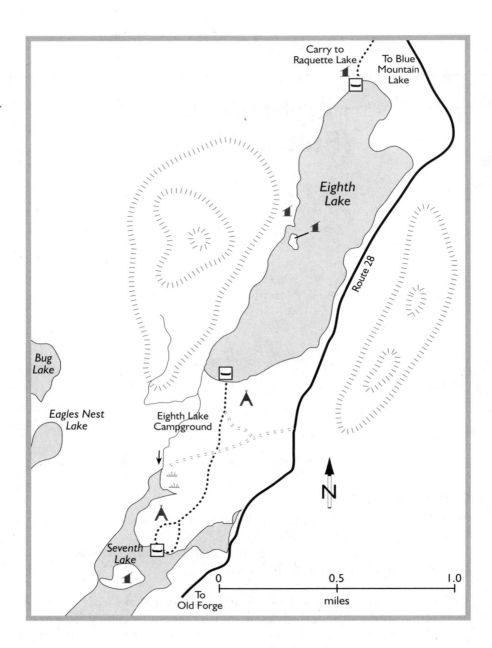

Carry to
Raquette Lake

To Blue
Mountain
Lake

Eighth
Lake

Route 28

Bug
Lake

Eagles Nest
Lake

Eighth Lake
Campground

N

Seventh
Lake

0   0.5   1.0

To
Old Forge   miles

The 90-mile guide-boat race from Old Forge to Saranac Lake draws overflow crowds as paddlers and rowers work their way up the chain into Brown's Tract Inlet, which joins the Raquette River drainage. Only on Eighth Lake, with its state-owned shoreline, can paddlers escape the development and powerboating that characterize the rest of the chain.

The invasion of PWC is more insidious than the invasion of Eurasian watermilfoil. The PWC exists for one purpose: thrill seeking, as operators jump wakes, drive 45 MPH or faster, tow children on tubes at high speed, run over swimmers, crash into each other and into boats, intrude on the peace and calm, and inject oil into the gas, polluting the atmosphere and water. In proportion to their numbers, PWC cause accidents and complaints about their behavior far more than other watercraft. When will we wake up and ban these cursed machines, at least from small lakes, ponds, and rivers?

Nestled in a valley with hills all around, and lying in a north-south orientation, Eighth Lake suffers less from prevailing westerly winds than the rest of the chain. The relative calm of Eighth Lake stood in

A black bear peers at us from its resting place in the woods near Eighth Lake.

Adirondack Park and Environs   305

sharp contrast to the wind-driven swells and whitecaps that dominated the surface of Seventh Lake when we paddled here.

Tame black ducks populate Eighth Lake, along with belted king-fisher, common merganser, and loon. The forested shores include northern white cedar, hemlock, red and striped maples, beech, yellow birch, and tall white pine that tower over everything else. The sole island has white pine, paper birch, northern white cedar, and nice rock outcroppings for swimming and sunning. Hobblebush populates much of the understory. Three shelters, independent of the campground and available on a first-come basis, occur on the island, on the nearby shore, and on the northwest corner next to the canoe carry.

The clear water means low biological productivity, and without marshy areas, you may run out of areas to explore and vistas to enjoy. Because you cannot paddle the outlet of Eighth Lake, you have to carry about 0.8 mile through the campground to Seventh Lake if on a long-distance paddle or wish to observe PWC frolics and seaplane takeoffs.

But if you crave wilderness adventure, paddle up Eighth Lake to the northwest corner and carry from there the 1.3 miles into Brown's Tract Inlet, a beautiful marshy stream that meanders east just over 2 miles, making its way to South Bay on Raquette Lake. From there, we would paddle northeast, skirting the left side of Big Island, and up the Marion River toward Utowana, Eagle, and Blue Mountain lakes (see Blue Mountain Lake section). Alternatively, you could paddle around to the right upon entering South Bay and on the east end paddle under Route 28 into the 2-mile-long South Inlet, another marshy stream, reputedly one of the most gorgeous in the Adirondacks. You would see a lot more than tame black ducks while paddling through these marshlands, we assure you.

When we paddled this area in the drought summer of 1995, low-water conditions and lack of rain reduced food availability somewhat, causing wildlife to move about more than usual. While here, we saw a fairly large black bear whiling away the afternoon, back to a large tree, pretty much unconcerned by the presence of our cameras about 50 feet away.

Although we did not see the abundant wildlife that you would likely see, for example, on the Marion River or North Branch of the Moose River, we did enjoy our only paddle on the Fulton Chain valley along the historic Old Forge to Saranac Lake guide route. We felt part of history as we hiked the extremely well worn path to Brown's Tract Inlet.

64

Limekiln Lake
Inlet and Ohio

Maps: New York Atlas Map 86:C2, USGS Quadrangle Old Forge

Area: 457 acres, maximum depth 72 feet

Habitat type: oligotrophic lake with marshy inlet stream

Fish: splake (state record 13 pounds 8 ounces caught here in 2004)

Expect to see: loon

Camping: App. A #100 (on-site)

Take note: surrounded by scenic hillsides

GETTING THERE

From Inlet village, go 0.7 mile east on Route 28, and turn right on Limekiln Road. Go 1.8 miles (2.5 miles), and turn right to the campground. Go 0.6 mile (3.1 miles) to the access.

Our first exploration began more than 40 years ago, when one of us paddled here as a boy. The lakeshore has changed some, but we were happy to see upon our return that state-owned lands surround most of Limekiln Lake, a rare jewel in the western Adirondack high country. Limited private lands on the northeast corner suffer from a fair amount of development, so you will see a number of motorboats during the summer— far more than we recall from the 1960s. Even so, Limekiln Lake sees much less traffic than most of the Fulton Chain vacation region. Nick's

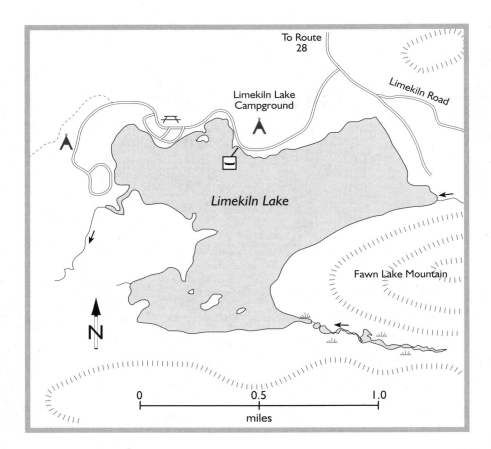

Lake Campground just outside of Old Forge fills up each night of the summer, whereas Limekiln Lake Campground often does not.

Despite the motorboats, Limekiln Lake provides a quality quietwater experience. Its high elevation (1,885 feet) and considerable depth make the waters oligotrophic, meaning very low biological productivity. The crystal-clear water allows you to peer into its depths and shows almost no evidence of tannic acid, which results from plant decay and turns the water yellowish brown.

Coves, inlets, islands, and bays characterize this small lake, and we enjoyed exploring each of them, studying the fauna and flora. Forested hillsides surround Limekiln with some modest vertical relief. Studying the high tree-species diversity around the shore provides a diversion from wildlife watching; we found red and sugar maples, tamarack, bal-

A marshy stream flows through beaver meadows into the southeast corner of Limekiln Lake.

sam fir, black and red spruces, hemlock, and white pine growing in profusion. Thick shrubbery dominates the understory.

In shallower waters, we found water shield, yellow pondlily, and other aquatic vegetation, but the dwarf fragrant waterlilies provided a real surprise. Distinguishing characteristics of the two dominant subspecies of fragrant waterlily include the following: *odorata* has purple leaf undersides and purple sepals, while *tuberosa* has green leaf undersides, green sepals, and leaves can grow to a foot across. The diminutive deep purple leaves—measuring no more than two or so inches—of the waterlilies in Limekiln Lake matched the minuscule flowers in size. We wondered whether the cold water of this high-altitude lake kept them from growing larger or whether this population of *odorata* has a genetic disposition to dwarfism.

Out on the main lake, loons dove for fish, and a common merganser family rested on a log, casting one wary eye at us as we paddled by. We suspect that the numerous black ducks hanging around the campground were looking for illegal handouts.

The small creek that flows into the southeast corner remains our favorite spot on the lake. As you paddle through the sinuous channel, note the large tamarack starting to fill in the marsh. We paddled by sphagnum islands loaded with carnivorous pitcher-plant and sundew, trying to eke out a little extra nitrogen from passing insects. You would have to travel widely to find a higher pitcher-plant density.

Balsam fir, black spruce, and yellow birch grow here, along with sheep laurel and other shrubs. Crush a leaf of one of the sweet gale plants that grow in profusion, and note its aromatic odor. We lingered here for a long while, watching the bright colors of a male yellow warbler with its red streaking on the breast. We listened to hoarse "chick-a-dee-dee" calls of foraging boreal chickadees. We studied bankside flowers and watched the sun dip behind the western hills. Mesmerized by the reflected glow from still waters, we hated to leave this tranquil spot.

65

Moss Lake
Webb

Maps: New York Atlas Map 86:B2, USGS Quadrangle Eagle Bay

Area: 115 acres

Habitat type: small, shallow, marshy lake

Fish: brook trout

Expect to see: osprey, loon

Camping: on-site wilderness camping permits 315-942-5789

GETTING THERE

From the junction of Routes 1 and 28 at Eagle Bay on Fourth Lake, go 2.0 miles north on Big Moose Road/Route 1 to the access on the left. Carry down to the water.

Simply gorgeous Moss Lake nestles beneath the rolling, forested peaks that typify this part of the Adirondacks. Its lack of development stands in stark contrast with the heavily developed and overused Fulton Chain just to the south. Though very small, Moss Lake can provide a very pleasant few hours of paddling, hiking, and enjoying the fauna and flora.

Surprisingly for the time of year, we saw a loon pair with chick during an early October visit. Though nearly grown, the chick must have hatched from a second nesting, after the first failed. Otherwise, the adults would have migrated to the coast by this time. The loon nests very early, giving it an opportunity to lay a second pair of eggs if the first

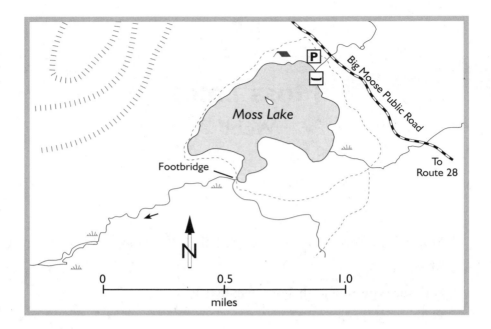

nest fails. They probably nest on the lake's sole island, where osprey also have nested in recent years on a dead pine tree.

The Moss Lake Camp for Girls occupied the lake and 600 surrounding acres from 1923 until 1972, spreading along northern and eastern shores and providing horseback riding, hiking, and canoeing. In 1973, Dr. George Longstaff, who developed the camp, sold the property to The Nature Conservancy, which subsequently deeded the land to the state to become part of the Adirondack Forest Preserve. During 1974 to 1978, a group of Ganienkeh Mohawks claimed title to and occupied the land but eventually moved the settlement north to the Canadian border. In 1979, the Department of Environmental Conservation razed the remaining buildings to return the lake to its primeval condition.

A 3-mile path—formerly the camp's bridle path, built in 1924—extends around the lake. Cross-country skiers use the trail in winter, and others hike it in summer. The trail meanders through mostly deciduous forest, dominated by sugar maple. We saw massive yellow birch and one enormous cherry, its roots folding over a large rock. A few large hemlock, spruce, and white pine added variety to the tree

Alex paddles back up the brushy outlet of Moss Lake.

canopy. The understory was thick with hobblebush (*Viburnum lantanoides*), ferns, and clubmosses.

The trees form a backdrop to the water-loving shrubs at the water's edge: leatherleaf, sweet gale, alder, and winterberry (a member of the holly family with bright red-orange fall-ripening berries attached directly to the branches without stalks). During our fall visit, a few scattered mountain ash added an extra spot of brilliance to the autumn foliage.

At the south end, a footbridge crosses over the outlet stream. To explore below the bridge, you have to lift your boat over. The sandy-bottomed channel meanders gently to the southwest through marshy vegetation. Fairly quickly, beaver dams block your progress. We carried across a couple small dams but did not explore far. With a little effort, one might be able to go as much as 1 mile down this creek before running into quickwater.

66

Stillwater Reservoir
Webb

Maps: New York Atlas Maps 85:A7 and 86:A1, USGS Quadrangles Beaver River, Eagle Bay, Number Four, Stillwater

Area: 6,195 acres, maximum depth 32 feet, average depth 6 feet

Habitat type: very large, shallow reservoir

Fish: splake, smallmouth bass

Expect to see: loon, waterfowl, great blue heron, wild turkey, deer

Camping: on-site wilderness camping

Take note: not for novice paddlers

GETTING THERE

From Lowville, go 17.4 miles east on River Road/Number Four Road, turn right on Stillwater Road, and go 8.1 miles (25.5 miles) to the access.

From Eagle Bay on Fourth Lake at the junction of Routes 1 and 28, go 17.3 miles north on Big Moose Road/Route 1, turn right on Stillwater Road, and go 0.5 mile (17.8 miles) to the access.

The Beaver River flows west out of Lake Lila—a wonderful paddling spot—into privately owned Nehasane Lake, down to Stillwater Reservoir, out into Moshier Lake, and into the lakes that comprise the Beaver River Canoe Route—Beaver Lake, Soft Maple Reservoir, Effley Falls Pond, Elmer Falls Pond, and Taylorville Pond. From there, the Beaver River meanders another dozen miles to its confluence with

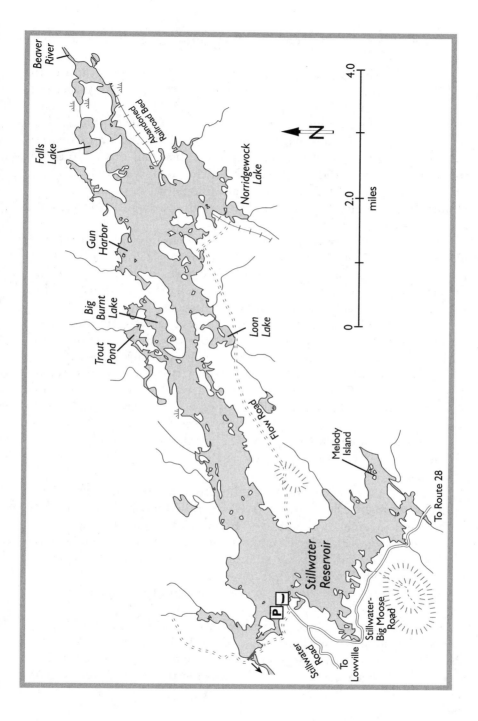

Beaver
River

Abandoned
Railroad Bed

Falls
Lake

Norridgewock
Lake

Gun
Harbor

N

Big
Burnt
Lake

Loon
Lake

Trout
Pond

Flow Road

Melody
Island

To Route 28

Stillwater
Reservoir

Stillwater-
Big Moose Road

To Lowville

Stillwater Road

P

0   2.0   4.0

miles

the Black River, which eventually flows into Lake Ontario at Black River Bay.

Along the river's heavily impounded route, many opportunities for paddling appear, including at Stillwater Reservoir, by far the largest body of water on Beaver River. The reservoir's 117 miles of shoreline and 45 islands beckon boaters in large numbers. In our trips to Stillwater, we observed about equal numbers of paddlers and motorboaters. In a rough survey, paddlers occupied more than half of the 46 campsites sprinkled around the reservoir. Many motorboaters visit this body of water just during the day to take advantage of the smallmouth bass fishing. Fortunately, the personal watercraft crowd has not appeared in great numbers . . . yet.

Even with 45 islands providing some shelter from the wind that blows off Lake Ontario, Stillwater Reservoir can roll along with huge waves. We strongly suggest that you paddle here only when the weather forecast includes a stagnant high-pressure cell. When the winds blow, paddle nearby Beaver River Canoe Route instead.

The first time we paddled here, a modest easterly air flow kicked up two-foot swells, but the second time the lake lived up to its name, with the surface barely rippling as arctic high pressure kept the winds at bay. The winds off Lake Ontario also carry a lot of moisture, and as the air cools as it ascends the Adirondack Plateau, it cannot hold as much moisture. Consequently, a lot of water wrings out along the western slopes, including at Stillwater Reservoir. Indeed, Stillwater also receives a huge amount of snow, carried aloft by winds over Lake Ontario; the record from the winter of 1971–1972 is 375 inches—more than 31 feet!

You can get away from most other boaters on Stillwater by paddling its connected lakes and bays. We paddled most of the shoreline, including a stretch of the Beaver River leading to Nehasane Lake. While paddling the lake's east end, we met a solo paddler who had paddled to Lake Lila and back. He spent four hours of this trek walking his boat through shallows during a low-water year. We recommend that the adventuresome paddle this in one direction, from Lake Lila down to Stillwater.

Our favorite locations on Stillwater include the southwest cove's Melody Island area; the sheltered coves of Trout Pond along the north shore; the deep, narrow, unnamed cove on the northeast; and Loon Lake along the southern shore, with its beautiful island for camping. We had

A lesser yellowlegs, a large sandpiper often seen in migration, runs along the shore.

to carry into Loon Lake, which you reach via a short, rocky stream that keeps out the motorized crowd.

The fishing must be good on Stillwater, as evidenced by the huge loon population. On one trip, we counted 34, including 4 young, as we paddled the southern shore from the access to the Beaver River mouth; of course, we missed some along the north shore. The small number of young did not surprise us because, even with 117 miles of shoreline, the lake does not provide a lot of good nesting sites. First, nest sites must be free from human and predator disturbance; second, fluctuating water levels drown nests or, more often, leaves them stranded; third, they nest on mounds of grass or other vegetation. As that dry summer proceeded, exposed rocky shorelines appeared, providing anything but ideal loon nesting habitat. Growing evidence shows that competition from unmated loons causes high infant mortality.

We observed a lot of wildlife here, including black duck, herring gull, raven, crow, great blue heron, lesser yellowlegs, spotted sandpiper, and dozens more bird species. We watched deer wander along the shore in many spots, but the biggest treat was to watch a wild turkey flock approach the shore either to get a drink or to pick up gravel to help grind food—you might need gravel too if you ate whole acorns.

Back in the protected coves we studied yellow-flowered bladderwort—an aquatic carnivorous plant—and several species of waterlily. Because marshes and swamp specialists do not appear in high numbers, Stillwater stands in marked contrast to our usual choice of paddling: swamps, marshes, bogs, and meandering, slow-flowing streams. The higher productivity of these latter habitats means more wildlife to view and plants to study. But here you can stretch your paddling muscles on a multiday trip, and it provides many nooks and crannies to explore—but keep your eye on that weather!

67

Beaver River Canoe Route
Croghan, Watson, and Webb

Maps: New York Atlas Map 85:A6, USGS Quadrangles Belfort, Number Four, Stillwater

Area: Soft Maple Reservoir 271 acres, Effley Falls Pond 294 acres, Beaver Lake 238 acres

Habitat type: interconnected small lakes with portages

Fish: brook trout, smallmouth bass

Expect to see: loon, deer, beaver

Camping: Brookfield Power provides water-accessible Soft Maple Campsite, 315-346-1756; Beaver River Canoe Route brochure, 877-856-7466 or e-mail nyrecreation@brookfieldpower.com

GETTING THERE

Beaver Lake. From Lowville, go 17.4 miles east on River Street/ Number Four Road, and turn right on Stillwater Road. Go 2.0 miles (19.4 miles), and turn left on Moshier Road. Go 0.6 mile (20.0 miles), and park on the right. Carry 0.3 mile to the water.

From Eagle Bay on Fourth Lake, go 17.0 miles north on Route 1/Big Moose Road, and turn left on Stillwater Road. Go 5.8 miles (22.8 miles), and turn right on Moshier Road.

Taylorville Pond. From the junction of Stillwater, Number 4, and Buck Point roads, go 0.5 mile north on Buck Point Road, and turn left on Soft Maple Road. Go 7.9 miles (8.4 miles)—passing Beaver Lake to Soft

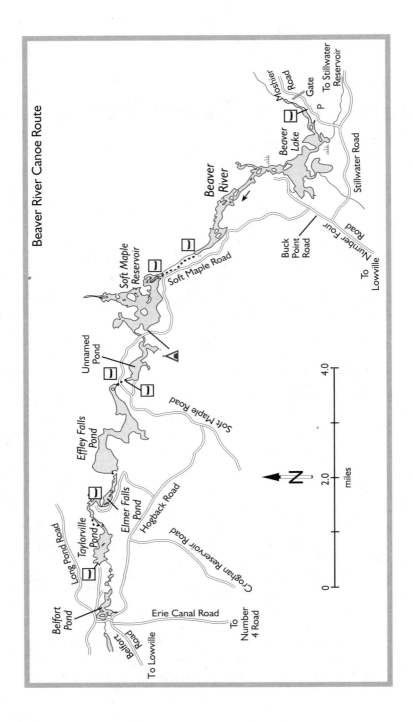

Beaver River Canoe Route

Maple carry at 2.5 miles (3.0 miles) and 3.3 miles (3.8 miles) and Effley Falls access at 6.0 miles (6.5 miles)—and turn right on Hogback Road. Go 4.3 miles (12.7 miles), and turn right on Erie Canal Road. Go 0.2 mile (12.9 miles), and turn right on Long Pond Road. Go 0.1 mile (13.0 miles), turn right on Taylorville Road, and go 1.0 mile (14.0 miles) to the access.

A series of connected reservoirs form the popular Beaver River Canoe Route. You can travel this route, starting at Moshier Falls, paddling east to west downstream through Beaver Lake, Soft Maple Reservoir, an unnamed reservoir, Effley Falls Pond, Elmer Falls Pond, and Taylorville Pond. Because of dams, only in a few spots does current impede upstream progress, should you decide to paddle the route both ways. During high-water conditions, fighting the current between Beaver Lake and Soft Maple Reservoir may prove difficult. Near the access at the beginning of every reservoir, water rushes out of turbines in proportion to power generated. At peak generation times, paddling against the current back to the put-in spot may be dangerous. Another consideration: on your return, all of the carries go straight uphill. We paddled this route in both directions and heartily recommend it as a one-way trip . . . downstream.

Beaver Lake

A study in contrasts, Beaver Lake starts at the Moshier Falls power plant, travels through an ever-widening marsh, necks down as it enters the main lake—which has a fair amount of development—and then enters a long, beautiful stretch of Beaver River, which in places has significant flow.

Just past the access, we saw two loon adults, along with a nearly grown offspring, in the pickerelweed and cattail-ringed marsh. If you have time, linger among the yellow pondlily, fragrant waterlily, and other aquatic plants that dot the huge swamp on the unpopulated southeast end. The extensive marshy areas that head off in all directions not only harbor a great deal of wildlife but also represent the only examples of this habitat on the canoe route.

As you approach the main lake, stay to the right to avoid the houses and to enter the Beaver River as it flows north out of the lake. Paddling around the lake represents profitless enterprise, that is, unless you want to see who can spot the most different kinds of boats. We saw canoe, kayak, pontoon boat, sailboat, outboard, inboard, stern drive, personal watercraft, bass boat, water-skier, floatplane, rowboat, and inner tube.

Fortunately, the next 3.5 miles take you down a relatively unpopulated broad channel, past occasional islands, with scenic wooded hillsides all around. Watch for Eastern kingbird—a black-and-white flycatcher with terminal white tail-band—perched on streamside branches, waiting to pounce on passing insects. The narrow leaves of water celery point the way downstream as a belted kingfisher flies before you. Flocks of cedar waxwing, with their conspicuous crests, alternately catch flies and search for ripened berries.

Of the entire canoe route, this passage remains our favorite. For those with limited time, we recommend that you stick to Beaver Lake and the Beaver River.

Soft Maple Reservoir

We paddled alone for an hour and then completed the long, 0.8-mile carry into Soft Maple Reservoir, where a pack of five personal watercraft greeted us. These two-strokers burn gas along with oil injected from a separate reservoir into the combustion chamber, producing a lot of noise and smell. Operating a two-cycle engine for an hour can generate as much air pollution as driving a car halfway across the country!

Soft Maple Reservoir, arguably once the most scenic lake on this route, suffers greatly from summer home development and has become overrun with powerboats and personal watercraft. We paddled across quickly. Unfortunately, Soft Maple harbors the route's only legal campsite—on the western shore just to the left of the peninsula that defines the lake's outlet.

We slowed down after clearing the peninsula to enjoy the yellow birch lining the shore at the outlet, which passes under an iron bridge into an unnamed reservoir. On our return trip, paddling back in the late afternoon, we saw here our only beaver on the Beaver River. This lonely fellow stayed close to the power plant, undoubtedly the area with the least human activity. It probably wandered here in the spring when parents drove away last year's brood to make way for new kits. It probably recognized its poor choice 'long about Memorial Day.

Unnamed Reservoir

A few well-kept, year-round houses greeted us as we paddled out onto this unnamed reservoir, peaceful and calm in comparison with our recent experience. Because no dam separates this body of water from Soft Maple, people might count this as a continuation of the previous reservoir. We hope this book starts a movement to secede. The two bodies of water bear no resemblance.

The generally wooded shore, with branches hanging out over the water, reminded us to slow down, that we intended to study plants and wildlife rather than boat wakes and paddle whirlpools, that, as Gandhi said, "There is more to life than simply increasing its pace." Although no marsh existed to draw in wildlife, we lingered here, enjoying the peaceful surroundings, as two people on a Sunfish searched in vain for a breeze. On our late afternoon return trip, the glasslike surface reflected the sun's inexorable march down through the trees to the horizon.

At the western end on the left side of a narrow channel, the carry heads off briefly but steeply uphill, followed by a half mile downhill to Effley Falls Pond.

Effley Falls Pond

Effley Falls Pond has some development but not nearly the traffic of Soft Maple. We stopped to talk to other paddlers and to some swimmers. And we saw nary a motorboat, much to the liking of the four loons swimming about.

We observed late summer monarch butterflies sucking nectar from clumps of purple aster to provide fuel for flight. The monarch, *Danaus plexippus*—one of a very few long-distance migratory insects—summers from southeast Alaska to Newfoundland and south throughout the United States and Canada. It also ranges to Argentina, Hawaii, and many other locations throughout the world. Remarkably, each fall monarchs migrate by the millions to Michoacán in central Mexico, southern California, and south Florida. They overwinter as adults, mate in late winter, and immediately begin their sometimes many-thousand-mile northward migration, an extraordinary undertaking, given that most butterfly adults live for only a few weeks. The heroic monarch hatches during the summer, grows through several caterpillar stages, pupates into an adult, flies from New York to central Mexico, hibernates among millions of other monarchs, mates, flies north to New York, lays its eggs, and dies!

Tracing individual flight paths among millions of migrating monarchs has not proved easy. By marking thousands of individuals in the Mexico highlands with wing tags, researchers then searched the northern

United States and Canada, hoping to recapture a few marked individuals. They found one in New York, and one marked in Toronto they later found in Mexico. Those overwintering in southern California migrate to the Great Basin and the Pacific Northwest.

What allows such a seemingly fragile species to survive the rigors of two such journeys? Part of the answer lies in its larval diet of milkweed leaves. Plants with milky sap often indicate the presence of poison. Milkweed contains chemicals called cardiac glycosides—heart poisons such as calactin, calotropin, and calotoxin. Of the monarchs examined in the Northeast, 90 percent had sequestered cardiac glycosides. Birds that eat larvae or adults generally vomit and then avoid eating any more. Monarchs rely on this food aversion to avoid predation on their long, slow flights. Flying at 12 MPH, monarchs would be easy prey during the 250- to 300-hour flight from New York to Mexico. When we see late-season monarchs fueling up on flower nectar, we look at them in awe, knowing the long perilous journey that awaits them.

Elmer Falls Pond

We regret that Elmer Falls Pond, with no development whatsoever, extends for just less than a mile. A slow, early-morning or late-afternoon paddle should provide glimpses of wildlife. We paddled quietly up to a doe with two spotted fawns that had come down for a late-afternoon drink under spreading hemlock boughs. A common merganser herded her flock of nine nearly mature young before us. The carry at the end goes over the right bank, steeply downhill into Taylorville Pond.

Taylorville Pond

Perhaps the nicest of the reservoirs—with its tree-lined grassy banks, fields of ferns under large, lacy green hemlock, red maple hanging out over water, and majestic white pine—Taylorville marks the canoe route end. The narrow upper channel necks down as it spills out onto the main lake, followed by a gorgeous forested island. Past the island, a power line looms in the distance, reminding paddlers that these reservoirs serve our insatiable need for power. Paddling the final lake in our hand-powered craft, listening to the haunting call of the loon, the epitome of northern wilderness, we should reflect on power usage in our lives. Do we drive fuel-efficient cars? Carpool? Take mass transit? What can we do to reduce our consumption of natural resources?

The character of the short drop into the main lake changes with water level; when we paddled here, we dropped less than a foot. But, coupled with narrow banks, the water moved swiftly, forming whirlpools in the churning water below. On our return to Beaver Lake, after a futile effort trying to paddle back up over the drop, we carried left (north), hopping out onto a gigantic pink granite boulder, hiking back a few hundred feet through a hemlock grove, and relaunching in the widened channel's slackened current.

We hated to leave this scenic spot with loon echoes bouncing off forested hillsides, nuthatch chattering softly from streamside, brilliant red cardinal flower beckoning from the bank, and the sweet smell of balsam fir wafting in from the woods.

68

Long Pond, Round Pond, and Oswegatchie River
Croghan

Maps: New York Atlas Map 85:A6, USGS Quadrangle Stillwater

Long Pond area: 146 acres, maximum depth 72 feet, river length 1.5 miles

Habitat type: small ponds and slow-flowing, marshy river

Fish: splake, brown and brook trout

Expect to see: loon, wood duck, raven, ruffed grouse, muskrat

Take note: to run Oswegatchie River, use Jamieson and Morris, *Adirondack Canoe Waters: North Flow*, 3rd edition (Adirondack Mountain Club, 1988)

GETTING THERE

From Lowville, go north on Route 812 to Croghan. When Route 812 goes left, go straight on Belfort Road to Erie Canal Road, turn left, cross the Beaver River bridge, and turn right on Long Pond Road.

Long and Round Ponds. Go 4.2 miles on Long Pond Road, and turn right on Prentice Road. Go 4.3 miles (8.5 miles), turn left, and go 0.1 mile (8.6 miles) to the access on the left.

Oswegatchie River. From the junction with Prentice Road, go 5.7 miles (9.9 miles) on Long Pond Road to the access. Hike 0.3 mile (10.2 miles)

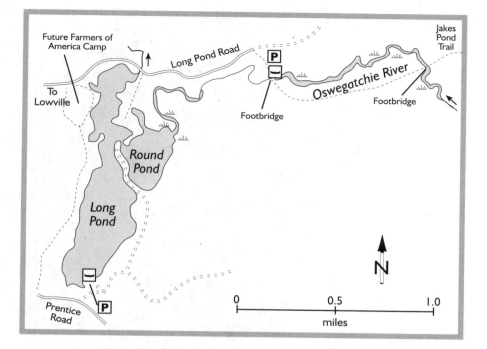

along Jakes Pond Trail, taking the left fork to the first footbridge; put-in on the far left side.

Long and Round ponds, in holes left by retreating glaciers, form two wide spots in the Oswegatchie River West Branch. We include these two ponds, along with an upstream portion of the Oswegatchie. You cannot paddle the river between the two ponds and the upstream section of river.

Long and Round Ponds

The Future Farmers of America maintain a camp on the northern shore of Long and Round ponds and own the land surrounding these ponds. Fortunately, they allow the public to paddle here, in a cooperative agreement with the Department of Environmental Conservation.

Arriving the night before our paddle, we camped nearby, dropping our sleeping bags on the ground, and listened to the loon's haunting call, echoing off the hillsides. A barred owl called its "who-cooks-for-you,

Dew-covered spider web on the inlet to Round Pond.

who-cooks-for-you" from the woods, and small mammals scurried through the dense brush. Still, we had no problem drifting off, soothed by the calls of the night.

We paddled here at first light, as mist drifted slowly across the water. We noticed a conspicuous browse line on the bankside hemlock that dominates Long Pond's south end. As we looked across, a deer ambled down for an early morning drink. The loon continued to call as we made our way north on still water.

Although many tree species grow along the shore, nearly pure stands grow in spots: hemlock along the east shore of Long Pond and red pine, punctuated by an occasional tall white pine, along the peninsula separating the two ponds. The generally shrubby shoreline gives way to a carpet of needles under the pines. Out in the water, fragrant waterlily carpets the protected coves, along with minor amounts of pickerelweed, some pondweed, and a few large patches of water shield.

A ruffed grouse drummed on a log off in the woods, and two ravens practiced their aerial acrobatics. A flock of yellow-rumped warblers cast about for insects, and barn swallows skimmed over the pond's surface. Two common mergansers tried to hide from us among the reeds of a shallow cove, and a belted kingfisher announced our presence to the early risers at the camp with its rattling cry. We felt slightly guilty about causing such a ruckus but later retracted those feelings: Tuesday is mechanized day at FFA camp!

While some campers took turns spinning around the lake on water skis, others took 15-minute floatplane rides—over and over, all morning long. Surprisingly, this did not affect the resident loons as much as it did us. We paddled up the inlet for its navigable half mile to watch the dew dry off streamside spiderwebs. We listened to white-throated sparrow and catbird call from the undergrowth, searched the water for beaver that own the lodge, studied purple elderberries, and then paddled back through tea-colored water to the access, under the floatplane's pontoons and through the ski-boat wake.

Along the way, we investigated the outflow under the bridge on Long Pond's north end. The current flows along here, tumbling down over a rock-strewn streambed. We turned around because paddling back up would be difficult at best.

Oswegatchie River

The contrast between these ponds and Oswegatchie River's upstream section stands out in our memory. Because you have to hike in to the river, few people paddle here among the tall tamarack and pine that dot the extensive marshland. Between the widened upstream river and the entrance to Round Pond, the river passes under a footbridge and cascades down over beautiful waterfalls. But upstream from the last cascade, the river barely flows through a sphagnum bog that covers a flat plateau. Because the huge surrounding marsh accumulates copious quantities of snow and water over the winter, water releases slowly, maintaining paddlable levels, even during dry summers.

Brushy banks covered with alder, leatherleaf, sweet gale, and other streamside vegetation lead to mats of floating aquatic plants. We carried up over a beaver dam and paddled through another. You can paddle back in for about a mile and a half, eventually ending in an enormous beaver

Fragrant waterlilies reflect early-morning light from the rippled surface of Round Pond.

meadow and sphagnum bog that extends off into the distance. As you near the second Jakes Pond Trail footbridge, you have to walk your boat through the shallows during times of low water. We had to negotiate around a bald-faced hornet nest attached to the downstream side of the second Jakes Pond Trail bridge.

Because we did not paddle here in early June, we missed the azalea bloom mentioned in the *Adirondack Canoe Waters: North Flow* guidebook. These showy flowers—in the heath family, along with rhododendron, mountain laurel, sheep laurel, blueberry, cranberry, and many other bog specialists—should enrich any paddling excursion.

Besides the beaver activity, expect to see beautiful wood ducks feeding on abundant aquatic vegetation that laces the tea-colored water. Muskrat harvest grasses, and deer come to the water's edge to drink. Birds flit about in profusion, and moose will tramp these swamps again. In recent years, this largest member of the deer family has returned to New York after more than a hundred years' absence. A feeling of remoteness and peacefulness surrounds this extraordinary place. If you want wilderness, this is a good place to find it.

69

Oswegatchie River

Fine

Maps: New York Atlas Map 94:D1, USGS Quadrangles Five Ponds and Newton Falls

Length: 13 miles from Inlet to High Falls

Habitat type: twisting wilderness stream through northern boreal forest

Fish: brook trout

Expect to see: osprey, wood duck, boreal chickadee, spruce grouse, gray jay, beaver, otter

Camping: on-site wilderness camping

Take note: to run another section of Oswegatchie River, use Jamieson and Morris, *Adirondack Canoe Waters: North Flow*, 3rd edition (Adirondack Mountain Club, 1988)

GETTING THERE

From Cranberry Lake village, go west on Route 3, 3.0 miles past the turnoff to Wanakena, and turn left on Sunny Lake Road (Inlet Road). Take an immediate sharp left, and go 3.2 miles (6.2 miles) to the road end at Inlet.

The remarkable Oswegatchie River upstream (right) from Inlet, an extraordinary canoe wilderness, drains the high country of the Five

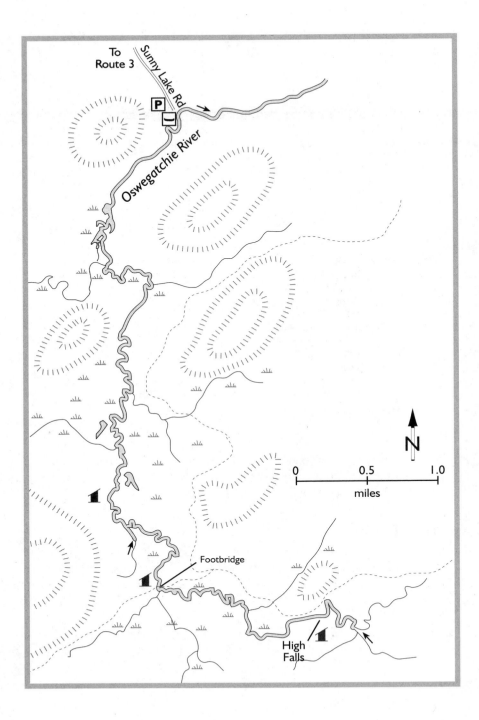

To
Route 3

Sunny Lake Rd

P

Oswegatchie River

N

0   0.5   1.0
miles

Footbridge

High
Falls

Ponds Wilderness Area. This is one of the few places in the Adirondacks without motors, so paddlers treasure this place; do not expect to paddle alone here.

This trip travels upstream (south) to High Falls and returns. You can paddle several miles beyond the falls, penetrating ever deeper into wilderness, but that has become a little more difficult. A violent windstorm ripped through this section of the Adirondacks in mid-July 1995.

We camped out near Inlet on the night of July 14, 1995, and had planned to paddle the Oswegatchie the next morning. As first light neared on the 15th, we awoke to great tent flapping. Desperately, we held onto the tent's fragile fabric. After a few minutes, the wind subsided, and we emerged to find the landscape littered with fallen trees. With all roads blocked by downed trees and power lines, we retreated outside the park to the north, the only direction with open roads.

When we returned to paddle the Oswegatchie three weeks later, we witnessed indescribable devastation. The Five Ponds Wilderness had been the epicenter of a storm that destroyed much of 1 million acres of timber. Just over 100,000 acres suffered greater than 60 percent tree loss, while the rest sustained about half that percentage loss.

Blown-over and snapped-off trees—all facing west to east—dominated much of the river's course. We skirted countless treetops, ducked under many leaners, and carried over several logjams. Many sections remained untouched, but then hundreds of acres of twisted wreckage confronted us as we rounded the next bend.

Hardly a tree remained standing on the right side of High Falls. One large cherry tree had crashed down on the lean-to on the right side; the lean-to had occupants—as it always does. Fortunately, the log structure held, protecting its occupants. Amazingly, none of the more than 30 paddlers and hikers in the wilderness died, though falling trees killed a camper at Eighth Lake Campground and another at Lake Lila.

Signs at the access warning, "Caution, Wind Damage, Unsafe Conditions," did not deter us or the several other paddlers we encountered. As we paddled out in the early morning mists through spirelike balsam firs, a beaver swam by, totally unconcerned by our presence, answering our question about what became of the wildlife during the storm. Beaver have done a good job pruning back the streamside alder.

As we penetrated farther into the wilderness, beaver meadows appeared on side channels. If you have time, carry up over the banks

Early-morning mists rise from the surface of the Oswegatchie River in the Five Ponds Wilderness Area.

through joe-pye weed into these meadows, as they provide excellent wildlife habitat. A bittern that had stationed itself upright to blend in with the streamside grass bolted skyward as we got too close. A snowshoe hare, wearing its summer browns, munched on grass, while flocks of cedar waxwing ate everything in sight, except the ripening winterberries whose bright red fruit persists well into winter because of low nutritional value. Birds and mammals prefer more nutritious fruit and insects. However, after depletion of other food sources, the waxwing and other wildlife do eat these berries, eventually scattering the plant's seeds to new locations in their droppings.

As we neared the first of five obstructions across the stream, an otter that sat feeding on a fish slid gracefully into the tea-colored water. Tannic and other organic acids liberated from decaying vegetation in the surrounding swamp turn the water into a rich yellow brown. Animal droppings on nearly every exposed rock tell us that this otter and the beaver we saw earlier have much company.

The surrounding boreal forest of tamarack, black spruce, white pine, and balsam fir provides habitat for rare northern species, includ-

Joe-pye weed

ing spruce grouse, gray jay, and boreal chickadee. We encountered only the boreal chickadee, with its gray cap and hoarse "chick-a-dee-dee" call. This habitat will eventually again include moose, as its wide cloven hooves and very long legs—the largest moose stand seven and a half feet at the shoulder—adapt them to life in beaver meadows.

A little way upstream, you reach a footbridge at the top of a riffle. At high-water levels, you have to carry over or pole through the riffle. Just after the footbridge, at campsite 22, a sign says "Spring" with an arrow pointing the way. Depending on water level, it can take all day—or longer—to reach High Falls. The downstream trip with the current and with lighter food packs should take well less than a full day. It takes more than three days to explore the wilderness fully. You may have to carry around an occasional logjam or beaver dam.

As we drifted back lazily with the current, we remarked at the abundant wildlife. In addition to the species noted earlier, we saw crow, catbird, yellow warbler, common yellowthroat, northern harrier skimming over the marsh surface, yellow-rumped warbler, downy woodpecker, wood duck, American redstart, black-and-white warbler, and magnolia warbler. A garter snake swam in S-shaped arcs across the river before us, and osprey and red-tailed hawk circled above. We wondered if their nest trees got blown down—at least the adults survived to build new nests next year. We would be back to check on their progress.

70

Cranberry Lake
Clifton, Colton, and Fine

Maps: New York Atlas Map 94:C2, USGS Quadrangles Cranberry Lake, Five Ponds, Newton Falls

Area: 6,995 acres (11 square miles), maximum depth 38 feet

Habitat type: large, shallow lake

Fish: brook trout, smallmouth bass

Expect to see: osprey, loon, waterfowl, great blue heron, beaver, otter

Camping: App. A #92 (on-site)

Take note: wind makes paddling treacherous; to run Oswegatchie River East Branch, use Jamieson and Morris, *Adirondack Canoe Waters: North Flow*, 3rd edition (Adirondack Mountain Club, 1988)

GETTING THERE
Northern access. From Cranberry Lake village, go west on Route 3 to the sign for the access on the left

Wanakena access. From the northern access road, go west 6.7 miles on Route 3, and turn left on Route 61. Go 0.9 mile (7.6 miles), turn left on Ranger School Road, and go 0.4 mile (8.0 miles) to the access on the right.

The third largest lake in the Adirondacks, Cranberry Lake might intimidate those familiar with Lake George and Great Sacandaga, with their

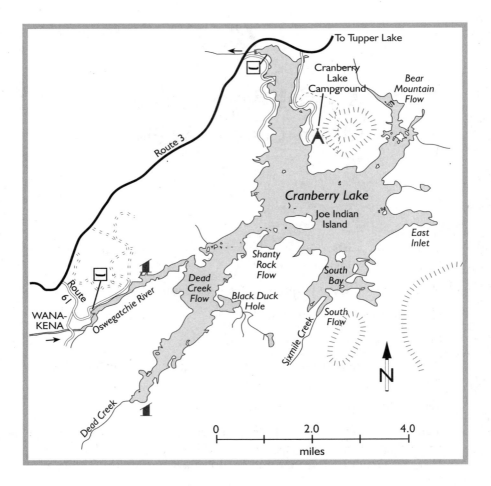

well-defined north-south channels that funnel even modest breezes into threatening swells. Though wind-driven swells on Cranberry's main body might swamp an open boat, it harbors many quiet coves that resemble a Rorschach ink blot, with jagged fingers containing 55 miles of shoreline running to the edges of the map in all directions. The two larger lakes attract hordes of large boats and personal watercraft, but Cranberry attracts far fewer boaters and about equal numbers of paddlers and motorboaters.

Cranberry's attraction lies in its protective islands that shelter quietwater paddlers from the wind and the 46 water-accessible campsites scattered about the shore and islands. Extensive marshes of Bear Mountain Swamp, a network of hiking trails in the surrounding Five Ponds Wilderness (118,000 acres) and Cranberry Lake Wild Forest (24,000 acres), abundant wildlife, and the lake's relative seclusion combine to make Cranberry one of the Adirondack's finest paddling destinations.

We prefer putting in on the quieter southwestern arm in Wanakena, where the Oswegatchie River East Branch enters the lake, thereby avoiding the congestion and development that characterize the village and surrounding shoreline. The Wanakena arm also provides access to more sheltered coves and bays, allowing you to avoid the main lake's windier open water.

On the Wanakena arm, hemlock lines the banks in places, sporting a conspicuous browse line where deer munch from the winter ice, particularly right across from the ranger school, which represents the last development on this arm of Cranberry Lake; indeed, the state owns and protects three-quarters of the lakeshore and most of the surrounding hillsides.

Numerous great blue heron patrolled the shallow coves, and hermit thrush sang from the understory in the early morning hours. An osprey fished the quiet waters of Shanty Rock Flow, and two flocks of common merganser tried to hide along the shores as we cruised by. Ring-billed gulls dive-bombed us if we got too close to their nests on bare granite boulders, and we watched a loon pair with a half-grown black chick swimming between them.

We picnicked on the smooth ledges surrounding the falls where Sixmile Creek enters South Flow. We hiked back along the trail leading away from the falls, searching the marshes for beaver; none seemed to be out in the middle of the day.

Granite boulders, some really huge, crowd the shoreline. Glacial erratics form small islands, even out in the middle of the main lake. Spruce, hemlock, tamarack, red maple, yellow birch, aspen, and many other tree species cover the hills that recede off into the distance.

Marshy areas exist at the back of Black Duck Hole on the east side of Dead Creek Flow and much more extensively in Bear Mountain Flow. When we paddled back into Black Duck Hole, black ducks dabbled for abundant succulent underwater vegetation. We watched an otter cavorting, and a huge beaver lodge provided the final confirmation that this area has abundant wildlife. A fellow paddler who visits Cranberry frequently said that he often sees otter in the lake's southern portions.

You can travel back for a couple of miles into Bear Mountain Flow to a very long line of black spruce that mark the end of the marsh, and you probably will paddle alone here. We turned around at the second beaver dam.

Extensive mats of small, red-tinged sundew cover the hummocks of Bear Mountain Flow, in as great a concentration as we have seen. As we looked carefully at these small, carnivorous plants, we could see the dewlike, sticky secretions on short stalks that crowd the outer margins of their rounded pads—their only leaves. Insects, attracted to these glistening secretions, become entrapped. A slight roll of the pad pushes the unlucky insects onto shorter stalks that contain digestive enzymes. The digested insects get incorporated into plant tissues, supplementing the meager nutrients available in swamps and bogs.

But large patches of a beautiful yellow-flowered bladderwort provided our biggest treat. Pushing gently on the long spur protruding from the rear of the flower opens the front two petals, revealing the interior reproductive parts. We often see both yellow- and, more rarely, purple-flowered bladderwort, particularly in shallow, stagnant water, with only the small bloom stalk above the surface. However, the bladderwort found here, genus *Utricularia*, shared the hummocks with sphagnum and sundew. One of the few terrestrial bladderworts, these plants trap insects on dry land, with their bladders immersed in mud, functioning much the same way as its aquatic cousins.

We spent several hours back in Bear Mountain Flow and saw nary another paddler. Ducks, great blue heron, and kingfisher kept us company. This was the last part of Cranberry Lake that we paddled, and the memory of the wonderful sights and sounds of the marsh kept our minds off the long paddle back to the Wanakena access.

Carnivorous Plants

The Table Is Turned

Carnivorous plants are fascinating—and a common sight as you paddle through New York's bogs and marshes. Specialized adaptations make them one of nature's true wonders and make us wonder how their meat-eating habit evolved.

Carnivory in plants apparently resulted from convergent evolution: the development of similar traits among unrelated species. Many different, completely unrelated plant families on nearly every continent have some carnivorous species. These plants have two characteristics in common: almost all live in mineral-poor soils and supplement meager soil nutrients with those from animals, and they use modified leaves to trap food.

Two main capture strategies have evolved: active and passive. Most people recognize the active capture strategy of the Venus's-flytrap, a plant that grows in sandy soils in a narrow band along the North and South Carolina coastal border. A few other carnivorous plants have adopted active capture strategies, and one grows abundantly—sometimes forming dense mats—in the quiet, shallow marshes and bogs of New York: bladderwort of the genus *Utricularia*. Bladderwort leaves consist of minute bladders that, upon stimulation, inflate and ingest insect larvae and other organisms, to be digested by plant enzymes.

Passive capture strategies have taken two main paths among the remaining carnivorous plants. Pitcher-plant—*Sarracenia purpurea*—collects rainwater in its funnel-shaped leaves. Insects, attracted to nectar secreted around the top of the pitcher, fall in. The plant's stiff, downward-pointing hairs keep most insects from climbing back out. Eventually, the insects drown, and a combination of plant and bacterial enzymes reduces the insects to absorbable nutrients.

Another passive-capture plant uses sticky surfaces to ensnare insects. Sundew (genus *Drosera*) forms tiny rosettes that protrude from a central root. Stalked glands of two types cover the modified-leaf surface. One type secretes a sticky substance that glistens like dew in the sun, giving the plant its name. Enzymes secreted by the second set of glands digests entrapped insects, drawn initially by the nectarlike secretions.

Each plant—bladderwort, pitcher-plant, and sundew—captures its intended victims in a different way, but each does so because, in nutrient-poor marshes and bogs, absorbing nitrogen and other minerals from insects and other prey gives it a selective advantage over other plants.

Do not be fooled by the black, fertile-looking soils of marshes and swamps. Black dirt like this in Iowa means fertile soil, but in bogs it means carbon from undecomposed plants. The tea-colored water, laden with organic acids from decaying vegetation and supplemented by acid rain, effectively washes out minerals. Although carbon dioxide and water remain plentiful, nitrogen, phosphorus, potassium, and other important elements get leached out or get bound up in underlying sphagnum and peat.

Bladderwort

Bladderwort grows in quiet, shallow waters or in shoreline muck. Keep an eye out for small yellow or purple snapdragon-like flowers, leading on short stalks to carnivorous underwater bladders. Most of the plant lives underwater in dense feathery mats, bearing hundreds of tiny (0.02 to 0.1 inch long), bulbous tarps that form the plant's leaves. The bladders have two concave sides and a trapdoor. When an insect larva or other small organism bumps into the door's guard hairs, the bladder's sides pop out, creating suction, the door swings open, and water along with the hapless critter get sucked in. All of this occurs in about 1/500 of a second, followed by slow digestion by plant enzymes.

In most ponds, mosquito larvae form the bulk of the plant's diet, but it also ingests other larvae, rotifers, protozoans, small crustaceans, and even tiny tadpoles. Plant tissues digest and absorb animal remains, causing the trap's sides to go concave again. With large prey, such as a tiny tadpole, the door closes around the organism, and part gets digested. The next time the hairs trigger, the plant ingests more of the organism, eventually sucking it all in.

Several species of bladderwort grow in New York, including two with purple flowers, one aquatic and one terrestrial, and possibly as many as 10 species with yellow flowers, mostly aquatic but including at least two terrestrials. We usually notice the presence of these plants when we see their snapdragon-like flowers protruding a few inches above the water's surface. Their dense underwater mats attest to their successful adaptation to nutrient-poor waters.

Pitcher-Plant

Although several other species of *Sarracenia* pitcher-plant exist in North America, the northern pitcher-plant, *Sarracenia purpurea,* has the widest distribution, growing from British Columbia to Nova Scotia, southward through the Great Lakes region, down the eastern coastal plain, crossing the Florida panhandle to the Mississippi River.

Initially green in spring, the pitcher-plant's funnel-shaped leaves turn progressively more purple, becoming deep maroon in fall, and return to green again in spring. Flowering occurs in June and July in New York, and single reddish flowers, borne on stout stalks, tower a foot or more above the pitcher cluster.

In contrast to most other species, the northern pitcher-plant does not have a hood to keep rain out. The curved pitchers recline, allowing rain to fall freely into the open hood. Because of dilution of the pitcher's contents, insects drown well before digestion occurs. The stiff, downward-pointing hairs in the plant's throat keep insects from climbing back out, and the relatively narrow funnel leaves little room for airborne escape. The upper pitcher walls sport a waxy coating, making for slippery footing. A combination of plant and bacterial enzymes degrade the unlucky insects, and their nutrients pass easily through the unwaxed surface of the lower pitcher.

Amazingly, several different types of organisms can live in the pitchers, unharmed by digestive juices. One harmless genus of mosquito, *Wyeomyia,* lives the aquatic part of its lifecycle in the pitcher, and other insects can escape by walking up the waxy cuticle and out over the downward-pointing hairs.

Sundew

To find sundew, look for tiny glistening drops at the ends of their traps. The smallest plants may measure only an inch across, making it easy to overlook them. Four species occur in our area, and we describe the most common species here: roundleaf sundew (*Drosera rotundifolia*).

This remarkable plant grows mainly in sphagnum bogs, from Alaska to northern California, across the Canadian Rockies and plains, through the Great Lakes, north throughout Labrador, south to Chesapeake Bay, and down through the Appalachians. The same plant grows in Europe, as well; Darwin devoted much of his book *Insectivorous Plants* to this one species. It averages about three inches across and about an inch high, with all of its leaves modified into sticky traps. A short leaf stalk ends in a flattened oval pad, covered with red, stalked glands. The longer glands secrete a sticky fluid, and the shorter glands secrete digestive enzymes. Insects, attracted to the nectarlike secretions, become trapped. Slowly, imperceptibly, the pad edges roll over slightly, placing the insect in contact with digestive juices.

The usually white but sometimes pink flowers hover well above the plant's leaves, borne on slender stalks. Although easy to miss, a little careful looking on sphagnum mats will show up many of these reddish rosettes. You should also see several small insects in various stages of digestion. And you, too, can wonder about how these plants developed the incredible ability to supplement the meager amount of available nutrients with those from insect prey.

71

Five Falls, Rainbow Falls, and Blake Falls Reservoirs
Colton and Parishville

Maps: New York Atlas Maps 94:A2 and 100:D2, USGS Quadrangles Carry Falls Reservoir, Rainbow Falls, Stark, Sylvan Falls

Area: Five Falls Reservoir 106 acres, maximum depth 40 feet; Rainbow Falls Reservoir 739 acres, maximum depth 45 feet; Blake Falls Reservoir 642 acres, maximum depth 45 feet

Habitat type: wooded reservoirs

Fish: smallmouth bass, northern pike, walleye

Expect to see: bald eagle, wild turkey, beaver, deer

Camping: McNeils Point Campsite, Blake Falls Reservoir, Brookfield Power, 877-856-7466 or e-mail nyrecreation@brookfieldpower.com

Take note: to run Raquette River, use Jamieson and Morris, *Adirondack Canoe Waters: North Flow*, 3rd edition (Adirondack Mountain Club, 1988)

GETTING THERE
From Potsdam, go south on Route 56 to South Colton.

Five Falls. Cross the Raquette River, and turn left on Snell Road. Turn immediately left on Three Falls Lane/Raquette River Road, and go 2.6 miles to Five Falls on the left.

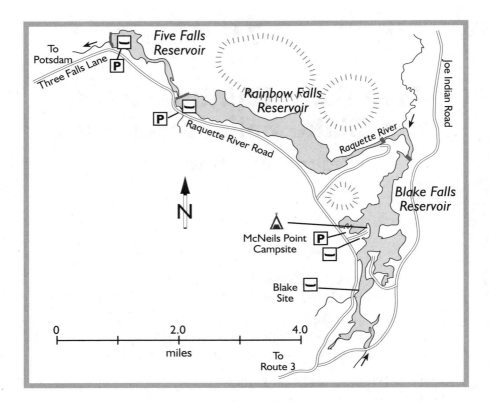

Rainbow Falls. From Five Falls, continue 1.4 miles (4.0 miles) to the access on the left.

Blake Falls. From Rainbow Falls, continue 3.8 miles (7.8 miles) to the McNeil Site or 4.7 miles (8.7 miles) to the Blake Site.

From the south, go north on Route 56 from Route 3, and turn right on Stark Road. Go 1.0 mile, turn left on Raquette River Road, and go 1.6 miles (2.6 miles) to the Blake Site or 2.5 miles (3.5 miles) to the McNeil Site.

On the northwestern edge of Adirondack Park, a series of seven reservoirs drowns out Raquette River rapids to provide electric power. What was once a beautiful wilderness river—second longest in the state after the Hudson—succumbed to our continuing thirst for power. Thankfully, Brookfield Power allows public use and provides picnic areas and campgrounds. We include here three connected intermediate reservoirs. With limited time, we would paddle Blake Falls, the nicest of the three.

Five Falls Reservoir

Small, quiet Five Falls receives little attention. If chaos reigns on the others, then we would paddle here. Where the main body necks down as you paddle around to the right from the access, note the rock formations near shore that extend out into the water, making passage difficult during times of low water.

The forested shoreline contains a wide variety of tree species, including both aspen—big-toothed and quaking—paper and yellow birches, red maple, red and white pines, northern white cedar, hemlock, and several others. A relatively open understory contains a large fern population.

We recognize aspen, members of the willow family, by its smooth, light green or yellow bark. In a light breeze, its leaves quake. It grows in association with pine and other conifers, and its golden yellow leaves in fall provide a beautiful contrast with the surrounding dark evergreens. Distinguish the two species by their leaves: quaking aspen (*Populus tremuloides*) has very fine teeth on its leaf margins, while big-toothed aspen (*Populus grandidentata*) has large serrations on the margins. Also, the big-toothed aspen trunk loses its smoothness as it grows larger.

Both species regenerate quickly after fire or other disturbance, serving as soil anchors. Quaking aspen also propagates readily by sending out root suckers, forming dense clones, all with the same genetic makeup. Taller species frequently crowd it out. In the West, with less crowding, individual trees may live for only 100 years, but the clone may survive for thousands, placing aspen (or at least its roots) among the oldest species on Earth. Furthermore, some scientists believe that an aspen clone is actually a single organism, interconnected by the root system. That would make some large western clones the largest organisms in the world—far outweighing the largest redwood, sequoia, and blue whale.

A few hundred species of wildlife—including moose, beaver, bear, elk, grouse, quail, and deer—rely on aspen for food from its bark, leaves, buds, flowers, and fruits. Coupled with its early successional soil-holding character, this food production makes aspen one of the most important tree species in the North Country.

We saw bustling among the branches, yellow warbler, black-throated green warbler, American redstart, and black-capped chickadee, while song sparrow and wood thrush hunted insects along the ground. A deer snorted at us from the brush, and we searched in vain for the beaver that had fed on tender aspen branches. We enjoyed paddling here among forested shores with a rich mixture of conifer and deciduous trees, but it does not take more than a few hours to paddle the entire shoreline.

Rainbow Falls Reservoir
Located between Five Falls and Blake Falls, Rainbow Falls takes much more time to explore. In spite of the houses that crowd the southern shore, we feel that paddling here still provides a quietwater experience, especially early and late in the season. The broad expanse of water near the dam on the west end gives way to an island that blocks the view of many of the houses. At the east end, the reservoir takes an abrupt left turn as it heads toward Blake Falls. The most beautiful area on the reservoir, this narrow arm sports forested shores and tall banks covered with lush vegetation, very similar in character to that found at Five Falls.

Paper birch, very similar to aspen in ecological niche, grows in profusion, and beaver hack away at them just as they do to aspen on Five Falls. In some sections, deer have created a conspicuous browse line by munching heavily on lakeside branches.

Besides the birds mentioned earlier, we saw red-eyed vireo, belted kingfisher, common loon, two families of common merganser, spotted sandpiper, black duck, and ring-billed gull.

Blake Falls Reservoir
By all odds the most scenic of the three reservoirs, Blake Falls provided us with the best looks at wildlife, even though we paddled here in mid-afternoon. Plant species also appear in greater abundance, and the aquatic habitat includes marshes, absent in the other reservoirs.

A wild turkey hen and her brood greeted us as we approached the water. This magnificent game bird, standing more than three feet tall, once inhabited most of the forested parts of eastern North America, foraging on acorns, chestnuts, beechnuts, seeds, and insects. With the clearing of forests, loss of the American chestnut to chestnut blight, and unregulated hunting, the wild turkey disappeared over much of its range. Recently reintroduced in many areas, the wild turkey now ranges over large tracts of New York.

As we approached the southern end, we spotted two mature bald eagles. Though we searched for their large nest of sticks, we never found it. Eagle nests may reach six or more feet in diameter, and the adults,

A majestic bald eagle clasps its perch in a hemlock on the south end of Blake Falls Reservoir.

which mate for life, usually return to the same nest, adding a new layer each year. Eventually, the nest may reach eight or more feet in depth and weigh up to a ton. Often found in dead trees that stand on partially rotted trunks, eagle nests make trees top-heavy, eventually bringing them down in windstorms.

As we paddled back to Blake Falls access, we reflected on the differences among the three reservoirs. Although the other two have relatively open understories filled with bracken and hay-scented ferns, Blake Falls has much more shrubbery. Its narrower channel lends it a more closed-in, riverlike feeling, making it seem smaller; indeed, because of peninsulas and meandering channels, from most locations it looks much smaller than the other two.

Back in the marshy areas—absent from the other two—we found swamp rose and swamp milkweed growing among many other wetland species. More conifer species grow here as well, including some large tamarack, spruce, balsam fir, and red and white pines. The lacy green foliage of hemlock hanging out over the water shades the shoreline in several areas.

72

Coles Creek
Louisville and Waddington

Maps: New York Atlas Map 99:A7, USGS Quadrangles Chase Mills and Louisville

Area: 680 acres

Habitat type: shallow, marshy dammed-up creek

Expect to see: great blue heron, deer

Camping: App. A #50 (on-site)

GETTING THERE

From Ogdensburg, go east on Route 37. Just after Coles Creek State Park entrance, turn right on Town Line Road, and go 0.3 mile to the access on the left. Or continue 1.5 miles (1.8 miles) to the Coles Creek bridge access.

From Masssena, go west on Route 37 to the Coles Creek causeway. Just past the marina on the right, turn left on Town Line road, and proceed as previously.

Coles Creek, flowing into the mighty St. Lawrence, has the distinction of being the northernmost body of water in this guidebook. A large earthen dam at its outlet backs up Coles Creek for several miles. Only truly tiny creeks feed the impoundment's southern end, which should make this body of water more a swamp than a flowage. Only about a mile away, Grass River drains a major portion of the northwest Adirondacks, taking away much of the water in Coles Creek's environs. However, the magnitude of

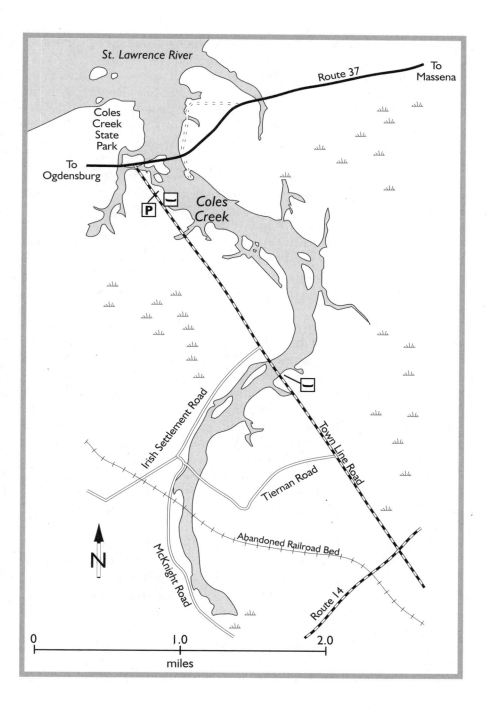

St. Lawrence River

Route 37

To Massena

Coles Creek State Park

To Ogdensburg

Coles Creek

P

Irish Settlement Road

Tiernan Road

Town Line Road

Abandoned Railroad Bed

McKnight Road

Route 14

N

| 0 | 1.0 | 2.0 |

miles

Adirondack Park and Environs 351

the northward-flowing water under the bridges and culverts surprised us, especially during low-water years.

The three causeways that bisect the waterway have low culverts or low stone bridges, not high enough to paddle under. Carrying over the two roads and the old railroad bed does not provide a challenge because the grades lie close to the water's surface. The several-mile-long waterway represents a real dichotomy: on the western shore, Canada goose and ring-billed gull gamboled in farmers' weedy fields, whereas the heavily wooded eastern shore with its jagged inlets has a much wilder feel to it. While a belted kingfisher guarded a cove's entrance, back in its depths lacy green hemlock boughs bent low over the water, lending a primeval feeling of dark isolation. As we watched a painted turtle slide off a log into the stagnant, pea green water, a great blue heron startled us as it bolted skyward, squawking away; we spotted these magnificent predators in nearly every cove and in many shallow, marshy locations. In two coves, we watched white-tailed deer drinking at the water's edge.

Tree-species diversity provides another contrast between the north and south ends of Coles Creek. Most everywhere, deciduous trees dominate the landscape. On the north, cottonwood, big-toothed aspen, paper and yellow birches, American beech, black gum, ash, maple, and basswood dot the shoreline, whereas on the south, large conifers have made inroads into hardwood dominance. Surprisingly, tamarack seems to be the biggest tree on the south end, with fair numbers of tall white pine and northern white cedar. Ferns abound in the southern understory, and sumac surrounds the old railroad grade. Near the far southern shore, the water and surrounding land turn swampy, with large patches of cattail and more and more aquatic vegetation, including pondweed, yellow pondlily, bulrush, and more. Bullfrogs called from the grassy shore and from among the lily pads.

We paddled back into every one of the many coves and around every island, finding great blue heron at every turn. Because of the depth of most of the coves, paddling the complete shoreline of Coles Creek presents quite a challenge for a daylong trip. As we emerged from the coves, the scene changed to common terns performing aerial acrobatics and yellowthroats singing in the underbrush. Loons dove for fish, and Eastern wood-pewees sang off in the woods. Some old beaver activity caused us to wonder why they disappeared. Will another colony move in to harvest the dominant hardwoods along the shore? Have conifers moved in on the southern end because of selective logging by beaver?

As we paddled back to the access, we noted another alien species starting its invasion: purple loosestrife. How soon will alien species crowd out our native species in these waters and shores? Only time will tell.

Western New York

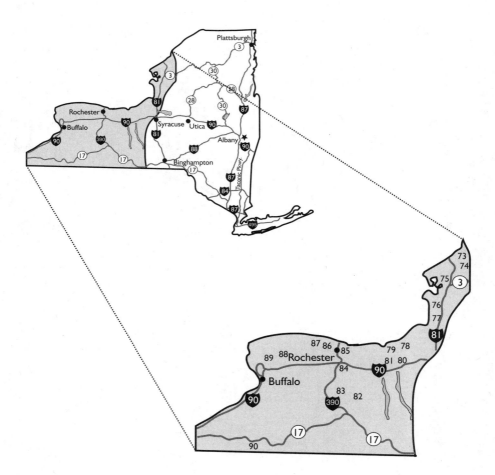

73

Crooked Creek

Alexandria and Hammond

Maps: New York Atlas Map 92:A1, USGS Quadrangles Chippewa Bay and Redwood

Habitat type: shallow, marshy, meandering creek

Fish: largemouth bass, northern pike

Expect to see: wild turkey, great blue heron, Canada goose, wood duck

Camping: App. A #47, 48, 52, 54, 57, 58, 61, and 64

GETTING THERE

From Ogdensburg, go south on Route 37, turn right on Route 12, and go to the Kring Point State Park entrance.

Route 12. From Kring Point State Park Road, go 1.6 miles north to the access over the Route 12 bridge on the right.

Route 1. From Kring Point State Park Road, go across Route 12 for 0.6 mile on Scribby Road, and turn left on Route 1. Go 0.3 mile (0.9 mile) to the access at the bridge.

Kring Point State Park, one of the first parks on the St. Lawrence River, dating to 1898, offers one of the most scenic campgrounds in the Thousand Islands Region and a wonderful base for exploring its streams and lakes. Half of the 108 camping sites front the water, and every site has a view of Goose Bay or the St. Lawrence. Because of its popularity, we strongly recommend reservations.

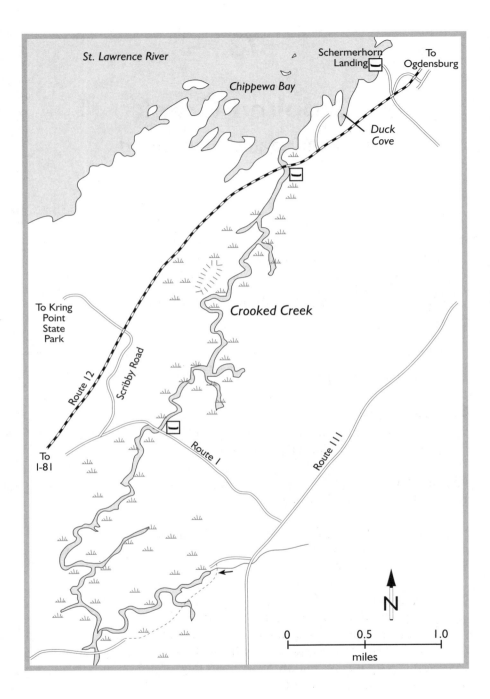

More than 1,700 islands dot the St. Lawrence, luring anglers from all over the East. Ironside Island—owned by The Nature Conservancy—just north of the park provides a home for the largest great blue heron rookery on the river. Dozens of treetop nests—some measuring six feet wide and four feet deep—dot the island. Only seasoned paddlers should venture out on the river, because of truly huge wakes churned up by commercial vessels traveling the Great Lakes and by large pleasure craft.

We recommend turning your attention inland to some of the small streams and lakes in the region. Meandering Crooked Creek, which wends its way through extensive marshlands just on the other side of Route 12 from Kring Point State Park, remains one of our favorites. Three access points provide opportunities for trips of different lengths. We had two cars and did a one-way trip downstream to Schermerhorn Landing. But first we put in at the Route 1 bridge and paddled upstream for just less than 3 miles, then paddled back downstream, under the Route 1 bridge, continuing down to Chippewa Bay. If you take a leisurely trip, stopping to explore side channels or to study the plants and abundant wildlife, this trip will take most of a day.

Cattails become your constant companion, but many other plant species, both aquatic and terrestrial, crop up to keep things from getting boring. Pine appears beyond the marsh's fringe, along with large red oak, but we focused more on the water. In one downstream section of the creek, tall cliffs—some rising 50 or 60 feet above the water—and massive slabs of pinkish rock add dramatic variety to an otherwise marshy paddle.

We found huge patches of bryozoa, an invertebrate in its own phylum (phyla include birds, mammals, reptiles, and so on). This bryozoan, in the genus *Pectinatella*, consists of huge, closely linked colonies of individuals called zooids. The zooids have protruding hairs, or cilia, that sweep the water to snare passing microscopic protozoans, algae, and diatoms. The slimy, gelatinous colonies look somewhat like translucent pineapples. An indicator species, its welcome presence points to pollution-free water.

Besides the ubiquitous cattails, we found rafts of yellow pondlily, lots of fragrant waterlily, a fair amount of floating heart in the upper reaches, and frequent large patches of yellow-flowered bladderwort in the tea-colored water.

We watched a red-tailed hawk pair circling lazily on afternoon thermals, rising skyward to get a better view of the surrounding fields. These rodent specialists have the widest range of all U.S. hawks, inhabiting every conceivable niche from desert to wet forest, sea level to mountain-top, coast to coast, and border to border. We also saw a few wild turkey, strutting in the fields.

We also looked for typical marsh species, including large numbers of great blue heron, common yellowthroat, and the most abundant bird, the red-winged blackbird. We very much enjoyed our lazy trip down the creek, and because of our pleasant experience, we really did not mind having to paddle the last little bit to Schermerhorn Landing out on crowded Chippewa Bay. If you plan a one-way trip ending at the land-ing, and if you get out onto a bay with wind-whipped waves, we strongly suggest that you paddle back upstream to the Route 12 bridge and walk the 1.4 miles to Schermerhorn Landing to retrieve your second vehicle.

74

Red Lake and Indian River

Theresa

Maps: New York Atlas Map 92:B2, USGS Quadrangles Muskel-lunge Lake and Redwood

Area: 366 acres, maximum depth 47 feet

Habitat type: winding, slow-flowing river and shallow lake

Fish: largemouth and smallmouth bass, walleye, northern pike

Expect to see: osprey, red-tailed hawk, great blue heron, wood duck, wild turkey

Camping: App. A #47, 48, 52, 54, 57, 58, 61, and 64

Take note: stay off Indian River during high water

GETTING THERE

From I-81, Exit 49, go 4.6 miles east on Routes 411 and 26 to Theresa, and turn left on Commercial Street. Go 0.1 mile (4.7 miles), and turn left on Bridge Street. Go 0.2 mile (4.9 miles), and turn left on Red Lake Road. Go 2.8 miles (7.7 miles), veer left on Red Lake Road, and go 0.9 mile (8.6 miles) to a fork. Go left 0.1 mile (8.7 miles) to Indian River or right 1.0 mile (9.6 miles) to Red Lake.

Red Lake

A great blue heron stood near the access where pickerelweed, bulrush, and grasses crowd the shoreline. Along much of the lake's southeastern side,

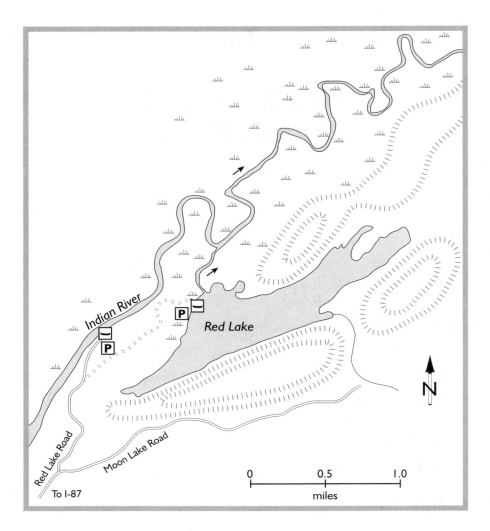

extensive cliffs extend upward from the water 100 feet or more. Many areas drip with polypody fern, lichens, and thick moss. On the more exposed cliff faces, look for delicate, lavender bell-like flowers of harebell, which has become established in the tiniest of cracks. Scarlet cardinal flower—always a favorite—grows in rocky soil closer to the water.

On less-steep banks, a diverse mix of conifer and deciduous trees—everything from northern white cedar to species usually found farther south, such as shagbark hickory and white oak—have taken hold. Hem-

Crimson cardinal flower in bloom along the banks of Indian River.

lock, white pine, paper birch, basswood, white ash, silver and sugar maples, and red oak also appear. High species diversity occurs here because it represents a transition between high-elevation Adirondacks and low-lying St. Lawrence floodplain.

Just northwest of the access, Red Lake flows slowly through a broad, deep outlet channel, passing between a marsh and a small hill, flowing for less than a half mile into Indian River. Thick vegetation covers the banks, but surprisingly little floating vegetation occurs in the channel.

Indian River

Flowing northeast toward Black Lake and the St. Lawrence, the river channel meanders extensively. Minimal midsummer current makes paddling in both directions fairly easy. In spring and after heavy rainfall, water levels rise quickly, as the Indian River and its tributaries drain a sizable portion of the western Adirondacks. After a steady rain, the river can rise a few feet in less than 24 hours. At high water, the river spreads out, providing access to bottomland, but current makes it more dangerous and difficult, if not impossible, to paddle in both directions.

Thick aquatic vegetation lines the river. Pickerelweed dominates in most areas, with patches of arrowhead mixed in. Cardinal flower and swamp milkweed grow in abundance, along with buttonbush—with white spherical flower clusters and sycamore-like seedpods.

Along a 5-mile stretch of river, we passed several beaver lodges, including a massive one with lots of cuttings. Mussel shells littered the bottom and shoreline. We saw red-tailed hawk, osprey, kingfisher, yellow warbler, common yellowthroat, white-throated sparrow, great blue heron, Eastern phoebe, Eastern wood-pewee, red-winged blackbird, grackle, and ring-billed gull. Painted turtles sought a few rays of sunlight on a mostly overcast afternoon.

As we rounded a bend, a group of turkey vultures erupted into flight. They had been feeding on the bloated carcass of a huge snapping turtle. The vultures' broad wings wafted essence of long-dead turtle onto the river as we beat a hasty retreat from the malodors.

75

Black River Bay
Brownsville and Hounsfield

Maps: New York Atlas Maps 83:D6 and 91:D6, USGS Quadrangles Dexter and Sackets Harbor

Habitat type: shallow, marshy bay

Fish: largemouth and smallmouth bass, northern pike

Expect to see: waterfowl, great blue heron, Caspian and black terns

Camping: App. A #59 and 65

Take note: winds can make paddling treacherous on the main bay

GETTING THERE
Military Road. From Watertown, go west on Route 3, and turn right on Route 180. Go 1.2 miles, and turn left on Military Road. Go 1.3 miles (2.5 miles) to the access on the right.

Muskellunge Creek. From the junction of Military Road and Route 180, go 0.3 mile (1.5 miles) north on Route 180 to the access on the left.

A shallow, marshy wildlife paradise, Dexter Wildlife Management Area protects Black River Bay from development. The northernmost wildlife management area on Lake Ontario's eastern shore, Dexter harbors many plants and animals and few paddlers.

We launched at sunup from the private campground on Black River, paddling southwest down to the bay. After clearing the campground,

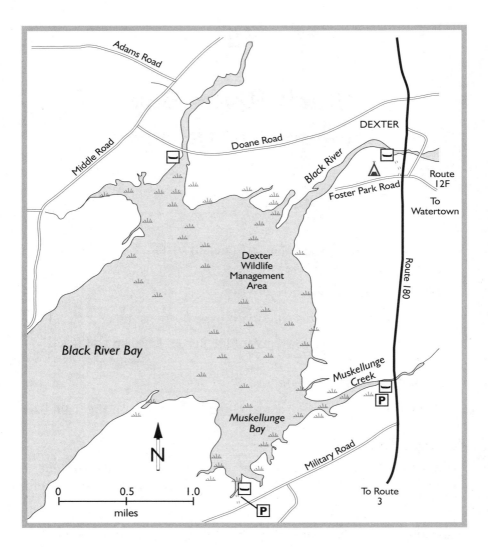

we paddled by a few small islands with beautiful fractured rock formations, eventually leading out onto a huge bay with Lake Ontario in the background. We were totally unprepared for the unfolding sight. Water shimmering on the horizon made it impossible to judge distance over the glasslike surface that lay before us. Ripples created by Caspian terns diving on fish barely stirred the surface waters. Rarely do we confront a body of water this large under such calm conditions.

When we paddled here in July, a high-pressure cell had stalled over the eastern Great Lakes, providing crystal-clear skies and, more importantly, absolutely windless conditions. In summer, afternoon breezes blowing eastward off Lake Ontario can whip up formidable waves that surge unimpeded up Black River Bay, making boating treacherous. Under windy conditions, we strongly recommend sticking to more protected Muskellunge Bay.

Along Black River Bay's northern edge, a northern water snake (*Nerodia sipedon*) swam along with us for a short distance before retreating into the cattails. Huge carp periodically startled us as they thrashed in the shallow, muddy water.

Much of Muskellunge Bay, particularly the southern end, contains intermittent dense stands of cattail that protect wildlife and paddlers from wind-driven waves. Here we found, literally, a dozen great blue herons fishing the shallows and several nesting black terns. When we got too close to one of the small cattail islands, three or four black terns dive-bombed us until we retreated quite a distance.

On the bay's east end, cattail-covered islands give way to willow-clad shores. Here, among the trees, we listened to the Eastern wood-pewee's "pee-o-wee"; the tufted titmouse's whistled "peet-er, peet-er, peet-er"; and the cardinal's "bir-dee, bir-dee, bir-dee." Beaver had dined recently on felled willow. A crow-sized pileated woodpecker flew in undulating flight over the water in front of us, alighting in a dead tree. But the real attraction remained the marsh.

We found the diminutive yellow pondlily, *Nuphar microphyllum*, with leaves less than five inches long and flowers less than an inch across. Floating heart, *Nymphoides cordata*, an aquatic gentian with small heart-shaped leaves and small white flowers, choked the channel in protected areas. Acres of white and yellow waterlilies, plants that do not grow in water deeper than four feet, confirmed the bay's shallowness.

Clumps of arrowhead and yellow-flowered bladderwort, especially along Muskellunge Creek, added to the interesting plants to study. We watched as many as five great blue herons fishing at once, and ducks scurried into the cattails as we approached. Spotted sandpipers bobbed along the shore, and barn swallows skimmed the water's surface for a morning drink. We watched a cormorant trying to deal with a fish way too large to swallow, as marsh wrens serenaded us with their melodious songs off in the cattails. We spent most of the morning paddling the entire shoreline of the bay's south end, a great place for quietwater paddlers to study plants and wildlife.

76

Lakeview Wildlife Management Area— North and South Colwell Ponds, Goose Pond, Floodwood Pond, and Lakeview Pond

Ellisburg

Maps: New York Atlas Map 83:C5, USGS Quadrangles Ellisburg and Henderson

Area: 3,461 acres in the Wildlife Management Area

Habitat type: shallow, marshy ponds; small, wooded streams

Fish: largemouth bass, northern pike, steelhead (spring), chinook salmon (fall)

Expect to see: black tern, waterfowl, muskrat, deer

Camping: App. A #14 and 63

Take note: 10 hp limit

GETTING THERE
Colwell Ponds. From I-81, Exit 36, go west on Route 13 to Route 3. Turn right, go 9.8 miles north, and turn left on Montario Point Road. Go 0.7 mile (10.5 miles), turn right, and go 0.3 mile (10.8 miles) to the access.

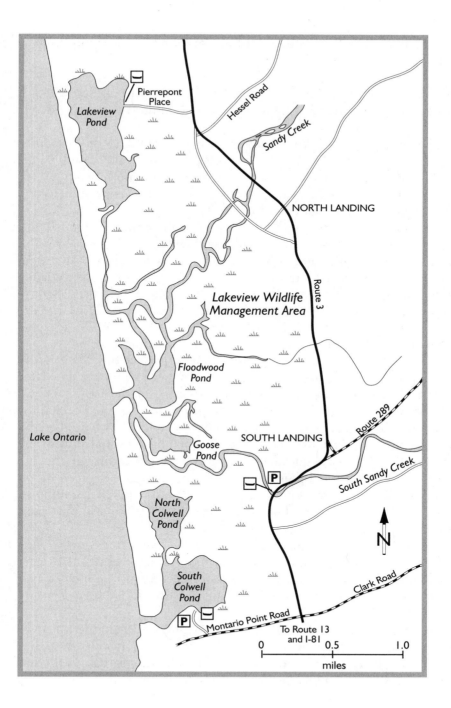

Pierrepont
Place

Lakeview
Pond

Hessel Road

Sandy Creek

NORTH LANDING

Route 3

Lakeview Wildlife
Management Area

Floodwood
Pond

Lake Ontario

Goose
Pond

SOUTH LANDING

Route 289

South Sandy Creek

P

North
Colwell
Pond

N

South
Colwell
Pond

Clark Road

P

Montario Point Road

To Route 13
and I-81

0   0.5   1.0

miles

South Sandy Creek. Continue 1.1 miles (10.9 miles) north on Route 3 to the access on the left.

Lakeview Pond. Continue 3.2 miles (14.1 miles) north on Route 3, and turn left on Pierrepont Place. Go 0.5 mile (14.6 miles) to the access.

Paddlers may enter Lakeview Wildlife Management Area on the south, southeast, and north. The southern access provides access to only South and North Colwell ponds. The other two—one on South Sandy Creek and the other on Lakeview Pond—provide access to a series of interconnected creeks, sloughs, and ponds.

On your way to the South Colwell Pond off Montario Point Road, stop at the lookout tower on the right, and enjoy the view out over the marsh. Most of Lake Ontario's eastern shore harbored extensive wetlands. Although shortsighted humans drained some of these wetlands for agriculture and development, extensive pockets remain protected by a series of six state parks and wildlife management areas. The large expanse trailing off into the distance before you—Lakeview Wildlife Management Area—represents the largest of these remaining wetlands.

We paddled Colwell ponds in mid-June, a perfect time for wildlife viewing. Because little water flows through these scenic ponds, they later become choked with aquatic vegetation. Trees cover the barrier dunes, and narrow-leaved cattail rings the ponds, providing protected habitat for numerous white-tailed deer and multihued wood duck. As we paddled the shoreline in early morning, flocks of male wood duck exploded from the cattails with their very unducklike cries, and deer crashed through the cattails after we interrupted their morning drink. In contrast, green heron waited patiently over the water, suspended from low perches waiting to spear passing fish, and great blue heron stood stock-still out in the water, also waiting, but for somewhat larger passing fish.

Even in mid-June, aquatic plants crowded the water's surface, including an extensive patch of water crowfoot—a member of the buttercup family—with its small white flowers projecting just an inch or two above the water's surface. Note its submerged, threadlike leaves, evenly spaced along the stalk.

As we paddled out through a light morning mist hanging low over the water, a huge caddis fly hatch was on. Millions of tiny all-white flies flew erratically over the surface in a primordial mating ritual. As the sun rose in the sky, the caddis flies headed for the filtered light making its way through tall trees. Caddis fly larvae build underwater structures of small twigs or stones and feed on microscopic underwater plants and animals that drift by. When they hatch into adults, they can be identified by their wings running the length of their bodies, folded over their backs like tents.

As we watched the terns, seemingly for an hour, we also watched the pond's surface change from early-morning glasslike conditions to a wind-rippled surface. As the sun heats the land, warm air rises. To replace the rising mass, cooler replacement air drifts in from Lake Ontario's surface, quietly at first, building in strength throughout the morning and early afternoon. Toward evening, with the setting sun, the wind dies again and drifts toward calm.

Somewhat reluctantly, we left the terns and headed to South Sandy Creek. With two cars, paddlers could travel from the north end of Lakeview Pond, down through Floodwood and Goose Ponds, and up South Sandy Creek to the access. With winds out of the south, you might want to paddle this route in the opposite direction. With winds off Lake Ontario—the usual state of affairs—coastal dunes provide some protection from the wind, and travel direction becomes less important.

If you wish solitude, we recommend putting in at South Sandy Creek and paddling downstream into Goose Pond. Large willow and huge box elder crowd the water; several deadfalls—called structure by anglers—provide habitat for fish and turtles. We had no problem paddling around them. Surprisingly, we found a muskrat sitting out on a deadfall, just watching us as we glided by.

Resist the temptation to paddle by Goose Pond, a wild, wonderful place to study aquatic plants and ducks in solitude. Yellow pondlily mats the surface, and clumps of very-narrow-leaved arrowhead poke up in clusters, and pickerelweed appears in patches. Cattail, with hidden marsh wren singing its melodious song, rings the pond. More black terns skimmed the marsh's surface, while ducks fed near the edges. Deer cautiously edged out to the water for a drink.

Floodwood Pond has more open water than Goose Pond but has its share of aquatic plants. As you paddle north out of Floodwood, watch carefully for a narrow channel heading west that leads to Lakeview Pond. Yellow pondlilies cover this long, straight channel, providing outstanding habitat for pike, bass, turtles, and frogs.

We spent some time here trying to sort out the four resident species of *Nuphar* or yellow pondlily. We distinguished the two larger-flow-

View from the lookout tower out over the flat coastal plain of the Lakeview Wildlife Management Area and Lake Ontario.

ered (1.5 to 2.5 inch wide), larger-leaved (8 to 15 inch long) species by how the leaf lobes leave the submerged stalk. In *Nuphar advena*, the lobes diverge at about a 45-degree angle, while the lobes on *N. variegata* cross each other. *N. microphyllum*, as its name suggests, has leaves less than 5 inches long and flowers less than an inch wide. The fourth species, *N.xrubrodiscum*, the most difficult to identify, has 5- to 8-inch-long leaves, 1 to 1.5 inch-wide flowers, stigma with more than 10 rays (fewer than 10 in *N. microphyllum*), and leaf notch about half the midrib length (two-thirds in *N. microphyllum*). In practice, the last two species gave us fits, perhaps because *N. rubrodiscum* may be a hybrid of *N. microphyllum* and another *Nuphar* species.

Returning from Lakeview Pond, you can turn left (northeast) onto Sandy Creek. We paddled up Sandy Creek to North Landing to the string of camps and houses on the island where the creek divides. Given the huge expanse of wetland wilderness waiting for exploration downstream, we decided to turn around. On the way back, watch for the relatively wide human-made connector that leads from Sandy Creek into the top of Floodwood Pond. When you get to the pilings at the end of the connector, a left turn (northeast) takes you up into the far reaches of the marsh, whereas a right turn (south-southwest) takes you back down toward Goose Pond.

77

Deer Creek Marsh
Richland

Maps: New York Atlas Map 83:D5, USGS Quadrangle Pulaski

Area: 1,195 acres in the Wildlife Management Area

Habitat type: shallow, slow-flowing creek

Fish: largemouth and smallmouth bass, northern pike

Expect to see: waterfowl, great blue heron, snapping turtle, beaver, muskrat, deer

Camping: App. A #14 and 63

GETTING THERE

From I-81, Exit 36, go west on Route 13 to Route 3. Turn right, and go 1.8 miles north to the access on the left. Hike 125 yards down to the water.

Deer Creek meanders through one of the extensive marshes that line the shores of eastern Lake Ontario. Fortunately, many of these marshes have protection from development by inclusion in six state parks or wildlife management areas. Although the creek affords a view of only a tiny portion of Deer Creek Wildlife Management Area, we found that the accessible area abounds with wildlife. True to its name, a deer drank from the creek as we paddled along; upon spotting us, it crashed off through the thick cattails, waving its white tail at us in annoyance.

Because Deer Creek remains unobtrusive—sometimes with no outlet to the lake—not many people boat here, compared with the heavy fishing and recreational use of Salmon River, just to the south. Thus,

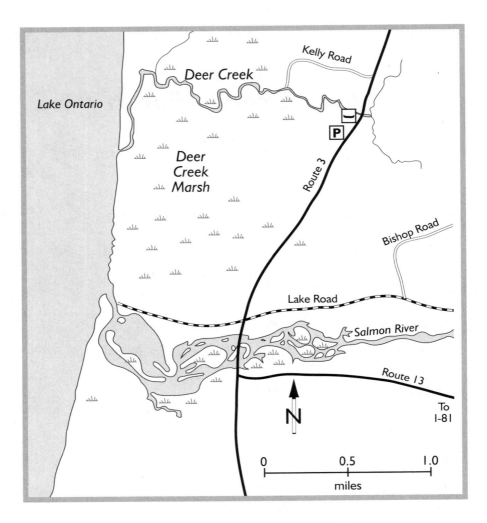

wildlife has not become nocturnal. When we paddled here in June, we saw at least a dozen muskrat harvesting grass in the late afternoon sun; one unconcerned fellow sat out in plain view and watched us with a wary eye as we paddled by. On our return trip, we surprised a beaver cutting alder branches along the shore. After staring at us for a few moments, it slid into the water as we glided by. Satisfied that we did not belong in its environs, it whacked the water vigorously, sending showers into the air in front of us.

A sandbar temporarily keeps Deer Creek from draining into Lake Ontario. Occasional storms alternately open and close access to the lake.

Numerous female snapping turtles—some certainly weighing 25 or 30 pounds—had climbed out onto the soft banks to lay eggs. As we rounded a bend, we spotted one excavating a nest near the top of a huge beaver lodge. Though we tried not to disturb her, she spotted us and, amazingly, just let go and rolled like a rock, tumbling snout over tail down the side of the lodge, ending with a large splash in the water.

Snapping turtles inhabit freshwater marshes and streams from southern Canada to the Gulf Coast and from the Atlantic to the Rockies. They usually climb out on land only to lay eggs; rarely do they bask like other turtles. If you have confronted a big one on land—a huge one can reach 60 pounds—you probably know they act aggressively and will snap at anything nearby with a powerful bite that can easily sever errant fingers. Surprisingly, they remain docile in water; when stepped on, they just retract their heads into the shell. Indeed, some people hunt them by walking barefoot in muddy areas, feeling with their toes for the carapace's sawtoothed rear edge. Having found the nonlethal end, they yank the turtle out of the water by its long tail. Having no firsthand knowledge of this technique, we should not be held responsible for any mishaps!

We also saw great blue heron patiently stalking the shallows; at one point, we saw three of these majestic birds in the air at once. A veery called from the woods, and a rufous-sided towhee piped up from the brush. Marsh wrens, occasionally popping up into sight, sang melodiously from the reeds, and a female mallard with her brood paddled back into the protection of the surrounding marsh. Red-winged blackbirds, by all odds the most common marsh bird, dangled from cattail stems as we slipped by.

Down by Lake Ontario, spotted sandpipers ran along the tall barrier dunes; a colony of bank swallows had carved nest cavities into the steeper sides of the dunes. Invading cottonwoods struggled to hold the dunes together, warding off erosion from rain and harsh winter winds off the lake. The "outlet" turned out to be an exposed sandbar—littered with the tiny dead shells of invading zebra mussels. These bars build up because winds from the west blow on most days across Lake Ontario's shallow end, carrying along sand and the rest of the lake bottom to deposit along shore, choking off channels and building dunes. New channels get cut both by large storms off the lake and by inland runoff after major rains. We no longer wondered why no current flowed on Deer Creek.

The creek itself presents a study in contrasts. Alternately flowing by alder and oak, through narrow then wide channels, by cattail swamp and coastal sand dunes, it provides a rich variety of habitat for plants, the basis of the food chain. Besides the alder and white oak, we saw jewel-weed with its delicate leaves, mighty hemlock, clumps of yellow iris, and a huge variety of aquatic vegetation. This area and the other lakeshore parks and wildlife management areas contain the largest variety of waterlilies in the United States outside of Florida, including two species with white flowers and four varieties with yellow flowers.

Instead of paddling directly back to the access, we continued on upstream, passing under the Route 3 bridge. As we passed under, a raft of nesting barn swallows exploded out from under the bridge. We could paddle only a little way upstream, out into farm country, before the creek became impassable, but we did see a couple of broods of Canada goose and wood duck above the bridge. As we paddled back to the access in the waning sun, as it reflected on the placid water, we reflected on the huge amount of wildlife that we had seen in this biologically rich wildlife management area.

78

Sterling Valley Creek/ The Pond

Sterling

Maps: New York Atlas Map 74:B1, USGS Quadrangle Fair Haven

Length: 7 miles

Habitat type: shallow, marshy, meandering streams

Fish: largemouth bass, northern pike

Expect to see: great blue heron, waterfowl, beaver, muskrat, deer

Camping: App. A #18 (on-site)

GETTING THERE

From Oswego, go west on Route 104. When the road divides, turn right on Route 104A. In Fair Haven, turn right into Fair Haven Beach State Park, and go 1.8 miles to the access area on the right. To avoid paying the park fee, launch from Farden Road (see map).

Sterling Valley Creek drains the hills east and south of Fair Haven Beach State Park. The tributaries flow together into Sterling Valley, nearing the end of their journey to Lake Ontario, spilling out over an extensive marsh. This marsh—and many like it along Lake Ontario's broad plain—provides wonderful habitat for fish and waterfowl. Although the waterfowl back in the tules, particularly the beautiful wood duck and ring-necked duck, try to escape human notice, those inhabiting The Pond have grown quite used to human presence. Signs suggest that

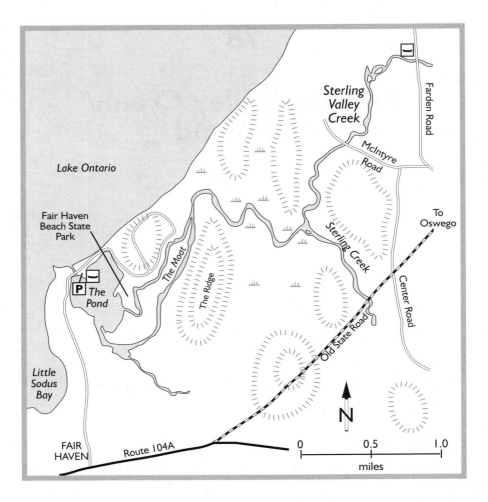

feeding the abundant Canada geese and mallards will cost you more than the price of the food (illegal = fine).

Several broods of mallard and Canada goose munched away on the abundant vegetation. Out in the middle, a common moorhen grazed on fanwort floating in the surface film. The moorhen resembles its relative, the American coot, except that it has a red bill, whereas the coot has a white one. Members of the rail family, they both swim and graze on aquatic plants just like ducks.

Yellow pondlily occurred in great mats, and duckweed—one of the smallest flowering plants—had started to fill in any available

This delicate, iridescent green damselfly folds its wings vertically over its back, in contrast with dragonflies that hold their wings out to the side.

open water when we visited. By summer's end, paddling here can be a challenge.

The Moat, an impenetrable swamp filled with downed trees and duckweed, provides abundant habitat for numerous wood duck. As you paddle up the creek, an island ringed with cattail separates The Moat from the creek. We suggest that you paddle back through one of the several cuts through the island—particularly on the northern end—to The Moat. We watched numerous wood duck feeding on aquatic vegetation and turtles basking on logs.

In addition, we saw many ring-necked ducks and common mergansers. Barn swallows swooped over the water's surface, alternately catching insects on the wing and dipping for a drink. Red-winged blackbirds sang from the cattails, their weight bending the slender stalks, and kingbirds darted out from streamside perches to catch some of the all-too-abundant insect life.

Along Sterling Valley Creek, ramshackle cabins with boat docks askew lined the banks for a short way on the right. After clearing these, we paddled through an idyllic swamp to the fork, where Sterling Creek veered right into farm country and became impassable as it neared Old State Road. Sterling Valley Creek continued to meander several miles through the valley.

As we studied a beaver lodge with fresh cuttings and watched musk-rat feeding on grasses, two personal watercraft roared up this narrow creek. Two-strokers create awful noise and smell because they burn directly injected oil. They leave a huge wake and drive wildlife to cover. We should ban them from streams and ponds, as has happened in other states. If they want to roar around Lake Ontario, fine, but they have no business disrupting wildlife on small creeks such as Sterling Valley.

Paddling back in the setting sun to the access, past huge willows, red oak, paper birch, and hemlock, we wondered about the fate of this wild-life paradise. Disruptive recreation should be banned.

The Beaver

Resident Wetlands Engineer

The beaver, *Castor canadensis,* is one of the most remarkable animals found in New York's lakes, ponds, and streams. Unlike most other animals, beaver actively modify their environment. The sole representative of the family Castoridae, this 30- to 100-pound rodent—largest in North America—descends directly from a bear-sized ancestor that lived a million years ago.

Quietwater paddlers frequently see beaver dams and lodges, especially on more remote lakes and ponds. This industrious mammal uses branches pruned from streamside trees or downed timber to construct dams and lodges. Beaver now work mostly under cover of darkness, especially in areas heavily frequented by humans. In the wilds, however, many beaver work away in broad daylight. We mention in our descriptions where we have seen beaver abroad during the day.

Beaver build dams to raise a stream or pond's water level, providing the resident colony with access to trees growing farther away. The deeper water of their ponds also allows beaver to cache branches underwater for winter retrieval, even when thick layers of ice cover their winter stores. They also dig small canals through marsh and meadow to transport branches from distant trees. Just as we find paddling a canoe easier than carrying it, beaver prefer swimming with a branch—taking advantage of water's buoyancy—than carrying it overland. They usually prune off leafy twigs to reduce drag.

Studies show that the sound of flowing water guides beaver in their dam building—they jam sticks in the dam where they hear the gurgle of water. In one experiment, researchers played a tape of gurgling water; beaver responded by jamming sticks into locations that emanated sound, even though no water actually flowed there. Beaver dams can be very large, over 10 feet high and hundreds of feet long. The largest dam ever recorded, near the present town of Berlin, New Hampshire, spanned 4,000 feet and created a lake with 40 lodges!

Beaver dams benefit many other species, providing important habitat for waterfowl, fish, moose, muskrat, and other animals. Plus, the dams provide flood control, minimize erosion along streambanks, increase aquifer recharge, and improve water quality, both by allowing silt to settle out and by providing biological filtration through aquatic plants. We credit beaver with creating much of America's best farmland by damming watercourses, thus allowing nutrient-rich silt to accumulate over many years. As the ponds fill in, meadows form.

The beaver lodge includes an underwater entrance and usually two different platforms: a main floor about four inches above the water level and a sleeping shelf another two inches higher. Beaver may construct the lodge in a pond's center but more commonly site it on the edge. Before winter onset, beaver cover much of the lodge with mud—which they carry on their broad tails while swimming—that freezes to provide an almost impenetrable fortress. The river otter—the only predator that can get in—can swim through the underwater entrance. Beaver leave the peak more permeable for ventilation.

Near the lodge, in deep water, beaver store up a winter's worth of branches in an underwater food cache. They jam the branches butt-first into the mud to keep them under the ice and then swim out under the ice to bring back branches to eat.

The beaver has adapted remarkably well to its aquatic lifestyle. It has two layers of fur: long silky guard hairs and a dense woolly underfur. By regularly grooming this fur with a special comblike split toenail and keeping it oiled, water seldom totally wets the beaver's skin. Its nose and ears have special valves that keep them shut when underwater, and special skin folds in the mouth enable it to gnaw underwater and carry branches in its teeth without getting water down its throat. Back feet have fully webbed toes to provide propulsion underwater, and the tail provides important rudder control, helping it to swim in a straight line when dragging a large branch. Both the respiratory and circulatory systems have adapted to underwater swimming and enable a beaver to stay underwater for up to 15 minutes. Finally, as with other rodents, its teeth grow constantly and keep sharp through use.

Beaver generally mate for life and maintain an extended family structure. Young stay with their parents for two years, so both yearlings and the current year's kits live with the two parents in the lodge. Females usually bear two—sometimes three—kits between April and June. Born fully furred with eyes open, they can walk and swim almost right away, though they rarely leave the lodge until at least a month of age. Yearlings and both parents bring food to the kits as well as help with dam and lodge construction.

The demand for beaver pelts, more than any other factor, prompted the early European exploration of North America. Trappers nearly exterminated them by the late 1800s. In New York State, only one known active beaver colony—plus a few scattered individuals—remained in 1904. Then began what certainly must be one of the most successful endangered species reintroduction programs ever.

The state released 6 beaver in 1904 in the Old Forge area of the Adirondacks. In 1906, the state released another 25 animals imported from Yellowstone Park, and private landowners released 14 more on nearby private lands. By 1915, that tiny population had expanded to an estimated 15,000 to 20,000 animals. By 1924, the state opened a limited trapping season on beaver. In 1994, the Department of Environmental Conservation estimated the New York population to be 93,000 individuals in nearly 18,000 colonies.

As you paddle along the shoreline of lakes or quiet rivers, keep an eye out for telltale beaver sign, including gnaw marks on trees, distinctive conical stumps of cut trees, canals leading off into the marsh, alder branches trimmed back along narrow passages, and well-worn paths leading away from the water's edge where beaver have dragged more distant branches to the water.

We see beaver most often in the late evening or early morning. Paddle quietly toward a beaver lodge around dusk. Wait patiently, and you will likely see the animals emerge for evening feeding and perhaps construction work on a dam or lodge.

79

East Bay
Huron

Maps: New York Atlas Map 73:B6, USGS Quadrangle East Bay

Area: 290 acres, length 5.5 miles

Habitat type: shallow, marshy, meandering creeks

Expect to see: Canada goose, wood duck, muskrat, beaver

Camping: App. A #18

Take note: novice paddlers should avoid Lake Ontario

GETTING THERE

From Route 104 where Route 414 goes south, go north 3.5 miles on Lake Bluff Road to where it curves left and Garner Road goes straight. Go 6.2 miles (9.7 miles) on Garner Road, and go straight on East Bay Road for 0.1 mile (9.8 miles) to the access on the left, just before the creek.

To reach the second access, continue 0.2 mile (10.0 miles), turn left on Slaght Road, and go 0.2 mile (10.2 miles) to the access on the left.

You will see many animals—including great blue heron, marsh wren, wood duck, kingfisher, Canada goose, beaver, muskrat, painted turtle—in East Bay's long winding inlet channels. For a birder, botanist, or photographer, the bay's marshland provides tremendous opportunity for exploration.

Several slow-flowing inlet creeks meander through extensive cattail marshes. From the East Bay Road access, paddle toward the main bay, then take the arm to the left (west). Paddling here in late June, we spotted delicate rose pogonia orchids hidden among ferns on sphagnum

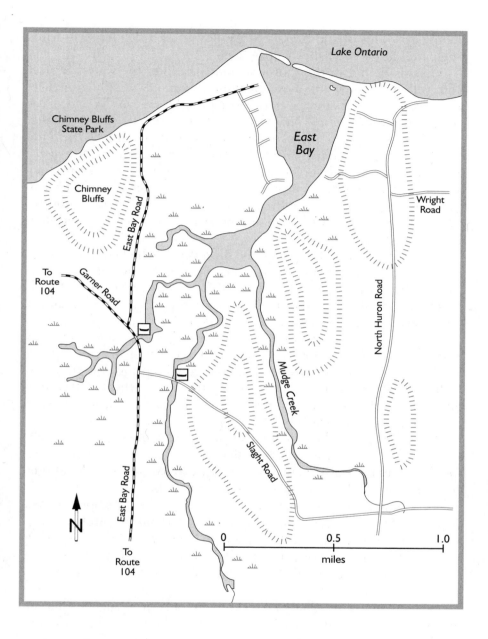

Lake Ontario

Chimney Bluffs
State Park

Chimney
Bluffs

East
Bay

Wright
Road

East Bay Road

To
Route
104

Garner Road

North Huron Road

Mudge Creek

Slaght Road

East Bay Road

To
Route
104

N

0   0.5   1.0
miles

hummocks. This orchid bears a single flower on a slender stem with a single oval leaf about halfway up.

Cattails dominate the shoreline and waterlilies the water's surface. Both yellow pondlily and more common tuberous waterlily grow here. Two subspecies of fragrant waterlily occur in this region: *Nymphaea odorata* subspecies *odorata* and *Nymphaea odorata* ssp. *tuberosa*. Though guidebooks list them separately, taxonomists have recently lumped them into one species. You can distinguish *tuberosa* from the more common *odorata* lilies: *tuberosa* pads have green undersides, flowers have green sepals, and both are often quite large, whereas the usually smaller *odorata* pads have purple-tinged undersides and sepals. East Bay had some of the biggest *tuberosa* we have seen, with leaves as much as 17 inches across and stems a half-inch thick.

Interestingly, after blooming, the flowers get pulled underwater by a coiling action of the stems, which protects the seed head and permits the seeds to ripen over a period of three or four weeks. After ripening, the seed head, or aril, breaks free and floats to the surface, where it gradually decomposes and releases its seeds to the pond bottom.

You will also see arrowhead, pickerelweed, nettle, alder, blue flag, morning glory, swamp loosestrife—a native cousin of the pesky purple loosestrife that has taken over wetlands throughout the eastern United States—duckweed, fanwort, and bladderwort. Where the land rises from the water, deciduous trees dominate: red oak, basswood, beech, sassafras, red maple, and yellow birch, to mention a few.

We saw the most bird life in Mudge Creek, including several dozen wood duck. Usually you see them flying away far ahead, because they spook very easily, but by paddling quietly, you can sometimes get quite close. The wood duck now abounds in our marshes, after nearly suffering extermination at the turn of the century, saved by the Migratory Waterfowl Act that protects migrating birds except during carefully timed waterfowl hunting seasons. The wood duck got a further boost beginning in 1940 with the construction of wood duck nesting boxes—a practice begun in Massachusetts after most dead trees used for nesting got knocked down by the 1938 hurricane.

As we paddled up Mudge Creek, an armada of about 75 adult and immature Canada geese surprised us round a bend, heading toward us. Upon spotting us, they began bobbing their heads in concern, a comical spectacle that had the desired effect. After watching the geese for about 10 minutes, we turned around to leave them in peace.

Merganser with chicks

We also saw huge carp, surface feeding amid the waterlilies, humped backs extending out of the water an inch or more. We drifted over almost on top of one particularly large individual—and got a great look; it finally noticed us and took off, its wake imparting a noticeable rock to our boat.

We saw the most beaver activity in the inlet creek extending farthest south, upstream from the Slaght Road access. Paddling late in the day, we saw four beaver and several lodges.

East Bay's north end suffers from development, and you may encounter water-skiers and personal watercraft. When we visited, we paddled through the breachway onto Lake Ontario, but the two excavators—one antique quietly rusting in the shade of a willow—provided evidence that the breachway may close occasionally. On a calm day, paddling out onto Ontario and around the point to the west offers a real treat.

Chimney Bluffs, about a mile down the shoreline from the breachway, contains a remarkable geologic feature that definitely rates a visit—either by water in very calm conditions or by East Bay Road. Dramatic, 150-feet-tall, eroding, reddish sandstone spires look more like they belong in Utah or Arizona. Some knife-edge ridges and spires run so thin you wonder how they still stand. You can walk or paddle along Chimney Bluffs shore, or explore above by trails.

80

Howland Island (Seneca River)

Conquest

Maps: New York Atlas Map 74:D1, USGS Quadrangle Montezuma

Length: 10 miles, 3,600 acres in Howland Island Wildlife Management Area

Habitat type: shallow, slow-flowing river

Fish: largemouth and smallmouth bass, northern pike

Expect to see: bald eagle, osprey, waterfowl, great blue heron

Wildlife Refuge and Camping: Montezuma National Wildlife Refuge, 315-568-5987, www.fws.gov/r5mnwr; camping App. A #17 and 18

Take note: shallow water in drought years; avoid during waterfowl hunting season

GETTING THERE

Footbridge. From I-90, Exit 40, go south on Route 34, and turn right (west) on Route 31. In Port Byron, turn right (north) on Route 38. Go 1.8 miles, and turn left on Howland Island Road. Go 1.8 miles (3.6 miles) to the Erie Canal footbridge.

Haiti Island. From Port Byron, go 3.0 miles north on Route 38 to the access on the left, just before the bridge.

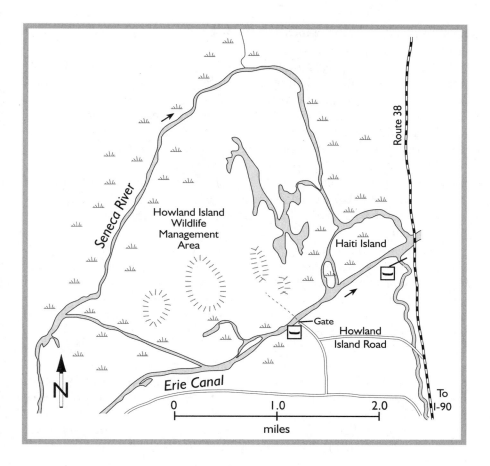

The Erie Canal takes a shortcut across a deep Seneca River bend, neatly enclosing the Howland Island Wildlife Management Area and providing a wonderful 10-mile loop trip. Although you may encounter a few motorboats on the canal, most stay off the Seneca. Portions of the river, particularly the long stretch that heads southwest to northeast, suffer from siltation. When we paddled here in the 1995 drought year, we hit bottom with every paddle stroke for a few miles. In wetter years, the higher water level should provide sufficient depth.

Under calm conditions, toss a coin to choose your travel direction, but if the wind blows from the west or northwest, we would paddle counterclockwise. The western half of the loop, in contrast with the heavily wooded eastern half, has low banks and few trees to block the wind. We tried to paddle clockwise into a stiff northwest wind and wished we had chosen to go the other way.

Although we thought that the day would bring mostly a study of plants, given our late morning start—when most birds and mammals rest—instead it brought us great looks at two monarchs: the great blue heron, monarch of the marsh, and the bald eagle, monarch of the skies.

Ducks and geese abound in this marshy paradise, but rarely have we seen as many great blue heron standing stately, knee-deep in water, patiently waiting to harpoon passing fish. Though we did not keep count, we must have seen more than a dozen. If this were not sufficient inducement to paddle here, we also spotted two bald eagles. The first one—a mature adult with white head and tail—soared effortlessly on huge broad wings.

The second bird, judging from the white flecking on the underside, must have been a second- or third-year bird. First-year birds remain nearly completely brown, but older birds turn progressively whiter on the head and tail, reaching full adult plumage in four to five years. This bird, soaring ever higher, seemed totally oblivious to the raucous harassment engendered by several crows that tried to drive the eagle from their territory. The attacking crows seemed sparrow-sized compared with the massive eagle.

Thirty years ago, such a sight almost never occurred. DDT, introduced in the 1940s to control mosquitoes and other pests, and its breakdown products accumulated in the environment and caused reproductive failure. The eagle has traveled a long road to recovery in New York, from no successful hatchings for many years before 1976, to producing only three young in 1987, to fledging 30 birds from 19 nests in 1995, to fledging 112 birds from 92 nests in 2005. Because of the amazing success in New York and elsewhere, the U.S. Fish and Wildlife Service removed the nation's symbol from the Endangered Species List and placed it on the Threatened List.

Despite the bald eagle success, shortsighted economic interests continue to press for weakening of the Endangered Species Act. Most people would much rather see an eagle doing aerial battle with crows, a peregrine falcon stooping on a pigeon, and a California condor floating with the clouds than see some favored business get the green light to destroy the preferred habitat of an endangered species for short-term economic gain for a few individuals. We all pay for such largesse by living in an altered environment very much less beautiful, interesting, and wild. Those who enjoy the outdoors—be they quietwater paddlers, hikers, or sportsmen—

Canada geese abound at Howland Island Wildlife Management Area.

should make their voices heard: a strong Endangered Species Act will help to preserve the environment for future generations to enjoy.

Lots more awaits you on your paddle around Howland Island. In addition to beaver activity, we saw a groundhog in a tree eating leaves! Admittedly, the tree trunk had bent down to a low angle, but this raises questions about the name "groundhog."

We never tired of paddling through huge patches of fragrant waterlily on the north side, nor of the chattering call of kingfishers as they fled before us. Great crested flycatchers darted off their streamside perches to snatch insects that fluttered on the breezes, and dozens of wood duck provided dramatic sparkles of color. If you hear what appears to be a robin calling from the higher foliage, take another look. It easily could be a beautiful rose-breasted grosbeak; we saw several along the way.

We are fortunate that we can paddle such a wonderful wildlife area. The nearby Montezuma National Wildlife Refuge—well worth a visit—provides similar habitat but no paddling. It has self-guided auto trails, foot trails, and observation towers. One can often spot bald eagles at Montezuma, as well.

81

Clyde River
Galen

Maps: New York Atlas Map 73:D6, USGS Quadrangle Lyons

Length: 10.5 miles

Habitat type: small, shallow stream

Fish: largemouth and smallmouth bass, northern pike

Expect to see: great blue heron, kingbird, oriole

Camping: App. A #17

Take note: snags and aquatic vegetation make for slow going

GETTING THERE

From I-90, Exit 42, go 5.0 miles north on Route 14, and turn right on Zohn Alloway Road. Go 1.1 miles (6.1 miles), and turn right on Schwartz Road. Go 1.1 miles (7.2 miles), and turn right on Lyons-Marengo Road. Go 2.0 miles (9.2 miles), and turn left on River Road. Go 1.2 miles (10.4 miles) to the first of several accesses; best is the last (13.5 miles).

Forgotten by time, the Clyde River gave up much of its water and its character to the Erie Canal. Portions of it still run along with the canal. We do not cover those sections here because they include channelized water and too much boat traffic. Instead, we include the headwaters of the Clyde, if they can be called such. With almost no flow, the river collects snags and mountains of aquatic vegetation as summer wears on. Still, something primeval beckons one to paddle the Clyde.

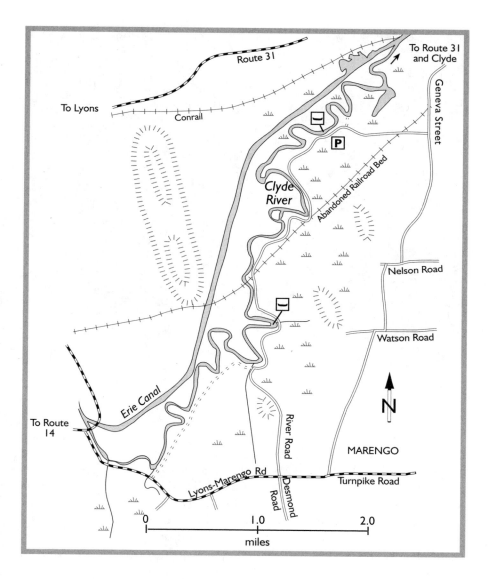

River Road parallels one shore, and the other shore marks the beginning of deep, dark, brushy forests with towering trees and hanging vines. Fields and occasional cottages line the eastern shore, making the western shore vastly more interesting. Paddling the Clyde up and back, we found ourselves clinging to the western shore, except where drowned logs dictated detouring to the other side.

A tiger swallowtail perches on the leaves and flowers of a hawthorn.

While vultures circled lazily overhead, great blue heron fished the productive waters. From the northern access, we paddled about 5 miles upstream and back down, without seeing any other fishers besides birds and turtles, which were taking a break, basking on logs. While tree swallows skimmed the surface to drink, bullfrogs called from the lily pads. We stopped to photograph colorful Baltimore orioles hanging from branches as they stooped to suck nectar from flowers with their narrow, pointed bills. Kingbirds patrolled the water, fluttering about to catch moths and other insects on the wing.

The dark swamp water harbored many fish that darted away, seeking cover under acres of floating vegetation. Along the far bank, ferns and swamp rose fought for light under a canopy of tall silver maple, ash, shagbark hickory, white oak, basswood, and many others. Hawthorns with showy clusters of white flowers bloomed along the banks. Back in the woods, Eastern wood-pewees whistled "pea-o-whee," and campgrounds. We include here three connected intermediate reservoirs. With limited time, we would paddle Blake Falls, the nicest of the three.

Five Falls Reservoir

Small, quiet Five Falls receives little attention. If chaos reigns on the others, then we would paddle here. Where the main body necks down as you paddle around to the right from the access, note the rock formations near shore that extend out into the water, making passage difficult during times of low water.

The forested shoreline contains a wide variety of tree species, including both aspen—big-toothed and quaking—paper and yellow birches, red maple, red and white pines, northern white cedar, hemlock, and several others. A relatively open understory contains a large fern population.

We recognize aspen, members of the willow family, by its smooth, light green or yellow bark. In a light breeze, its leaves quake. It grows in association with pine and other conifers, and its golden yellow leaves in fall provide a beautiful contrast with the surrounding dark evergreens. Distinguish the two species by their leaves: quaking aspen (*Populus tremuloides*) has very fine teeth on its leaf margins, while big-toothed aspen (*Populus grandidentata*) has large serrations on the margins. Also, the big-toothed aspen trunk loses its smoothness as it grows larger.

Both species regenerate quickly after fire or other disturbance, serving as soil anchors. Quaking aspen also propagates readily by sending out root suckers, forming dense clones, all with the same genetic makeup. Taller species frequently crowd it out. In the West, with less crowding, individual trees may live for only 100 years, but the clone may survive for thousands, placing aspen (or at least its roots) among the oldest species on Earth. Furthermore, some scientists believe that an aspen clone is actually a single organism, interconnected by the root system. That would make some large western clones the largest organisms in the world—far outweighing the largest redwood, sequoia, and blue whale.

A few hundred species of wildlife—including moose, beaver, bear, elk, grouse, quail, and deer—rely on aspen for food from its bark, leaves, buds, flowers, and fruits. Coupled with its early successional soil-holding character, this food production makes aspen one of the most important tree species in the North Country.

We saw bustling among the branches, yellow warbler, black-throated green warbler, American redstart, and black-capped chickadee, while song sparrow and wood thrush hunted insects along the ground. A deer snorted at us from the brush, and we searched in vain for the beaver that had fed on tender aspen branches. We enjoyed paddling here among forested shores with a rich mixture of conifer and deciduous trees, but it does not take more than a few hours to paddle the entire shoreline.

Rainbow Falls Reservoir
Located between Five Falls and Blake Falls, Rainbow Falls takes much more time to explore. In spite of the houses that crowd the southern shore, we feel that paddling here still provides a quietwater experience, especially early and late in the season. The broad expanse of water near the dam on the west end gives way to an island that blocks the view of many of the houses. At the east end, the reservoir takes an abrupt left turn as it heads toward Blake Falls. The most beautiful area on the reservoir, this narrow arm sports forested shores and tall banks covered with lush vegetation, very similar in character to that found at Five Falls.

Paper birch, very similar to aspen in ecological niche, grows in profusion, and beaver hack away at them just as they do to aspen on Five Falls. In some sections, deer have created a conspicuous browse line by munching heavily on lakeside branches.

Besides the birds mentioned earlier, we saw red-eyed vireo, belted kingfisher, common loon, two families of common merganser, spotted sandpiper, black duck, and ring-billed gull.

Blake Falls Reservoir
By all odds the most scenic of the three reservoirs, Blake Falls provided us with the best looks at wildlife, even though we paddled here in mid-afternoon. Plant species also appear in greater abundance, and the aquatic habitat includes marshes, absent in the other reservoirs.

A wild turkey hen and her brood greeted us as we approached the water. This magnificent game bird, standing more than three feet tall, once inhabited most of the forested parts of eastern North America, foraging on acorns, chestnuts, beechnuts, seeds, and insects. With the clearing of forests, loss of the American chestnut to chestnut blight, and unregulated hunting, the wild turkey disappeared over much of its range. Recently reintroduced in many areas, the wild turkey now ranges over large tracts of New York.

As we approached the southern end, we spotted two mature bald eagles. Though we searched for their large nest of sticks, we never found it. Eagle nests may reach six or more feet in diameter, and the adults, veeries whistled their cascading, flutelike notes. Many more bird species announced their territories, including gray catbird, northern cardinal, yellow warbler, common yellowthroat, Eastern phoebe, mourning dove, red-winged blackbird, rose-breasted grosbeak, great crested flycatcher, and American goldfinch.

It took quite a while to reconcile the two banks of the river, one with development, the other impenetrable jungle. We can only wonder what this wonderful swamp must have contained in pre-colonial times. Because people have forgotten this waterway, you probably will paddle here alone, perhaps joined by an occasional angler. Often, the fisher is just the great blue heron.

82

West River

Italy

Maps: New York Atlas Map 58:C3, USGS Quadrangle Middlesex

Length: 3.5 miles

Habitat type: slow-flowing stream through a wide swamp

Fish: largemouth and smallmouth bass

Expect to see: waterfowl, turtles, muskrat, beaver

Camping: App. A #20 and 22

GETTING THERE

From Naples, at the junction of Routes 21 and 245, go 3.5 miles east on Route 245 to the access on the left. We prefer the hand-carry access: continue for 0.5 mile (4.0 miles), turn left on Sunnyside Road, and go 0.1 mile (4.1 miles) to the access on the left.

The Department of Environmental Conservation protects the West River, which flows—pretty much imperceptibly—into the south end of Canandaigua Lake. Part of the 6,100-acre High Tor Wildlife Management Area, the stream contains two portions, both worth exploring. When the wind has turned big lakes to a foaming froth, paddle here instead.

Putting in at the Sunnyside Road access, stay to the right (east) and head upstream under both bridges, taking you into the heart of the High Tor Wildlife Management Area and, more importantly, away from motorboats. The sinewy West River reaches back upstream about 2.0 weed-choked miles before you reach the first beaver dam. We did not explore

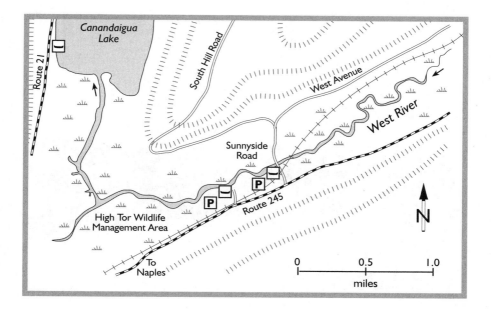

beyond it, although it looked as though you could go quite a bit farther. This beaver dam provided the first inkling that we were paddling
upstream, given the seemingly nonexistent current. A sea of aquatic vegetation covers the entire river, from bank to bank, even where the river
is 100 feet across.

Duckweed, a minuscule stemless flowering plant, covers the underwater vegetation in great floating mats. Tuberous waterlilies and yellow
pondlilies occur in profusion out in the water, with arrowhead lining
the shore. Extensive cattail stands course through the shallows, broken
occasionally by clumps of dwarf silver maple, alder, large willow hanging out over the water, and lower-growing vegetation. We found large
clusters of beautiful pink swamp rose, yellow iris, swamp milkweed, and
many other flowering plants.

But wildlife provides the real attraction. Evidence of beaver activity appeared everywhere, and we saw muskrat both swimming and harvesting grasses. Turtles poked their heads up through the vegetation
seemingly every few feet; we surprised several huge snapping turtles,
which dove for cover under the boat. We saw great blue heron, green
heron, kingfisher, great crested flycatcher, Eastern phoebe, red-winged
blackbird, and many other bird species. We saw more than 100 ducks,

The slow-moving, marshy West River flows into the south end of Canandaigua Lake.

including mostly wood duck. If you are lucky, you may catch sight of small, brightly colored hooded merganser; it competes with the wood duck for cavity nesting sites. A Canada goose family grazed the shoreline as well. Two young great horned owls sat on a log hanging out over the water.

Because this represents a very wild, truly productive environment, we strongly recommend against paddling upstream—downstream is okay at any time—from the hand-carry access during nesting season (before July 1). We paddled here in mid-July.

Downstream from the hand-carry access, motorboats maintain an open channel. We would avoid this area on summer weekends. Although vegetation along the lower river remains pretty much the same as above the access, wildlife appears with less frequency, no doubt driven away by boat traffic. You can also see layered farms on the hillsides off in the distance, whereas above the bridges we saw no development.

At the hand-carry access, a plaque reads, "Nundawao. Legendary site of the first Seneca Indian Village just across the river. This was the birthplace of the Seneca, members of the Iroquois nation."

83

Hemlock Lake and Canadice Lake
Canadice, Conesus, and Livonia

Maps: New York Atlas Map 58:C1, USGS Quadrangles Honeoye and Springwater

Area: Hemlock Lake 1,800 acres, Canadice Lake 650 acres

Habitat type: deep, long, water-supply reservoirs

Fish: brown, lake, and rainbow trout; landlocked salmon (Hemlock); largemouth and smallmouth bass; pickerel

Expect to see: bald eagle, osprey, red-tailed hawk

Camping: App. A #22

Take note: north or south winds make paddling treacherous; free self-service permit required; City of Rochester, Water and Lighting Bureau, 585-428-3646

GETTING THERE

Hemlock Lake and Permits. From Rochester, go south on Route 15A. Where Route 20A goes left, go 0.7 mile south on Route 15A, and turn right on Rix Hill Road. Follow signs to the self-service permit station. To reach the northern access, go around to the right by the maintenance garages and then about 1 mile on East Lake Road.

Southern access. Continue 7.9 miles (8.6 miles) south on Route 15A, and turn right sharply back on the access road.

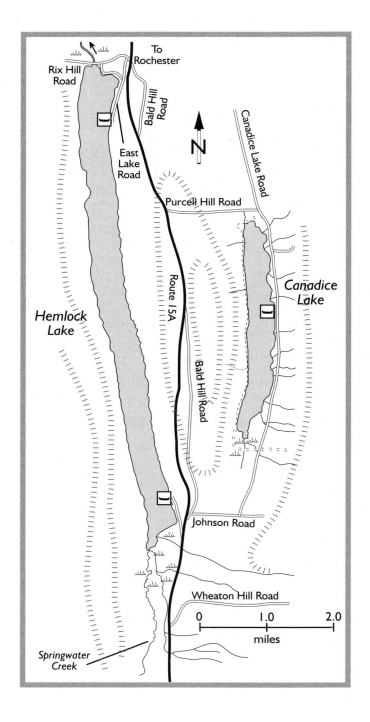

To
Rochester

Rix Hill
Road

Bald Hill Road

East
Lake
Road

N

Canadice Lake Road

Purcell Hill Road

Route 15A

Hemlock
Lake

Canadice
Lake

Bald Hill Road

Johnson Road

Wheaton Hill Road

0   1.0   2.0

miles

Springwater
Creek

Canadice Lake. From Rix Hill Road, go 2.5 miles (3.2 miles) south on Route 15A, and turn left on Purcell Hill Road. Go 1.4 miles (4.6 miles), and turn right on Canadice Lake Road. Go 1.4 miles (6.0 miles) to the access on the right.

Hemlock and Canadice lakes stand out as rare jewels, the only Finger Lakes not ringed by roads or dominated by development and personal watercraft. Alas, preservation did not result from farsighted conservation efforts but because they serve as water-supply reservoirs for the city of Rochester, which limits access and controls uses.

Hemlock Lake

Only a couple of structures mar the view of the hillsides surrounding Hemlock Lake, and although the city allows motors, it limits boats to 16 feet (except canoes) and to 10 horsepower. A picnic area perches on the north end of this 8-mile-long, north-south-oriented lake, but boats may not go north of the northern access (about a mile from the north end).

After getting a permit, you may want to travel down to the southern access for two reasons: first, the southern section, including Springwater Creek and marsh, provides more interesting paddling; second, the prevailing summer winds usually blow from the south, protecting those waters from wind. When winds blow, we suggest that you paddle nearby West River at the south end of Canandaigua Lake.

Rochester imposes several more restrictions, which we will not recount here, except for one. To halt the spread of zebra mussel—Eurasian import to the Great Lakes region in the ballasts of ships—you may not launch your boat in Hemlock Lake within three days of having it in other waters. These very destructive bivalves have reproduced prolifically in the Great Lakes, attaching themselves in many-deep clusters to water intakes and other marine structures, eventually clogging water passages.

While giving out warnings we should mention that, although this is an unspoiled lake, thirsty Rochester does draw down the level in summer, revealing ugly barren shores, especially in dry years. In wet years, the level may remain quite high even in the middle of July. If you know people in Rochester, ask them to help preserve the lake by installing low-flow toilets and showerheads and sink aerators and by using water judiciously.

Hardwoods, such as aspen, willow, red and white oaks, walnut, and sycamore, dominate the Hemlock Lake shoreline. Occasional pine, mostly

Flowering dogwood blooms in the spring on the hillsides surrounding Hemlock and Canadice lakes.

red, appear here and there, and a well-developed understory fights for light along the shore. Surprisingly, the quite-clear water harbors a relatively large amount of submerged aquatic vegetation, even out in the open lake. The Springwater Creek marsh at the south end consists of a wide expanse of cattails, grasses, and waterlilies. During times of high water, you can paddle down into it quite a way. It starts way over on the western shore and continues south.

When we paddled here, we saw ring-billed gull, a nesting red-tailed hawk pair, spotted sandpiper bobbing on rocks, belted kingfisher, Eastern phoebe, great crested flycatcher, and tons of tree and barn swallows skimming the water's surface, snatching up airborne insects. You may also see the main attraction, a nesting pair of bald eagles.

Canadice Lake

Much of what we said about Hemlock remains true for Canadice. According to local anglers, even a modest breeze can kick up rollers on Canadice. Because it has a north-south orientation with steep hillsides all around, winds get funneled up and down the lake, even when they blow from off-axis directions.

Canadice, slightly more than 3 miles long and less than a half mile wide, nestles in a deep valley, ringed with forested hillsides rising more than 1,000 feet above the lake's surface. A lone house appears near the northern shore, the only development visible from the water. Drawdown reveals a rock-filled shore, instead of exposed muddy banks, making the view a lot less ugly. Although a road travels down the eastern lakeshore, it contains very light local traffic only.

While crows and red and gray squirrels harassed a perched red-tailed hawk, fish jumped out in the open water, rising for a late-May fly hatch. A few anglers searched for the lunker trout that inhabit the depths. We were content to absorb the sights of dogwood blooming on the hillsides and the songs of northern oriole and black-throated green warbler emanating from the treetops. Heart-shaped leaves of bankside cottonwoods rattled in the light breeze as we peered back into the undergrowth, trying to catch sight of veery, yellowthroat, or other ground-dwelling songbirds.

We enjoyed our early season paddle here, thankful that Rochester had not drawn the water down appreciably. Given the proximity to lakes infested with zebra mussels—Conesus, Canandaigua, Keuka, Seneca, and Ontario—we wondered how long it would take for Hemlock and Canadice to become infested with the destructive bivalves. Will the warnings about zebra mussels at the access have any effect on their appearance here? Can the larvae hitchhike on the legs of long-legged waders such as the great blue heron? We all will have to wait to see how this plays out here and in our other favorite waters.

84

Mendon Ponds
Mendon

Maps: New York Atlas Map 72:D1, USGS Quadrangle Pittsford

Area: Hundred Acre Pond 120 acres, Deep Pond 30 acres

Habitat type: small, shallow ponds

Expect to see: waterfowl

Camping: App. A #27

Take note: Mendon Ponds Park, www.monroecounty.gov/parks

GETTING THERE

From Rochester, go south on Route 65 for 0.6 mile past the bridge over I-90, and turn left on Canfield Road. Go 1.1 miles (1.7 miles), and turn right on Douglas Road. Go 0.8 mile (2.5 miles), to the access on the right.

Mendon Ponds Park lies close to Rochester, just a mile south of the Thruway. Although not a wilderness environment, it provides a great place for family recreation, a place to teach children about plants, wildlife, geology, and canoeing. The 1,000-acre wetland area has much to teach us about climate cycles and geology. The surrounding bog, underlain with peat, provides an outstanding example of the rare kettle-hole bog community.

Kettle hole ponds, remnants of the last Ice Age, formed as glaciers retreated, leaving behind huge chunks of ice buried in glacial till. The melting ice formed kettle holes, which gradually filled in

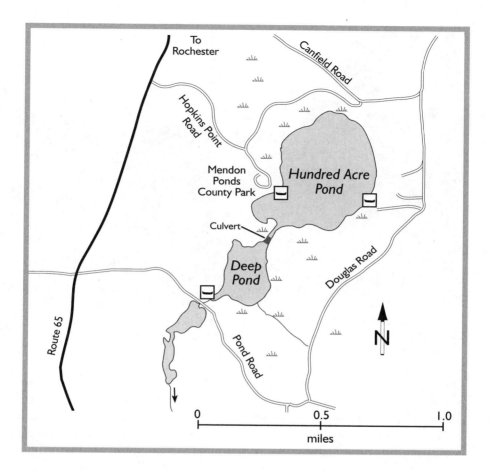

with sphagnum over thousands of years, forming peatlands. As the leading edges of glaciers retreated, they left behind low sediment ridges called eskers, which we can see here and in many other areas of the North Country. Eskers formed when under-ice rivers flowed through glacial cracks, depositing sediment along their borders.

The park rents canoes at the Hundred Acre Pond access site off Route 65; other recreation and picnicking opportunities abound at the park. Launch your boat at one of three access points: from the canoe rental facility, from the opposite shore on Hundred Acre Pond, or from the southwest corner of Deep Pond, off Route 65 on Pond Road.

Acres of fragrant waterlily dominate the southern end of Hundred Acre Pond, a kettle hole left by a melting glacier at the end of the last Ice Age.

During our mid-July visit, anglers told us that in some summers the ponds become completely choked with aquatic vegetation. Clearly, with ever-increasing accumulations of dead plant material during each annual cycle, the ponds march inexorably to the filled-in bog condition, where a floating mat of sphagnum supports bog specialists, adapted to acidic conditions. Eventually, trees encroach as the bog fills in, squeezing out the water.

Norway spruce, red pine, silver maple, ash, oak, and others grow well back from the water, with occasional willows on the shore. Cattails crowd the banks in shallow water, and arrowhead grows in huge patches where cattails have not yet crowded it out.

We saw ducks, great blue heron, red-winged blackbird, and common yellowthroat. A hermit thrush called from the dense undergrowth, and several species of swallow skimmed the water's surface for a drink on a sweltering July day. Several Eastern kingbirds patrolled the airways, performing the excellent service of snaring deerflies on the wing. Large flocks of Canada goose simultaneously mowed the grass and fertilized it, probably saving the county park a great deal of work.

As we approached the carry into Deep Pond at the south end of Hundred Acre Pond, a huge beaver lodge and lots of beaver activity greeted us. Traversing into the more secluded Deep Pond from Hundred Acre Pond should be a breeze; one could just paddle through the culvert that separates them. However, the beaver in the area must be really hard up, because they had chosen to dam up this culvert, thus requiring us to carry up and over the separating embankment.

We tried to paddle into the weed-choked southeastern cove on Deep Pond but couldn't penetrate more than 50 feet, because yellow pondlily and fragrant waterlily, along with arrowhead, some rushes, and a few cattails, choked the waterway. In this more secluded area, we watched turtles bask and enjoyed the beauty of swamp rose and swamp milkweed. We found it hard to believe such tranquil surroundings exist on the very outskirts of Rochester.

85

Genesee River Gorge
Rochester

Maps: New York Atlas Maps 71:C7 and 72:C1, USGS Quadrangles Rochester East and Rochester West

Length: 4 miles

Habitat type: wide, deep, slow-flowing river

Expect to see: great blue heron, turtle, beaver

Camping: App. A #27

Take note: motorboats dominate the downstream section

GETTING THERE

From Main Street in Rochester, go about 5 miles north on State Street/ Lake Avenue, and turn right at the stoplight on Boxart Street, at the sign for Turning Point Park. Go 0.5 mile to the parking area inside the gate (check the closing time). Carry a quarter mile to the river; a portage cart works fine.

The Genesee River's lower section, from Genesee Dock at Turning Point Park to the spectacular falls 4 miles upstream (south), offers a wonderful morning or afternoon paddle within Rochester's city limits. The river— wide and deep for most of this section—really surprised us, given its urban setting. Large boats ply these waters—indeed, a cement tanker had docked just north of the park when we visited—but most boat traffic stays north of Turning Point Park and heads out onto Lake Ontario.

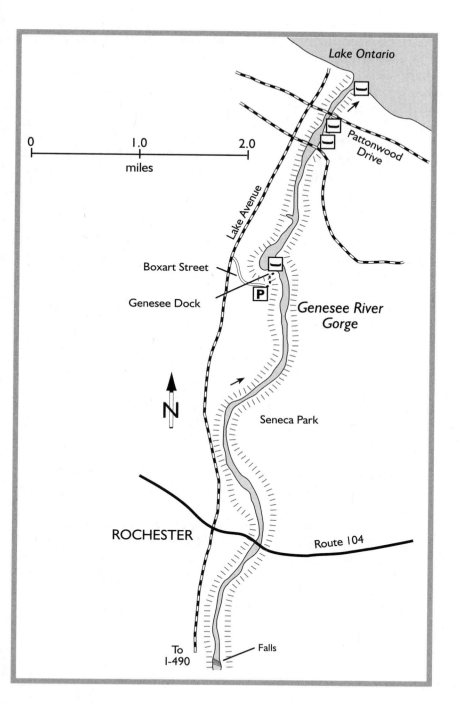

Lake Ontario

0   1.0   2.0
miles

Lake Avenue

Pattonwood Drive

Boxart Street

Genesee Dock

P

Genesee River Gorge

N

Seneca Park

ROCHESTER

Route 104

To I-490

Falls

With the river's high banks, a paddler here feels remarkably separated from the surrounding city. You pass under a few bridges—including Route 104—and what appears to be a piped aqueduct, pass a large Kodak water treatment plant on the right, and catch a glimpse of a few large buildings and smokestacks. But mostly you paddle here separated from the urban congestion a quarter mile to the east or west. The canyon walls somehow muffle the noise as well; we really felt quite alone here—albeit during a paddle quite late in the day. The occasional rusting engine block, shopping cart, and partially floating tire reminded us that civilization lingers not far away, however.

Heading south, the initially marshy shores grow thick with cattail, with willow here and there. On higher terrain, deciduous trees dominate: red and white oaks, basswood, maple, walnut, and sassafras. In some areas tall, red, sandstone cliffs probably serve the local kingfishers well. When we paddled here late in June, large carp spawned at the water's surface—sometimes you can paddle quite close and get a good view of these huge fish. We also saw snapping turtle, painted turtle, and a beaver during our upstream exploration.

Eventually, the marsh gives way to a more abrupt shoreline, rising steeply from the river. About 4 miles from the put-in, you pass an island on the left, the current picks up, and you have to dodge protruding rocks. Depending on flow, you may be able to continue paddling upstream here, or you can beach your boat and walk along the shoreline. A wide cirque of red cliffs appears ahead, and around the bend to the left the northernmost falls on the river roars off in the distance. Though not quite as dramatic as Upper Falls (just a little farther south), this one falls a greater distance, providing a spectacular sight. Water cascades over a broad brim, dropping approximately 150 feet into a widened section of the gorge.

We did not paddle north of Turning Point Park. Closer to Lake Ontario, high banks disappear, development encroaches, and powerboats dominate the water—not our idea of a good time. We prefer watching beaver forage on cattails as dusk approaches, studying basking painted turtles through binoculars, and spotting herons fishing the marsh. You can almost forget that New York's third-largest city churns away above you.

86

Buck Pond

Greece

Maps: New York Atlas Map 71:B7, USGS Quadrangle, Braddock Heights

Area: 550 acres

Habitat type: cattail swamp

Expect to see: osprey, black tern, wood duck, great blue heron, marsh wren

Camping: App. A #27

Take note: novice paddlers should not venture out onto Lake Ontario

GETTING THERE

From Rochester, go west on Lake Ontario State Parkway, and exit on Long Pond Road. Go 1.1 miles north, and turn right on Edgemere Drive. Go 1.3 miles (2.4 miles) to the access on the right.

Backed up against Lake Ontario and only a few miles from Rochester, Buck Pond offers a pleasant escape from civilization. Though most of the marsh lies within earshot of automobiles and motorboats, you will feel alone here exploring the rich, bird-filled marsh. The few buildings on the northeastern shore and vacation traffic along Edgemere Drive do not seem to spoil its wild character.

Though less than a mile across, Buck Pond offers long, winding, inlet channels and hidden coves to explore that could occupy you for several

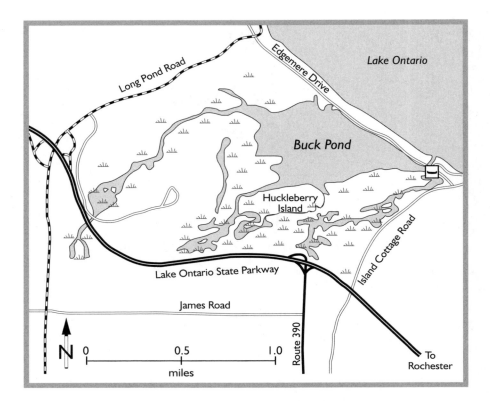

hours. By early summer, marsh vegetation—cattail, bulrush, bur-reed, swamp loosestrife, arrowhead, pickerelweed, fanwort, duckweed, tuberous waterlily—chokes the shallower channels. Although cattail dominates the shoreline, a rich diversity provides for the needs of the marsh ecosystem's many animals. At the end of June, we could still paddle up the western inlet—where the current seemed nonexistent—and under the Lake Ontario State Parkway, though thick vegetation impeded our progress in a few places.

We found paddling around Huckleberry Island to the west harder but well worth the effort. Open water gradually disappears amid the thick cattail stands as you pass the island and head southwest. Watch for a stately great blue heron or osprey perched on the dead tree overlooking the marsh from Huckleberry Island. We saw several dozen wood ducks back here; watched great blue herons fishing; happened on a secretive,

Thick vegetation, mostly cattail, dominates the winding channels of Buck Pond.

rarely seen least bittern amid the cattails; and enjoyed the song of the marsh wrens—we even watched one slipping in and out of its hidden nest woven of cattail leaves.

The least accessible section extends east from the access, then around to the south and southwest along Island Cottage Road. Though we could not get through the thick waterlilies here, we watched a dozen black terns swooping and diving for small fish in the shallows. The only mostly black tern, with silvery wings, this uncommon species nests on freshwater marshes. To protect its young, keep your distance.

In addition to birdlife, we saw lots of painted turtles, particularly in the westernmost section, huge carp splashing at the water's surface, and fleeting glimpses of a few lunker largemouth bass. Indeed, the fishing looked excellent.

Paddling in spring before cattail emergence, you can see more of the marshy inlets and coves, and without the floating and submerged vegetation, you can explore a much larger area, possibly making your way around Huckleberry Island.

Paddling here on a day when the wind barely rippled the surface, we used the opportunity to paddle under the Edgemere Drive bridge and onto

Lake Ontario. You may have to carry your boat over a narrow sandbar. Ontario, though smallest of the Great Lakes, ranks fourteenth largest in the world, nearly as big as New Jersey. It feels more like the ocean than a freshwater lake. Along the shore, note the quantity of washed up zebra mussel shells. This recently introduced nuisance species continues to wreak havoc throughout the Great Lakes.

87

Salmon Creek and West Creek
Greece and Parma

Maps: New York Atlas Map 71:B7, USGS Quadrangles Braddock Heights and Hilton

Length: 6 miles

Habitat type: shallow, marshy creeks

Fish: largemouth bass, northern pike

Expect to see: waterfowl, moorhen, great blue heron, black tern

Camping: App. A #27

Take note: avoid the main part of Braddock Bay

GETTING THERE

From Rochester, go west on Lake Ontario State Parkway, and exit on Route 261, going southwest, away from Manitou Beach. Route 261 turns left, and Curtis Road goes off right. From here, Braddock Bait and Tackle, Willow Inn, and Docksiders are just a few hundred yards down on the left. The first two charge five dollars to launch; Docksiders is free.

Braddock Bay, an inlet of Lake Ontario, lies just a few miles east of Rochester. Thirty or so creeks flow into the lake from Braddock Bay to Round Pond, 4 miles away, drawing from at least 150 square miles of flat coastal plain. These bays constitute wetlands of regional significance. Indeed, the state protects 2,125 acres as the Braddock Bay Fish

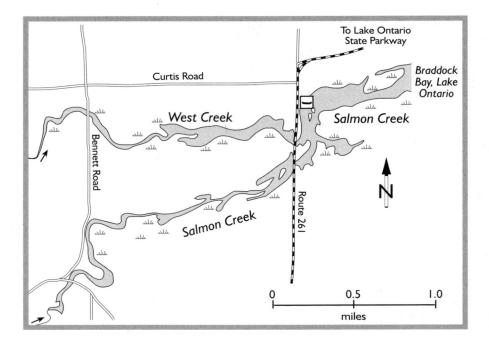

and Wildlife Management Area, covering most of the marshes north of the Lake Ontario Parkway from Rose Marsh on the west to Buck Pond on the east.

Unfortunately, protection does not extend to most of Braddock Bay, which bristles with crowded marinas, development, large boats, and the dreaded personal watercraft. No paddler should paddle out into Braddock Bay on a July or August weekend for fear of getting run over or swamped. Fortunately, an alternative exists. One can paddle two relatively unspoiled tributaries—West Creek and Salmon Creek—or nearby Buck Pond (see previous entry).

Paddle south a short distance, and cross under Route 261, putting you on West Creek; the bridge over Salmon Creek lies a few hundred feet farther south. Try to time your passage so that no cars cross the bridge while you are underneath; the noise can be quite loud, especially under the Salmon Creek bridge. These low-clearance bridges exclude most boats other than canoes and kayaks. Further, weeds choke the two creeks so that props on motors would foul instantly.

Cattails dominate the marshes surrounding the creek, and pickerelweed and acres of waterlilies crowd the channel. We watched several red-winged blackbirds chase a red-tailed hawk from the cattails where it had stooped, looking for a meal. Hawks appear in abundance, especially during migration. In 1987, observers counted more than 100,000 raptors during spring migration, which peaks in late April.

Tree species include towering Norway spruce, huge willows, and ash. Grapevines drape over the vegetation along the banks, and sumac appears here and there. Flocks of cedar waxwing and several species of swallow patrol the waterway, picking off insects born of these fertile waters, while great blue heron fish the shallows. Painted turtles dive for cover as you approach, and acres of tuberous and fragrant waterlily flowers will greet you if you paddle in the morning.

You can paddle upstream through clear water and undisturbed habitat for about a mile and a half, all the way to the bridge on Bennett Road. After that, the creek gets too shallow for paddling. If you have time, paddle back downstream, cross back under the Route 261 bridge, turn south for a few hundred feet, recross back under Route 261, and paddle up Salmon Creek. While you are out in the south end of Braddock Bay, explore the extensive marsh, teeming with wildlife. If you get too close to the tiny islands where black terns nest, they will dive-bomb your boat. After one warning, we steered clear and watched them glide effortlessly over the water. A black bird with silvery wings, this tern has become increasingly rare over most of its breeding range, which stretches from coast to coast in the northern United States and Canada.

Salmon Creek has more water in it than West Creek, and consequently, aquatic vegetation does not choke the main channel nearly as much. The longer Salmon also has more side channels to explore and fewer cattails, which can get boring after awhile. You can paddle upstream almost to the high school before riffles block your way. Common moorhens take time from grazing on aquatic plants to scurry back into the cattails as you approach. Kingfishers fly upstream from perch to perch, announcing your presence as they go. The unusual box elder, the only maple with a three-leaflet compound leaf, hangs out over the water in many places. Thick vines drape over the shoreline vegetation, and a rope swing dangles from a hemlock out over the water like a vine, inviting you to drop into a 7-foot-deep pool on hot, sultry summer days.

88

Oak Orchard Creek
Alabama and Shelby

Maps: New York Atlas Map 70:D2, USGS Quadrangles Knowlesville, Medina, Oakfield

Length: 6 miles one way

Habitat type: shallow, marshy, slow-flowing stream

Fish: smallmouth bass, northern pike

Expect to see: bald eagle, waterfowl, great blue heron

Camping: App. A #26, 28, and 35

Take note: Iroquois National Wildlife Refuge, 585-948-5445, www.fws.gov/northeast/iroquois; no motors allowed

GETTING THERE

Iroquois National Wildlife Refuge Visitor Center. From I-90, Exit 48A, go north on Route 77/Route 63. From where Route 77 goes left, go 0.8 mile north on Route 63, and turn left on Casey Road to the Visitor Center.

Oak Orchard Creek. From the junction of Casey Road and Route 63, go less than 0.1 mile (0.9 mile) north on Route 63, and turn right on Roberts Road. Go 2.5 miles (3.4 miles), turn left on Knowlesville Road, and go 1.5 miles (4.9 miles) to the access at the Oak Orchard Creek bridge.

If you want a truly wonderful experience in western New York, go to the Oak Orchard area in the spring or fall when thousands of migrating geese, ducks, and swans descend on three wildlife refuges surrounding

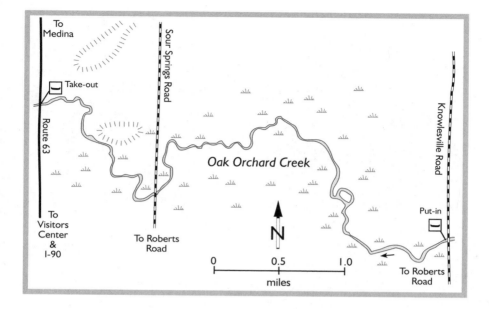

To Medina

Take-out

Sour Springs Road

Route 63

Oak Orchard Creek

Knowlesville Road

Put-in

To Visitors Center & I-90

To Roberts Road

N

Put-in

0   0.5   1.0

miles

To Roberts Road

the creek. More than 100,000 Canada geese have descended here during spring migration. In the mid-1980s, the bald eagle also returned to Iroquois, and in 1994, a pair nested within sight of the visitor center and fledged three young, an extraordinary event. Since the first edition of this book, at least 20 more eagles have fledged there. In the last 10 years, nests blew down, and eagles constructed new ones. In 2005, three nests produced an astounding 7 eaglets.

The refuges include two state-owned Wildlife Management Areas, Oak Orchard on the east and Tonawanda on the west, with Iroquois National Wildlife Refuge (NWR) sandwiched in between, comprising 20,000 acres of protected wetlands. Oak Orchard Creek meanders from east to west through Oak Orchard Wildlife Management Area (WMA) and Iroquois NWR before turning north, heading for Lake Ontario. The section included here flows through Iroquois NWR.

Paddle west from Knowlesville Road, the dividing line between Oak Orchard WMA and Iroquois NWR. One might be tempted to use two cars and to make this a one-way trip. We advise against this except during high water or in the spring before aquatic plants choke the channel. Check stream conditions at the visitor center before embarking on such an adventure; sections may be impassable or extremely slow going.

Canada geese keep a lookout for danger as their downy goslings feed on tender springtime shoots.

In mid-July, the lazy current allows tons of duckweed—a minuscule, free-floating, flowering plant—to clog the waterway, especially behind beaver dams and logjams, making paddling exceedingly difficult. Still, despite the duckweed and downed trees, we love paddling here among myriad plants, animals, and birds.

As you leave the access, look for giant cottonwoods that send seed-carrying cotton balls on the wind, drifting out over the water. The creek starts out about 30 feet wide but widens to 40 to 50 feet across as tree-lined banks of willow, ash, and silver maple give way to dense stands of cattail. Occasional beaver lodges and a few dams dot the waterway. As you pass, wood duck, coot, and other waterfowl scurry into the protective cattails, as common yellowthroat and hermit thrush call from the dense undergrowth.

Beautiful stands of swamp rose and swamp milkweed grace the shores in places, and arrowhead and *Rumex* poke up from the shallows. During high water, side channels off the main creek flood the adjoining land, providing greater access to these very productive wetlands. Besides touring the area by boat, we recommend that you visit the waterfowl-viewing areas if you are here in the spring or fall.

89

Tonawanda Creek

Amherst, Clarence, Lockport, Newstead, Pendleton, and Royalton

Maps: New York Atlas Map 69:D7, USGS Quadrangles Clarence Center, Tonawanda East, Wolcottsville

Length: 20 miles

Habitat type: slow-flowing stream

Fish: largemouth and smallmouth bass, northern pike, walleye

Expect to see: great blue heron, waterfowl, beaver, muskrat, deer

Camping: App. A #26, 34, and 35

Take note: logjams may require carries on steep muddy banks

GETTING THERE

Route 270. From Buffalo, go north on Route 263 (Buffalo-Millersport Road), and turn left on Route 270 (Campbell Boulevard). Go 3.5 miles, and turn right on Tonawanda Creek Road. Access is on the left just after the turn.

Route 78. From Buffalo, go north on Route 263. From the junction with Route 270, continue 5.6 miles on Route 263, and turn left on Route 78. Go 0.1 mile (5.7 miles), cross the bridge over Tonawanda Creek, and turn left onto the widened shoulder; be careful here when entering and leaving the highway, as traffic is usually horrendous.

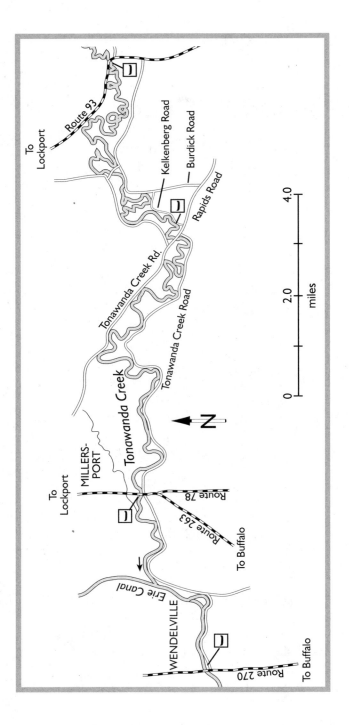

Kelkenberg Road. From Route 78, go 7.1 miles (12.7 miles) east on Tonawanda Creek Road south, and turn right on Rapids Road. Go about 200 yards, turn left on Kelkenberg Road, and go 0.1 mile (12.8 miles) to the access on the left.

Route 93. Go another 1.2 miles (14.0 miles), and turn left on Burdick Road/Tonawanda Creek Road. Go 3.5 miles (17.5 miles) to Route 93, turn left, and go 0.6 mile (18.1 miles) to the bridge, where you can launch from either side.

Tonawanda Creek runs northward to Batavia from its source in Wyoming County south of Attica, then turns west, eventually emptying into the Niagara River just north of Buffalo. Before reaching the river, however, it joins the Erie Canal in Pendleton (near the downstream end of this section). Although some whitewater exists in the creek's upper reaches, the 20-mile section included here drops less than one foot per meandering mile, resulting in modest to no measurable current most of the time.

A study in contrasts, Tonawanda Creek alternates between ferns and fields, camps and woodlots, wooded shores and muddy banks, clear sailing and annoying logjams. Beaver have contributed quite a bit to the logjams, some longstanding, judging by the jewelweed growing out of some logs. Though houses do not crowd the banks in the upper reaches and few motorboats ply these waters, below Route 78 in Millersport development increases significantly.

Where tree density remains low, beautiful, aroma-laden honeysuckle alternates with irises and dame's rockets—a widespread escape from cultivation. Willows lean out over the water, nearly closing the canopy. Wild grapevines drape over much of the shoreline vegetation. Three maples grow in profusion: mostly silver maple, along with lesser amounts of red maple and box elder. Other common trees include ash, basswood, white oak, black walnut, and cottonwood.

We never tired of the songs of three dominant birds: Baltimore oriole with its melodious, treetop song; red-winged blackbird singing "cong-ka-ree" from the tops of cattails; and the loud "witchety, witchety, witchety" sung from the undergrowth by the diminutive common yellowthroat, a small yellow warbler with a black mask through the eyes. Other birds include cardinal, grackle, song sparrow, mallard, robin, gray catbird, mourning dove, bobolink, American goldfinch, crow, Eastern phoebe, black-capped chickadee, house wren, and blue jay.

Turtles basked on the many logs we passed, while groundhogs munched on streamside grass. Raccoon tracks on the muddy banks told of nighttime foraging, and occasional discarded tires reminded us that many people view the nation's streams as more of a dump than as a recreational asset. As a light rain began, runoff from muddy banks and agricultural fields turned the clear water clay-colored nearly instantly. One wonders where this huge silt burden eventually leads.

We also never tired of the endless meanderings, although much of the shoreline looked the same. The stream straightened in the lower reaches, and we made more progress. We least enjoyed the last stretch between Millersport and Wendelville, particularly after the Erie Canal joined from the north.

Still, this whole reach provides enjoyable paddling and a wonderful resource for the quietwater enthusiast in an area with little else to offer. While glaciers carved out the Finger Lakes to the east and south and molded the Great Lakes, it left this area flat and without many ponds and small lakes. So we should all remain thankful for Tonawanda Creek and do our best to keep it untrammeled for future generations.

90

Allegheny Reservoir
Cold Spring, Elko, and South Valley

Maps: New York Atlas Map 41:D5, USGS Quadrangles Little Valley, Red House, Steamburg

Area: 12,000 acres

Habitat type: large reservoir

Fish: smallmouth bass, muskellunge, northern pike, walleye

Expect to see: waterfowl

Camping: App. A #1 and 2 (on-site)

Take note: wind makes paddling on the main reservoir treacherous; Seneca-Iroquois National Museum, Salamanca, 716-945-1760, www.senecamuseum.org

GETTING THERE

From Route 17, Exit 18, go south on Route 280 to Friends Boat Launch, Allegany State Park, on the right.

Located almost entirely within the Allegany Indian Reservation, Allegheny Reservoir represents one of the few quietwater paddling resources in southwestern New York. A dam just over the border in Pennsylvania caused inundation of a many-mile stretch of the scenic Allegheny River. The river begins in Pennsylvania, swings northward and flows west through New York for about 50 miles, exits into Pennsylvania through the reservoir, and eventually joins the Monongahela to form the Ohio River at Pittsburgh.

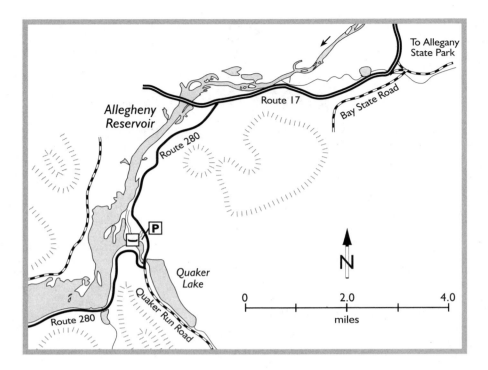

Portions of the reservoir's eastern shore belong to Allegany State Park, a huge state park that includes a nice camping area, which fills up nearly every day of the summer, and two popular swimming areas: Quaker Beach on Quaker Lake, just a mile from the access, and Red House Beach on Red House Lake.

Leaving behind the Norway spruce, with its drooping branches, and large white pine at the access, paddle to the left over to the Quaker Lake outfall to look at the water cascading over the dam. Along the way, note the pine groves on the hillsides. Scrub vegetation, including lots of willow, grows down to the waterline along the left shoreline, and tall silver maple, white pine, hickory, oak, and hemlock climb the hillsides along the right.

Back at the access, two coves appear on the right just before you get to the main reservoir. Willow dominates the shoreline here as well, with silver maple farther back and basswood and aspen on higher ground. The first cove to the right contains many camps and boats. A peninsula forms the far shore, but high water sometimes cuts off the peninsula, forming an island. The camp on the peninsula's high spot includes ducks, chickens, and mounds of trash. The second peninsula is a lot more scenic.

Moving out into the main reservoir, we noted that the shoreline in this area remains pretty much intact, punctuated only occasionally with camps. Wooded hillsides receding into the distance provide a scenic backdrop. Upon entering the reservoir, three choices immediately confront you: paddling upstream toward Salamanca, downstream toward Pennsylvania, or to the opposite shore. No matter which direction you choose, you should enjoy miles of scenery and plenty of wildlife.

Paddling here during high water in early July, we could barely detect any current on the main reservoir. A breeze, just sufficient to ripple the water's surface, blew us gently upstream, while a northern cardinal called from the dense undergrowth. American redstarts, acting more like flycatchers than warblers, darted out to snare insects on the wing. Barn and tree swallows skimmed the water's surface, doing their best to reduce the hordes of insects produced by these productive waters.

Some warnings: the state requires all people in boats less than 16 feet and in all canoes to wear personal floatation devices (PFDs); the state would like all of us to take precautions against importing exotic species such as Eurasian watermilfoil, water chestnut, and zebra mussels into Allegheny Reservoir and other nearby bodies of water.

Appendix A

Camping and Cabin Information, New York State Parks, and New York State Forest Preserves

RESERVATIONS
www.reserveamerica.com; 800-456-2267

INFORMATION
Office of Parks, Recreation and Historic Preservation
Empire State Plaza
Agency Building 1
Albany, NY 12238
General Information on State Parks: 518-474-0456, 518-486-1899
    TDD; nysparks.state.ny.us/parks/

New York State Department of Environmental Conservation
Public Affairs and Education
625 Broadway
Albany, NY 12233-4500
General Information: 518-457-3521
Campground and Cabin Information Only: 518-457-2500
Backcountry Camping: 518-402-9428
www.dec.state.ny.us/website/do/or2top.htm

LISTING OF STATE PARKS BY REGION

Office of Parks, Recreation and Historic Preservation
State Park Campgrounds

Allegany Region—716-354-9101

1	NY Atlas 41:5D	Allegany: Quaker	716-354-2182	Rte. 17, Exit 18, 11 mi. w. of Salamanca
2	NY Atlas 41:6D	Allegany: Red House	716-354-9121	Rte. 17, Exit 19, 7 mi. w. of Salamanca
3	NY Atlas 39:7A	Lake Erie	716-792-9214	Rte. 5, 7 mi. w. of Dunkirk

Central Region—315-492-1756

4	NY Atlas 62:D2	Bowman Lake	607-334-2718	off Rte. 220, 8 mi. w. of Oxford
5	NY Atlas 48:C1	Chenango Valley	607-648-5251	Rte. 369, 12 mi. n. of Binghamton
6	NY Atlas 62:A1	Chittenango Falls	315-655-9620	Rte. 13, 4 mi. n. of Cazenovia
7	NY Atlas 77:B4	Delta Lake	315-337-4670	Rte. 46, 6 mi. ne. of Rome
8	NY Atlas 63:D6	Gilbert Lake	607-432-2114	Rtes. 205 & 51, 12 mi. nw. of Oneonta
9	NY Atlas 64:B2	Glimmerglass	607-547-8662	4 mi. s. of Rte. 20, E. Springfield
10	NY Atlas 75:D7	Green Lakes	315-637-6111	Rtes. 290 & 5, 10 mi. e. of Syracuse
11	NY Atlas 63:D5	Hunts Pond	607-859-2249	off Rte. 8, 2 mi. n. of S. New Berlin
12	NY Atlas 49:C4	Oquaga Creek	607-467-4160	off Rte. 206, 11 mi. s. of Sidney
13	NY Atlas 77:A5	Pixley Falls	315-942-4713	Rte. 46, 6 mi. s. of Boonville

| 14 | NY Atlas 83:D5 | Selkirk Shores | 315-298-5737 | Rte. 3, 3 mi. w. of Pulaski |
| 15 | NY Atlas 76:C2 | Verona Beach | 315-762-4463 | Rte. 13, 7 mi. nw. of Oneida |

Finger Lakes Region—607-387-7041

16	NY Atlas 46:A2	Buttermilk Falls	607-273-5761	Rte. 13 s. of Ithaca
17	NY Atlas 59:A7	Cayuga Lake	315-568-5163	Rte. 89, 3 mi. e. of Seneca Falls
18	NY Atlas 74:B1	Fair Haven Beach	315-947-5205	Rte. 104A, 2 mi. n. of Fair Haven
19	NY Atlas 60:C3	Fillmore Glen	315-497-0130	Rte. 38, 1 mi. s. of Moravia
20	NY Atlas 59:5D	Keuka Lake	315-536-3666	Rte. 54A, 6 mi. sw. of Penn Yan
21	NY Atlas 59:C6	Sampson	315-585-6392	Rte. 96A, 11 mi. s. of E. Geneva
22	NY Atlas 57:D7	Stony Brook	585-335-8111	Rte. 36, 3 mi. s. of Dansville
23	NY Atlas 60:D2	Taughannock Falls	607-387-6739	Rte. 89, 8 mi. n. of Ithaca
24	NY Atlas 46:A2	Robert H. Treman	607-273-3440	Rte. 13, 5 mi. sw. of Ithaca
25	NY Atlas 45:B6	Watkins Glen	607-535-4511	Rte. 14, main entrance, village of Watkins Glen

Genesee Region—585-493-3600

26	NY Atlas 56:A1	Darien Lakes	585-547-9242	Harlow Rd., Darien Center
27	NY Atlas 71:B5	Hamlin Beach	585-964-2462	Lake Ontario St. Parkway, 25 mi. w. of Rochester
28	NY Atlas 70:B3	Lakeside Beach	585-682-4888	Lake Ontario St. Parkway, 35 mi. w. of Rochester
29	NY Atlas 57:D4	Letchworth	585-493-3600	I-390 Exit 7, 35 mi. s. of Rochester

Long Island Region—631-669-1000

30	NY Atlas 26:C3	Heckscher	631-581-2100	Heckscher St. Parkway, E. Islip
31	NY Atlas 29:B5	Hither Hills	631-668-2554	Montauk Highway, Montauk
32	NY Atlas 27:A6	Wildwood	631-929-4314	N. Country Rd., Wading River

Niagara Frontier Region—716-278-1770

33	NY Atlas 54:D3	Evangola	716-549-1802	Rte. 5, 27 mi. sw. of Buffalo, Irving
34	NY Atlas 68:B4	Four Mile Creek	716-745-3802	Rte. 18 or Robert Moses Parkway, 4 mi. ne. of Youngstown
35	NY Atlas 70:B1	Golden Hill	716-795-3885	Lower Lake Rd., off Rte. 269, Barker

Palisades Region—845-786-2701

36	NY Atlas 32:C3	Harriman: Beaver Pond	845-947-2792	Palisades Pkwy, Exit 16
37	NY Atlas 32:C3	Harriman: Sebago Cabins	845-351-2360	Palisades Pkwy, Exit 16

Saratoga-Capital Region—518-584-2000

38	NY Atlas 80:C4	Moreau Lake	518-793-0511	I-87, Exit 17S, S. Glens Falls
39	NY Atlas 65:D5	Max V. Shaul	518-827-4711	Rte. 30, 6 mi. s. of Middleburgh
40	NY Atlas 66:C1	Thompson's Lake	518-872-1674	Rte. 157, 18 mi. w. of Albany

Taconic Region—845-889-4100

41	NY Atlas 33:A5	Clarence Fahnestock	845-225-7207	Rte. 301, off Taconic Parkway
42	NY Atlas 52:D4	Lake Taghkanic	518-851-3631	Rte. 82 at Taconic Parkway, 11 mi. s. of Hudson

43	NY Atlas 36:B4	Margaret Lewis Norrie	845-889-4646	Rte. 9, 4 mi. n. of Hyde Park
44	NY Atlas 37:A7	Rudd Pond	518-789-3059	off Rte. 22, 2 mi. n. of Millerton
45	NY Atlas 53:D5	Taconic: Copake Falls	518-329-3993	east of Rte. 22, Copake Falls

Thousand Islands Region—315-482-2593

46	NY Atlas 91:C5	Burnham Point	315-654-2324	Rte. 12E, 4 mi. e. of Cape Vincent
47	NY Atlas 91:B6	Canoe-Picnic Point	315-654-2522	access by boat only, Grindstone Island
48	NY Atlas 92:A1	Cedar Island	315-482-3331	access by boat only, Cedar Island
49	NY Atlas 91:C5	Cedar Point	315-654-2522	Rte. 12E, 6 mi. w. of Clayton
50	NY Atlas 99:A6	Coles Creek	315-388-5636	Rte. 37, 4 mi. e. of Waddington
51	NY Atlas 103:C6	Cumberland Bay	518-563-5240	Rte. 314, 1 mi. e. of Plattsburgh
52	NY Atlas 91:B7	Dewolf Point	315-482-2012	I-81, Exit 51, 2 mi. n. of Alexandria Bay
53	NY Atlas 98:C4	Eel Weir	315-393-1138	Rte. 812, 7 mi. s. of Ogdensburg
54	NY Atlas 91:B7	Grass Point	315-686-4472	Rte. 12, 1 mi. w. of I-81, Alexandria Bay
55	NY Atlas 94:A1	Higley Flow	315-262-2880	Rte. 56, 2 mi. e. of S. Colton
56	NY Atlas 98:D2	Jacques Cartier	315-375-6371	Rte. 12, 3 mi. w. of Morristown
57	NY Atlas 91:B7	Keewaydin	315-482-3331	Rte. 12, 1 mi. w. of Alexandria Bay
58	NY Atlas 92:A1	Kring Point	315-482-2444	Rte. 12, 6 mi. e. of Alexandria Bay

59	NY Atlas 91:D5	Long Point	315-649-5258	Rte. 12E, 8 mi. w. of Three Mile Bay
60	NY Atlas 103:D5	Macomb Reservation	518-643-9952	off Rte. 22B, 2 mi. w. of Schuyler Falls
61	NY Atlas 91:B7	Mary Island	315-654-2522	access by boat only, Alexandria Bay
62	NY Atlas 100:A2	Robert Moses	315-769-8663	off Rte. 37, 3 mi. n. of Massena
63	NY Atlas 83:B5	Southwick Beach	315-846-5338	off Rte. 3, 2 mi. w. of Woodville
64	NY Atlas 91:B6	Wellesley Island	315-482-2722	I-81, Exit 51, 4 mi. w. of Alexandria Bay
65	NY Atlas 83:A5	Westcott Beach	315-646-2239	Rte. 3, 3 mi. w. of Sackets Harbor
66	NY Atlas 84:C4	Whetstone Gulf	315-376-6630	Rte. 26, 6 mi. s. of Lowville

DEPARTMENT OF ENVIRONMENTAL CONSERVATION
Forest Preserve Public Campgrounds

Adirondacks

Warrensburg—518-623-1200

67	NY Atlas 88:C3	Eagle Point	518-494-2220	Rte. 9, 2 mi. n. of Pottersville
68	NY Atlas 80:A4	Hearthstone Point	518-668-5193	Rte. 9N, 2 mi. n. of Lake George Village
69	NY Atlas 80:A4	Lake George Battleground	518-668-3348	Rte. 9, 1/4 mi. s. of Lake George Village
70	NY Atlas 81:A4	Lake George Islands:		
		Glen Island	518-644-9696	Bolton Landing
		Long Island	518-656-9426	Cleverdale
		Narrow Island	518-499-1288	Huletts Landing

| 71 | NY Atlas 80:B3 | Luzerne | 518-696-2031 | Rte. 9N, 8 mi. sw. of Lake George Village |
| 72 | NY Atlas 89:B6 | Rogers Rock | 518-585-6746 | Rte. 9N, 3 mi. n. of Hague |

Raybrook—518-897-1309

73	NY Atlas 103:D6	Ausable Point	518-561-7080	Rte. 9, 12 mi. s. of Plattsburgh
74	NY Atlas 102:D1	Buck Pond	518-891-3449	off Rte. 86, 6 mi. n. of Gabriels
75	NY Atlas 97:D6	Crown Point	518-597-3603	off Rte. 9N, 8 mi. n. of Crown Point
76	NY Atlas 95:B5	Fish Creek Pond	518-891-4560	Rte. 30, 12 mi. e. of Tupper Lake
77	NY Atlas 87:A5	Lake Eaton	518-624-2641	Rte. 30, 2 mi. w. of Long Lake
78	NY Atlas 87:A7	Lake Harris	518-582-2503	Rte. 28N, 3 mi. n. of Newcomb
79	NY Atlas 97:C5	Lincoln Pond	518-942-5292	Rte. 7, 6 mi. s. of Elizabethtown
80	NY Atlas 101:D6	Meacham Lake	518-483-5116	Rte. 30, 19 mi. n. of Clear Lake Jct.
81	NY Atlas 96:B1	Meadowbrook	518-891-4351	Rte. 86, 2 mi. e. of Saranac Lake
82	NY Atlas 88:A4	Paradox Lake	518-532-7451	Rte. 74, 2 mi. e. of Severance
83	NY Atlas 97:A5	Poke-O-Moonshine	518-834-9045	Rte. 9, 6 mi. s. of Keeseville
84	NY Atlas 89:B5	Putnam Pond	518-585-7280	off Rte. 74, 6 mi. w. of Ticonderoga
85	NY Atlas 95:B5	Rollins Pond	518-891-3239	Rte. 30, 12 mi. e. of Tupper Lake
86	NY Atlas 95:B7	Saranac Lake Islands	518-891-3170	Rte. 3, 5 mi. w. of Saranac Lake village

87	NY Atlas 97:D4	Sharp Bridge	518-532-7538	Rte. 9, 15 mi. n. of Schroon Lake
88	NY Atlas 96:A3	Taylor Pond	518-647-5250	Silver Lake Rd., 9 mi. nw. of Au Sable Forks
89	NY Atlas 96:B3	Wilmington Notch	518-946-7172	Rte. 86, 3.5 mi. w. of Wilmington

Herkimer—315-866-6330

| 90 | NY Atlas 86:C1 | Alger Island | 315-369-3224 | Rte. 28, 8 mi. e. of Old Forge |
| 91 | NY Atlas 86:C1 | Nicks Lake | 315-369-3314 | off Rte. 28, 1.5 mi. sw. of Old Forge |

Canton—315-265-3090

| 92 | NY Atlas 94:C2 | Cranberry Lake | 315-848-2315 | off Rte. 3, 1.5 mi. s. of Cranberry Lake Village |

Indian Lake—518-648-5616

93	NY Atlas 86:B3	Brown Tract Pond	315-354-4412	Rte. 28, 7 mi. e. of Eagle Bay
94	NY Atlas 86:B3	Eighth Lake	315-354-4120	Rte. 28, 5 mi. w. of Raquette Lake
95	NY Atlas 87:A4	Forked Lake	518-624-6646	off Rte. 30, 3 mi. w. of Deerland Village
96	NY Atlas 86:B4	Golden Beach	315-354-4230	Rte. 28, 3 mi. n. of Raquette Lake
97	NY Atlas 87:C6	Indian Lake Islands	518-648-5300	Rte. 30, 14 mi. n. of Speculator
98	NY Atlas 87:B5	Lake Durant	518-352-7797	Rt. 28, 2 mi. e. of Blue Mountain Lake
99	NY Atlas 87:C5	Lewey Lake	518-648-5266	Rte. 30, 14 mi. n. of Speculator
100	NY Atlas 86:C2	Limekiln Lake	315-357-4401	off Rte. 28, 3 mi. se. of Inlet
101	NY Atlas 86:B4	Tioga Point	315-354-4230	Raquette Lake

Northville—518-863-4545

102	NY Atlas 79:D5	Caroga Lake	518-835-4241	Rte. 29A, 9 mi. nw. of Gloversville
103	NY Atlas 79:A4	Little Sand Point	518-548-7585	off Rte. 8, 3 mi. w. of Piseco
104	NY Atlas 79:A5	Moffitt Beach	518-548-7102	Rte. 8, 4 mi. w. of Speculator
105	NY Atlas 79:C7	Northampton Beach	518-863-6000	Rte. 30, 1.5 mi. s. of Northville
106	NY Atlas 78:A4	Point Comfort	518-548-7586	off Rte. 8, 4 mi. w. of Piseco
107	NY Atlas 79:A4	Poplar Point	518-548-8031	off Rte. 8, 2 mi. w. of Piseco
108	NY Atlas 79:B6	Sacandaga	518-924-4121	Rte. 30, 4 mi. s. of Wells

Catskills

Schenectady—518-357-2234

109	NY Atlas 49:D7	Bear Spring Mountain	607-865-6989	off Rte. 206, 5 mi. se. of Walton
110	NY Atlas 51:C7	Devil's Tombstone	845-688-7160	Rte. 214, 4 mi. s. of Hunter
111	NY Atlas 50:D3	Little Pond	845-439-5480	off Rte. 17, 14 mi. nw. of Livingston Manor
112	NY Atlas 52:C1	North/South Lake	518-589-5058	off Rte. 23A, 3 mi. ne. of Haines Falls

New Paltz—845-256-3099

113	NY Atlas 34:A4	Beaverkill	845-439-4281	off Rte. 17, 7 mi. nw. of Livingston Manor
114	NY Atlas 51:D6	Kenneth L. Wilson	845-679-7020	off Rte. 28, 4 mi. e. of Mt. Tremper on Rt. 40
115	NY Atlas 35:A5	Mongaup Pond	845-439-4233	off Rte. 17, 3 mi. n. of DeBruce
116	NY Atlas 51:D6	Woodland Valley	845-688-7647	off Rte. 28, 6 mi. sw. of Phonecia

Suffolk County Parks with Campgrounds

East End

117	NY Atlas 28:B4	Cedar Point	631-244-7275	Cedar Point, 6 mi. n. of East Hampton
118	NY Atlas 27:B7	Cupsogue	631-852-8111	Barrier island sw. of Westhampton Beach
119	NY Atlas 27:A7	Indian Island	631-244-7275	Rte. 105 Riverhead
120	NY Atlas 28:C1	Sears Bellows	631-244-7275	Off Rte. 24 nw. of Hampton Bays
121	NY Atlas 28:D2	Shinnecock East (beach vehicle camping only)	631-852-8899	Sw. of Southampton on barrier spit
122	NY Atlas 29:B6	Theodore Roosevelt (beach vehicle camping only)	631-244-7275	E. side of Lake Montauk

West End

123	NY Atlas 26:B3	Blydenburgh (county residents only)	631-854-3712	S. edge of Smithtown between Rtes. 25 and 347
124	NY Atlas 27:B5	Cathedral Pines	631-852-5502	On Longwood Rd. n. of Yaphank
125	NY Atlas 27:C6	Smith Point	631-244-7275	On Fire Island at end of Wm. Floyd Pkwy.
126	NY Atlas	Southaven	631-854-1414	On Carmans River just n. of Sunrise Hwy.

Federal National Forests and Seashores

127	NY Atlas 27:C6	Fire Island National Seashore	631-289-4810	On Fire Island
128	NY Atlas 45:A7	Finger Lakes National Forest	607-546-4470	On County Rte. 2 ne. of Watkins Glen

Nassau County Campgrounds

129	NY Atlas 26:B1	Battle Row	516-572-8690	Claremont Rd. in old Bethpage
130	NY Atlas 25:D7	Nickerson Beach (county residents only)	516-571-7724	Lido Blvd., Long Beach

PASSPORTS & PASSES

Empire Passport: Provides yearlong vehicle entry to state parks and recreation areas. Purchase can be made at participating facilities or by mail from Office of Parks (address at the beginning of this appendix).

Golden Park Program: Provides New York State residents 62 or older free entry weekdays, holidays excluded; simply show New York driver's license or Nondriver Identification Card.

Access Pass: New York State residents with permanent disabilities are provided to state parks and recreation areas. Access passes can be purchased by mail from Office of Parks (address at the beginning of this appendix).

Appendix B

Bibliography

Armstrong, Kathie, and Chet Harvey, *Canoe and Kayak Guide: East-Central New York State*, 1st revised ed., Adirondack Mountain Club, 2005.

Darwin, Charles, *Insectivorous Plants*, University Press of the Pacific, 2002.

DeLorme Mapping Company, *The New York Atlas and Gazetteer*, 7th ed., 2003.

Ehling, William, *Canoeing Central New York*, Backcountry Publications, 1982.

Freeman, Mark, *Canoe Guide to Western and Central New York State*, Adirondack Mountain Club, 1993.

Hampton, Bruce, and David Cole, *Soft Paths: How to Enjoy the Wilderness without Harming It*, 3rd ed., Stackpole Books, 2003.

Hutchinson, Derek, *Basic Book of Sea Kayaking*, 2nd ed., Falcon, 2007.

Hutchinson, Derek, *The Complete Book of Sea Kayaking*, 5th ed., Falcon, 2004.

Jacobson, Cliff, *Basic Essentials Canoeing*, 2nd ed., Globe Pequot Press, 1999.

Jamieson, Paul, *Adirondack Pilgrimage*, Adirondack Mountain Club, 1988.

Jamieson, Paul, and Donald Morris, *Adirondack Canoe Waters: North Flow*, 3rd ed., Adirondack Mountain Club, 1988.

Jerome, Christine, *Adirondack Passage: The Cruise of the Canoe Sairy Gamp*, Adirondack Mountain Club, 1998.

Lanza, Michael, *Ultimate Guide to Backcountry Travel*, AMC Books, 1999.

Marsh, George Perkins, *Man and Nature*, University of Washington Press, 2003.

Murray, William H. H., *Adventures in the Wilderness; or, Camp-Life in the Adirondacks*, Adirondack Museum, 1970.

New York State Department of Environmental Conservation publications locator: www.dec.state.ny.us/website/locator/index.html

Proskine, Alec, *Adirondack Canoe Waters: South & West Flow*, 2nd ed., Adirondack Mountain Club, 1989.

Roberts, Harry, and Steve Salins, *Basic Essentials Canoe Paddling*, 3rd ed., Falcon, 2006.

Roosevelt, Theodore, *The Summer Birds of the Adirondacks in Franklin County, N.Y.*, printed privately, 1877.

Sears, George Washington, and Dan Brenan, *Canoeing the Adirondacks with Nessmuk: The Adirondack Letters of George Washington Sears*, Syracuse University Press, 1993.

Seidman, David, *The Essential Sea Kayaker*, 2nd ed., Ragged Mountain Press, 2001.

Walter, George, *The Loomis Gang*, North Country Books, 1985.

Appendix C

About the Appalachian Mountain Club

Founded in 1876, the AMC is the nation's oldest outdoor recreation and conservation organization. The AMC promotes the protection, enjoyment, and wise use of the mountains, rivers, and trails of the Northeast outdoors.

People
We are nearly 90,000 members in 12 chapters, 20,000 volunteers, and over 450 full time and seasonal staff. Our chapters reach from Maine to Washington, D.C.

Outdoor Adventure and Fun
We offer more than 8,000 trips each year, from local chapter activities to major excursions worldwide, for every ability level and outdoor interest—from hiking and climbing to paddling, snowshoeing, and skiing.

Great Places to Stay
We host more than 138,000 guest nights each year at our AMC Lodges, Huts, Camps, Shelters, and Campgrounds. Each AMC Destination is a model for environmental education and stewardship.

Opportunities for Learning
We teach people the skills to be safe outdoors and to care for the natural world around us through programs for children, teens, and adults, as well as outdoor leadership training.

Caring for Trails

We maintain more than 1,500 miles of trails throughout the Northeast, including nearly 350 miles of the Appalachian Trail in five states.

Protecting Wild Places

We advocate for land and riverway conservation, monitor air quality, and work to protect alpine and forest ecosystems throughout the Northern Forest and Highlands regions.

Engaging the Public

We seek to educate and inform our own members and an additional 1.5 million people annually through AMC Books, our website, our White Mountain visitor centers, and AMC Destinations.

Join Us!

Members support our mission while enjoying great AMC programs, our award-winning AMC Outdoors magazine, and special discounts. Visit www.outdoors.org or call 617-523-0636 for more information.

THE APPALACHIAN MOUNTAIN CLUB
Recreation • Education • Conservation
www.outdoors.org

Appendix D

Alphabetical List of Bodies of Water

About the Authors

John Hayes, a former professor of biochemistry and environmental science at Marlboro College in Vermont, is now Dean of Arts & Sciences at Pacific University in Oregon. Besides exploring the lakes and rivers of his new home in the Northwest, he has paddled Minnesota's Boundary Waters Canoe Area, Georgia's Okefenokee Swamp, Florida's Everglades, as well as throughout the Northeast. Hayes has written for *National Geographic Traveler* and has edited numerous solar energy conference proceedings. He was book review editor of the *Passive Solar Journal* and served as Vice Chair of the American Solar Energy Society. He has led natural history field trips to Central America, Mexico, the Southwest's deserts, the Rockies, the Everglades, Borneo, and Africa. He and Wilson are co-authors of paddling guides to New York and all New England states.

Alex Wilson is founder and president of BuildingGreen, Inc., in Brattleboro, Vermont, an 18-person company dedicated to reducing environmental impacts of the built environment. BuildingGreen has published *Environmental Building News* since 1992, publishes the most comprehensive directory of green building products (*GreenSpec*®), and offers various other print and online resources on green building. Wilson also writes widely for other magazines, including *Fine Homebuilding, Architectural Record,* and *Landscape Architecture,* and he is author or coauthor of various books, including the *Consumer Guide to Home Energy Savings* (ACEEE, 8th edition 2003), *Green Development: Integrating Ecology and Real Estate* (John Wiley, 1998), and his latest, *Your Green Home* (New Society, 2006). He is also an instructor at the Boston Architectural College. Wilson served on the board of the U.S. Green Building Council for five years and is currently a trustee of The Nature Conservancy—Vermont Chapter. He has long been an avid quietwater paddler and naturalist.